YOUTH INJUSTICE:
CANADIAN PERSPECTIVES

EDITED BY

THOMAS O'REILLY-FLEMING
BARRY CLARK

CANADIAN SCHOLARS' PRESS INC.   TORONTO   1993

Youth Injustice: Canadian Perspectives

First published in 1993 by
Canadian Scholars' Press Inc.
180 Bloor St. W., Ste. 402
Toronto, Ontario
M5S 2V6

Canadian Cataloguing in Publication Data

Main entry under title:

Youth Injustice: Canadian Perspectives

Includes bibliographical references.
ISBN 1-55130-009-5

1. Juvenile justice, Administration of - Canada. 2. Juvenile delinquency - Canada. I. O'Reilly-Fleming, Thomas, 1951 - . II. Clark, Barry, 1944 - .

KE99445.Y68   1992   345.71'08   C92-095541-X
KF9771.Y68   1992

Printed and bound in Canada

Book design/layout by Steven Hain, Toronto

 OTABIND The pages in this book open easily and lie flat, a result of the Otabind bookbinding process. Otabind combines advanced adhesive technology and a free-floating cover to achieve books that last longer and are bound to stay open.

This book is dedicated to our
wives and children;
Patricia and Elaine, Kate,
Patrick, Thomas and Samantha.

For William Noble Fleming
Whose courage and humanity
are a source of inspiration.

"Let the Deed Show"

ACKNOWLEDGEMENTS

There are a number of people to whom we owe a considerable debt and without whose effort this book would not have come to fruition. Tim Wayne, the editor for Canadian Scholars' Press was open to the idea of this book, enthusiastic and supportive throughout the editorial process. Pamela Hamilton was a professional of the first degree in getting us through the production and copyedit phases of the manuscript, and made the book a pleasure to work on. Emeritus Professor A. Stuart Nease, Past President, Jim Preston, and the Board of Directors of The John Howard Society of Windsor and Essex County were a source of much needed encouragement during our initial forays into this area.

Max Hedley, Head of the Department of Sociology and Anthropology, University of Windsor encouraged our work in this area. We are grateful to Mary Lou Dietz, Chair of the Criminology Program, and all of the members of the department for their support in our scholarly endeavours. The Council of Deans kindly awarded me a sabbatical of which this is one of the fruits. Dean Kate McCrone, Faculty of Social Science was supportive of my efforts in this and other projects that I have undertaken in the past two years, and this greatly facilitated the completion of this book. I would also like to extend my thanks to Dean Lois Smedick.

Mr. William Bateman and Dr. David Nimmo provided me with a forum in which to test out some of the materials that eventually came to form essential parts of this book, and I deeply appreciate their support and encouragement.

L.A. Visano and Kevin McCormick, two fine colleagues from the Department of Sociology, York University, originally introduced us to Canadian Scholars' Press and encouraged us to undertake this project. Their technical and other advice was crucial to the completion of this book.

Shannon Flegel, Andrew John Lindsay, Gina Sampson, Danielle Soulliere, and Scott Tempest of my Thursday night graduate seminar assisted valiantly with proofreading of various portions of the manuscript. We are especially thankful of their help. The secretarial staff of The Department of Sociology, University of Windsor, Perry, Andria, Sue and Carmel took our messages and assisted with technical matters, and we would not have met our deadlines without them. My mother and father, Alice and William Fleming, provided room and board while I visited Toronto. My other parents, Rod and

Mary O'Reilly deserve a special thanks.

Both Barry Clark and I want to thank our wives and children for their patience with our obsessions. Kate was my little helper throughout this project.

Thomas O'Reilly-Fleming
Windsor, Ontario
September 9, 1992

TABLE OF CONTENTS

OVERVIEW:
Youth Injustice, Society and the State

The introduction of the Young Offenders Act (YOA) to Canada in 1984 supposedly heralded a new era in our societal approach to youthful lawbreakers. While one might assume that the cumulative knowledge of three-quarters of a century of dealing with young people in trouble with the law would have moved our knowledge and practice substantively further along the road of progressive development, the YOA actually succeeded in refocusing our approach away from the needs of young people in conflict with their society to a reliance upon the law, its agents and mechanisms of control to deal with youths as though they were adult offenders. The new thrust of the YOA has returned to earlier models of control emphasizing the unholy triumvirate of crime, punishment and responsibility.

A central organizing feature of this book is to redress the mistaken concept that youth in Canadian society have been the recipients of justice emanating from the criminal justice system. Rather they have been the recipients of a series of injustices often carried out in the name of progress, or reflecting the new political atmosphere of the 'exceptional state.' The movement from a needs-based justice system for juveniles, which placed rehabilitation above the supposed need of society to punish, to a distinctly retributive system has resulted in an ever-increasing net of control being thrown over young people. While our current system again returns to more historically grounded themes of individual pathology which have political currency in contemporary society, the broader political-economic roots of adolescent offending have been largely ignored. This occurs not only at the level of apprehension and sentencing but in a general malaise regarding the building of alternatives to custody, particularly in Ontario.

Although the literature on youth crime is growing in Canada there are still several significant gaps in our knowledge. We know little about the specific factors that contribute to youthful offending by minority groups. This has lead to significant problems in terms of policing of minority youth in Canada, a situation that will worsen if, as a society, we are unwilling or unable to pay more than lipservice to the concept of equality within a multi-racial society. Consider the Toronto high school which the noted social work professor, Wilson Head, visited in May of 1992. On the morning of his visit the principal confiscated two handguns. Head, interviewing one young man asked him what he wanted to do in the future. His response was, "I'm not gonna live past 25."

Research has not been forthcoming on one of the most vital aspects of juvenile crime, the interaction between police and juveniles. We know virtually nothing about the ways in which youth and the police construct their everyday interactions. As the point of entry of juveniles into the criminal justice system this is a key juncture which is deserving of academic attention. Another area of concern is that of police handling of "under twelve", children who commit acts that if they were over the age of twelve would qualify as crimes. While those under twelve are considered *doli incapax* under Canadian law, current Canadian police practices in handling children who run afoul of community standards require research attention.

A work by Tullio Caputo, a researcher who has both published widely on the subject of young offenders, as well as been involved at the level of praxis in this field, introduces the book. His chapter was chosen to introduce this volume as it represents a key analysis of the development of our justice system's approach to juvenile offenders and also reflects the approach of the contributors to this volume, setting the tone, as it were, for the argument developed throughout this book. It also informs us of the importance of grounding our research and policies in historically informed research. The Juvenile Delinquents Act (JDA) has shifted from an initial long-term period of attention to the problems of youth and their need for positive intervention from the community to an approach that is characterized predominantly by punishment. The movement in legislative direction that Caputo meticulously documents demonstrates clearly the shift from concern to correction, and from community responsibility to personal pathology, in that juveniles are no longer seen as the products of a society that has in some sense failed them, but rather as authors of their own personal destruction. At one level this perpetuates a myth of cultural opportunity, that is, that the individual chooses his/her actions and shifts our attention away from the structural to the wholly personal. While concerns about youth and the conditions that produce delinquency may be much debated by politicians in the press, youth swarmings and riots in Toronto in 1992 demonstrated that it is only when large scale violence erupts that much of anything is done.

Caputo's article is the starting point for any serious student of the evolution, or perhaps more accurately, devolution of our juvenile 'justice' system. It would not be accurate to characterize the entirety of the YOA as a draconian piece of legislation bent upon the punishment of young people in conflict with our society. The YOA, as Caputo notes, has brought certain safeguards and benefits to young people. The removal of 'status' offenses such as truancy and promiscuous behaviour have recognized the principle that young people should not be the objects of criminal laws that do not effect adults or which are based upon sexual behaviour (between adolescent consenting partners). During the 1970s judges in the provincial family court system began to become aware that their expertise as social workers was not sufficient to cope with the increasingly litigious atmosphere of the family court. Youths who were charged began to appear with legal counsel in court and to argue the more technical points of law before judges who did not possess advanced legal training. This effectively circumvented the whole idea of *parens patriae,* or the "state as parent," as judges were forced into a more narrow role of adjudicating the law as it applied to juveniles. The YOA began its life, as Caputo's research has shown, as a response to the limitations of the JDA and the evolving nature of the adversarial representation of charged children and teenagers.

Other problems with the JDA were evident, but not any less controversial. Under the JDA children from the age of seven could be charged, an age limit that was to be altered to 12 under the YOA. Police organizations were particularly opposed to this piece of legislation, fearing a kind of "mini-criminal" would be permitted to flourish if no police intervention backed by the force of law were available.

The YOA heralded a new emphasis on due process for the young offender but this was overshadowed by the concentration on punishment within the criminal justice system. As various researchers have shown, the number of young offenders being held in custody has been rising since the introduction of the YOA. While sentences have become shorter, the impacts are significant in the life of young people. The YOA, Caputo argues, does not have the mechanisms in place to deal with the youthful deviant since little, if any, attention is paid to the "structural reality" that they experience in Canadian society. It is as though judicial and correctional officials as well as policymakers have deliberately turned a blind eye to the conditions that create and contribute to youth delinquency in society preferring, as it were, to punish the symptoms rather than the cause of rising youth crime. Since an overwhelming percentage of youth offending in Canada involves property offenses, particularly break and entry, it is surprising, or perhaps not that academic researchers, the media and the general public have not sought to address the conditions in which delinquency arises. One simple example underscores this point; the price of going to the movies is roughly ten dollars at the time of writing; a simple lunch at a burger restaurant retails for over $5. It is expensive for a young person to live day-to-day in our society and many children and teens do not possess the economic wherewithal to live a decent life. A life filled with denial is likely to transform itself into a life filled with anger at some point as many young people are asked to be "have-nots" in a society that places an overwhelming emphasis on material worth as a measure of the success of one's life. While conditions in Canada have not reached the depths of those experiences in inner city American where children kill other children because they want the jacket or shoes the other is wearing, there is certainly compelling evidence for those on the front line of social efforts that all is not well.

Caputo develops two examples of the kinds of problems that are impacting in levels of youth offending. The first is the high levels of unemployment that young people are experiencing. In the summer of 1992 'official' estimates of unemployment amongst youth 16-24 ran at 18% while the number was likely much higher given those who had simply given up looking for work or were underemployed. Secondly, Caputo further explores the issue of the increasing length of dependency that we have developed for young people in our society. No longer do young people seek full-time work as children of ten or twelve years of age as might have youngsters in the first decades of this century. We require young people to remain in school for longer periods. The age of consent for sexual relations remains at eighteen as does the age for voter eligibility. Young people may not legally buy or imbibe alcohol until the age of nineteen. In this contradictory stage of life young people are asked to be increasingly responsible by the YOA yet denied this role in almost all other aspects of their daily lives by other legal structures. This contradiction is deeply felt by many young people, in fact most young people experience a period of rebellion during the latter stages of their teen years. Caputo argues finally, and with conviction, for an alternative strategy predicated upon a community-based strategy, as well as a new focus on "broader social processes." It is likely that until we address these wider issues as a society that we will effectively deal with those young people who come into conflict with our law in increasing numbers.

Rehabilitation in our juvenile justice system is now regarded as the folly of a more liberal era, and "get tough" policies have replaced attempts to ameliorate the effects of cultural disadvantage, poverty, family rupture and various other social maladies. In the United States under Reagan/Bush the "thousand points of light" have turned out to be no more than illusions in the darkness for many young persons' desperate lives. Many youngsters have pondered how you see these lights from the ghettos of southeast Los Angeles, Miami, Detroit, or even in the shadows of the White House in Washington. This movement, variously referred to as 'just deserts' or the 'justice-as-fairness' model is a misnomer as are many of the terms associated with juvenile offenders. Fairness is relative to the economic position of youth in society. We know that poor youth and adults end up occupying the places in our growing prison systems whereas few "white collar" offenders, ever receive hard time for their activities. Rather than delivering justice these philosophies have had exactly the opposite effect; while arrests have fallen in states employing this philosophy incarcerations continue to rise. This is the case in Canada, where the "short, sharp shock," that is, increasing use of short sentences of three months or less have become the norm.

This is a book which is privileged to have contributions by the leading Canadian researchers in the field of young offenders. Their chapters, the majority of which have been published in The Canadian Journal of Criminology, which remains the leading journal for the publication of research on issues affecting youths and the law, share a commonality in their attention to the 'injustice' delivered under the rubric of 'justice' to young people in this country. The articles deal with a wide variety of topics which examine youth behaviour outside of the criminal justice system from the sale of sex, through the apprehension stages of policing, to the courtroom. The understanding youths have of court procedures, the inadequacies of current treatment programmes and legislation, the fate of rehabilitative programmes, the structure of alternative measures programmes, minority youth offenders, issues of criminal liability in children, and youth gangs are explored in this volume. We hope to achieve with this book a volume that will not only assist researchers but draw together in coherent form cutting edge ideas in theory and research from the last decade in Canada with an emphasis on work since the implementation of the YOA. As we have already stated, there are several key areas in which no published literature yet exists and hopefully, this volume can act as a catalyst to researchers to address these vacuums.

As editors we combine experience in both the academic understanding of juveniles in conflict with society as well as praxis work on the front line with young people. We have included in this volume individuals whose work has primarily reflected a connection between theoretical and praxis issues. We argue that is only by broadening the dialogue on the substantive issues that produce youth injustice that we will be able to move on as a society and provide justice for all.

CHAPTER 1
The Young Offenders Act: Children's Rights, Children's Wrongs

T.C. CAPUTO*

This paper presents an overview of juvenile justice in Canada, including the passage of the Juvenile Delinquents Act in 1908 and its replacement with the Young Offenders Act in 1984. This development reflects a shift in philosophy from a welfare orientation to a greater concern with criminal behaviour and the accountibility of young offenders. The implications of this change are discussed in light of the potential benefits that various provisions of the Young Offenders Act have for young people, including the granting of various rights and the guarantee of due process. These are contrasted with the consequences that an emphaisis on the criminal behaviour of young people can have for the juvenile justice system. Evidence is presented which suggests that more young people are being incarcerated and for longer periods of time under the Young Offenders Act. It is argued that the Young Offenders Act is unable to deal effectively with the problems of young people since it does not address the structural reality that they experience in this society. High unemployment and an increasingly lengthy period of dependency are discussed as two examples of the barriers restricting the normal passage from adolescence to adulthood for many young people. Suggestions for an alternative strategy are offered which incorporate elements of a comunity-based strategy as well as a focus on broader social processes.

INTRODUCTION

The Young Offenders Act received royal assent on July 7, 1982 and was proclaimed law on April 2, 1984. The passage of this legislation marked the beginning of a new era of juvenile justice in Canada. It brought to a close the seventy four year history of the *Juvenile Delinquents Act* (JDA) and signalled a fundamental shift in the philosophy underlying our treatment of young people (Archambault, 1983; Lillies, 1983; Nasmith, 1983; Thompson, 1983).

This paper examines the development of a distinct system of juvenile justice in Canada including the passage of the *Juvenile Delinquents Act* and the creation and implementation of the new *Young Offenders Act* (YOA). Central to this discussion is a consideration of the idealogical and philosophical assumptions which underlie this legislation (Doern and Phidd, 1983: 51-59). Those assumptions warrant our attention, for their significance sometimes extends beyond the realm of juvenile justice as "it has often been the case in recent years that popular concepts of practice in juvenile justice have made inroads into the adult criminal justice system" (Ekstedt and Griffiths, 1984: 331).

ESTABLISHING A JUVENILE JUSTICE SYSTEM IN CANADA

The establishment of a separate system of justice for young peope in Canada followed similar developments in a number of western countries. This development was based, in part, on the "discovery" of childhood which Aries (1962) describes as taking place in western Europe between the sixteenth and nineteenth centuries. Prior to this, few distinctions were made on the basis of age and young people were fully integrated into the main stream of social life. A high infant mortality rate discouraged emotional investment and the "old tendencies were either to ignore children or exploit them" (Empey, 1982: 38). This began to change as middle class families started to define their children as innocent and sensitive beings who required nurturance and protection. That is, children "became categorized as a special class with special needs" (Rooke and Schnell, 1983: 8).

This development reflects the growing prosperity of middle class families that were able to forego the economic contribution of their children while directing an increasing proportion of family resources towards child rearing.

Yet as Rooke and Schnell (1983) note, once the concept of childhood was widespread among the middle class, it came to be viewed as a normal part of life that should be available to all children. Those groups without childhood were defined as inferior and in need of assistance. This definition of the situation contributed to the development of a child rescue movement spearheaded by middle class reformers (Leon, 1977; Rooke and Schnell, 1983).

In his assessment of the "child savers" in the United States, Platt (1969) points out that there was more to the development of a separate justice system for juveniles than a humanistic desire to help unfortunate children. He argues that this reflects a change in the political economy from the laissez-faire to monopoly capitalism and a concomitant change from repressive control to welfare state benevolence. According to Platt,

> the "child saving" movement which developed in the United States during the latter part of the nineteenth century was not a humanistic enterprise on behalf of the working class against the established order. On the contrary, its impetus came primarily from the middle and upper classes who were instrumental in devising new forms of social control to protect their power and privelage (1977: xx).[1]

This analysis can be applied equally to the idealogical and political changes which were taking place in Canada during the last decades of the nineteenth century, and especially as this relates to the treatment afforded young people. Earlier in the century, reformers "generally believed that only a long period of compulsary and segregated training, discipline and schooling would change the character of the pre-delinquent or delinquent young person" (Sutherland, 1976: 100). The new reformers, however, looked to the family as the vehicle for rehabilitation. It was thought that a healthy family, including an appropriate foster family, was the ideal environment for rehabilitating those young people who had been involved in delinquent behaviour. While the state had been reluctant in the past to interfere in family matters, the changes brought about by these reformers placed childrearing practices under the jurisdiction of the court and permitted the state to intervene when families failed to raise their children "properly". "Juvenile delinquency can thus be analyzed as the creation of an emergent dominating Canadian capitalist class intent on maintaining control of working youth in burgeoning industrial cities" (West, 1984: 52).[2]

J.J. Kelso, a young Toronto journalist, was one of the most vocal proponents of a family-centred system for dealing with children with problems

(Sutherland, 1976: 112). Working with the like minded reformers, Kelso was active in the Children's Court Movement which sought to create a juvenile justice system that reflected their beliefs in a family centrered approach. They opposed the institutionalization of children and in their view, the "baneful influence of bad homes" was one of the most serious causes of crime. For this reason, they argued that the traditional "rights of parents" could be forfeited by gross neglect or by such continued gross misconduct as must work the ruin of their children" (Sutherland, 1976: 109). The passage by the federal government of the first *Juvenile Delinquents Act* of 1908 represented the crowning achievement of the Children's Court Movement (Currie, 1986: 63).

THE JUVENILE DELINQUENTS ACT (JDA)

The philosophy underlying the *Juvenile Delinquents Act* is known as *parens patriae*. It establishes the juvenile court as the surrogate parent that is able to intervene if other social institutions such as the family or the school fail to raise the child in an appropriate manner. This paternalistic philosophy and the statute based on it cast the court in the role of a firm but understanding parent. A central feature of this legislation is its image of children. During the latter part of the nineteenth century, reformers defined children as poor, innocent beings, who were in need of protection from the corrupting influences of society. While they may have been involved in undesirable behaviour, children were more in need of care and nurturance than punishment. Adjective such as "poor", "unfortunate," and "blameless" had been used by reformers in their campaign to eliminate the imprisonment of children. "In effect, prison reformers created for themselves a complex and ambiguous figure of a blameless child who is nevertheless guilty" (Houston, 1987: 177).

This image is evident both in the way that delinquency is defined in the *Juvenile Delnquents Act* and in the way that delinquents are to be treated. For example, Section 2 of the JDA defines a juvenile delinquent in the following way:

> "juvenile delinquents" means any child who violates any provision of
> the Criminal Code or of any federal or provincial statute, or of any
> by-law or ordinance of any municipality, or who is guilty of sexual
> immorality or any similar form of vice, or who is liable by reason of
> any other act to be committed to an industrial school or juvenile
> reformatory under any federal or provincial statute...

This definition encompasses both the violation of laws that apply to adults and a set of special "status offences" which apply only to children. Children are defined in this legislation as boys and girls under the age of sixteen or a maximum age established by individual provinces. Section 3(2) of the JDA states that those children adjudged to have committed a delinquency should not be dealt with as offenders, but as being in a condition of delinquency and in need of help, guidance, and proper supervision. The general orientation of this legislation is clearly expressed in Section 38 which states the following:

> This Act shall be liberally construed in order that its purpose may be carried out, namely, that the care and custody and discipline of a juvenile delinquent shall approximate as nearly as may be that which should be given be his parents, and that as far as practicable every juvenile delinquent shall be treated not as a criminal, but as a misdirected and misguided child, and one needing aid, encouragement, help and assistance.

Judges were granted a great deal of discretion under the *Juvenile Delinquents Act.* all cases involving children had to come before a juvenile court. In exceptional cases involving indictable offences under the criminal code, a juvenile court judge could decide to transfer the child to adult court provided that the child was fourteen or older and that this was for the "good of the child and where the interests ofthe commuity demanded it" (*Juvenile Delinquents Act*, Section 9(1)).

Hearings could be heard in private under the JDA, and neither the names of the children involved nor their identities could be revealed. These hearings could be informal since they were not bound by the same strict procedural rules that governed adult courts. Parents or guradians had a right to be present at these hearings; however, they could also be held repsonsible for the behaviour of their children. Children could not be detained in the same place as adults but had to be sent to special detention homes or shelters which were to be used exclusively for children. Probation oficers, under the control of the judge, could assist the court in representing the child at the hearings by providing any information the court might require or by being available to take charge of the child before or after the hearing, as directed by the court. The court was to act in the best interests of the child at all times.

Subsection 20 of the JDA outlines the various dispositions available to the court. these include the following:

a)   suspended final sentence;

b)   adjourn the hearing or disposition of the case from time to time
     for any definite or indefinite period;

c)   impose a fine not exceeding twenty-five dollars, which may be
     paid in periodical amounts or otherwise;

d)   commit the child to the care or custody of a probation officer or
     any other suitable person;

e)   allow the child to remain in its home, subject to visitation of a
     probation officer, such child to report to the court or to the pro-
     bation officer as often as may be required;

f)   cause the child to be placed in a suitable family home as a foster
     home, subject to the friendly supervision of a probation officer
     and the further order of the court;

g)   impose upon the delinquent such further or other conditions as
     may be deemed advisable;

h)   commit the child to the charge of any children's aid society,
     duly organized under an Act of the legislature of the province...;

i)   commit the child to an industrial school duly approved by the
     lieutenant governor in council.

Section 20 of the JDA states further that the parents and the municipality may
be ordered to contribute child support. The court could also cause the delinquent to be brought before it up to the time that the child reached the age of
twenty-one.

This range of dispositions gave juvenile court judges tremendous latitude
in dealing with juvenile delinquents. Sentences could be of indeterminate
length and the only provision guiding judicial discretion was that it be exercised in the best interests of the child.

In spite of its laudable goals, the *Juvenile Delinquents Act* came under
increasing scrutiny and by the early 1960s, a number of groups began to call
for changes to the legislation (Corrado, 1983). The two main criticisms of the
Juvenile Delinquents Act focussed on the extensive power it granted the
court for dealing with young people and its apparent inefficiency in preventing
delinquency and rehabilitating delinquents. The informality of the system permitted the potential abuse of children's rights since there were few constraints
on judicial discretion. This was especially evident in the indeterminate sen-
tances available under the *Juvenile Delinquents Act* since they allowed the

court to intervene in a young person's life to a much greater extent than was possible under the adult system.

A number of legal and constitutional changes also began to undermine many of the practies existing under the JDA. For example, the affirmation of children's rights by the Gault decision in 1967 in the United States meant that children in that country were entitled to the same due process safeguards available to adults. Gerald Gault was a fourteen year old boy who had been arrested for making an obscene phone call. Lundmann (1984: 99) notes that Gault was sentanced to six years in a State Industrial School. The same offence for an adult carried a maximum sentence of six months! The Supreme Court of the United States eventually overturned this decision and ruled that "juveniles have a right to receive counsel, to confront and to cross-examine witnesses, to remain silent, to be given a transcript of the hearing, and the right to an appeal" (Lundman, 1984: 99). This guaranteed young people many of the due process safeguards already enjoyed by adults and in the process moved the juvenile justice system in the United States much closer to the adversarial adult system.

As is the case in numerous areas, developments in the United States often influence what takes place in Canada (West, 1984: xiv). This is particularly evident in the development of juvenile justice in Canada as Canadian reformers often conferred with their counterparts in the United States and examined American programs and practices before implementing their own (see Sutherland, 1976 and Rooke ans Schnell, 1983). It is in this sense that the Gault decision had important implications for juvenile justice in Canada.

Currie (1986) discusses the emergence of the Children's Liberation Movement in the 1960s in Canada which actively sought reforms such as those contained in the Gault decision. She states that,

> juvenile justice became increasingly criticized at two levels. Not only did juvenile justice fail to protect and rehabilitate children, but it also failed to provide children with the protection afforded adults. Attention centred on the fact that violations of the act included offences—called status offences—that applied only to minors and would not be punishable if committed by an adult (Currie, 1986: 65).

Other criticisms included the fact that the decision to bring a child into court was often made by a parent or social worker (Currie, 1986). No violations of the law were necessary for this action to be taken since it required only that a determination be made that the child was unmanageable or beyond parental control. Furthermore, the role played by lawyers in criminal courts was performed by probation officers or case workers in juvenile court and they were concerned with such things as "truancy, school performance, attitude, and promiscuity during presentence investigation" (Currie, 1986:65). Again the commission of an offence was not the key factor since what was important was whether or not the child's behaviour was conforming to an ideal standard. The Act was also criticized for the variability which existed across the country in the age limits for defining juvenile delinquents. Behaviour that could be considered delinquent in one province could be defined as criminal in another. There were few checks on those that exercised discretion in the juvenile justice system such as the police, the courts and those that adminstered court dispositions. Furthermore, review procedures of court dispositions were inadequate under the JDA. No legislative authority existed for the practice of diversion nor were there safeguards for young people dealt with by alternative measures to the formal court system (Caplan, 1981:1-3 cited in Havemann, 1986).

"The weakening of the principle of parens patriae began as the Act was attacked for violating basic constitutional rights, and agitation for a change gained widespread support" (Currie, 1986:65). This was given further impetus with the adoption of the *Charter of Rights and Freedoms* which made it illegal to treat people differently on the basis of their age. Consequently, many of the practices and procedures extant under the JDA were rendered inoperable.

There was growing disillusionment during the 1960s and early 1970s both in Canada and in the United States, with the rehabilitative philosophy of the juvenile courts. For example, after an extensive review of the research on delinquency treatment programs, Trojanowicz (1978) concluded that these programs did not achieve their goals of rehabilitation and crime prevention. Similar conclusions were reached by Empey (1982) and Lundmann (1984). Critics called for the abandonment of the rehabilitative philosohpy of the JDa in favour of one which emphasized punishment and deterrence (Von Hirsch, 1976; Wilson, 1975).

During this period a number of reforms were introduced which were based on the work of the Labelling theorists (Matza, 1964; Lemert, 1967; Becker, 1963). These theorists pointed out that while most young people become involved in some form of delinquent behaviour at one time or another in their lives, only a small number of these juveniles are ever apprehended and processed by the courts. Powerful labels are attached to those that experience official processing; the juveniles themselves, the authorities and others may respond to those labels.[3]

The Labelling theorists were concerned with the potentially negative consequences which could result from a child being officially processed and labelled a delinquent. The reforms inspired by the Labelling theorists sought to protect young people from the negative consequences of official labelling by diverting them from the court system. A number of "diversion" programs were established with the co-operation of the police and the courts, to keep delinquents out of the court system where possible, and to deal with them less formally. More drastic proposals went beyond the diversion and envisioned "judicious non-intervention" (Lemert, 1967) by the courts while others called for "fadical non-intervention" (Schor, 1973) and the complete reconstruction of the juvenile justice system.

The "diversion" reforms which were implemented did little to ameliorate the situation that children faced. Critics pointed out that rather than improving conditions for children, diversion and related programs had actually exacerbated the problem (Berlin and Allard, 1980; O'Brien, 1984). For example, young people enjoyed no additional rights or protection as a result of diversion, and in many cases these programs actually led to a widening of the net of control over them. Court intervention into children's lives vontinued to exceed what was possible under existing legislation for adults. Furthermore, these continued programs could not claim to be any more effective than previous programs had been in preventing delinquency, or for that matter, any more effective than doing nothing at all (Empey, 1982).

The ongoing criticism of the ineffectiveness of the juvenile justice system led to further calls for reform. This process was begun in earnest by the middle 1970s as the government embarked upon an extensive period of consultation aimed at developing new juvenile justice legislation (Corrado, 1983; Solicitor General, 1975). An attempt was made to survey the views of various interest groups, and to arrive at a politically acceptable compromise by incorporating various elements of the competing theoretical and philosophical positions into new juvenile justice legislation.

Many of the concerns voiced in the debate over changes made to the *Juvenile Delinquents Act* reflected the vastly different approaches which exist on issues surrounding the development of criminal justice policy. A variety of models have been used to summarize the various perspectives advanced (see Reid and Reitsma-Street, 1984; Empey, 1982). The two major models which will be elaborated here are the welfare model and the justice model.

The welfare model is based on the philosophy of the positivist school of criminology which began to grow in popularity near the end of the nineteenth century. Positivist theorists held that crime was the result of physiological, psychological, environmental factors over which individuals had little control (Lombroso, 1912, Lombroso-Ferrerro, 1911; Vold, 1958). Instead of punishment, they recommended that criminals be treated by scientifically trained experts. This approach is evident in the paternalistic philosophy which underlies the JDA, since delinquents were not to be punished but rehabilitated through the administration of proper treatment. Proponents of this model are primarily concerned with the needs and well-being of children. Many social work and child welfare professionals as well as numerous juvenile court judges share this view (Bennett, 1985). This group has been described as the welfare lobby (Havemann, 1986).

The proponents of the welfare model argues that the JDA was ineffective because it was not given sufficient resources to work properly (Morris *et al.*, 1980). John Gilbert, M.P. (Toronto, Broadview) made this explicit in his comments in the House of Commons. He stated

> The difficulty is not in the basic philosophy of the *Juvenile Delinquents Act*, but in the failure of society to give the juvenile court adequate resources to fulfiil the aims of the philosophy, the philosophy of wanted young people to become law abiding citizens and directing treatment with regard to their rehabilitation (Commons Debates, 1971. Vol. 3:2381).

Proponents of the welfare model supported the ability of the system to tailor programs to the specific needs of children through the use of trial reports and a range of intervention strategies. They praised the informality and ability of the system which allowed the court to deal creatively with young people and their problems. However, they were aware of the potential for abuse in the system and they recognized the need to safeguard children's rights.

An opposing view is presented by the advocates of the justice model. This model is based on the philosophy of the classical school of criminology which held that people were hedonistic beings who sought to maximize their pleasure and minimize their pain (Beccaria 1774; Bentham, 1775). Crime was understood by classical theorists as a rational and calculated activity in which people engaged to obtain pleasurable ends. They felt that all that was needed to prevent crime was to ensure that the pain inflicted on criminals as punishment for their misdeeds, sufficiently outweighed the pleasure they attained through illegal activity so as to make further illegal activity unattractive. The classical theorists pointed out that punishment need not be brutal or severe to achieve this end, but that it be swift, certain, and graded (Phillipson, 1970;

Sylveter, 1972). Empey (1982) has outlined two versions of the justice model which represent contemporary expressions of classical theory. He calls these the "utilitarian perspective" and the "just deserts perspective".

The utilitarian perspective follows classical theory in calling for a return to a punishment-deterrence approach to crime (van den Haag, 1975; Wilson, 1975). Advocates of this approach argue that the courts have been too lenient and that sentences must be increased to act as an effective deterrent to crime (Trepanier, 1983). These ideas form the basis of the law and order lobby. The just deserts perspective, on the other hand, is critical of the ineffectiveness of the rehabilitation strategy of the welfare model and the extensive interference allowed into children's lives (Gray, 1981). According to this perspective, the courts should restrict themselves to dealing with the criminal behaviour of juveniles while leaving other needs to the appropriate child welfare authorities. Young people convicted of crime should be punished by the courts and they should understand this punishment to be a just desert of their criminal activity. Just deserts advocates believed that status offences should be eliminated and that children should be given the same rights as adults if they are to be treated as responsible individuals by the courts. These ideas form the basis of the children's rights lobby.

CREATING THE YOUNG OFFENDERS ACT

The apparent dramatic increase in incidence of juvenile delinquency during the 1950s led to a growing awareness of, and concern over, this problem. Amid increasing criticism of the JDA, and mounting presssure to act, the government established a special committee to examine the problem of juvenile delinquency.[4] The statistics displayed in Table 1 indicate that the amount of juvenile crime did, in fact, rise dramatically during the 1950s and 1960s. However, Table 1 also shows that adult crime rates rose just as sharply and that these figures represent a more general trend rather than something peculiar to the juvenile population.

A 1986 Senate report on youth examines this issue and notes that "part of the reported increase in crimes committed by young people can be attributed to more effective police surveillance and a greater determination to bring young people to justice" (Special Senate Committee on Youth, 1986). This view is shared by McDonald (1969) who also challenges the conventional wisdom concerning juvenile crime during this period. She examines data from 1950 to 1966 and argues that the increase in juvenile crime statistics is due to

Table 1
Selected Crime and Population Statistics

Year	Juveniles Charged Number	Juveniles Charged Rate/100,000	Adults Charged (Indictable offences) Number	Adults Charged Rate/100,000	Population 15 - 19 Number (000s)	Percent	Population 20 - 24 Number (000s)	Percent	Canada Total (000s)
1981	187,253	770.1	866,418	3563.4	2314.9	9.52	2343.6	9.63	24,314.7
1980	192,463	800.5	821,870	3418.4	2359.2	9.80	2305.7	9.50	24,042.5
1977	89,617	385.3	686,481	2951.5	2281.3	9.80	2197.8	9.44	23,257.7
1972	65,115	298.7	514,213	2358.6	2167.2	9.94	1922.0	8.96	21,801.5
1962	31,913	171.8	359,413	1935.4	1510.5	8.13	1211.7	6.52	18,570.0

Source: Adopted from Biron and Gauvreau (1984) and Canada Year Books (Ottawa: Government of Canada).

Table 2
Unemployment by Sex, Age and Race

Sex and Age Group	Unemployed '000 1979	1980	1981	1982	1983	Rate 1979	1980	1981	1982	1983
Total	836	865	898	1,314	1,448	7.4	7.5	7.5	11.0	11.9
Men	449	476	494	778	859	6.6	6.9	7.0	11.1	12.1
Women	387	389	404	537	590	8.8	8.4	8.3	10.9	11.6
Age 15-24	388	404	407	555	579	12.9	13.2	13.2	18.8	19.9
Men	214	225	233	331	345	13.2	13.7	14.1	21.1	22.4
Women	174	179	175	224	234	12.7	12.6	12.3	16.1	17.0
Age 25 +	447	462	491	759	869	5.4	5.4	5.6	8.4	9.4
Men	235	251	262	447	514	4.5	4.8	4.8	8.2	9.2
Women	212	210	229	313	335	7.0	6.5	6.7	8.8	9.6

Source: Statistics Canada (1985)

the fact Canadian authorities were "permitting progressively less deviance on the parts of citizens, especially juveniles" (quoted in Sutherland, 1976:142). She points out that law enforcement officials began to prosecute trivial infractions during this period, especially if they involved juveniles.

Concern over juvenile delinquency continued to grow throughout the 1960s and early 1970s as opposition members pressed the government for changes to the JDA. This may have been influenced by the visibility and the rebelliousness of the emerging youth culture of the period. Despite continued calls for reform, however, no changes were made to the legislation.

Table 3
Suicide rate by sex and age

Sex and age group	1961	1966	1971	1976	1981
Total	11.5	18.3	28.8	37.2	39.1
Men	9.0	15.3	23.1	29.0	33.2
Women	2.5	3.0	5.7	8.2	5.9
Age 15-19	14.9	17.1	23.7	25.6	28.1
Men	11.9	12.8	17.3	18.4	21.3
Women	3.0	4.3	6.4	7.2	6.8
Age 20-24	4.6	7.3	15.8	21.1	25.0
Men	3.7	6.0	12.7	16.8	21.2
Women	0.9	1.3	3.1	4.3	3.8
Total	836	865	898	1,314	1,448

Source: Adopted from *Youth: A Plan of Action*, Special Senate Committee on Youth (1986).

During the middle and late 1970s inordinately high unemployment rates exacerbated the problems faced by young people. Some observers began to talk about a "lost generation" who faced the possibility of going through life moving from one marginal job to another with unemployment and welfare in between. The magnitude of this problem can be seen in the employment statistics for the period which are presented in Table 2. The problems of the young people were examined in 1984 by the special Senate committee on youth, and Table 3 presents the statistics on suicide reported in this study.

It is clear from the data presented in Table 2 that the prospects for many young people were quite dismal during this period. The unemployment rate for people between the ages of 15 and 24 was slightly more than double the rate reported for people 25 and older. Table 3 indicates that the rate of suicide was alarmingly high for young people and this may reflect a growing sense of despair. Increasing rates of delinquency may represent another response to the situation faced by many young people as they find it increasingly difficult to fit into adult society.

During this extended period of economic recession, law and order campaigns gained momentum in Canada and the United States as well as in a number of western countries (Horson, 1981). Many of the tenets of the justice model found ready acceptance in this climate and calls for the increased protection of society, the punishment of criminal behaviour, and the return of capital punishment became popular. Cullen *et al.* point out that in the United States, crime provided an opportunity that issue-seeking politicians found easy to embrace.

> Once launched, the "get tough" movement proved self-reinforcing and difficult to counteract. As national and local political elites joined the bandwagon, they gave legitimacy to and nurtured the growth of the public's punitive sentiments. It was now fashionable to be a conservative on crime issues. This in turn placed politicians (including judges) who harboured more humanistic attitudes in a precarious position. To appear "soft on crime" would make them vulnerable to political attack (Cullen *et al.*, 1985:22)

Fattah (1982) makes similar assessment of the situation in Canada. He suggests that Canadian politicans have played upon the fears of the public by adopting the law and order rhetoric. Indeed, several recent studies of public perceptions fo crime indicate that Canadians grossly overestimate the amount of crime involving violence (Doob and Roberts, 1982; Wanner and Caputo, forthcoming). This may make them more receptive to the arguments raised by the law and order lobby.

An attempt was made during the creation of the new juvenile justice legislation, to retain some of the parens patriae philosophy of the JDA while heedding the criticism raised by proponents of the justice model. "The justice model allowed the Liberal government to co-opt the demands for individual accountability, protection for society, and tough deterrent measures against the new dangerous class voiced by the Opposition and the law and order lobby as its own. Both Government and Opposition attempted to make points off a "get tough" aproach" (Havemann, 1986:230).

This approach was made explicit by Robert Kaplan, the Soliciter General of Canada at the time, at a meeting of the House of Commons, Select Committee of Legal and Constitutional Affairs. He stated the following:

> we are attempting with this legislation to toughen the kiddie-court image of the juvenile court and make it a place where a mature young person will be punished and held accountable to society for what he has done...those young people who were indicating that the kiddie-court could not really control them and they did not have to get serious until they faced up to adult jurisdiction, will, if these courts develop the way we intend them to develop, be given something to think about when they appear before the youth court (quoted in Havemann, 1986:230).

The dual concerns of the justice model and the welfare model are evident in various provisions of the *Young Offenders Act,* a brief outline of the *Young Offenders Act* is presented below.

THE YOUNG OFFENDERS ACT (YOA)

The *Young Offenders Act* contains a different approach to juvenile justice than that found in the *Juvenile Delinquents Act.* The most obvious difference is that the term "juvenile delinquent" has been replaced by the term "young offender". This represents more than a simple change in terminology, however, since the new legislation places much more emphasis on the criminal behaviour of young people. The "status offences" which existed under the JDA have been eliminated in the YOA and many of the changes instituted move the juvenile justice system closer to the adversarial model of the adult system.

Subsection 3 of the *Young Offenders Act* is a unique section, called The Declaration of Principles, that contains eight items which are intended to outline policy for Canada with respect to young offenders. This section included the following provisions:

a) while young persons shold not in all instances be held acount-able in the same manner or suffer the same consequences as adults, young persons who commit offences should nonetheless bear responsibility for their contraventions;

b) society must, although it has the responsibilty to take reason-able measures to prevent criminal conduct by young persons, be afforded the necessary protection from illegal behaviour;

c) young persons who commit offences require supervision, disci-pline, and control, but, because of their state of dependency and level of development and maturity, they also have special needs and require guidance and assistance;

d) where it is not inconsistent with the protection of society, taking no measures or taking measures other than judicial proceedings under this Act should be considered for young persons who have committed offences;

e) young persons have rights and freedoms in their own right, including those stated by the Canadian Charter of Rights, and in particular a right to be heard in the course of, and to participate in, the processes that lead to decisions that affect them, and young persons should have special guarantees of their rights and freedoms;

f) in the application of this Act, the rights and freedoms of young persons included a right to the least possible interference with freedom that is consistent with the protection of society, having regards to the needs of young persons and the interests of their families;

g) young persons have the right, in every instance where they have rights or freedoms that may be affected by this Act, to be informed as to what those rights are; and,

h) parents have responsibility for the care and supervision of their children, and, for that reason, young persons should be removed from parental supervisions either partly or entrirely only when measures that provide for continuing parental super-vision are inappropriate.

In addition to the provisions outlined in the Declaration of Principle, the YOA has introduced a number of other significant changes to the juvenile justice system. To begin with, the Act formalizes many of the procedures of the juvenile court as it sets out in detail the procedures that are to be followed in various proceedings. It establishes minimum and maximum ages for young offenders across Canada, namely people between the ages of 12 and 17. Trials may now by held in public, although the identity of young offenders may not be revealed. The YOA includes a provision which guarantees young people charged with an offence the right to retain and instruct counsel. The parents of a young person accused of a crime are to be notified if the young person has been arrested and is being detained in custody. The court may order medical or psychological reports and under certain circumstances, the results of these may be witheld from the accused. The police are empowered by this legislation to photograph and fingerprint young people convisted of offences and these records may be kept for two years, in the case of summary convictions, and five years in the case of indictable offences. The Act also contains specific provisions for transferring young offenders to ordinary (adult) court.

The *Young Offenders Act* also contains a number of changes in the dispositions which are available to the court. These range from absolute discharge and fines, to secure custody orders. The maximum fine has been raised from $25 under the JDA, to $1,000 under the YOA. The young persons can be committed to custody for a maximum period of two years but this may be raised to three years if the persons has been convicted of an offence for which the punishment allowed in the Criminal code is imprisionment for life. The YOA also includes a section entitled "Alternative Measures" which may be used instead of judicial procceddings under specific circumstances. The Act outlines who is eligible for Alternative Measures, seeks to ensure that no coercion is used to force accused young offenders to participate in Alternative Measures and being used only in those cases for which sufficient evidence exists to proceed to prosecution.

ASSESSING THE YOUNG OFFENDERS ACT

Overall, the changes incorporated into the YOA move the juvenile justice system in Canada much closed to the adversarial adult system of justice. While there is some recognition of the special circumstances and needs of young people, the formalization of procedures, the addition of defence lawyers and the emphasis on criminal behaviour reflect the dominance of the justice model orientation in this legislation. The provisions in the YOA whioch enhance children's rights are a welcome addition to the juvenile justice system. However, these new rights may have come at a high cost if the system is more formal and adversarial in nature. "More rights are granted but considerably more responsibilities are imposed. Without sufficient resources the punishment aspect may be resorted to by the courts by default of having few palatable alternatives" (Wardell, 1985:388).

The criminal justice orientation of the YOA has been described by Leschied and Jaffe (1985) in their study of youth courts in nine southern Ontario countries during the first eight months after the YOA was implemented. Their results indicate that the level of charges remained about the same even though the police no longer charged persons 7-11 years of age under the YOA. More importantly, custodial dispositions showed a significant increase during this period. They also found that periods of pre-trial and pre-disposition detention has increased. In addition, the authors state that there was a 30 per cent increase in requests for social histories which they suggest are made in anticipation of an order for custody. This was in contrast to a 50 per cent decrease in requests for clinical assessments which they point out is surprising since there were no sections referring to this service under the JDA, whereas the need and purpose of clincial assessments is spelled out in detail in section 13 of the YOA. Leschied and Jaffe state:

> The preliminary findings reported in this study reflect the correctional theme of the YOA, with its emphasis on custody and minimization of treatment intervention. These findings reflect a major shift away from the parens patriae, rehabilitative emphasis of the JDA (Leschied and Jaffe, 1985:5).

In a subsequent article, Leschied and Gendreau (1986) note that there is a curious shortage of official documentation concerning the implementation of the YOA. The evidence that is available, however, shows that far more young people have been incarcerated since the YOA came into effect and that they are being held in custody for longer periods of time.

In Alberta, during the first six months of 1985 a total of 9,538 charges were laid against young persons under the age of sixteen. for the same period last year only 4,667 charges were laid against the same group. This represents a rate of increase of about 104% over 1984. For the last five years the conviction rate has been steady at around 75% of those charged.

The trend in Ontario is equally bleak ... custodial sentences during the first year of the Young Offenders Act averaged 250 days in that province; an increase of 115% over the figure for the last year of the Juvenie Delinquents Act (*John Howard Society Reporter*, 1985).

The results of investigative reporting presented in the mass media have documented similar finds. An article from the *Toronto Star* indicates that

> Average sentences for young lawbreakers in Ontario have more than doubled under Canada's Young Offenders Act.... In Ontario, the average sentence for offenders aged 12 to 15 has increased 135 percent for those being sent to training schools and 210 percent for those sentenced to group homes—open custody...(*Toronto Star*, August 6, 1985, A9).

Another article states:

> Despite all the talk about regarding the special needs of youngsters, and using custody as a last resort, the federal government by its very approval of the ACT had called on judges to lay down a firm hand. the Act in itself is a process by which to lock up youngsters. Therefore, a kid with a lengthy list of crimes is out of luck regardless of the reasons for his behaviour (*Calgary Herald*, July 26:A6).

The Alternative Measures section of the Act provides another example of the justice model emphasis of this legislation. This section of the Act is designed to keep young people out of the official system. However, the impact of Alternative Measures is restricted since they are reserved for first time non-serious offenders and are unavailable for repeat or more serious offenders. Many of the people who are eligible for Alternative Measures were already being dealt with informally under the JDA and the new legislation does little to address the problems of more serious young offenders. Furthermore, many jurisdictions have no Alternative Measures in place while in others, they are administered by the government with little community involvement. In each of these instances, the ideal behind this section of the legislation is far from met and the usefulness of Alternative Measures in this form is questionable.

The Alternative Measures section of the legislation is subject to a number of criticisms which apply well to various sections of the Act. For example, due to the fact that implementation of this federal law is left up to individual provinces, different ideologies and fiscal capabilities may lead to major discreoencies in how the same offence, committed by a similar type of individual, is dealt with in different provinces (Thompson, 1983; White, 1985). In addition, provisions such as Alternative Measures and legal representation favour the urban areas of the country where these resources are more plentiful. Moreover, the Act permits the use of Alternative Measures but does not require them.

In a recent Ontario case, a young persons applied to have the charges against him dismissed on the grounds that his rights had been infringed because Ontario had no Alternative Measures programs. The court agreed and dismissed the charges against him ruling that his rights had been infringed upon because the facts in the case indicated that he might have been considered for Alternative Measures had they been available in the province (*Weekly Digest of Family Law,* 1986: Issue 50, Dec. 15:6). This type of decision by the courts may have a significant impact on the way that they YOA is implemented in various parts of the country.

Wardeel (1986: 128-158) examines the implementation of a number of sections of the YOA such as sentencing; alternative measures; applications for transfer to adult court; and issues related to the rights granted young people under this legislation. He indicates that there is considerable variability in the way that the Act is being implemented across the country as well as in the way it is being interpreted by the judiciary. He presents a pessimistic assessment of the trend toward responsibility and accountibility and argues for mre emphasis on some of the parens patriae principles contained in the Act.

Doob (1983) has also expressed some concern over the implementation of the YOA and focusses on how the Act may change the way that police respond to young people. The decision to use Alternative Measures is made by the crown under the YOA while the police made these decisions under the JDA. The loss of this power may result in the police charging many more juveniles than they normally would have. Doob (1983) refers to this as turning police decisions into "non-decisions" since they may now apply the rules automatically and charge young offenders, as opposed to exercising some discretion. The net effect may be an increase in formality and a greater emphasis on the criminal behaviour of young people.

Early indications of the functioning of the YOA in Alberta suggest that these concerns may be warrented.

> ...over the past seven months, less than four percent of all young suspects have been selected for alternative programs...88 young offenders have been recommended for alternative measures since

April.... Over the same period, however, 2,227 teenagers appeared in court on formal criminal charges (*Calgary Herald,* November 123, 1985: 1-2).

House of Commons, Alan Redway M.P.(York East) reported that the Chief of Police of Metropolitan Toronto had informed him that "his forces hands are tied in dealing with some 300 cases involving arson, theft, assault, and sexual assault, because the suspects are under 12 years of age" (Canada House of Commons Debates, 1985, Vol. 3:4143).

At the other end of the spectrum, the ability of the system to deal with "teen thugs" has been questioned. It is pointed out that hardened 16 and 17 year old offenders must be dealt with under the juvenile legislation which has less serious penalties than the adult system. The lack of suitable procedures and safeguards for dealing with dangerous young offenders is also noted. Many provinces lack adequate facilities for young offenders and especially for those requiring special handling. Furthermore, the wisdom of houseing younger, more inexperienced offenders with older, more hardened teenagers is also questioned.

The maximum three year penalty available under the YOA has received a great deal of criticism for being too lenient as well. A sensational case in Toronto fuelled this controversy. The case involved a 14 year old boy from Scarborough, Ontario who murdered three people. He was subsequently convicted and given the maximum sentence available under the YOA, three years. This received widespread attention both in the press and in the House of Commons until an Appeals Court judge agreed to re-open the case.

Both children's rights activists and advocates of the welfare model have responded to the charges that the YOA is too lenient and that it doesn't give the authorities sufficient power to protect society. They point out, for example, that the case of the 14-year old boy who was sentenced to three years for murder gives an erroneous picture of the dispositions available under the YOA since the youth court is empowered to transfer cases to adult court under certain circumstances. The case in question is an instance when this could have been done. Gordon Tower, Parliamentary Secretary to the Solicitor General of Canada, pointed out the misconception over the leniency of the YOA when he stated in the House of Commons that a transfer to adult court meant that a young offender would "be subject to all the penalities that an adult would face, up to and including life imprisonment" (Cabada, House of Commons Debates, 1986. Vol, 7:9874).

The severity of the two and three year maximum sentences available under the YOA is also misleading since many of the procedures which modify sentences under the adult system, such as automatic sentence reduction and early release are unavailable under the YOA. Thus, in some cases, young offenders are still receiving harsher treatment than they would receive for similar offences under the adult system.

Children's rights advocates have also pointed out the potential problems with the practice of photographing and fingerprinting young offenders and of storing and controlling these records (Globe and Mail, 1984:14). These practices may be contrary to the Charter of Rights and Freedoms since they permit an undue invasion of privacy. At a more practical level, they charge that it is ludicrous to fingerprint and take "mug shots" of children.

As noted above, the Young Offenders Act has been critized by advocates of both the justice model and the welfare model. However, in the wake of "increasing pressure from law enforcement officers, provincial attourneys general and Tory backbenchers" (Calgary Herald, Oct. 19, 1985:A7), the government introduced Bill C-106 which proposed various reforms which reflect the concerns of the justice model. These changes were proclaimed law on September 1, 1986 except for the changes related to juvenile records which were implemented on November 1, 1986. They include: the ability of the court to impose consecutive sentences for new crimes committed before any sentence for previous crimes is completed; police access to juvenile records for continuign investigations; permissions for the courts to publicize the name of a young suspect who is at large; police rights to detain suspects longer before trials; and a streamlining of custody procedures making it easier to transfer custody to another. These changes are aimed at eliminating some of the administrative problems of the YOA and enhancing the ability of the authorities to enforce the law.

DISCUSSION: THE CONTROVERSY OVER CRIMINAL JUSTICE POLICY IN CANADA

In spite of the retention of some provisions drawn from the welfare model, the main thrust of the Young Offenders Act was such as to signal a fundamental shift away from the parens patriae doctrine which had dominated juvenile justice policy throughout most of this century (Leschied and Gendreau, 1986). Further evidence of this shift is evident in the nature of the admendments to the YOA which have been able to exert a great deal of influence during this period of conservatism in Canada. Their influence has not been restricted to the *Young Offenders Act*, but has appeared in numerous justice issues in recent years. Forexample, Bill C-18, the *Criminal Law Amendment Act*, increases the penalties for impaired driving and seeks to enhance the ability of the authorities to enforce laws related to prostitution (Canada, House of Commons Debates, 1984, Vol. 1:1383).

As noted above, crime provides politicians with an opportunity which many find difficult to resist. The problem is that while most people agree that crime is undesirable, there is little agreement on what the source of the problem is and how best to deal with it. The strategy of focusing on the sensational aspects of crime makes rational debates in this area difficult. Given the current conservative mood and the predominance of the law and order lobby, its resources of the collectivity to deal with the problems of their members. While an extensive discussion of such a community based system is beyond the scope of the present paper, the system which is envisioned would take into account the social, political and economic factors which adversely affect communities.

Iadicola (1986:153) discusses what he calls a "comprehensive model of community crime control" which he says contains two central components: geographical organization and social organization. He states that "the community is the geographical and social location in which crime takes place. The condition of the community determines the choices available to individuals responding to their conditions...[and] an organized community can serve as a means to change these constraints" (Iadicola, 1986:156).

Communities often organize in response to immediate or pressing needs such as crime or pollution etc. An organized base formed in this way, can be used to address other community concerns. As communities develop a collective identity and a sense of shared purpose, they are able to define and solve their own problems. They can also expand their organizational networks and gain control over more institutional and community resources.

While this model may be idealistic, there are numerous examples of communities that have successfully organized to deal with collective problems. For example, crime prevention programs have become common throughout Canada and various communities have organized to deal with problems of poverty and hunger. The possibility exists for these communities to expand their activites in a variety of directions.

> Where jobs are scarce, neighbourhoods have experimented with
> establishing cooperative industries. Where safe and adequate hous-

> ing is scarce, neighbourhoods have experimented with cooperatively
> owned apartment buildings. Where retail services have been lacking,
> neighborhoods have established food co-ops or actively sought to
> establish privately owned stores in their neighbourhood...Thus
> through organizing geographically and socially, residents acquire
> power to address neighbourhood problems which are directly rooted
> in the contradictions inherent in capitalist society (Iadicola,
> 1986:157).

Establishing a community based system with these ideals in mind, results in a fundamentally different approach to justice issues than that which currently exists. The community will have to deal more generally with the problems experienced by its own young people and ameliorative action may need to be geared less to the transgressions of specific individuals and more to the factors affecting all young people in the community such as education and employment which ensure community participation in the institutions that affect their young people directly, such as schools and the juvenile justice system. Placing more power in the hands of community members is a goal of this approach.

Analyzing the problem in this way may be more appropriate than continuing to search for solutions based on individual treatment strategies. An emphasis on individual treatment of symptoms while underlying causes are ignored. A structural analysis of the problem allows an examination of the social, polical and economic processes which may be adversely affecting young people (see West, 1959).

Research has shown that incidence of crime increase through the teen years and early twenties and level off at age 24 (Empey, 1982). Assuming that there is nothing special about being 24, the explanation for this change must be sought in the experiences of the participants. It is around this time that young people leave their parental homes and strike out on their own. They set up housekeeping, acquire goods and begin to accept the responsbilities faced by most adults in this society. However, for the first time they are able to make their own decisions and control their own lives. They are no longer subject to parental or school authority.

This process works for a majority of young people who progress normally through adolescence and into adulthood, and it is my contention that this may work for many more. Structural factors, however, unduly extend the already lenthy period of dependency and powerlessness of adolescents. Young people must be able to able to move into legitimate adult roles and participate as fully constituted members of their society."Youth must be given an opportunity to see in their work an intrinsic social value so that young people may come to have a stake in their society rather than being rejected by it" (Wardell, 1986:152). At the moment, this possibility does not exist for a growing number of young people.

The powerlessness, the lengthening period of dependency, and the inability of embarking on a career, represent significant obstacles for many young people. These factors must be taken into account if we are to find solutions to the problems faced by young people. Strategies based on treating and punishing individuals have had little success in the past and offer little promise for the future.

ENDNOTES

*I would like to thank my colleagues J.R. Ponting, A. Brannigan and S. Goldberg, as well as the anonymous referees for their thoughtful comments and suggestions on an earlier draft.

1.   For an analysis of this in the American case see Kolko, 1963 and Weinstein, 1968.

2.   An extensive discussion of this is presented in West (1984:23-53). For a similar analysis of the temperence movement see Gusfield (1963).

3.   Lemert (1951:76) defines secondary deviance as deviant behaviour which occurs in response to a label that has been successfully applied to an individual.

4.   Havemann (1986:224n) notes that a 1961 Report of the Planning Committee of the Department of Justice anticipated the inadaquacy of the Juvenile Delinquents Act for dealing with the consequences of the post-war 'baby boom' as a youth crime problem.

REFERENCES

Benthan, Jeremy (1775) Principles of Law. In J. Browning (ed.), *The Works of Jeremy Bentham Volume 1* (New York: Russell and Russell).

Berlin, M. and H. Allard (1980) Diversion of Children From the Juvenile Courts, *Canadian Journal of Family Law*, 3:349-60.

Biron, L. and D. Gauvreau (1984) *Portrait of Youth Crime* (Ottawa: Secretary of States, Social Trends Analysis Directorate).

Brannigan, Augustine (1984) *Crimes, Courts and Corrections* (Toronto: Holt, Rinehart and Winston).

Calgary Herald (1985a) Beatty Vows Changes to Young Offenders Act, October 19, A9.

_____, (1985b) Few Young Offenders Getting Second Chance, November 12, 1-2.

_____, (1986) Courts Getting Blame For Young Offender Tangles, July 26, A6

Caplan, A. (1981) A Research Programme for the Evaluation of the Young Offenders Act (Ottawa: MInistry of the Solicitor General of Canada).

Chan, J.B. and R.V. Ericson (1981) *Decarceration and the Economy of Penal Reform* (Toronto: centre of Criminology, University of Toronto).

Clarke, Dean H. (1982) Justifications for Punishment, *Contemporary Crises,* 6:27-62

Cohen, S. (1979) The Punitive City: Notes on the Dispersal of Social Control, *Contemporary Crises,* 33:339-63

Corrado, Raymond R. (1983) Introduction, in Corrado, Trepanier and LeBlanc (eds.), *Current Issues in Juvenile Justice* (Toronto: Butterworths).

Cullen, F.T., G.A. Clark and J.F. Wozniak (1985) Explaining the Get Tough Movement: Can the Public be Blamed? *Federal Probation,* 49:16-24.

Currie, Dawn (1986) The Transformation of Juvenile Justice in Canada: A Study of Bill C-61 in Brian D. MacLean (ed.), *The Political Economy of Crime* (Scarborough: Prentice-Hall)

Gray, Charlotte (1981) No More Juvenile Delinquents, *Alberta Report,* December: 18-9.

Greenberg, D.F. (1975) Problems in Community Correction, *Issues in Criminology,* 10:1-33.

Gusfield, J.R. (1963) *Symbolic Crusade: Status Politics and the American*

Temperance Movement (Urbana: University of Illinois).

Havemann, Paul (1986) From Child Saving to Child Blaming: The Political Economy of the Young Offenders Act, in S. Brickley and E. Comack (eds.), *The Social Basis of Law* (Toronto: Garmond Press).

Horton, John (1981) The Rise of the Right: A Global View, *Crime and Social Justice*, Summer.

Houston, S. (1978) The Victorian Origins of Juvenile Delinquency, in W.K. Greenaway and S.L. Brickey (eds.), *Law and Social Control in Canada* (Toronto: Prentice-Hall).

Hylton, John. (1982) Rhetoric and Reality: A Critical Appraisal of Community Correctional Programs, *Crime and Delinquency*, 28:341-73.

Iadicola, Peter (1986) Community Crime Control Strategies, *Crime and Social Justice*, 25:125-65.

Kolko, Gabriel (1963) *The Triumph of Conservatism* (New York: The Free Press).

Lemert, Edwin M. (1967) The Juvenile Court - Quest and Realities. Pp. 91-106 in the *President's Commission of Law Enforcement and Administration of Justice, Juvenile Delinquency and Youth Crime* (Washington DC: U.S. Government Printing Office).

Leon, Jeffrey S. (1977) The Development of Juvenile Justice: A Background for Reform. *Osgoode Hall Law Journal*, 15:71-106.

Leschied, Alan W. and Peter G. Jaffe (1985) *Implications of the Young Offenders Act in Modifying the Juvenile Justice System: Some Early Trends* (London Family Court Clinic).

Leschied, Alan and Paul Gendreau (1986) The Declining Role of Rehabilitation in Canadian Juvenile Justice: Implications of Underlying Theory in the Young Offenders Act. *The Canadian Journal of Criminology*, 28:315-22.

Lilles, H. (1983) The Beginning of a New Era, *Provincial Judges Journal*, 7:2: 21-6.

Lombroso-Ferrerro, Gina (1911) *Criminal Man According to the Classification of Cesere Lombroso* (Montclair: Patterson Smith, 1972).

Lundman, Richard J. (1984) *Prevention and Control of Juvenile Delinquency* (New York: Oxford University Press).

Matza, David (1964) *Delinquency and Drift* (New York: John Wiley and Sons).

McDonald, Lynn(1969) "Crime and Punishment in Canada: A Teat of the

"Conventional Wisdom", *Canadian Review of Sociology and Anthropology* VI, November.

Mills, C. Wright (1959) *The Sociological Imagination*, (New York: Oxford Uniersity Press).

P. and H. Giller, *et. al.* (1980) *Justice for Children* (London: McMillan).

Nasmith, A.P. (1983) "Paternalism circumscribed," *Provincial Judges Journal*, 7: 23-10.

O'Brein, Daniel (1984) "Juvenile diversion: an issues perspective from the Atlantic provinces," *Canadian Jornal of Crminology*, 26:2:217-30.

Pfohl, Stephen J. (1985) *Three Criminal Law REformers* (Montclair: New Jersey: Patterson Smith).

Platt, Anthony (1969) *The Child Savers* (Chicago: Chicago University Press).

Reid, Susan A. and M. Reitsma-Street (1984) "Assumptions and implications of the new Canadian legislation for young offenders," *Canadian Criminology Forum*, 7:1-19.

Reporter (1985) "Young Offenders Act Statistical Report" (Edmonton: John Howard Society fo Alberta), 2-4, December.

Rooke, Patricia T. and R.L. Schnell (1983) *Discarding the Asylum: From Child Rescue to the Welfare State in English-Canada (1800-1950)* (Lanham: University of America Press).

Rothman, D. (1980) *Conscience and Convenience: The Asylum and ITs Alternatives in Progressive America* (Toronto: Little, Brown, and Company).

Schur, Edwin M. (1973) *Radical Nonintervention Retingking the Delinquency Problem* (Englewood Cliffs: Prentice-Hall).

Solicitor Genreal of Canada (1975) *Young Persons in Conflict With the Law* (Ottawa: Ministry of Solicitor General).

Special Senate Committee on Youth (1986) *Youth: A Plan of Action* (Ottawa: Statistics Canada).

_____, (1985) *Canada Yearbook* (Ottawa: Ministry of Supply and Services).

Sutherland, N. (1976) *Children in English-Canadian Society: Framing the Twentieth Century Consensus* (Toronto: University of Toronto Press).

Sylvester, Sawyer F. Jr. (1972) *The Heritage of Modern Criminology* (Cambridge, Massachusets: Schenkman Publishing Company).

Thompson, G.M. (1983) Commentary on the Young Offenders Act, *Provincial Judges Journal*, 72, 27-34.

Toronto Star (1985) Young Offenders Jailed Longer Under the New Law Ontario Official Says, August 6, A9.

Trepanier (eds.), *Current Issues in Juvenile Justice* (Toronto: Butterworths).

Trojanowitz, R. (1978) *Juvenile Delinquency: Concepts and Control* (Englewood Cliffs, New Jersey: Prentice -Hall).

can den Haag, E. (1975) *Punishing Criminals* (New York: Basic Books).

Vold, George G. (1958) *Theoretical Criminology* (New York: Oxford University Press).

Von Hirsch A. (1976) *Doing Justice: The Choice of Punishments* (New York: Hill and Wang).Wanner, R. and T.C. Caputo (forthcoming) Punitiveness, Fear of Crime and Perceptions of Violence, *The Canadian Journal of Sociology.*

Wardell, W. (1985) The Young Offenders Act, *Saskatchewan Law Review*, 47:2:381-8.

_____, (1986) The Young Offenders Act: A Report Card 1984-1986, in D. Currie and B. MAcLean (ed.), *The Administration of Justice* (Saskatoon: Social Science Research Unit).

Weinstein, James (1968) *The Corporate Ideal in The Liberal State 1900-1918* (Boston: Beacon Press).

West, W. Gorodn (1984) *Young Offenders and the State: A Canadian Perspective* (Toronto: Butterworths).

White, C.A. (1985) Young Offenders Act: Growing Pains for New Law, *Canada and the World*, December, 51:26-7.

Wilson, James Q. (1975) *Thinking About Crime* (New York: Vintage Books).

CHAPTER 2
Dialectics and Delinquency

DEAN E. FREASE

INTRODUCTION

Many dialectical theoreticians have argued that generalizations and deterministic forms of explanations are unacceptable. In part, their case rests on the specific qualities of specific events and their need to understand the details. This paper is clearly not in that tradition. Rather, it rests on generalizations. It attempts to be more than a description of a single group of youngsters. Relationships exist which affect groups of different sizes and so generalizations and deterministic assumptions can be correctly applied in certain situations. What the reader will find is not documented proof in the sense of a empirical effort but rather logical proof in the sense of theory.

The term dialectic, in its most general meaning, refers to a struggle of opposites. Dialectical theory more specifically points to the universality of these opposites. We can not think of good without the concept of evil, for example. Each concept implies its opposite. Once this is understood a number of additional points may be discussed. Thus, gradual quantitative changes in a context of struggle may give rise to important qualitative changes. Take the idea of the unity of opposites—what this key dialectical notion points to is that opposing forces are locked in a kind of mortal combat from which neither may flee except by vanquishment. Finally, consider the famous idea:

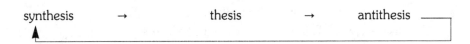

synthesis   →   thesis   →   antithesis

This, then, is how I think the idea of the dialectic should be considered here.

"Dialectics and Delinquency" was reproduced by permission of the *Canadian Journal of Criminology*, Vol. 29 (3), pages 249-255. Copyright by the Canadian Criminal Justice Association.

After I had written this paper, a recent book by Schwendinger and Schwendinger came into my view. While there are few obvious and specific links between this paper and the Schwendingers' book, the possibility of making those connections are clearly there. The book provides a number of concrete examples of what this paper points out in theory. That, however, awaits another article.

This is not a long paper. I have purposely kept it short because I think it better to consider a few points with some intensity than many out of focus.

In many situations, the modern delinquent gang appears to act as a functional equivalent to the ancient companionage in which shared responsibility dominates. This is perhaps most clearly seen when inter-gang relations are examined. Virtually all gang members are regarded as equally culpable in the view of the rival groups' membership.

For example, if a state of "war" exists between two gangs which was triggered by the intended harm of member A of one group, then any member of that group is considered a legitimate victim by the opposing gang. It need not be member A. Similarly, the gang member can call upon the gang for support, effective attachment and as a status source. Obligations and shared responsibilities are a part of the requirements of group membership.

In many groups of delinquents, a common feature is diversity. Diversity of style, of character, of ritual, of myth, of speech, of wardrobe and of stride, and, certainly, diversity of attitude and behavior. These differences are not the kinds of differences which a collection of youngsters can easily do without. They are necessary to the quality of the group and perhaps even to its survival.

It does seem clear that a collection of youngsters cannot be constantly involved in law violating behavior, nor can it be involved constantly in law abiding behavior. After all, each of us breaks the law. Not even professional criminals would consider the former a reasonable form of behavior—"Crazies" simply have no place in a stable organization.

Youngsters are unlikely to be convinced of the utility of non-stop conflict with conventional society—episodic delinquency seems to have advantages, so some youngsters argue against law violating behavior, while, at other times and in other situations, some youngsters, maybe the same ones, argue for law violation.

In this case, both councils, the council of war and the council of peace, are held together in mutual dependence. The existence of the gang is jeopardized without the presence of both. Each may be the necessary condition of the other.

It is this difference of viewpoint that makes internal conflict likely. The contending parties are locked into the same whole. There is little chance of avoiding the conflict. Regardless of the outcome, neither side comes away from the battlefield unscathed. Their attitudes have been confronted and the character of each side will have been penetrated and influenced in many ways.

It may be precisely these kinds of internal conflicts which bring about subtle and small incremental shifts in gang behavior. It is hard to imagine any significant change occurring in the absence of conflict.

The "push-and-shove" of everyday gang conflict involves a relationship of superordination-subordination between the contending groups. At times, they may appear in equilibrium, but in all likelihood this stage quickly passes into one of domination again. This relationship may be "unstable" in that events swirling around the members are undergoing continuous change and replacement of dominant group themes.

When things appear to be stable, change is actually occurring though on a quantitative rather than a qualitative level. Too often, social scientists fail to see change even when significant transformations are about to unfold. This observation certainly does not exclude stability. Change is constant and stability/equilibrium may only be fleeting. Just as a teetertotter swings through its fulcrum point so social situations are for a moment stable.

If one dominant group theme is replaced by another, we can say that *a change of types has taken place*. If the group which favors more law conforming behavior replaces the group of more dedicated delinquents, the entire gang may be said to have undergone a *qualitative change*. Of course, this temporary relationship can be just as readily reversed, so that delinquency rates increase. This change in kind may result from a shift in the internal balance of power. Such a change in kind, while it occurs in the last instance rapidly, may be preceded by a series of *quantitative changes*. Thus, a group of youngsters, who were best characterized as a play group in the early days of their association, by slow change and through more frequent law violating behavior, eventually take on the style and requirements of a gang. The qualitative change of kind was preceded by quantitative increases of action.

Once this reversal from a play group to a delinquent group has taken place, then the previously dominant consensus becomes subordinated and the previously subordinated becomes the dominant. It becomes more than a question of a simple shift of power; rather, entirely new relationships are created. New internal conflicts develop and new battles for leadership, power and consensus unfold.

But is it only an internal spark which brings about the motivating force for

development? Might not external forces such as the police, legislative committees, and other efforts by the control system also play a role?

Groups of youngsters, like any other social group, are regularly involved
with each other as well as with others external to the group. Each of these
meetings can influence the group as a whole in a number of ways. External
causes play a role in the changes which occur. However, at the same time,
external forces play a different role than the internal group mechanisms.
Specifically, the character of gang development may be determined internally
while external causes may condition change, which is to say they become
operative through internal causes.

Therefore, the kinds of conflicts between school and friends or between
friends and parents allow for the larger society to affect the lives of the youngsters. Because of conditions present internally to youth culture, through links
to conventional society, the external environment has a capacity for influencing delinquency.

Generally, when considering shifts from delinquency to nondelinquency or
from behavior whose dominant feature is nondelinquent to behavior whose
dominant characteristic is delinquent, these shifts may be explained from the
standpoint of internal gang concerns. Furthermore, the particular and specific
conflict on which the previous behavior was based may determine what new
quality emerges. It appears that external considerations affect generally only
the small, quantitative shifts which occur. That is, spacial and temporal beginning points as well as the change rate.

For example, the life cycle of a gang may be retarded, speeded up or even
reversed by a variety of purely external forces such as police efforts, social
work efforts, school efforts and parental concerns, but the path and final
appearance may be determined by the internal conflicts in the gang itself.

We can regard this entire process of conflict resolution as the replacement
of one quality by another, of an old quality by a new. An old dominant quality
is replaced by a new and opposite quality. It is in this context that each party
has a clear and separate image.

On the social battlefield, just as each party has its own character so the
conflict may take on trappings unique to that specific conflict as a result of the
special mix of contending groups. To determine how each conflict will work
out, one has to have a detailed knowledge of any particular situation.
Regardless of which group prevails, a point should be reached in their struggle
whereby quantitative increments result in qualitative change and, the whole
becomes more than the sum of its parts. It is at this point that we can say the
new form begins to appear in focus and the new quality becomes evident.

What contours develop depends for the most part on external pressures.

The development of a new quality may be expected to occur in a relatively short period of time. This is so because small quantitative changes over time eventually result in a new presence. Once this occurs. new behaviors come to the situation, new social roles develop, new characterizations to old roles occur and, fundamentally, new effects may be seen. Prior to the qualitative change, much groundwork was laid unnoticed.

The "sudden" appearance of the political criminal, for example. was in reality a long-time-coming. The kinds of conflict resolution which created the political criminal may be different from the kinds of conflict resolution which produce burglars. To understand each requires a detailed knowledge of prior conflicts present in their personal histories. Once a nonpolitical prisoner has assumed the shading and consciousness of political man; once the qualitative leap is made, the process of further development may be potentially slow. The process may not only proceed along a political path, it can also be halted or be reversed completely. We can refer to the case of reversal or arrested development as a tertiary stage of non-maturation in the sense that the initial stage or quantitative shifts occurred as did the secondary or qualitative stage; however, the new quality failed to mature. In the case of a politically motivated offender, the kinds of conflict which s/he will confront from established authority generally will be of a much different nature than will be the situation facing the nonpolitical offender.

Largely because of the threat posed to the legitimate order by some political offenders, the antagonism which confronts them may be more intense than that which faces the traditional property or personal offender. Conflicts then between groups and within groups may differ. Conflicts between a revolutionary group and the authorities differ from the conflicts within the revolutionary group.

Furthermore, in certain conditions, individuals are capable of a behavioral inversion. What this potentially means, in the context of delinquency, is that most delinquents eventually become transformed into nondelinquent adults or, for that matter, even nondelinquent teenagers. The reverse is also true, but probably with less frequency. Within a gang, opposites may tend to merge and become transformed into their mirror image.

It may be helpful to regard groups within a gang as being at different points on a continuum of change, anchored at one end by the group member who makes a permanent break with the gang. Change of attitude and behavior occur in the group. However, during the initial stage, these incremental changes are difficult to see and so give the appearance of stability. The two stages may be present at the same time with the qualitative change state pulling the last few small incremental attitudinal shifts across the line into the difference-of-kind zone. The allure of the final break may be enough to transport a youngster across the few remaining shifts in quick order. So then the total time necessary to travel quantitatively may be differentially distributed over the continuum, being relatively slow at first but gaining speed toward the end.

If one group does transform itself into its opposite, it follows that, at some point, each is identical with the other. However, there is nothing automatic about the process. If the conditions are unfavorable, no change will occur.

SUMMARY

What I have asserted is that reality in general and gang delinquency in the specific case are not static. Groups contain contradictory forces and the conflict of these opposites fuel their reality in constant change.

I have tried to be reasonably faithful to certain key elements in dialectical theory, notably a) how gradual quantitative changes may give rise to important quantitative changes; b) how contending and opposite forces may be held together in unity of opposites, and; c) how that struggle of opposites result in one group neutralizing the other but at the same time be effected by its opposite. In turn, the victorious group is confronted by a group which developed from it—all in sequence, and so it goes as group history unfolds.

REFERENCES

Liebow. Elliot. 1967. *Talley's Corner*. Toronto: Little Brown and Company.

Mao Tse-Tung. 1953. *On Contradictio* . New York: International Publishers.

Reasons, Charles E. 1974. "The Politicizing of Crime: The Criminal and the Criminologist," *The Journal of Criminal Law and Criminology*. Vol. 64. No. 4.

Schwendinger. H. and J.R. Schwendinger. 1985. *Adolescent Subcultures* and *Delinquency*. Toronto: Praeger Press.

Thrasher, Frederic M. 1966. *The Gang*. Abridged edition. Second impression. Chicago: University of Chicago Press.

Whyte. William. 1965. *Street Corner Society*. Chicago: University of Chicago Press.

CHAPTER 3
The Declining Role of Rehabilitation in Canadian Juvenile Justice: Implications of Underlying Theory in the Young Offenders Act[1]

ALAN W. LESCHIED
PAUL GENDREAU

The implementation of the *Young Offenders Act (YOA)* in Canada has been the subject of considerable controversy. From one point of view, this is a natural development since the legislation affects various political jurisdictions. The preoccupation with the politics of implementation, however, has prevented a much needed critical analysis of the underlying theoretical assumptions of the YOA. The logistical and political issues surrounding the YOA pale in comparison to the serious consequences the legislation has for those involved in managing not only the criminal justice system but, more importantly, the clients themselves.

The philosophy underlying the YOA is strongly based on punishment not rehabilitation. In many respects, the state has legitimized the neglect of young persons who were previously cared for under the *Juvenile Delinquents Acts* (JDA). This is strong language and at odds with YOA visionaries who trumpeted the legislation as progressive, seemingly unique to Canadian criminal justice. Rather, Canada has once again borrowed social policy from the United States. We will draw upon recent evidence generated from one Canadian jurisdiction clearly implicating the YOA as a harbinger of benign neglect.

"The Declining Role of Rehabilitation in Canadian Juvenile Justice: Implications of Underlying Theory in the Young Offenders Act" was reproduced by permission of the *Canadian Journal of Criminology*, Vol. 28 (3), pages 315-322. Copyright by the Canadian Criminal Justice Association.

PHILOSOPHICAL ANTECEDENTS

The reader is directed to more eloquent summaries of the recent history of criminal justice theory in the United States.[2, 7, 8, 18, 21] Until recently, juvenile justice philosophy relied heavily on traditional liberal values which provide that the state should not only protect the citizen's liberty but be an instrument of benevolence wherever social deprivation has occurred. In the opinion of many, not only has the war on crime, poverty, and other social pestilences failed, but the state has unwittingly permitted intolerable abuses to be perpetrated against the people it has claimed to help. Recent historical changes have meant a collapse of this liberal ideal. No longer does criminal justice hold the rehabilitation of offenders as the ideal. It was Martinson[17] who sounded the death knell of rehabilitation with his assertion that "nothing works".

Disaffected liberals agreeing with Martinson argued that, if "nothing worked", we should at least avoid doing harm and that any punishment meted out to offender should be a "just desert". We should be concerned with justice not mercy. Rehabilitation efforts were seen, in retrospect, as being degrading to offenders. Therefore, we should do less, not more. This viewpoint found immediate favour with two other potent interest groups: neo-conservatives who desired the full rule of law applied to offenders, and civil libertarians who decried the hypocrisy of the supposedly benevolent state institutions who abused the rights of the dispossessed.[2]

The new model of criminal justice has been labelled a number of different things ranging from "just deserts" to "justice-as-fairness" to "radical non-intervention".[4] This justice model has presented a number of policy recommendations such as decriminalization, lowering the age of accountability, abolishing the juvenile court, determinate sentencing, graded punishment based on the crime and past record, help for victims, and restitution. These policies signalled the advent of proceduralism which, in effect, stripped the juvenile court of its intended purpose to service young offenders leaving the system with a miniature criminal court duplicating adult court. On the adult side, a number of states have adopted some version of this justice model by imposing guidelines to cut down discretion, abolish parole boards, etc.

DOING JUSTICE IN THE U.S.

The most recent evidence on the effects of the "justice-as-fairness" model has produced mixed results.[6, 7, 11] Fairness of sentencing has not occurred. In urban areas, there is now more plea bargaining than ever before and discretion has moved downwards in the system making it less easily detected. Plea bargaining may occur in up to 90% of cases. In rural areas, where plea bargaining is less frequent, length of sentences has increased.

Judges continue to have some discretion despite the imposition of dispositional guidelines, but with the abolishment of parole boards there is no review for discrepant decision making. Previously, parole boards could ensure equity.

Determinate sentencing presumably was going to improve the quality of institutional life as inmates would know with certainty when they would be released. Some data[10] indicates, however, that inmates serving longer sentences were not in favor of determinate sentencing. They do not want their opportunities for getting out decreased.

There has been no discernable change in crime rates in those states using the justice model.

In the United States, there is some data attesting to the fact that, at least with juvenile offenders, incarcerations are increasing while arrests are down. Expenditures for institutions has increased with the concomitant increase in average lengths of stay for juveniles. In addition, there appears to be some racial bias with more incarcerated youths being blacks and Hispanics whereas the number of white incarcerated youths is decreasing.

It would appear that justice model proponents have fallen prey to ultra conservatives who believe the overriding goal of the criminal justice system is social protection and safety, to the exclusion of the concerns of the offender. Prison populations appear to be increasing amongst adults as a result of the action of legislators who increase sentences in response to each public outcry over a heinous crime. Indeed, Shane-Dubow[19] noted that the recent trends in sentencing have *invariably* been towards harsher penalties! Consequently, a number of states are reporting serious overcrowding and some have refused to take inmates because of the lack of space. In fact, some jurisdictions have started to "sneak in" a merit scheme such as 90 day release just to relieve overcrowding.

Proponents of the justice model have a strong sense of pessimism and are little concerned with service delivery issues; rather, deterrence is the preferred topic under study. Despairingly, there is virtually no theorizing about rehabilitative services in criminal justice academia in the United States at this time.[6]

To be fair, out of this despairing scenario, there are some mixed effects. Survey data reported by Cullen[6] has shown that while many in the U.S. believe that punishment is a goal of the criminal justice system, respondents still want rehabilitation services to be offered.

THE CANADIAN SITUATION

We are not unique. The YOA mimics many of the policies directly emanating out of the justice model in the United States. The Solicitor General is quoted as stating that, while youths will have more legal rights, victims will get more out of the criminal justice system since a new range of penalties such as financial compensation and restitution for the victim will be provided; again direct policy implications from the justice model. The Juvenile Delinquent's Act, which was replaced by the YOA, was described as "benevolent tyranny".

Nicholas Bala[3], a distinguished expert in the law as it affects children and families, has commented that the JDA was influenced by the positivist school of criminology. Bala, amongst others, has stated that this school assumed people could be treated under a welfare oriented philosophy whereby those responsible for making decisions about a child's life were given very substantial discretion to impose dispositions in "the best interests of the child". The fundamental questioning by sociologists and criminologists whether treatment-based systems really worked and a concern by lawyers and other advocates of children's rights about the lack of "due process" led to the subsequent revocation of the JDA. According to Bala, the YOA can best be understood as a response to the problems arising from the JDA, and a continuation and culmination of a process of reform commenced by the courts and provincial governments over a period of almost 20 years. The YOA ensures that young people receive due process. The Act suggests that the goal of juvenile justice is the imposition of criminal sanctions and not the promotion of the welfare of children. The criminal law focus of the YOA is apparent in the shift away from indeterminate custodial dispositions based on need to determinate custodial dispositions based on notions of punishment. Central to the legislation is the idea of minimal interference and the young person's informed rights. Moreover, the discretion of decision makers is to be structured; that decisions about young persons are to be made by judges rather than those in the juvenile corrections system.

There is a part of the "Declaration of Principle" of the YOA which comments on the fact that young offenders have special needs requiring guidance and assistance. Therefore, in Canada, the just deserts philosophy has some ambivalence about it and is sometimes referred to as "creative tension". Even in this regard, one is reminded of the statement by various justice as fairness proponents in the United States that offenders should be given services "if they want them".

EMPIRICAL DATA

What has been disturbing in this country has been the lack of empirical data generated by the criminal justice system on the effects of the YOA. If one believes that the trends in the United States can be replicated in Canada, then we should expect less treatment service delivery and increased incarceration in various forms.

Recent data describing changes in one Canadian jurisdiction would seem to reaffirm some of the theoretical concepts of the justice-as-fairness model.

A study by Leschied and Jaffe[14] indicated that sentences for children, age 12 to 15, have increased 135% for those being sent to training schools (closed custody) and 210% for those sentenced to group homes (open custody). A youth now spends an average of 6-9 months in some form of custody compared to 3-6 months under the discretionary system of the JDA. Other provinces such as Manitoba, Saskatchewan, British Columbia, and Nova Scotia apparently are reporting similar trends.[20, 9]

Other data reported by Leschied and Jaffe, point to the fact that, under the JDA, committal to training schools accounted for 5% of dispositions and, now, under the YOA, custody committals now account for twice that percentage.

The use of secure detention apparently has changed. In one 20-bed secure detention unit, the average length of stay has increased by approximately 21%; extended periods of both pre-trial and pre-disposition detention has caused an increased percentage of youths remaining for 15-30 days.

There has been a marked decrease in the use of treatment services. An extremely limited number of treatment orders have been made, (5) under section 20 (I) and, of the 5 orders made, two were terminated at the request of the young persons who withdrew their consent. The year previous, there were approximately 200 such treatment dispositions made.

Thus, these trends indicate a "correctional" response is preferred over the needs-based rehabilitative response by the court under the JDA. Custody has been expanded; the number of young persons in secure custody are identical to those in training schools under the JDA. Moreover, young persons in open custody appear to have been drawn from those who may have been previously ordered into the care of a CAS or place in a treatment centre.

Another trend towards a correctional response is illustrated by the number of requests for psychiatric/psychological reports (S. 13) and social histories (S.

14). An increase in social histories is coincidental with increases in custody committals because, before a committal can be made, a social history must be provided to the court. Requests for social histories under the YOA is 30% more than was the case for the JDA. Over 50% of social histories requested were in anticipation of an order for custody.

Finally, the increased use of detention appears to be tied to the increased application of due process which has prolonged the court process and the extended period of time required for the completion of social histories while the youth is being detained.

Compounding all of the problems in the area of rehabilitation is the consent to treatment issue. The YOA ignores the fact that a young person's criminal acting out behaviour is related to pathological conditions and does not address underlying issues which could be related to subsequent antisocial behaviour.[15] The judge is hamstrung in that a ruling cannot be made based on his knowledge and experience without first acceding to the wishes of the youth. Consent presumes that children can speak to an issue which they cannot comprehend because they are too immature.[12, 13] The child being able to withdraw consent at any time is a major impediment to therapeutic processes being undertaken and the courts cannot order the most appropriate disposition for the child. The disposition used, where consent is not forthcoming, appears to be open custody which is not able to provide the type of intervention necessary.

If any constructive action is to be taken in the area of consent, it should be on the basis that the *court* is in a better position to rule on the necessity for treatment than the child. Surely, a youth court judge can decide if the treatment order is abusive of the young person's rights. While defense counsel can argue that a young person's need for treatment should be a community concern independent of an appearance before the youth court, in reality, a young person's offence may be the only concrete and legally sound piece of evidence to convince the young person and his or her family that help is necessary; help that is required but not welcomed. Finding the delicate balance in such cases should rest with the judge and not with an adolescent in severe crisis.

FUTURE OUTLOOK

In this country, some blame the courts for failing to live up to the spirit of the legislation by stressing punishment at the expense of rehabilitation. Bala recently stated that many of the complaints about juvenile justice in Canada

should not be directed towards the YOA but towards those provincial governments which have only grudgingly moved in the direction of minimal compliance or failed to seize many of the opportunities created by the YOA for innovative responses to the problems of young offenders.

The legislation in its present form has created difficulties for proponents of
rehabilitation and it is hoped some constructive alternatives will be found to
the present predicament. But with the insistence that discretion is evil and the
concomitant promulgation of individual rights at any cost, we will likely see
more spectacular abuses of basic *human rights* with the incessant insistence
upon *individual rights*. The adversarial model we now have in place leaves us
very little room to manoeuvre. Children will not have benevolent institutions to
be their advocates. Witness the case of the 12 year old girl in California who
was placed in solitary confinement because she would not testify against her
father on allegations of sexual abuse.[18] Or the recent case, reviewed in the
London Free Press[16], regarding the charges of sexual assault and gross inde-
cency against a teenager who, confessing the acts to his mother, had the
charges against him dismissed since the mother, acting as a person in authority, did not advise her son of his legal rights to have counsel.

In an article entitled "Can Juvenile Justice Survive?", Conrad[5] stated

"We know very well how to bring boys and girls to justice, once we've
caught them, but our ideas about what to do with them then are conspicuous
for their banality and incompetence.... It is depressing to contemplate our
inability to help them in any way other than keeping them for a while (in custody) away from the commission of other crimes" (p. 553).

It is hoped that future amendments to the YOA will consider the need for
a more balanced integration of civil rights and rehabilitation in order to fulfill
the visionaries' quest for truly progressive juvenile justice legislation in Canada.

ENDNOTES

1.   Reprint requests should be addressed to Alan Leschied, London Family
     Court Clinic. 80 Dundas Street. P.O. Box 5600. Terminal A. London,
     Ontario N6A 2P3. The second author is seconded to the Department of
     Justice, Wellington, New Zealand. Portions of this paper have been pre-
     sented by one or both authors at Toronto, and Chaffey's Locks in
     Ontario, Halifax, Nova Scotia, Cincinnati, Ohio, and Wellington, New
     Zealand.

2.   Allen, F.A. *The decline of the rehabilitative ideal: Penal policy and
     social purpose.* New Haven: Yale University Press. 1981.

3.   Bala, N. "The young offender's act: Why a new era in juvenile justice?"
     Presented at the Canadian Psychological Association annual meeting.
     Halifax, Nova Scotia. 1985.

4.   Carney, L.P. *Corrections: Treatment and philosophy.* Englewood
     Cliffs,. N.J.: Prentice-Hall. 1980.

5.   Conrad, J.P. "Can juvenile justice survive?" *Crime and Delinquency.*
     544-554. 1981.

6.   Cullen, F.T. "Does rehabilitation work? The origins and meaning of a
     troublesome question". Presented at the University of Ottawa,
     Department of Psychology, Ottawa, Ontario. 1985.

7.   Cullen, F.T. and K.E. Gilbert. *Reaffirming Rehabilitation.* Cincinnati:
     Anderson Publishing. 1984.

8.   Empey, L.T. *American delinquency: Its meaning and construction.*
     Homewood, Ill: Dorsey. 1982.

9.   Garber, L. "Panel discussion of the effects of the Y.O.A. on the Nova
     Scotia juvenile justice system." Presented to Canadian Court
     Administrators Conference. Halifax, Nova Scotia. 1985.

10. Goodstein, L. and J. Hudack. "Importance to prisoners of predictability
     of release: A test of a presumed benefit of the determinate sentence."
     Criminal Justice and Behaviour. 9. 217-228. 1982.

11. Goodstein, L. J.H. Kramer and L. Nuss. "Defining determinacy:
     Components of the sentencing process ensuring equity and release cer-
     tainty". *Justice Quarterly. 1.* 47-73. 1984.

12. Grisso, T. and L. Vierling. "Minor's consent to treatment: A developmental perspective." *Professional Psychology.* 9. 412-427. 1978.

13. Leschied, A.W. and C. Hyatt. "Perspective: Section 21(1) of the young offender's act and the consent to treatment." *Canadian Journal of Criminology.* 28. 69-78. 1985.

14. Leschied, A.W. and P.G. Jaffe. "Implications of the Young Offender's Act in Modifying the juvenile justice system." In N. Bala and H. Lilles (eds). *The young offender's act update.* Toronto: Butterworths. 1985.

15. Leschied. A.W., and P.G. Jaffe. "Consent to treatment under the young offender's act: A case study." *Canadian Psychology.* In Press.

16. *London Free Press.* "Mom failed to read son his rights: Charges dumped because she became 'authority'." August 7, 1985.

17. Martinson, R. "California research at the crossroads". *Crime and Delinquency* 22. 180-191. 1976.

18. McNally, R.B. "The juvenile justice system: A legacy of failure." *Federal Probation.* 48. 29-33. 1984.

19. Shane-Dubow, S. "Sentencing reform in the United States: history, content, and effect." Presented at the National Conference on Sentencing. Baltimore, MD. 1984.

20. *Toronto Star.* "Young offenders jailed longer under new law, Ontario official says." August 6, 1985.

21. Travis, L.F. and F.T. Cullen. "Radical non-intervention: The myth of doing no harm." *Federal Probation.* 48. 29-32. 1984.

CHAPTER 4
Assumptions and Implications of New Canadian Legislation for Young Offenders

SUSAN A. REID
MARGE REITSMA-STREET

INTRODUCTION

The creation, development and implementation of social policy are influenced by beliefs and assumptions about man, society and the state (Miller, 1973; George & Wilding, 1976: 16-20). Social policy may be defined as the "principles that govern action towards given ends" which affect men, women, and children in their social and economic relationships (Titmuss, 1974: 23). This definition of social policy includes programmes which promote well-being, life, quality and fellowship as well as those programmes which control disobedience, disorder and threats to life and property. It is not easy, however, to draw the distinction between the control and welfare components within a social policy (Lerman, 1977; Higgins, 1980). A critical examination of beliefs and assumptions within social policies promotes a more realistic awareness of the complex contradictions woven into them (Rein, 1976: 16). Furthermore, the exploration of assumptions helps to anticipate intended as well as unintended consequences (Gil, 1976: 34).

Reflections on the 1908 *Juvenile Delinquents Act (JDA)* (R.S.C., C.J-3) over the past twenty-five years point to difficulties in separating the welfare from the social control components of a social policy. For example, under section 20 (3) of the *JDA* a child found to be "delinquent" could be potentially under the supervision of a judge from the age of seven to the age of twenty-one years. "Supervision" by a judge included the provision of "help, guidance and assistance" as well as the control of the young person's movements and decision-making. An analysis of the contradictory philosophy and provisions of the *JDA* also illuminates a number of unintended, disturbing consequences of Canadian policy for young offenders. For example, a youth found guilty of a minor offence might spend several months in a training school while an adult found guilty of the same offence may receive, at most, a small fine (MacDonald, 1971; Wilson, 1982).

These contradictions, in combination with changing societal beliefs regarding youth and crime, spurred interest in modifying the *JDA*. The change process however, was an extremely slow one: the first initiative was taken in 1960, but it was twenty-four years before new legislation, the *Young Offenders Act (YOA)* (S.C. 1981-82-83, c. 110), was proclaimed. One reason for the delay was the conflict in assumptions held by bureaucratic, political and professional individuals and organizations regarding the purposes of the juvenile justice system. This conflict, and the intensive debates surrounding the *YOA* are summarized in the following remarks made by Judge Omer Archambault, Director of the federal Solicitor General's Young Offenders' Policy Unit from 1976-1983:

> The *Young Offenders Act*...is in response to this evolution of cultural values and attitudes towards criminal justice. The legislation is based on a new set of fundamental assumptions reflecting this evolution and inspired...by extensive knowledge of human behaviour generally and the moral and psychological development of children in particular. (Archambault, 1983: 3)

This paper explores the assumptions and potential consequences of the new Canadian federal policy for the young offenders under the *Young Offenders Act*. First, a brief history of the Act is outlined. Second, four sets of assumptions regarding man, society and the purpose of the juvenile justice policy are presented. Next, the values assumed in the eight principles of the *YOA* are analyzed by independent raters and compared to these four sets of assumptions. The final section discusses several implications that may emerge from the particular combination of assumptions in the new Act.

HISTORY OF THE YOUNG OFFENDERS ACT

Just before midnight on June 19, 1908, the first *Juvenile Delinquents Act* in Canada was passed following a ten minute debate. The deceptively swift passage of this Act in the House of Commons had been, however, preceded by years of controversy regarding the treatment of juvenile offenders and several attempts to pass provincial and federal legislation (Sutherland, 1976; Leon, 1977; Houston, 1972). The controversy and debate which preceded the passage of the *JDA* were mirrored in the debates and alliances to promote change prior to the enactment of the *YOA*.

As already indicated, there was an extensive consultation process lasting nearly twenty-four years prior to the enactment of the *YOA*. Reports on juvenile delinquency and six legislative proposals, namely the 1967 Draft Act, the 1970 Bill C-192, the 1975 Liberal proposals, the 1977 Conservative proposals, and the 1981 Bill C-61 were debated in numerous conferences, working groups, bureaucratic and political committees and professional organizations at both the federal level[1] and within each provincial jurisdiction. One of the primary reasons for the delay in passage of the new legislation was the debate over philosophical orientation. Issues raised included: "the best interests of the child" versus "the protection of society"; "punishment" versus "treatment"; "flexible adjudication" versus "procedural rights"; and "federal" versus "provincial" jurisdictions.[2]

Four Models of Juvenile Justice

Opinions regarding policies and programmes for young offenders are predicted on sets of assumptions which can be classified into four models identified as Crime Control, Justice, Welfare and Community Change. A "Model" is defined as a "general mental construct about a social phenomenon...constructed to generate propositions about the relationships between phenomena" (Djao, 1983: 8). The four models are designed to summarize systematically common members of society (Packer, 1964).

The four models can be summarized as follows: Crime Control - responsibility of the state and courts to maintain order for society; Justice - procedures or interference with freedom specifically limited and based on consent as much as possible; Welfare - societal responsibility to attend to the needs of the youth and family; and Community Change - societal responsibility to promote welfare and prevent youthful crime. While the four models are similar in many respects, their differences allow them to be placed on a broader continuum with opposing poles which have been labeled as conservative right versus socialist left (Miller, 1973), residual versus institutional (Wilensky & Lebeaux, 1976:138-140), or anti-collectivist versus collectivist (George & Wilding, 1976:21, 62). Impressionistically, the Crime Control model sits on the far right end of the continuum, the Justice and Welfare models jostle a bit to the right, welfare a bit to the left and the Community Change model on the far left.

Crime Control Model

This model (Catton, 1975; Horton, 1981) gives priority to the security and maintenance of the moral, economic and political order and freedoms of a community, defined by the exceptions of the governing groups, whether they be democratically elected or revolutionary dictatorships. Basic order must be maintained both within, and at the boundaries of a society. A youth is seen as a miniature adult freely deciding to engage in disapproved conduct and thereby posing a threat to the social and economic relationships within society. Under this model, laws defining criminal behaviour are flexible and broad, encompassing any behaviour perceived as immoral, unmanageable or threatening to the collective order. The police, court personnel, and penal agents are key actors in the implementation of the crime control model, frequently requesting more resources. The process of stopping, containing, fact-finding, adjudicating and punishing violators is speedy and efficient utilizing both informal and routine procedures. Minimal opportunity for procedural challenge or appeal is provided for the offender. Social defence, deterrence, retribution and punishment are essential justifications for the control model with procedures being weighted in favour of society.

Justice Model

The Justice model draws upon classical criminology, beginning with the pioneering work of Beccaria's *Essay on Crime and Punishment* in 1804 (Mannheim, 1972) and gaining credence in the 19th century within Western Europe and the colonies. The years since the early 1960s have seen a re-affirmation of this model for all people, regardless of race or age (Faust & Brantingham, 1974; Morris *et al.*, 1980).

In this model, priority is given to perceptible social control processes administered by judicial bodies independent of political and economic influence. Protection is ensured for both the individual and society though a collection of autonomously acting, self-seeking individuals who contract with each other through the State to preserve the peace. Youth are perceived as rational, responsible and to a degree, in control of their behaviour. Specific behaviours threatening social or economic relationships are codified into offences with fixed, proportionate punishments. The judicial process of adjudication and disposition is administered without regard to race, sex or socioeconomic position, in the context of a fair, open trial. A young persons remains innocent until guilt is established beyond a reasonable doubt. Provisions for legal counsel, cross-examination and public scrutiny are available. To compensate for the young person's age at the time of the offence and the fact that he/she may lack the necessary *mens rea* (i.e. guilty mind) to be convicted of the offence, diminished responsibility, proportionately lighter sentences than those given to adults and the use of additional expert adult assistance throughout the trial process are legitimized by law.

The Justice model shares with the Crime Control model a focus on deterrence and social defence. In contrast, however, the Justice model weighs the proceedings in favour of the individual by considering deterrence, reparation and compensation as more important justifications for intervention than retribution or punishment.

Welfare Model

At the end of the 19th century the Welfare model emerged, drawing upon the positivist school of criminology (Platt, 1969; Rothman, 1980). This model, sometimes referred to as the Family Model (Griffiths, 1970), assumes youth are shaped primarily by their environment and are not quite the freely-determined individuals espoused by the Crime Control or Justice models. The primary goal of juvenile justice built on welfare assumptions is prevention of the antisocial syndrome (APA, 1980:31). Modifying criminogenic environments, particularly the family environment, and rehabilitating the antisocial youth are the major means of prevention. Comprehensive investigation of the whole youth is essential in planning an appropriate disposition. The final disposition can be easily modified to fit the changing needs and circumstances of the young person. Both privately sponsored and public social scientists, welfare workers and teachers are involved in the investigation, trial, treatment and rehabilitation process. Lord Kilbrandon gave succinct expression to the Welfare model in an influential report, *Children and Young Persons*, which led to the creation of the welfare-oriented Scottish Children's Panels of 1968:

> ...on purely practical grounds it would therefore appear that emphasis ought to be given to preventative and remedial measures at the earliest possible stage if more serious delinquencies are not to develop. That implies above all the application of an educative principle, which cannot hope to operate with any measure of success except under a procedure which from the outset seeks to establish the individual child's needs in light of the fullest possible information as to

his circumstances, personal and environment (Scottish Home & Health Department, 1964, s. 78:39).

Community Change Model

This model draws from the economic determinism of 19th century Marxist theory and the mid 20th century social conflict and phenomenological perspectives (Snider & West, 1980; Sinclair, 1983). The primary environments of family, school and neighbourhood are significantly shaped by the major norms developed and differentially applied by the political, economic and social ruling groups in a society. The model assumes society is not a

> static conception of pathological and/or anomic individuals colliding with a simple taken-for-granted set of institutional orders, but rather...a conception of the complex interaction between developments in institutional and social structures. (Taylor, Walton & Young, 1973:226, 227)

The aim of policies built on the Community or Societal Change model is to change the processes that lead to inequality, poverty and delinquency: youthful crime is prevented by promoting the welfare of all youth. Legislation and institutions must ensure equal distribution of educational, medical and employment opportunities. Fundamental revisions are required in the policies and programmes of legal and penal establishments to ensure fair and equal assistance to those few youths who truly threaten society's social and economic relationships.

The only way in which policies based on this model can be implemented is with a complete change of the capitalist `socioeconomic system (Quinney, 1977:16). As Krisberg (1975:18) has noted of other efforts aimed at correcting the individual:

> Piecemeal reform efforts, when applied to social issues such as crime, racism, poverty or mental illness, support the myth that progress and improvement can occur without major restructuring of the social order.... The standards of practicality are always taken from those who rule and who wish to preserve their status quo.

While a complete restructuring of society is not possible without a revolution, there are a number of steps which can be taken in the interim. For example, Miller (1973:23) advocates increased "local control, decentralization, community control, a new populism, and citizen power". In other words, more community and citizen involvement in the prevention and control of crime will lead to policies which take into account the welfare of all individuals.

PROVISIONS OF THE *YOUNG OFFENDERS ACT*

The Crime Control, Justice, Welfare and Community Change models of juvenile justice described above provide the framework for examining the assumptions about youth, society, crime and law in the YOA. Specifically, a content analysis is conducted of the Declaration of Principle in the YOA (Section 3), with reference to the four models. Before turning to the analysis, the YOA provisions are briefly summarized as follows:

(1) Offences (s. 2(1))

The previous single charge of delinquency is replaced with all the specific summary conviction and indictable offences against the *Criminal Code* and other federal statutes and regulations. Offences against provincial and municipal laws do not fall under the provisions of the YOA and status offences have been completely eliminated.

(2) Age (s. 2(1))

The age of criminal responsibility is now uniform across Canada with a minimum age of twelve years. Young people from the age of twelve to under eighteen years will be dealt with by the Youth Court. Youth who are fourteen years or older may be transferred to adult court doe indictable offences if it is deemed to be in the interest of both the youth and society.

(3) Rights (s. 3 (1) (e) (g); sections 7,8,10,11)

Young people have the same rights to due process of law and equal treatment under the *Canadian Charter of Rights and Freedoms*. These rights include: notification of charges, judicial interim release (bail), legal representation including the decision to enter an alternative measures programme, appeal of a finding and disposition. Further rights and guarantees are provided to account for the young person's dependent status and age. These guarantees included the participation of the family in all stages of the proceedings, detention facilities separate from adults if at all possible, and anonymity of young persons in the media.

(4) Alternative Measures (s. 4)

Youth will be offered the choice of alternative measures (where they are available) to the formal court process if such a program is consistent with the protection of society and is entered into voluntarily with a young person who has accepted responsibility for the offence in question.

(5) Procedures

The procedures for arrest, detention, bail and predispositional reports as set out for adults in the *Criminal Code* will now be applicable to young offenders. The only proviso is that courts will be separate from adults and be conducted by youth court judges. Detention facilities, if at all possible, are to be separate from adult offenders as well.

(6) Records (sections 40-46)

Records and finger print files are to be destroyed if the youth is found not guilty, the charges are dismissed or following a crime free period (from two to five years) after the completion of a disposition.

(7) Dispositions (sections 20-26, 28-34)

A wide range of dispositions (sentences) are provided with a maximum of three years in custody for offences in which an adult would receive life imprisonment. If custody is being considered as a disposition the court must conduct a predispositional evaluation and prepare a predispositional report to be used in the final decision. Dispositions undergo regular reviews by courts, or where available, review committees. Upon review, dispositions can be altered if necessary or appropriate.

ANALYSIS OF THE YOA PRINCIPLES

The "most significant differences between the JDA and the YOA can be identified by comparing the underlying principles of the former with the Declaration of Principle found in s. 3 of the YOA" (Lilles, 1983:21). This significant difference is one reason why we chose to examine closely the Declaration of Principle; the second reason is our assumption that explicit principles are overt indicators of the more covert values and assumptions that guide the implementation of legislation and social policy.

In the 1982 government publication outlining the YOA, the then Solicitor

General Robert Kaplan gave the following summary of the principles:

> The Act balances the rights of society, the responsibility that young
> offenders must bear for their actions and the specific needs and
> rights of our young people. In doing so, it is in keeping with the phi-
> losophy and circumstances of our time (Canada, 1982:1).

The authors first examined the eight subsections of the Declaration of
Principle to determine how similar each subsection was to the four models of
juvenile justice. Since several subsections appeared to fall under more than
one model, a content analysis of the phrases within each subsection was conducted to provide categorization by only one model. Table 1 presents the subsections of the Declaration of Principle divided into thirteen phrases and the
authors' perception of which model most closely represented the assumptions
within each phrase. The two authors made their ratings independently, and
they repeated the rating procedure two weeks later. Similar ratings were
reached each time, although a "close second rating" was noted for aspects of
three of the thirteen phrases as illustrated in Table 1 by the use of asterisks.

The authors categorized four phrases as falling under the Justice model of
juvenile justice, four phrases as representing the Crime Control model, four
phrases as indicative of the assumptions of the Welfare model, and only one
phrase showing similarity to the Community Change mode. Phrases 1 (i.e.
young person's accountability) and 8 (i.e. young person's rights) which were
most similar to the Justice model were also rated as containing elements which
could be categorized under the Welfare model. Similarly, phrase 7 (i.e. non-
intervention) was rated primarily under the Welfare model with some assumptions also falling under the Justice model.

Subsequent to the authors' categorization of the phrases of the
Declaration of Principles, three classes of undergraduate students enrolled in a
course on juvenile justice at the University of Toronto and the University of
Guelph were given a thirty minute lecture on the four models of juvenile justice. The students (N=48) received a summary sheet which highlighted the
main points presented in the lecture. Each student was then given the thirteen
phrases in random order and was asked to indicate which of the four models
most clearly illustrated each phrase. The number and percentage of students
selecting various models for each phrase is presented in Table 2. Also listed
are results of the chi-square test performed on the two models chosen most
frequently by the students for each of the thirteen phrases.

Table 1
The Thirteen Phrases of the YOA's
Declaration of Principle
Categorized by the Four Models of Juvenile Justice
According to the Authors

Number	Phrase	Author's Categorization
1	*While young persons should not in all instances be held accountable in the same manner or suffer the same consequences for their behaviour as adults,* young persons who commit offences should nonetheless bear responsibility for their contraventions. (s.3 (1) (a))	Justice (Welfare)*
2	Society must...be afforded the necessary protection from illegal behaviour. (s. 3 (1) (b))	Crime Control
3	(Society) has the responsibility to take reasonable measures to prevent criminal conduct by young persons. (s. 3 (1) (b))	Community Change
4	Young persons who commit offences require supervision, discipline and control. (s. 3 (1) (c))	Crime Control
5	(Young persons) . . . because of their state of depency and level of development and maturity, they also have special needs and require guidance and assistance. (s. 3 (1) (c))	Welfare
6	Where it is not inconsistent with the protection of society. (s. 3 (1) (d))	Crime Control
7	..."taking no measures or taking measures other than judicial proceedings under this Act should be considered for dealing with young persons who have committed offences. (s. 3 (1) (d))	Welfare (Justice)*

Table 1 (continued)

Number	Phrase	Author's Categorization
8	Young persons have rights and freedoms in their own right, including those stated in the Canadian Charter of Rights and Freedoms or in the Canadian Bill of Rights, and in particular, a right to be heard in the course of, and to participate in the processes that leads to decisions that affect them, and* young persons should have special guarentees of their rights and freedoms. (s. 3 (1) (a))	Justice (Welfare)*
9	In the application of this Act, the rights and freedoms of young persons include a right to the least possible interference with freedom. (s. 3 (1) (f))	Justice
10	...that is consistent with the protection of society. (s. 3 (1) (f))	Crime Control
11	...having regard to the needs of young persons and the best interests of their families. (s. 3 (1) (f))	Welfare
12	Young persons have the right in every instance where they have rights or freedoms that may be affected by this Act, to be informed as to what those rights and freedoms are. (s. 3 (1) (g))	Justice
13	Parents have responsibility for the care and supervision of their children and for that reason, young persons should be removed from parental supervision, either partly or entirely only when measures that provide for continuing sipervision are inappropriate. (s. 3 (1) (g))	Welfare

* Phrases within the asterisks were also considered appropriate to a second model of juvenile justice.

Table 2
The Thirteen Phrases of the YOA's
Declaration of Principle
Categorized by the Four Models of Juvenile Justice
According to 48 Undergraduate Students

Phrase		Model of Juvenile Justice					Significant
Number	Control	Justice	Welfare	Community	Change		Differences[a]
	n	%	n	%	n	%	n	%	x^2 p < .01
1	22	45.8	25	52.1	1	2.1	0	0.0	0.096 n.a.
2	46	95.8	1	2.1	1	2.1	0	0.0	20.166 sig.
3	22	45.8	2	4.2	1	0.0	24	50.0	0.043 n.a.
4	22	45.8	3	6.8	22	45.8	1	2.1	0.000 n.a.
5	0	0.0	0	0.0	46	95.8	2	4.2	20.166 sig.
6	37	77.1	3	6.3	1	2.1	7	14.6	10.227 sig.
*7	5	10.6	10	21.3	15	31.9	17	36.2	0.063 n.a.
8	0	0.0	48	100.0	0	0.0	0	0.0	— sig.
9	1	2.1	42	87.5	4	8.3	1	2.1	10.888 sig.
10	35	72.9	7	14.6	0	0.0	6	12.5	9.333 sig.
11	0	0.0	0	0.0	47	97.9	1	2.1	22.042 sig.
12	0	0.0	47	97.9	1	2.1	0	0.0	22.042 sig.
13	1	2.1	2	4.2	41	85.4	4	8.3	15.211 sig.

[a] *Chi square calculated to test differences between the two models where applicable, chosen most frequently by the students.*

* *n=47; data for one subject was discarded due to coding errors.*

The description of the four models of juvenile justice and the phrases of the Declaration of Principle in the YOA were sufficiently clear that students independently categorized all thirteen phrases into only one or two models. Over 70% of the students agreed that just one model was indicated in nine of the thirteen phrases (p < .01). (Hereafter, these nine phrases will be referred to as the congruent phrases). The students categorized three of the nine congruent phrases under the Justice model, three under the Crime Control model and the remaining three under the Welfare model of juvenile justice. The equal number of phrases categorized into the three models of Justice, Crime Control and Welfare supported the authors' initial categorization of the thirteen phrases.

The student rating of phrases 1 and 7 also supported the "close second rating" shown in the authors categorized phrase 3 (i.e. society's responsibility to prevent youthful crime) as falling under the Community Change model, agreement was shown by 50% of the student raters while the other students felt this phrase fell under the Crime Control model. Similarly, phrase 4 (i.e., requirement of discipline, control and supervision) was categorized by the authors as falling under the Crime Control model with 50% of the students agreeing with this rating and 50% indicating that this phrase was more similar to the assumptions of the Welfare model.

There are several limitations to these findings. First, an independent check of the authors' understanding of the four models is necessary, as is a check on the categorization of the eight subsections of the principles into the thirteen phrases. Second, a simple frequency count of congruent phrases per model is only a rough estimate of model importance as one phrase may conceptually be more influential than another phrase. Third, it is possible that the implementors of the YOA will perceive the principles of section 3 globally, rather than differentiate them into categories as subsumed in this paper. We did not explore global perceptions of the Declaration of Principles in the YOA, nor the possibility of the dominance of one model in such a global assessment. Fourth, there may be little relationship between the principles as outlined in section 3 of the Act and the provisions which follow. A careful analysis of the optional and mandatory provisions of the Act and how much provisions reflect the espoused principles is certainly necessary, but beyond the scope of this paper.

DISCUSSION

This paper is based on the assumption that perceptions concerning youth, society and the state influence juvenile justice policy formulation and its subsequent implementation. An examination of the principles of the *Young Offenders Act* suggest three findings: (1) Most of the assumptions reflected in the Declaration of Principles are comphrensible and are understood in a similar fashion by independent raters; (2) The assumptions in the principles repre-

sent various models of juvenile justice which differ markedly in their perceptions regarding the causes and responses to crime; and (3) The assumptions in
the principles reflect more than the dual focus on Justice and Welfare models
as has been suggested (Lilles, 1983:21), with the assumptions of the Crime
Control, Justice and Welfare models each being granted equal prominence.

> The Statement of Principle adds considerations of accountability by
> the young offender (albeit less than for adults), protection of the pub-
> lic and guarantees of rights and freedoms with minimum interference
> with freedom to the previous treatment objectives of the JDA. The
> accumulation of these principles, old and new, seems to call for a
> delicate balancing act by the court. (Nasmith, 1983:10)

While our findings support Judge Nasmith's opinion that the principles of the
YOA call for a delicate balancing act, this "balance" is to be implemented in
light of the resolution of virtually dichotomous issues: youth's accountability for
their actions with society's responsibility for crime prevention; society's protection from crime with the needs and rights of youth being equally addressed.
Furthermore, the YOA states that in the implementation of the Act, the provisions shall be "liberally construed" so that "young people will be dealt with in
accordance with the **principles**" (s.3(2) emphasis added).

One major impetus to reform the *Juvenile Delinquents Act* was the concern regarding the incredible disparity in age jurisdiction, dispositional practices, and service delivery to juvenile delinquents both within and between the
provinces (Canada, 1965: para. 62-65). The YOA ameliorates some of these
disparities through the insistence upon a uniform maximum age jurisdiction
and the provision of due process protections within the new Youth Courts.
Other provisions in the YOA, however, may serve to increase the much criticized disparity between the provinces, who are required to enforce the legislation. For example, it is up to the discretion of the provinces to determine
whether or not alternative measures to formal court proceedings (s.4), community and treatment-oriented dispositions (s.20 (c) to (i); s.21 (6); s. 21 (9); s. 22
(1); s.29 (1)), review boards (s.30) and Youth Juvenile Committees (s.69) will
be provided.

Even in the absence of conclusive data on the value of any one set of principles of the effectiveness and efficiency of any juvenile justice system, governments still proceed to make changes in their legislation and policies regarding
youth. For example, California went from a primarily welfare-oriented system
for young offenders to one premised on justice assumptions in 1960 (Lemert,

1970), while several years later both England and Scotland changed in the opposite direction from systems predominantly based on justice assumptions to ones premised on welfare principles (Bottoms, 1974; Martin, Murray & Fox, 1981).

These striking system reversals, and the many less striking ones in other countries, are in part due to the unintended consequences of any model, often starkly captured by an extreme situation, not intended, but certainly possible within the system (Mitford, 1974; Wooden, 1976). Awareness of these unintended consequences promotes questioning, reassessments and the possibility of new ideas (or old ideas resurrected) being put on the agenda of the decision makers. For example, in 1967, the Supreme Court of the United States handed down a decision in *Re Gault* that juvenile delinquents must be provided with at least minimal procedural safeguards in the adjudication and disposition process. This decision came from a *habeus corpus* appeal iniated by the parents of a young boy who had been detained in a reform school for six years following an uncontested trial over a neighbour's complaint regarding an obscene phone call (*Re Gault* 387 U.S. 1, 1967). This example clearly shows the consequences of one model, in this case the Welfare Model, in extreme form. The consequences were magnified by the opinions of the media, the public and ultimately the Court who passed down a decision which altered the policy for young offenders.

To avoid potential extremes, policy-makers are under pressure to develop policies that at least appear to blend the values of several models (Asquith, 1983:8). In the last thirty years most of the attempts to change juvenile justice policy in English-speaking states have attempted to address the problem of blending the values of several models while struggling to avoid the potential extremes of any one model.[3]

This ongoing tension among sets of assumptions may be inevitable, an perhaps even desirable in an attempt to reach a juvenile justice system which will meet the needs of society and youth:

> There are significant indications that a new system of juvenile justice is emerging—a system which can preserve the advancements in the behavioural sciences can be utilized in the treatment of troublesome youth, but only within a legal framework of justice, that protects the individual rights of such youth and precludes authoritative intervention in their lives without a crucially important reason for doing so. (Faust & Brantingham, 1974:25)

The juvenile justice system may now be engaging in an honest struggle with real problems by providing a meeting point for the different approaches (Parsloe, 1976:74,75).

A number of commentators of the YOA suggest that a new system of juvenile justice has been reached with this Canadian legislation (Kaplan, 1982; Wilson, 1982; Archembault, 1983; Nasmith, 1983; Lilles, 1983). It has also been suggested that the YOA goes one step further in its ability to adapt to change through the upcoming years

> ...it can be said that the Act is then able more easily to adapt as soci-
> etal views change: today one stresses those principles and provisions
> which suggest a "criminal code for children"; tomorrow, when and if
> the pendulum shifts once again, the needs-oriented provisions...can
> be emphasized (Thompson, 1983:27).

By way of summary, then, it can be argued that they inclusion of the assumptions of three models of juvenile justice in the YOA may avoid the unintended consequences of the extremes of any one model and provide something for everyone and for all occasions. Moreover, the flexibility of several sets of assumptions may be useful in developing a creative response to individual cases which come before the Youth Courts.

This positive interpretation regarding the compromise and the flexibility in the YOA, however, underestimates the problems inherent in the lack of priority assumptions in the new Act. There are no points of resolution for the persons and bureaucracies responsible for implementing the YOA, and there are many possibilities for discretion. Since the principles provide a rationale for every possible direction, it is more likely that other factors, such as bureaucracies' access to funds and the ideologies of those responsible for enforcing the new Act, will influence the implementation of the provisions. As Parker *et al.* conclude in their review of the discretion of the 1969 English law for young offenders: diversity and dissonance prevail since the police, magistrate, and social workers "vie for influence and tilt decisions towards their own ideological and organizational preference" (1980:236).

The Canadian Foundation for Children and the Law expressed concern about the lack of priority in the Principles section of the new Act and voiced their concerns in a brief to the Standing Committee on Justice and Legal Affairs during the consultation period prior to enactment of the YOA:

> The requirement in s. 3(2) that the Act be liberally construed is

somewhat at variance with its detailed drafting. The scope for liberal construction is reduced where quite specific provisions have been enacted. In that many of these detailed provisions are not designed to protect the procedural and substantive rights of young persons, liberality in their application is not necessarily a virtue, especially in service to principles expressed without priority in s. 3(1). This leaves it open to each youth court judge to determine priorities, such as societal protection from illegal behaviour, and liberally to sacrifice enacted protections of young persons to serve that end. (Justice for Children, 1981:8).

The tense struggle over the lack of priority in the stated principles in the YOA has already erupted in Ontario during 1984. Under the JDA, the provinces were given the discretion to choose a maximum upper age limit between 16 and 18 years (s.2), and Ontario opted for the age of sixteen as the upper age jurisdiction of the juvenile court. The Ministry of Correctional Services was responsible for the enforcement of laws related to young persons over the age of sixteen years while the Ministry of Community and Social Services, as of 1977, was responsible for those youth under the age of sixteen. Given the mandate under the YOA for a uniform maximum age jurisdiction of under eighteen years, a struggle ensued between the two provincial ministries regarding the approaches to be used in dealing with youth, the appropriation of funds for young offenders and the delivery of services to young people who had previously been dealt with under two distinct "correctional" systems. The Ministry of Correctional Services wanted to maintain its authority over the sixteen and seventeen year old offenders and extend its jurisdiction to all young offenders while the Ministry of Community and Social Services wanted to maintain the integrated programmes for youth which had been developed and extend these programmes to the older age group. Both ministries utilized the assumptions of the principles in the YOA to justify their prospective positions. The issue was resolved by maintaining the jurisdictional boundaries of the two ministries as they had existed prior to the enactment of the YOA: the Ministry of Correctional Services retained authority over the older youth, and the Ministry of Community and Social Services retained the jurisdiction for the younger age group. It appears that this compromise is more a case of organizational necessity and budgetary constraints than a "delicate balancing" of the principles of the YOA.[4]

Further difficulties arise in attempting to balance the principles of the new Act when one considers the fact that implementation of the YOA comes at a time of economic restraint and a conservative mood (Leman, 1980; Horton, 1981). At present in Canada, there was eight conservative provincial governments and a recently elected federal conservative government which boasts a large majority. The philosophy of these governments included individual responsibility, fiscal restraint and private enterprise which are not necessarily conducive to the assumptions of the Welfare and Community Change models of juvenile justice. In addition, with greater social and financial vulnerability permeating Canadian society, there is a tendency on the part of many to express greater concern with law and order (Hylton, 1981). The assumptions of the Crime Control model, then, are readily supported to allay a perceived vulnerability and to strengthen the threatened legitimacy of the government (Hall et al., 1978). It is this "perceived" fear rather than any real increase in crime that thwarts compromise and leads to a subsequent emphasis on Crime Control solutions (Jankovic, 1980; Taylor, 1983; Krisberg et al., 1984).

It is suggested that without a priority among the principles in the YOA, the mandatory Justice provisions may be honored at least in form, but the Crime Control provisions will be stressed in practice. It is expected that formal court proceedings, fines, probation and custodial dispositions will take precedence over more "welfare-orientated" proceedings and dispositional alternatives such as community service orders and conditional discharges. The reasons for this suggested direction are not efficiency or cost but rather the flexibility, creativity and time required to orchestrate such alternatives among the various organizations responsible for implementation. The Welfare and Community Change dispositions require more of these resources than the Crime Control or Justice alternatives.

Briefly, it has been suggested that while one strong priority in the intention of legislation for juvenile offenders may lead to the extreme discussed above, at least some differentiation and prioritization is necessary. If there is no priority, and a "fifty-one" per cent is all that is conceptualized, it will be difficult to resolve ongoing tensions between the individuals and bureaucracies responsible for implementing the new Act. Decisions will not take place according to consciously promoted ideals but will rely on the values and mandates of those who enforce the provisions of legislation.

Suggested scenarios for prioritizing the principles in YOA are as follows:

(1)	the justice principles can predominate during the adjudication stage of the proceedings (i.e. the determination of guilt) while the Community Change principles can be utilized in efforts to prevent youthful crime;

(2) The Welfare and Justice principles can take precedence over the Crime Control principles in cases of victimless crimes or where the young person involved has had less than four police contacts (Wolfgang *et al.*, 1972:89);

(3) The least possible interference with the freedom principle (i.e. Justice) and the voluntary acceptance of treatment which matches the needs of the youth involved (i.e. Welfare) can take primacy with respect to dispositional alternatives for the majority of young offenders; and

(4) The mandatory Welfare principle and Crime Control principles are only suitable for the less than ten per cent of apprehended youth who engage in serious acts and who are classified as chronic recidivists (Lab, 1984; West, 1984:56-66).

This paper has raised the issue of the effect of assumptions and beliefs about youth, society and the state in relation to the development and implementation of social policy for young offenders. The principles of the new federal legislation for young offenders in Canada were analyzed in terms of four models of juvenile justice. It was concluded that the stated philosophy of the YOA reflects assumptions from three somewhat contradictory models of juvenile justice. Possible implication of these apparent contradictions were discussed in terms of the delicate balancing of principles and the tense struggle among the individuals and bureaucracies empowered to implement the new legislation. While the YOA is still in its infancy and change is possible in years to come, the balancing will be difficult at this time because of contemporary economic and social vulnerabilities within Canadian society. Furthermore, the legislation itself allows much latitude in interpretation due to its requirement of "liberal construction", a lack of priority given to the principles of the Act, and the inclusion of optional provisions throughout the body of the statute. It is therefore more likely that instead of a delicate balancing of principles, implementation of the YOA will be guided by standard operating procedures within juvenile justice bureaucracies, the primacy of mandatory as opposed to optional provisions and the financing available in each region and province throughout Canada, allocated for experimentation with new and creative programmes.

ENDNOTES

1. The following list provides a summary of the major reports, committees
    conferences, legislative bills and proposals which proceeded the YOA at
    the federal level of government:

    Department of Justice on Juvenile Delinquency appointed on November
    6, 1976 and reported in 377 page report *Juvenile Delinquents in
    Canada* in 1965; 1967 a draft bill based on recommendations from the
    1965 report, "An Act Respecting Children and Young Persons"; the
    first federal-provincial conference on juvenile delinquency was held on
    January 10-11, 1968; November 16, 1970 first reading of Bill C-192
    withdrawn due to steady opposition; October 5, 1973 Cabinet formed
    Joint Review Committee Group consisting of department of Solicitor
    General and National Health and Welfare; 1974 held second federal-
    provincial conference to discuss recommendations of joint review
    groups; 1975 the report and Legislative proposals "Young Persons in
    Conflict with the Law" was published; 1976 formed an interdepartmen-
    tal working group to draft proposals from recommendations of the
    1975 report; 1977 draft proposals from recommendations of the 1975
    report; 1977 published "Highlights of Proposed New Legislation for
    Young Offenders" and distributed 15,000 copies; 1979 Conservative
    government drafted set of legislative proposals; 1981 Cill C-61 had first
    reading on February 16, 1981; 1983 YOA given royal assent on July
    7, 1983; April 1, 1984 YOA proclaimed in force.

    See also: M. Reitsma-Street, "Policy formulation in the Canadian juve-
    nile justice system: The Transformation of the 1980 *Juvenile
    Delinquents Act* into the 1982 *Young Offenders Act*. Unpublished
    manuscript. Centre of Criminology, University of Toronto, February,
    1984.

2. For references to the debates see:

    House of Commons Debates. Third Session 28th Parl., vol. 115, no.
    27, Nov. 16, 1970: 1171; no. 53, Jan. 13, 1971: 2370-2390; no.
    103, March 24, 1971: 4373-4588; no. 112, April 6, 1971: 4961-5;
    no. 27, no. 343, May 17, 1982: 17486.

    House of Commons Debates First Session 32nd Parl. Vol. 124, no.

184, Feb. 16, 1981a: 7258; no. 184, April 15: 9307-9328; no. 188, May 12, 1981: 9493-9524; no. 200, May 29, 1981: 10072-91; no. 202, June 2, 1981: 10023-10024; no. 343, May 17, 1982: 17486.

3.   See for example:

England: Report of the Committee on Children an Young Persons (Ingleby) Cmnd, 1191, HMSO, 1960; Scotland: Report on Children and Young Persons (Kilbrandon), Cmnd, 2306, 1964; United States: The President's Commission on Law Enforcement and Administration of Justice: Task Force on Juvenile Delinquency and Youth Crime (deB. Katzenbach), Washington, Government Printing Office, 1967; Ireland: Report of the children and Young Persons Review Group (Black) Belfast, HMSO, 1979.

4.   S.A. Reid, "The New 'Age' of Juveniles Under the *Young Offenders Act:* Reaching the Decision and Anticipating the Problems" Unpublished manuscript. Centre of Criminology, University of Toronto, 1983. See also, "Juvenile Justice System split into two age groups," *The Globe and Mail*, December 18, 1984:8; "Unequal Treatment" *The Globe and Mail* (Editorial), January 9, 1985; "Highlights of the NJC Meeting", May 1983, *Contact*, 2 (1), 1983:4-5.

REFERENCES

APA, 1980. *Diagnostic and Statistical Manual of Mental Disorders.* (3rd edition) Washington: American Psychiatric Association.

Archembault, O., 1983. "Young Offenders Act: Philosophy and Principles." *Provincial Judges Journal* 7 (2): 1-7.

Asquith, S., 1983. *Children and Justice: Decision-Making in Children's Hearings and Juvenile Courts.* Edinburgh: Edinburgh University Press.

Babbie, E., 1983. *The Practice of Social Research* (3rd ed.). Belmont, California: Wadsworth.

Bottoms, A.E., 1974. "On the decriminalization of English juvenile courts." in R. Hood (ed.) *Crime, Criminology and Public Policy.* London: Heinemann.

Canada, Department of Justice on Juvenile Delinquency, 1965. *Juvenile Delinquency in Canada.* Ottawa: Queen's Printer.

Canada, Solicitor General, 1982. *The Young Offenders Act, 1982: Highlights.* Ottawa: Supply and Services Canada.

Catton, K., 1975/76. "Models of procedure and the juvenile courts." *Criminal Law Quarterly* 18: 181-201.

Djao, A.W., 1983. *Inequality and Social Policy.* Toronto: Wiley.

Faust, F.L. and P.J. Brantingham, 1974. *Juvenile Justice Philosophy.* St. Paul, Minn.: West

George, V. and P. Wilding, 1976. *Ideology and Social Welfare.* Boston: Little.

Gil, D., 1976. *Unraveling Social Policy* (revised). Cambridge, Mass., Schenkman.

Grifiths, J., 1970. "Ideology in criminal procedure or a third model of the criminal process." *Yale Law Journal* 79:359.

Hall, S., Critcher, C., Jefferson, T. Clarke, J., and Roberts, B., 1978. *Policing the Crisis.* London: The MacMillan Press.

Higgins, J., 1980. "Social control theories of social policy." *Journal of Social Policy* 9: 1-23.

Horton, J., 1981. "The rise of the right." *Crime and Social Justice* 15:7-17.

Houston, S.E., 1972. "Victorian origins of juvenile delinquency: A Canadian experience." *History of Education Quarterly* 12:254-280.

Hylton, J., 1981. "The growth of punishment: Imprisonment and community corrections in Canada." *Crime and Social Justice* 15:18-28.

Inter-Ministry Implementation Project, 1981. *Implementing Bill C-61 The Young Offenders Act: An Ontario Consultation Paper.* Toronto: Ontario Inter-Ministry Implementation Project.

Jankovic, I., 1980. "Labor market and imprisonment" in T. Platt and P. Takagi (eds.) *Punishment and Penal Discipline.* Berkeley: Crime and Social Justice Associates.

Justice for Children, 1981. *Brief on the Young Offenders Act, Bill C-61.* Toronto: Canadian Foundation for Children and the Law.

_____, *Response to Ontario Consultation Paper on Implementing Bill C-61 The Young Offenders Act.* Toronto: Canadian Foundation for Children and the Law.

Kaplan, R., 1982. *House of Commons Standing Committee on Justice and Legal Affairs.* Issue 65:9.

Krisberg, B., 1975. *Crime and Privilege: Toward a New Criminology.* Englwood Cliffs, N.J.: Prentice-Hall.

Krisberg, B. and P. Litsky and I. Schwartz, 1984. "Youth in confinement: Justice by geography." *Journal of Research in Crime and Delinquency* 21 (2):153-181.

Lab, S.P., 1984. "Patterns of juvenile misbehaviour." *Crime and Delinquency* 30 (2):293-308.

Leman, C., 1980. *The Collapse of Welfare Reform: Political Institutions, Policy and the Poor in Canada and the United States.* Cambridge: MIT Press.

Lemert, E., 1970. *Social Action and Legal Change: Revolution Within the Juvenile Court.* Chicago: Aldine.

Leon, J., 1977. "The development of Canadian juvenile justice: A background for reforms." *Osgoode Hall Law Journal* 15:71-106.

Lerman, P., 1977. "Delinquency and social policy." *Crime and Delinquency* 23:383-393.

Lilles, J.A., 1983 "Beginning a new era." *Provincial Judges Journal* 7 (2): 21-26.

MacDonald, J.A., 1971. "A critique of Bill C-192: The Young Offenders Act." *Canadian Journal of Criminology and Corrections* 13:166-180.

Mannheim, H. (ed.), 1972. *Pioneers in Criminology* (revised). Montclair, New Jersey: Patterson Smith.

Martin, F.M. and S.J. Fox, and K. Murray, 1981. *Children Out of Court*. Edinburgh: Scottish Academic Press.

Miller, W.B., 1973. "Ideology and criminal justice policy." *Journal of Criminal Law and Criminology* 64: 141-162.

Mitford, J., 1974. *Kind and Usual Punishment*. New York: Alfred A. Knopf.

Morris, A. and H. Giller and L. Szwed and H. Geach, 1980. *Justice for Children*. London: MacMillan.

Nasmith, A.P., 1983. "Paternalism circumscribed." *Provincial Judges Journal* 7 (2): 8-12.

Packer, H., 1964. "Two models of the criminal process." *University of Pennsylvania Law Review* 113: 1-69.

Parker, H. Casburn, M., and Turnbull, D., 1980. "The production of punitive juvenile justice." *British Journal of Criminology*, 20 (3):236-260.

Parsloe, P., 1976. "Social work and the justice model," *British Journal of Social Work* 6:71-89.

Platt, A.M., 1969. *The Child Savers*. Chicago: University of Chicago Press.

Quinney, R. 1977. *Class, State and Crime*. New York: David McKay.

Rein, M., 1976. *Social Science and Public Policy*. Harmondsworth, Middlesex: Penguin.

Rothman, D.I., 1980. *Conscience and Convenience*. Boston: Little, Brown.

Scottish Home and Health Department and Scottish Education Department, 1964. *Children and Young Persons* (Cmnd.2306). Edinburgh: Her Majesty's Stationary Office.

Sinclair, C.M., 1983. "A radical/Marxist interpretation of juvenile justice in the United States." *Federal Probation* 46:20-27.

Snider, L.T. and W.G. West, 1980. "Crime and delinquency: A critical approach to law in the Canadian state." in R.J. Ossenberg (ed.) *Power and Change in Canada*. Toronto: McClelland and Stewart.

Solomon, P.H., 1981. "The policy process in Canadian criminal justice." *Canadian Journal of Criminology*. 23: pp. 5-25.

Sutherland, N. 1976. *Children in English Canadian Society: Framing the Twntieth Century Consensus*. Toronto: University of Toronto Press.

Taylor, I., 1983. *Crime, Capitalism and Community*. Toronto: Butterworths.

Taylor, I., P. Walton, and J. Young, 1973. *The New Criminology: For a social theory of deviance*. London: Routledge and Kegan Paul.

Thompson, G.M., 1983. "Commentary on the Young Offenders Act." *Provincial Judges Journal* 7 (2):27-34.

Titmuss, R.M., 1974. *Social Policy*. London: George Allen and Unwin.

West, W.G., 1984. *Young Offenders and the State*. Toronto: Butterworths.

Wilensky, R.L. and C.N. Lebeaux, 1965. *Industrial Society and Social Welfare* (2nd ed.). New York: Free Press.

Wilson, L.C., 1982. *Juvenile Courts in Canada*. Toronto: Carswell.

Wolfgang, M.E. and R.M. Figlio and T. Sellin, 1972. *Delinquency in a Birth Cohort*. Chicago: University of Chicago Press.

Wooden, K., 1976. *Weeping in the Playtime of Others*. New York: McGraw Hill.

CHAPTER 5
Youth's Knowledge And Attitudes About The Young Offenders Act: Does Anyone Care What They Think? [1]

PETER G. JAFFE
ALAN D. W. LESCHIED
JANE L. FARTHING

One strange irony about the *Young Offenders* Act (YOA) is that no one has really consulted with the group most affected by this legislation: adolescents. There is no shortage of individuals prepared to speak on behalf of the needs and rights of young persons. Before and after the implementation of the YOA, legislators heard from lawyers, judges, police officers, probation officers, and social service and mental health professionals about the real and perceived impact of this legislation. Although only limited data has been available to analyze the changes the YOA produced in comparison to the *Juvenile Delinquents* Act, the overall response has been critical of the legislation and of provincial implementation. However, there are no data on the views of the consumers of the YOA.

A number of researchers have indicated that knowledge and public views of the law serve as an important basis for the behaviour and attitudes amongst children and adolescents.[4, 9, 6]

Saunders[11] has noted that an increased awareness and knowledge of the law results in more favourable attitudes towards it. Maher and Stein[8] noted that when juvenile offenders were given more knowledge about the law even this group developed more positive attitudes towards the law.

The recently proclaimed YOA in Canada (proclaimed into law April 1, 1984) provides a unique opportunity to study the knowledge of young persons directly affected by this new piece of legislation.

The YOA is a dramatic departure from the JDA (proclaimed 1908) in three major areas: first, it emphasizes the importance of the accountability and responsibility of young persons for their behaviour; second, it insures the protection of legal rights for all young persons from the point of police contact through the court process; third, it de-emphasizes the role of treatment/rehabilitation in the mediation of delinquent behavior.[7]

The intent of the present study was to examine the knowledge and attitudes regarding the YOA among a group of young persons who, due to their age, (12-18), are affected by the legislation.

METHOD

Subjects

The methods utilized in the present study required a group of young persons to complete a questionnaire on a number of aspects of the Young Offenders Act.[2] The subjects were 351 students (180 males; 171 females). The average age was 15 years, with a range of 12 to 18 years. The subjects were drawn from two schools in London, Ontario (I elementary; I secondary).

Materials

A 12 item questionnaire was given to all of the students in the sample. Knowledge and attitudes regarding the philosophy of the YOA and where this information was obtained by the young persons (i.e. media, personal experience) was elicited.

Procedure

The students were told that there was new legislation dealing with the criminal behaviour of young people and that it would be interesting to note their knowledge and opinions about it. The young persons were then administered the questionnaire with the understanding that their answers would remain anonymous. The vocabulary of the questionnaire was geared to a grade 5 level of reading and comprehension. The students completed the questionnaire within 15 to 20 minutes. After completion, students were shown a brief videotape produced by the federal Ministry of the Solicitor General on the highlights of the YOA. A group discussion about the YOA took place in the remaining class time.

RESULTS

Frequencies and percentages were calculated of the students' responses to the questionnaire. Chi square analysis was used to examine within group differences based on age and sex. In an effort to gain information on the group under study, part of the questionnaire asked students about their own experience in Youth Court and primary source of their knowledge regarding the YOA. Approximately 16% of the respondents had been in trouble with the law. Of this group, 75% had contact with the police, but had not been charged. For those who proceeded to court, 14.6% were given probation or some other form of court disposition other than institutionalization and 10.6% had a charge that was later dismissed. The most common type of crime committed by this group was shoplifting. Drinking and other crimes such as assault, vandalism, and break and enter were also reported. 61.3% of the students knew someone who had been involved with the law. Close friends accounted for 30.5%, whereas relatives accounted for 19.3%, and acquaintances accounted for the remainder. Approximately ten per cent of the students questioned had no knowledge of the YOA.

Table 1
Source of Youths' Knowledge of the YOA

Items	Percentage
None	10.8
Television	44.7
Newspapers/magazines	39.6
Friends	22.5
Teachers	28.8
Parents	24.2
Personal experience	8.0
Public presentations	10.5
Other	7.4

Note. N = 306

Table 2 provides a summary of the students' responses to the factual questions about the YOA. The percentage of correct responses for the twelve questions ranged between 7.8% to 58.8%. Students had inaccurate information in a number of key areas. Almost two-thirds of the students believed that young offenders should receive counselling or treatment when it is ordered by the judge. Only 7.8% knew that the law now states that if young offenders do not want treatment, they do not have to receive such interventions. 40.1% agreed that young offenders should be rehabilitated and not punished, 26.8% disagreed with the rehabilitative approach. Only 8.6% of the respondents agreed with the provision of destruction of records after two years.

The students agreed with the law on three questions. They believed that young offenders should be sent to adult court when the crime committed is serious, when the offender is over 14, and when ordered to do so by the court. Also in agreement with the law, young persons were aware of their right to legal counsel, and for the ordering of parents to appear in court.

Overall, opinions of the students agreed with their knowledge of the law. However, some differences did emerge. The majority of students thought that 10 should be the youngest age and 18 should be the oldest age to appear in Youth Court. Approximately one-third of the students thought that young offenders should be tried in adult court when the crime was serious. Agreement with the philosophy of the YOA was endorsed by approximately half the students.[3] The other half of the students endorsed the philosophy of the JDA.

Within Group Difference

Within group differences factored for age produced significant differences on two of the twelve questions related to opinions of the YOA. Older adolescents (17 to 18 years of age), in contrast to their younger counterparts, were more likely to believe that young offenders should attend for treatment if ordered by the court ($X^2(8) = 17.02$, $p < .03$) and that records should be destroyed when the young offender becomes of adult age ($X^2(6) = 14.13$, $p < .03$).

Chi square analysis using sex as a factor produced differences in two areas. Females tended to be more lenient with repeat offenders who had three police occurrences ($X^2(4) = 12.31$, $p < .02$), and also felt more strongly that young offenders should have legal representation ($X^2(4) = 12.12$, $p < .02$).

Table 2
Mode Scores and Percentages For Questions
According to Knowledge and Opinion of the Law

Items		Knowledge	Right Answer	Opinion
Youngest age		12.84[a]		
to appear in	mode	12	12	10
Youth Court	%	21.8	21.8	17.0
Oldest age		17.15		
to appear in	mode	17	17	18
Youth Court	%	26.6	22.6	26.1
Maximum penalty				
for first	mode	1 year	2 years	1 year
contact	%	43.1	20.9	44.6
Maximum penalty				
for third	mode	5 years	3 years	5 years
contact	%	40.5	26.1	39 7
Going to	mode	all	b	serious crime
Adult Court	%	29.6		30.3
Right to	mode	yes	b	yes
Legal Counsel	%	58.8		59.7
Parents being	mode	ordered to	b	ordered to
allowed in court	%	51.3		49.1
Counselling	mode	if judge orders	not if does not want	if judge orders
treatment	%	60.7	7.8	58.8
Police	mode	kept	destroyed	kept
records	%	46.6	8.6	52.6

Note. N = 351

[a] means

[b] same answer as the knowledge response

Discussion

The aim of the present study was to examine students' knowledge and opinions of the YOA through administration of a questionnaire examining their knowledge and opinions.

The most obvious conclusion from the present study is that within the present group of adolescents only minimal, accurate knowledge is known about the criminal justice legislation which affects them. In the majority of areas investigated by the questions on the YOA, close to 75% of the respondents did not have accurate information. One in ten of the respondents reported that they knew nothing at all about the YOA. This finding is surprising given the amount of publicity the YOA has received. Access to information through the media appears to be the most popular source. However, concern has been expressed for the accuracy of some of the media's coverage of the Young Offenders Act.[5] Sources of information which tend to show less bias in their orientation, such as through the school, are relied on less frequently. This low percentage of informed adolescents is in considerable contrast to reports of the general level of knowledge of the law by persons in one Ontario community. Ribordy'[o] administered a questionnaire regarding six enacted pieces of legislation including the *Young Offenders Act* to assess knowledge and opinions about the law. These results indicated that 92% of respondents felt they were sufficiently or somewhat informed about the law and were able to correctly respond to specific questions about the law in 71% of the questions asked. These percentages are in stark contrast to the low percentage of adolescents who were able to respond correctly to questions on the *Young Offenders Act,* and the even lower percentage who considered themselves informed about the YOA.

The second conclusion drawn from the present study suggests that, in a number of areas, young people disagree with the legislation which has been established. Key areas in this regard indicate that young persons feel that age ten is a more appropriate minimum age for accountability under legislation than the legislated age 12. Additionally, respondents believed that young offenders should not have the ability to waive a disposition of treatment when it has been endorsed by the court. A significant number of students believed that rehabilitation should be a goal of juvenile justice and, in this regard, almost half of the respondents endorsed the philosophy of the JDA as the preferred approach to young offenders. Areas of agreement indicate that young persons perceive their right to legal representation and that parents should be ordered to be a part of the youth's court process.

Somewhat contradictory to the emphasis given rehabilitation was the emphasis placed by the present group on harsher means of punishment given to repeat offenders. Respondents endorsed punishment for a third time offender which was much harsher than what would be meted out by a youth court judge. This finding is a similar theme which is reported, again by Ribordy and his colleagues, who indicated that in their sample, one-third of the respondents felt that criminal justice legislation should be more punitive.

SUMMARY

If the thesis, set forth by Leblang and Saunders among others, is correct, that knowledge of the law results in more favourable attitudes toward it and is an important basis of behaviour, then Canadian society has its work cut out for it in educating a generation on new juvenile justice legislation. If education in the law can be a significant crime deterrent for young persons, then it would appear that this opportunity is largely being missed.

Overall. it is interesting to note how little students know about the legislation and how much they think it should be changed. Less than 30% of the students knew about the age range and the waiver to adult court procedures, and less than 10% knew what happens to police records and their ability to refuse mental health treatment. The students seem most informed about their right to a lawyer, which may reflect the impact of American norms on television.

The students' opinions appear closest to some of the reactions of police associations across the country to the YOA. Although they agree on the upper age limit and would even extend it to include 18 year olds, they believe young persons should be held more fully accountable for their misbehaviour at age 10 and that police records should be kept. Most students have more faith in the court's wisdom to order treatment for a young person than current legislators who suggest adolescents should decide when they require treatment, irrespective of the wishes of the court and the opinion of mental health professionals. In some ways, this group is expressing a belief in a "hybrid" of juvenile justice philosophy which combines the best parts of both the YOA and the JDA.

In our opinion, these findings should stimulate other groups who want to speak for young persons to seek out their wishes. Legislators may need to find a consultative process for adolescents to provide a perspective on laws that have a direct impact on their lives. Although laws may not be tailored to please young persons' wishes, their voices should be heard and consideration given to their ideas.

ENDNOTES

1. Reprint requests to the senior author, 80 Dundas Street, Box 5600, Station "A", London, Ontario, N6A 2P3. The authors acknowledge the cooperation of the London Board of Education in completing this research project.

2. Copies of the questionnaire are available from the senior author.

3. Philosophy of the *Juvenile Delinquents Act* and the Young Offenders Act was expressed as follows:

   a.) "...to be dealt as one in a condition of delinquency and. therefore, requiring help, guidance and proper supervision." In other words, the young offender needs someone to look after him or her.

   Or

   b.) "...while young persons should not in all instances be held account-able in the same manner or suffer the same consequences for their behaviour as adults, young persons who commit offences should nonetheless bear responsibility for their contravention." In other words, young offenders have the same rights as adults and are to be held responsible for their behaviour.

4. Boydell, C., and C. Grindstaff. "Public attitudes toward legal sanctions for drug and abortion offences". *Canadian Journal of Criminology and Corrections. 13*(3), 209-232, 1971.

5. Jaffe, P.G. and A.W. Leschied. "It's a better law than critics suggest". *London Free Press*. London, Ontario. 1985.

6. Leblang, T.L. "Impact of legal medical education on medical students' attitudes towards the law". *Journal of Medical Education. 60* (4), 279-287, 1985.

7. Leschied, A.W. and P.G. Jaffe. "Implications of the Young Offenders Act in modifying the juvenile justice system. Some early trends". In N. Bala and H. Lilles (eds.). *Young Offenders Act Update*. Toronto: Butterworths. 1986.

8. Maher, B. and E. Stein. "The delinquent's perception of the law and the community". In S. Wheeler (ed). *Controlling Delinquents*. New York: John Wiley and Sons. 1968.

9.   Nesdale, A. "The law and social attitudes: Effects of proposed changes in drug legislation on attitudes toward drug use". *Canadian Journal of Criminology.* 22 (2), 176-187, 1980.

10.   Ribordy, F.X. *Legal education and information: An Exploratory Study.* Ottawa: Department of Justice. 1986.

11.   Saunders, L. "Ignorance of the law among teenagers: Is it a barrier to the exertion of their rights as citizens?" *Adolescence. 16* (63), 711-726, 1981.

CHAPTER 6
Children's Knowledge of the Legal System: Are They Competent to Instruct Counsel?[1]

MICHELE PETERSON-BADALI
RONA ABRAMOVITCH

Young people's interactions with the legal system have a profound effect on their lives; however, their ability to use effectively their rights has received virtually no empirical examination. The present study examined age differences in young people's knowledge of legal concepts presumed to be important in terms of the capacity to instruct legal counsel. Forty-eight subjects in each of grades 5, 7, and 9, and 48 young adults participated in a structured interiew containing four scenarios, each depicting a young person who had committed a criminal offence, was charged, and retained a lawyer. Subjects were questioned regarding their knowledge of the role of defense counsel, lawyer-client confidentiality, the meanings of "plead Guilty" and "plead Not Guilty", and what happens during a trial. Results revealed that some aspects of legal knowledge were understood adequately by subjects at all ages (e.g., definitions of defense counsel's role, plea of Guilty) while subjects were uniformly ignorant of others (e.g., the meaning of "plead Not Guilty"). Subjects' responses to most of the questions improved with age (e.g., understanding of lawyer-client confidentiality, trial descriptions). Certain misconceptions also increased, rather than diminished, with age (e.g., meaning of a Not Guilty plea). Findings are discussed in terms of both developmental theory and practical implications for the legal system.

Children interact with the legal system in a number of contexts, and these interactions have a profound impact on their lives. For example, legal proceedings are undertaken to determine which parent a child will live with, whether a child will be removed from his or her family to live in a foster or group home, and whether a child is guilty of a criminal offence and thus subject to criminal sanctions, such as probation or incarceration. These legal decisions are potentially life-altering for children, and it is crucial that they be given the right to participate in the process which results in such decisions. Throughout the past two decades, there has been an increasing focus on the legal rights of children. Foremost among these is their right to be heard and represented in the legal proceedings which will affect their lives (Mitchell 1984).

With the extension to children of the right to "legal representation" comes the task of defining (or perhaps redefining) the term. Central to this construct is the relationship between client and lawyer. With respect to adult clients, legal representation involves "protecting the client's interests and carrying out the client's wishes" (Wilson and Tomlinson 1986:331). As persons who have not reached full cognitive and emotional maturity, however, children differ from adults in important ways which have traditionally limited their involvement with the legal system, and which likely have an impact on the nature of the solicitor-client relationship. Thus, the question of the child's ability to properly instruct legal counsel is an important issue to resolve if children's right to legal representation is to be more than a hollow promise.

A standard of competence to instruct counsel which is acceptable to legislators and the legal profession can best be generated within that profession. However, an exploration of children's abilities to engage in the activities which comprise instruction of counsel would be of assistance to the legal profession in establishing such a standard. Instruction of counsel involves a wide variety of competencies, including an understanding of one's legal rights, knowledge of the legal system and of the roles of legal personnel, as well as the ability to reason and make decisions based on legal criteria. Several writers (Read 1987; Catton 1978; Leon 1978) have suggested that children must possess at least some knowledge of the legal system and its key players in order to participate meaningfully in the legal process. Very little empirical data is available to address the question of young people's abilities in these areas. The sparse research concerning children's knowledge of their rights reveals that they fail to make the basic distinction between a 'right' and a 'privilege' prior to middle childhood—age 7-10 (Melton 1983), and that, for a majority of youths, understanding of the function and significance of specific rights (e.g., silence and counsel) fails to meet legal competence standards prior to ago 16 (Grisso 1981). Further, it appears that juveniles' understanding of their legal rights is overestimated, both by lawyers and by themselves (Lawrence 1983).

Somewhat more empirical data is available concerning young people's knowledge of the legal system, including basic concepts of due process, legal roles, and legal procedures. For example, with respect to understanding of procedural justice, there is evidence that children are aware of certain due process concepts (e.g., proof beyond reasonable doubt, mitigation) beginning in middle childhood, although the knowledge of older children is more extensive and refined than that of younger children (Gold, Darley, Hilton and Zanna 1984; Irving and Siegal 1983). The bulk of the literature exploring children's legal knowledge, however, has focused on age differences in the understanding of the purpose and function of various court structures and proceedings, as well as children's conceptions of the roles of various actors within the legal system. With respect to the former, American and Australian researchers have reported that young people's understanding of the purpose of court hearings improves with age (Cashmore and Bussey 1987; Saywitz 1989; Warren-Leubecker, Tate, Hinton, and Ozbek 1989). When Cashmore and Bussey (1987) asked 6 to 14-year-old Australian students "what is a court?", there was an increase with age in the frequency of references to court as a place where guilt (or innocence) is determined and, conversely, there was a decrease in the frequency of concrete, descriptive responses (e.g., "a place where there's a judge who sits high on a platform"). Similarly, in her interview study of 4 to 14-year-old American children, Saywitz (1989) found that subjects' awareness of the trial as a truth seeking process increased with age. While the majority of 4 to 7 year-old children conceived of the goal of the court process as the accomplishment of a specific act (e.g., to punish the criminal or to make a custody decision), children aged 8 to 11 years old "were aware that the court is a fact finding process that seeks to uncover the truth" (Saywitz 1989:151). These subjects did not understand, however, that sometimes the truth (reality) differs from the judge's or jury's decision about what happened because the evidence on which they based their decision was flawed, and this understanding was attained by only a minority of the 12 to 14-year-old subjects. Warren-Leubecker et al. (1989) also reported a developmental trend in children's understanding of why people go to court, although, as early as age 9 a majority of students gave the "very vague but accurate answer 'To settle arguments or solve problems'" (Warren-Leubecker et al. 1989:169). In a more ecologically valid interview study of 12 to 16 year-old Canadian young offenders, Read (1987) found that one-third of youths did not view the judge as an impartial figure in the trial process and half believed that the judge has unlimited discretion in decision-making. Sixty-two percent of the youths interviewed wished they knew more about court proceedings and their rights. Thus, in general, available research suggests that young children show confusion or ignorance about the court's function, although they have a general sense of the purpose of court. Their understanding increases substantially with age, however, and in some cases becomes less concrete and more abstract in nature. Not surprisingly, there are also differences in the ages at which various facts or concepts are acquired; while many children 6-8 years of age had a sense of what a court is and who is in charge, very few subjects expressed the distinction between the legal and empirical truth of a matter, even by age 14.

There has been a recent increase in the number of studies addressing children's understanding of important legal roles and legal terminology, and the impact of understanding (or, more commonly, misunderstanding) of these concepts on their ability to participate competently in the legal system. In interviews with children from kindergarten through Grade 6, Saywitz and Jaenicke (1987) found that a small minority of terms were understood by all subjects (judge, lie, police, remember, and promise), while a number of others reflected significant grade-related trends (e.g., lawyer, evidence, jury, oath, witness). Finally, the legally relevant definitions of a number of terms were not understood by any of the subjects (e.g., defendant, hearsay, charges). As subjects often defined the vocabulary items in terms of their more common usage (e.g., "court is a place where you play basketball"), the authors concluded that "child witnesses may frequently be operating under the false impression that they understand a term that they have, in fact, misconstrued" (Saywitz 1989:135). Other authors (Cashmore and Bussey 1987) have argued that children's understanding of the legal meanings of these terms may have been underestimated because the terms were not presented within a legal context. Several studies (e.g., Cashmore and Bussey 1987; Saywitz 1989) have attempted to address this weakness by providing subjects with explicit and concrete prompts in the form of pictures or models of courtrooms, which include those people commonly found in a court. Findings indicate that older subjects demonstrated more complete and more accurate knowledge than younger subjects, and that, on the whole, the description of court personnel given by young children was quite global and concrete (e.g., sitting, talking, helping). In addition, across several studies (Cashmore and Bussey 1987; Saywitz 1988; Warren-Leubecker et al. 1989), a consistent pattern emerged in terms of the order in which the various concepts were mastered: judge first, followed by lawyers (particularly the defense lawyer), and, finally, the jury.

Children's understanding of the roles and functions of legal personnel (particularly defense counsel) is central to their capacity to instruct legal counsel. Two aspects of the legal system are deemed critical in this respect: the notion of defense counsel as an advocate for the client, and the principle of lawyer-client confidentiality. Without understanding that defense counsel's express duty is to carry out the client's wishes, and that any information given in the context of the lawyer-client relationship is strictly private, an individual would be operating at a marked disadvantage within the adversarial context of criminal procedure. Research in the United States, Canada, and Australia suggests that although children may possess a basic understanding of the role of defense counsel, their understanding continues to improve with age. Data from Warren-Leubecker *et al.'s* (1989) study suggested a progression from complete lack of understanding or misconception (ages 3-8) to a more general understanding of the advocacy role (8-11) and, finally, to a very specific conception of the lawyer as a defender. Youths may also hold some specific misconceptions about the role of their lawyer. For example, in her study of Canadian young offenders, Read (1987) found that only 18% of youths knew that information given to their lawyer is confidential, and Cashmore and Bussey's (forthcoming a) Australian study yielded an even lower figure (3%). In addition, in a U.S. study of juveniles detained on non-felony charges, Grisso (1981) found that approximately a third of subjects who had little or no prior experience with the law believed that the role of defense counsel is to defend the interests of the innocent but not the guilty.

THE PRESENT STUDY

Whether the client is a child or an adult, much of the knowledge and understanding required for competent participation in the legal process is not likely to be part of his or her initial knowledge-base. Clearly, one of the tasks of the lawyer is to inform and educate his or her client in these essential facts and concepts, in order to allow the client to make as well-reasoned a choice as possible. In fact, it can been argued that "competence" to instruct counsel does not rest within the child-client, but within the interaction between lawyer and client; as Roesch, Webster and Eaves (1984:51) state, "fitness, to a considerable degree, can be taught". In order to promote competence to instruct counsel in their child-clients, lawyers need information about what children know about the legal system and, particularly, what misconceptions they may hold, in order to develop optimal ways of presenting necessary information and explaining important legal constructs. Therefore, the purpose of the present study was to examine age differences in children's knowledge of the legal issues considered important in terms of the ability to instruct counsel. During the course of individual interviews, subjects were questioned to ascertain their knowledge of a number of critical legal roles and concepts, including the role of defense counsel, lawyer-client confidentiality, and what it means to plead Guilty or Not Guilty. Although young people's understanding of the role of defense counsel has received some study, its centrality to their capacity to instruct counsel adequately makes it worthy of further exploration. Further, despite the fact that an accurate understanding of what it means to plead Guilty or Not Guilty would appear to be an important prerequisite to competent instruction, no research has addressed young people's knowledge of these concepts. Subjects in the present study also responded to the open-ended question "what is a trial", since although previous research has investigated young people's knowledge of legal actors and concepts through explicit questioning (e.g., Saywitz 1989; Saywitz and Jaenicke 1987), no study has examined children's spontaneously expressed knowledge about the legal system.

METHOD

Subjects

A total of 192 subjects participated in the interviews, consisting of 24 males and 24 females from each of Grade 5, Grade 7, Grade 9, and Grade 12 or 13 classes. The mean age of subjects was 10.7 years (range 9.5 to 11.25 years) for the Grade 5 group, 13.0 years (range 12.25 to 13.6 years) for the Grade 7 group, 14.7 years (range 14.1 to 15.9 years) for the Grade 9 group, and 19.1 years (range 18.0 to 23.75 years) for the young adult group. The majority of subjects were White and Canadian-born, and the sample was fairly evenly divided between High (professional, management), Middle (skilled labour) and Low (semi-skilled, unskilled labour) socioeconomic status (SES) groups. All subjects were volunteers drawn from public schools within a Board of Education located in Toronto, Canada.

Procedure

Each subject was presented with four brief scenarios which depicted a series of events leading up to the arrest of the story's protagonist (who was matched to the subject's gender) who had actually committed the offense for which he or she was charged, followed by a more in-depth description of the character's initial meeting with his or her lawyer. During the presentation of the first scenario, the subject was asked a series of standard interview questions (described below) designed to assess his or her legal knowledge.[2] In addition to the questions, the subject was presented with simple definitions and explanations of key concepts and legal processes (e.g., plea of Not Guilty, presumption of innocence, proof beyond reasonable doubt). Responses to the interview questions were categorized according to coding schemes designed to capture the content and sophistication of subjects' knowledge. The following are the declarative knowledge questions posed during the course of the first story presentation, together with the coding schemes created to analyze responses. (The complete versions of coding and scoring systems, including detailed examples of category instances, are available from the first author.)

What is the job of the Lawyer?

This question was designed to elicit subjects' understanding of the role of defense counsel. Responses were placed into one or more of the following major role categories: General Advocacy (e.g., to represent or help the client), Defense (i.e., to defend the client), Defense Misconceptions (e.g., to prove the client innocent/Not Guilty), Minimize Sanctions (e.g., to get the client out of trouble), and Information (e.g., to find out what happened). A small percentage of responses which could not be categorized according to this coding scheme formed the "Other" category.

(A) Is it a good idea for the story character to tell the lawyer the whole story? Why/why not? (B) Can his/her lawyer tell anybody else what was said in their meeting? Can s/he tell the story character's parents? The judge? The police?

These questions were designed to elicit subjects' understanding of the nature of the relationship between solicitor and client, i.e., that it is based on confidentiality and trust. An adequate response to question (A) would be affirmative, while an adequate response to question (B) would be negative in each case. The reasons which subjects gave for disclosing information to a lawyer were assigned to one or more of the following categories: Assist Defense (e.g., so the lawyer can help/defend the client), Provide Information (e.g., so the lawyer knows the facts), and Negative Sanctions (e.g., because the client/lawyer might get into trouble for not telling everything).

What does it mean to plead guilty? Not guilty?

This question was designed to ascertain subjects' understanding of plea options, particularly the plea of Not Guilty, since it is here that clients must separate moral and legal issues. An adequate definition of the Guilty plea contains the notion that the defendant admits the veracity of the charges. An adequate definition of the Not Guilty plea must include some distinction between the moral and legal definitions of guilt, e.g., the notion that moral blamelessness is not necessarily asserted, but that the client demands that the issue of legal guilt be determined by means of a trial. Subjects' definitions of 'Plead Guilty' were assigned to one of the following categories: Admit Guilt (e.g, "saying he did it", 'admitting responsibility'), Actual Guilt (i.e.,a definition of 'Guilty' rather than 'plead Guilty'), Proven Guilty (e.g., "when they prove you did it"), and Other. Definitions of "Plead Not Guilty" were assigned to one of the following categories: Accurate (i.e., expressing the concepts described above), Deny Guilt (e.g., "saying that you didn't do it"; "saying that you're innocent"), Found Not Guilty (e.g., "when they let you off"), and Other.

What happens in a trial?

This question was designed to elicit subjects' knowledge of the trial process, including the key actors involved (defense lawyer, crown attorney, judge) and events which take place (e.g., cross-examination, questioning of witnesses) as well as their understanding of important legal concepts underlying a criminal trial, specifically the presumption of the defendant's innocence and the Crown's onus to prove guilt beyond a reasonable doubt, as well as the defendant's protection from self-incrimination. Therefore, subjects' responses were first broadly categorized into Actors, Events, and Concepts/ Misconceptions. Within the Actors category subjects responses were analyzed for mention of lawyers (defense, prosecuting or unspecified), judge, jury, defendant, witnesses, and plaintiff. The Events category was also divided into sub-groups: Trial Procedures (e.g., cross-examination, presentation of evidence), Judge's Role (e.g., "judge keeps order", "judge talks to client"), Description of Setting (e.g., "takes place in court"), General Decisions (e.g., "judge decides what's going to happen"), Guilt Decisions (e.g., "judge decides if you're guilty or not") and Punishment Decisions (e.g., "judge/jury gives client a punishment"). The Concepts category was sub-divided according to the type of concepts mentioned: Adversarial (e.g., "there are two sides"; "prosecutor tries to prove guilt"), Due Process (e.g., "each side tells its story", "decision is based on evidence"), and Procedural (e.g., "hearsay evidence is unacceptable"). The Misconceptions category was similarly divided into Due Process misconceptions (e.g., "the lawyer tries to prove client's innocence") and Procedural misconceptions (e.g., "the plaintiff sues the defendant").

The above measures relied entirely on subjects' ability to verbalize their knowledge. Therefore, it was important to examine the extent to which verbal skill, independent of age, was associated with subjects' demonstrations of knowledge. In order to obtain a measure of verbal ability, subjects under 18 years of age were administered the Vocabulary subtest of the Wechsler Intelligence Scale for Children-Revised (WISC-R).[3]

Reliability of coding, scoring and rating systems

In order to assess the inter-rater reliability of the coding system, an undergraduate psychology student acted as an independent rater for approximately 20% (N=40) or the interview protocols. In addition, intra-rater reliability was examined by the investigator, who re-coded approximately 10% (N=20) of the interview protocols (a subset of the 40 used by the second rater). Intra-rater agreement for all but 2 of the variables was over 80%, and in most cases exceeded 90%. Not surprisingly, inter-rater agreement was somewhat lower (ranging from 70%-100%) but exceeded 80% for a majority of the variables.

RESULTS AND DISCUSSION

Data analysis consisted mainly of log linear analysis of frequencies. Log linear analysis is a generalization of the chi square statistic for cross-tabulated data with more than two factors (which thus allows for an examination of interactions among factors). The independent variable of primary interest in these analyses was Grade, which was combined in turn with Sex and SES in two separate sets of analyses.In addition, chi square analyses examined the effect of Verbal Ability on subjects' legal knowledge; subjects in Grades 5, 7, and 9 were divided into High and Low Verbal ability groups based on a median split of WISC-R scores (collapsed over the three grades), in order to allow for an assessment of the effect of Verbal Ability independent of the subjects' grade. A p-value of .01 was chosen as the cutoff for significance in all analyses. Only significant effects are discussed.

Role of Lawyer

In response to the question "what is the job of X's lawyer", subjects' answers were quite evenly divided across the categories, with 20-30% of subjects providing responses in each category. When these responses were analyzed by grade, no significant differences emerged. The only age trend to approach significance was in terms of misconceptions (p=.02); while only 6% of the Grade 5 students expressed specific misconceptions about the lawyer's role, 29% of Grade 7's, 21% of Grade 9's, and 25% of the young adults expressed such misconceptions. The most common misconception related to the advocacy function; specifically, a number of subjects stated that the lawyer's job is to prove his or her client's innocence. In addition, the only significant effect of SES in the study emerged with respect to this question; more High SES subjects included a description of the lawyer as a provider of information than did subjects in either the Middle or Low SES groups.

The characterizations given by subjects in the present study are strikingly similar to those given by Cashmore and Bussey's 11 to 17-year-old Australian subjects (forthcoming b), who were asked "why do they give children a duty solicitor?". The majority of subjects in their study also described the defense lawyer either in general helping terms or more specific advocacy terms. In addition, the lack of developmental differences found in the present study can be compared to the data from Warren-Leubecker et al.'s (1989) study of 3 to 13-year-olds, which revealed that subjects in early childhood either had no idea or expressed misconceptions about a lawyer's role, while subjects in middle childhood expressed a general understanding of the advocacy role, and those in early adolescence focused more exclusively on the defense aspects of a lawyer's role. Taken together, these data suggest that children have already developed a reasonably accurate understanding of the lawyer's advocacy role by the end of middle childhood.

Disclosing Information to a Lawyer

When asked whether the client should tell his or her lawyer everything that happened, virtually all of the subjects (98%) said "yes". When asked why, however, various explanations were proposed, which varied significantly with grade. As Table 1 shows, the Assist Defense response was mentioned more frequently as Grade increased, and conversely, the Negative Sanctions explanation decreased with age. The Provide Information statement was expressed equally by the Grade 5, 7, and 9 subjects but not at all by the young adults. These findings are consistent with other legal research (e.g., Cashmore and Bussey 1987; Saywitz 1989), which suggests that younger children's actions are motivated by fear of punishment rather than for the purpose of achieving some positive goal.

Table 1
Percentage of subjects giving Assist Defense, Provide Information, and Negative Sanction rationales for disclosing information to a lawyer

Grade	Rationales		
	Assist Defense	Provide Information	Negative Sanctions
Grade 5	40	15	48
Grade 7	44	12.5	27
Grade 9	52	12.5	25
Adult	79	0	15
Total	54	10	29
Chi Sq.	19.7**	11.8**	13.8*

** $p < .01$

CONFIDENTIALITY

When subjects were asked whether the lawyer could tell anybody else what a client said, only a minority overall responded that he or she could (15%). This percentage declined significantly with age (25% of Grade 5's, 17% of Grade 7's and 9's and 4% of adults thought lawyers could tell ($X^2(3) = 10.6$, p=.01), and, conversely, the percentage of subjects who felt the information was confidential increased with age (67% of Grade 5, 77% of Grade 7, 83%

of Grade 9 and 96% of the young adult sample, respectively). Thus, lawyer-client confidentiality appears to be a relatively familiar concept to even the youngest subjects, with two-thirds correctly stating that lawyers cannot tell others what a client divulges. This knowledge also improves with age to the point where virtually all (96%) of young adults correctly answer the question.

In order to further probe their knowledge, subjects were asked about confidentiality in relation to specific individuals: the client's parents, the judge, and the police. Table 2 summarizes these findings. In general, subjects' confidentiality strictures relaxed when probed in terms of specific parties. When asked the question in general terms, only 15% of subjects responded that lawyers could divulge client information: however, 35% responded that the lawyer could tell police what his or her client said, 52% felt that the judge could be told, and 66% stated that the lawyer could tell parents. These misconceptions declined significantly with Grade, however (see Table 2). Despite the decline with age, it is interesting to note how many young adults retain the misconception that lawyers can break confidentiality and tell their parents what they have said. These results are consistent with both Read's (1987) and Cashmore and Bussey's (forthcoming b) findings that very few young offenders were aware that their relationship with defense council was a confidential one. These data suggest that lawyers must explicitly explain the principle of confidentiality to their clients. In addition, it suggests that which questions are asked influences the perceived quality of understanding; lawyers need to go beyond an open ended question and should probe their child clients more thoroughly about their beliefs in order to get a more accurate estimate of their understanding.

What does it mean to plead guilty?

When asked to define what 'pleading guilty' means, 72% of subjects correctly stated that it involves an admission of wrongdoing, or an acknowledgment that the charge was true. Fourteen percent stated that it meant that the person actually was guilty (in the moral sense), but gave no indication that an admission or statement was involved. In other words, they defined "guilty" rather than "plead guilty". Six percent of subjects confused pleading guilty with being proven guilty; 8% of subjects did not know or gave unclassifiable responses. When these results are divided by grade, it was apparent that understanding the notion of an admission of wrongdoing increased substantially after Grade 5 (from 46% to 79%), and plateaued by Grade 7. Indeed, a log linear analysis (which contrasted Admit Guilt with all other definitions) revealed a significant effect of Grade (x^2 (3)=20.5, p<.001). A minority of subjects at all ages (10-17%) confused a plea of Guilty with actual guilt. In addition, the Grade 5 students were more likely than the older subjects to confuse pleading guilty with being proven guilty.

Table 2
Percentage of subjects who believe that confidentiality can be broken with parents, judge, and police

Person	Grade					
	5	7	9	Adult	Total	Chi Sq
Parent	90	71	56	46	66	26.8**
Judge	73	65	44	25	52	30.0**
Police	63	46	25	6	35	43.9

** $p < .01$

What does it mean to plead not guilty?

Only 2% of the subjects accurately defined a plea of Not Guilty. The majority of subjects (63%) viewed pleading Not Guilty as a denial of guilt or a claim of innocence (i.e., the logical obverse of what it means to plead Guilty); 6% of subjects stated that it meant being found innocent, or not guilty in court. The notion that pleading Not Guilty is a denial of guilt increased sharply, from 31% in Grade 5 to 73% in Grade 7, 69% in Grade 9, and 79% in the Young Adult group (x^2 (3) for Deny Guilt vs. all other definitions = 28.7, p< .001).

This finding represents another example of Saywitz' (1989) contention that misconceptions about the legal system may increase, rather than decrease, with age. Further, it suggests that lawyers need to ascertain their clients' understanding of plea, clearly inform them of the meaning of these acts, and actively probe clients for comprehension of these definitions.

Table 3
Percentage of subjects who mentioned actors
in their trial description

Actor	Grade					
	Grade 5	Grade 7	Grade 9	Adult	Total	Chi sq
Defense Attorney	10	29	44	60	36	30.8
Crown Attorney	2	21	31	50	26	35.5**
Unspec. Attorney	25	33	12	10	20	10.6**
Judge	71	85	77	90	81	6.7
Jury	10	31	40	60	35	29.7**
Defendant	8	15	21	42	21	17.4**
Witness	31	21	21	33	27	3.3
Plaintiff	10	10	10	15	11	0.6
Others	10	8	6	15	10	2.0

** $p < .01$

What happens during a trial?

Three different aspects of subjects' descriptions of a trial were analyzed: actors, events, and concepts or misconceptions. As Table 3 shows, subjects mentioned a variety of different actors in the course of their descriptions but the only actor mentioned by the majority of the sample was the judge (81%). Log linear analyses revealed that the defense lawyer, crown attorney/prosecutor, defendant, and jury were mentioned by significantly more subjects as grade increased, a finding consistent with Warren-Leubecker et al. (1989). The frequency with which the terms judge, lawyer, and jury were mentioned is also consistent with previous data, which suggests that "children develop the concept of Judge before that of Lawyer, which is in turn developed before that of Jury" (Warren-Leubecker *et al.* 1989). Finally, the number of subjects who mentioned a lawyer without specifying whether he or she was in a defending or prosecution role declined significantly with grade, suggesting that, with age, children develop a greater precision in their understanding of the various kinds of lawyers.

Table 4
Percentage of subjects who mentioned events
in their trial descriptions

Events	Grade					
	Grade 5	Grade 7	Grade 9	Adult	Total	Chi Sq
Trial Procedures	77	81	75	73	77	1.0
Judge's Role	21	0	8	25	20	6.4
General Decisions	12	10	4	6	8	2.8
Guilt Decisions	48	60	50	81	60	14.8**
Punishments Decisions	29	35	33	35	33	0.6
Describe Setting	31	29	25	6	23	12.7**

** $p<.01$

Subjects also mentioned a variety of events which occur during the course of a trial. As Table 4 shows, the most frequently mentioned events were court procedures (e.g., present evidence, call witnesses) and decisions regarding the defendant's guilt. Log linear analyses revealed that the latter was mentioned by significantly more subjects as grade increased. In contrast, the number of subjects who included a description of the physical setting of the trial decreased markedly after Grade 9.

Finally, Table 5 presents the percentage of subjects in each grade who mentioned the various classes of concepts and misconceptions. Slightly more than half of all the subjects mentioned at least one adversarial concept, and a third of the subjects mentioned at least one due process concept. Twenty percent of subjects held some due process misconception (the most frequent being that the job of a defense lawyer is to prove a client's innocence). Both concepts and misconceptions with respect to trial procedures were infrequently mentioned at all grade levels.

Table 5
Percentage of subjects who mentioned concepts and misconceptions in their trial descriptions

grade

	Grade 5	Grade 7	Grade 9	adult	Total	Chi Sq.
Concepts						
Adversarial	35	42	52	79	52	22.7
Due Process	10	19	31	64	31	38.1
Procedural	0	0	0	6	2	8.5
Misconceptions						
Due Process	10	17	23	29	20	6.1
Procedural	8	4	4	8	6	1.5

** *p<.01*

Log linear analyses revealed a significant increase with grade in the number of subjects who mentioned concepts relating to the adversarial nature of a trial and to due process elements within a trial. There was no grade trend with respect to procedural concepts. It should be noted that only in the Young Adult group were such concepts mentioned (by 6% of subjects). In addition, there were no significant differences with grade in the mention of misconceptions about what happens during a trial. It is interesting to note a trend (p = .10) for due process misconceptions to be mentioned more frequently with age.

Taken together, these results suggest that subjects' trial descriptions became less concrete and behavioural, and more abstract and conceptual with age. Whereas the youngest subjects often described the physical layout of the courtroom (e.g., "people sit around in the courtroom and the judge—they take somebody to stand and talk to him..."), the 14 year-old and young adult subjects focused their description on the conceptual bases of the criminal trial (e.g., "due process... you need it so they can't just say 'you're guilty' and throw away the key"). This trend is consistent with developmental changes in other domains of social and non-social cognition (Flavell 1985). The tendency for younger children to give concrete, perceptually-based descriptions was also reported by Saywitz (1989) in connection with children's understanding of the roles of legal personnel. She found that her youngest subjects (4-7 years of age) "described how legal personnel behaved in global terms, such as talking, sitting, and helping" (Saywitz 1989:149), whereas her 8-11 year-old subjects offered conceptually based descriptions of legal roles. Similarly, Cashmore and Bussey (1987) reported a decrease with age in the number of subjects who gave "descriptive responses" of the court. The older subjects in the present study were also more likely to state that court is a place where guilt is determined than were the younger subjects, a result which is consistent with Cashmore and Bussey's (1987) findings.

Verbal ability

In addition to the developmental trends discussed above, most of the dependent variables revealed significant effects of verbal ability. In most cases, the Grade 5, 7, and 9 subjects who fell into the High Verbal Ability group showed more accurate legal knowledge than those in the Low Verbal Ability group. For example, more High Verbal Ability subjects than Low Verbal Ability subjects accurately defined a Guilty plea ($x^2(1)=26.7$, p<.001). The number of subjects who mentioned the defense lawyer ($x^2(1)=14.4$, p<.001), crown attorney ($x^2(1)=22.8$, p<.001), and jury ($x^2(1)=7.6$, p<.01) was also significantly greater in the High Verbal Ability group than in the Low Verbal Ability group. Finally, a greater number of subjects in the High Verbal Ability group mentioned adversarial ($x^2(1)=23.8$, $p<.001$) and due process ($x^2(1)=9.2$, $p<.01$) concepts in their trial descriptions.

These findings are not surprising given the positive correlation between age, cognitive level, and verbal ability. It raises the possibility that the developmental trends reported above resulted, not from changes in knowledge structures, but from differences in expressive language skills; the younger subjects may have been prevented from expressing their knowledge by virtue of their less developed verbal skills. Several findings suggest that this is not entirely the case. First, although there were a number of significant effects of verbal ability on legal knowledge, grade emerged as a significant factor even more often; further, no effects of verbal ability emerged where grade effects were absent. Secondly, in some cases, the Low Verbal Ability group was not simply less able to express knowledge, but actually retained less mature and accurate understanding of legal issues than peers in the High Verbal Ability group. For example, when subjects were asked why they would want to "tell the whole story" to their lawyer, a significantly greater number of subjects in the High Verbal Ability group than in the Low Verbal Ability group suggested that doing so would help their lawyer to prepare a better defense ($x^2(1)=8.5$, $p<.01$). Conversely, more Low Verbal Ability subjects than High Verbal Ability subjects expressed fear of punishment for not revealing all as their rationale ($x^2(1)=9.4$, $p<.01$). Similarly, a greater number of subjects in the High Verbal Ability group than in the Low Verbal Ability group upheld the concept of lawyer-client confidentiality when probed about disclosure to the police ($x^2(1)=17.3$, $p<.001$), the judge ($x^2(1)=6.5$, $p=.01$), and parents ($x^2(1)=13.8$, $p<.001$), despite the fact that only yes/no responses were required to demonstrate their knowledge. Finally, in some cases the High Verbal Ability group actually demonstrated a greater adherence to misconceptions than the Low Verbal Ability group, a finding which is difficult to explain in terms of their increased expressive language ability. For example, when asked to define a plea of Not Guilty, significantly more High Verbal Ability subjects gave responses falling into the Deny Guilt category than did Low Verbal Ability students ($x^2(1)=19.7$, $p<.001$).

GENERAL DISCUSSION

The results of the present study replicated findings reported elsewhere in the literature which have indicated that, as age increases, there is a general trend towards greater legal sophistication. However, the knowledge demonstrated by subjects was quite variable across the various legal concepts addressed. For example, with respect to the lawyer-client relationship, a majority of even the youngest subjects demonstrated an adequate understanding of the concept of defense counsel as an advocate in the criminal process. In contrast, youths showed substantial ignorance of the principle of lawyer-client confidentiality when probed regarding the lawyer's ability to reveal information to specific parties, although it should be noted that many of the young adults also erred in their judgements regarding privilege. Similarly, with respect to their knowledge of plea, while 80% of subjects 12 years of age and over correctly defined a plea of Guilty, virtually no subjects at any age demonstrated accurate understanding of the Not Guilty plea. Thus, the extent of young people's competence appears to vary depending on the particular legal concept or principle under question.

The foregoing discussion considered competence in absolute terms, referring to the percentage of subjects who demonstrated adequate knowledge of several important legal concepts. The appropriate standard for comparison of young people's knowledge is not some ideal level of knowledge, but the capacity demonstrated by adults, who are presumed by law to be competent to give legal instruction. When one judges the competence of young people in relation to that of adults, their are few areas in which marked differences between the two groups emerged. As the above discussion illustrates, the areas of legal knowledge which were most problematic for young people also posed considerable difficulty for the young adults. Furthermore, there were some areas in which legal misconceptions were actually more prevalent among older subjects than among the younger students.

Virtually all of the misconceptions expressed by subjects throughout the interview related to the concept of presumption of innocence; many of the students had difficulty understanding and recalling that an accused is presumed innocent unless the prosecution can prove otherwise, expressing instead the notion that once charged, a defendant must prove his or her innocence of a crime. In some cases, this misconception was actually more prevalent in the older subjects than in the younger children. Some writers (e.g., Saywitz 1989) have suggested that inaccurate television portrayals of the legal process may be responsible for this phenomenon. However this misconception is acquired, the present finding suggests that lawyers need to explain the principle of presumption of innocence to their young clients in a concrete manner, making clear its implications for the conduct of their defense. The fact that young people hold specific misconceptions regarding the legal system also suggests that, in general, lawyers need to ascertain their clients' knowledge state early in the lawyer-client relationship, in order to identify knowledge gaps and specific mis-conceptions. Further, lawyers will need to differentiate their information-giving to clients; a different kind of response may be necessary to provide young clients with information where it is absent, as opposed to repairing specific misunderstandings regarding the trial process or legal concepts. Whether and at what age lawyers can hope to gain their clients' understanding or the pre-sumption of innocence principle and other important legal concepts is a topic for further study.

In contrast to the numerous effects of grade and verbal ability which emerged in the present study, with one exception, there were no effects of either gender or socioeconomic status on subjects' legal knowledge. These results are consistent with existing literature, which has generally failed to find such effects. The one well-known exception with respect to socioeconomic status is Melton's (1983) finding that low SES 8-year-old children showed a less mature understanding of what a right is than their high SES peers. Melton interpreted this finding in terms of differential access to opportunities on the part of these two groups to experience and exercise their rights. In this vein, a more homogeneous access to legal information could account for the lack of SES differences in legal knowledge reported in this and other studies.

The present study, in addition to the bulk of existing research, focused on the legal knowledge of a cross-section of students; virtually none of the stu-dents in this study reported having had direct involvement with the juvenile legal system. Given the dearth of empirical data regarding young people's legal knowledge, researchers have focused on the easily-accessible population of "regular" school children in order to ascertain legal knowledge and under-standing under "ideal" conditions. The rationale expressed is that if students demonstrate ignorance, poor understanding, and misconceptions under the relatively stress-free conditions of the school research interview, then youths detained on criminal charges may fare even more poorly, as a result of both intrinsic and state-related factors. For example, youths detained on criminal charges are subject to a highly stressful experience, which may interfere with their ability to process information. Thus, it is argued that the results of the present study may represent the optimal level of knowledge expressed by sub-jects of different ages, and that, if anything, young offenders may show poorer legal knowledge and understanding than was apparent here. Some support for this argument is available from previous studies (Saywitz and Jaenicke 1987; Grisso 1981) which found that youths with experience in the legal system actually demonstrated poorer understanding of legal concepts than those who have never participated in the system. Despite this evidence, a common notion expressed by the public and popular press is one of the street-wise youth who manipulates the juvenile legal system with an experienced canniness in order to protect his or her interests. Thus, in contrast to the argument expressed above, it seems possible that young people who have been involved in the legal system will actually demonstrate superior knowledge and understanding in relation to those who have never had involvement with the criminal system, by virtue of their direct experience with the concepts, principles, and actors in that system. In order to directly examine these opposing positions, a young offender group is clearly the relevant population for study. Whether young offenders, as a group, are legally advantaged or disadvantaged relative to the general population remains to be seen.

ENDNOTES

1. The present study was conduced by the first author in partial fulfillment of the requirements of the Ph.D. program in the Department of Education (Ontario Institute for Studies in Education) at the University of Toronto.

2. Data regarding subjects' ultimate plea choices in each of the four scenarios, as well as the reasoning behind their decisions, is presented elsewhere (Peterson-Badali and Abramovitch, submitted for publication).

3. The WISC-R is normed for children up to 17 years of age. Therefore, the test was not administered to young adult subjects.

REFERENCES

Cashmore, J. and K. Bussey. 1987. Children's conception of the witness role. Paper presented at the International Conference on Children's Evidence, Cambridge University Faculty of Law.

Forthcoming a. Children's perceptions of the outcome and decision-making process in Children's Court criminal cases.

Forthcoming b. The perceptions of children and duty solicitors in children's criminal cases.

Catton, K. 1978. Children in the courts: A selected empirical review. *Canadian Journal of Family Law* 1: 329-362.

Flavell, J. 1985. Cognitive Development (Second Edition). Englewood Cliffs, NJ.: Prentice Hall.

Gold, L., J. Darley, J. Hilton, and M. Zanna. 1984. Children's perceptions of procedural justice. *Child Development* 55: 1752-1759.

Grisso, T. 1981. Juveniles' Waiver of Rights: Legal and Psychological Competence. New York: Plenum Press.

Irving, K. and M. Siegal. 1983. Mitigating circumstances in children's perceptions of criminal justice: The case of an inability to control events. British Journal of *Developmental Psychology* 1: 179-188.

Lawrence, R. A. 1983. The role of legal counsel in juveniles' understanding of their rights. *Juvenile and Family Court Journal* 34: 49-58.

Leon, J. S. 1978. Recent developments in legal representation of children: A growing concern with the concept of capacity. *Canadian Journal of Family Law* 1: 375-432.

Melton, G. 1983. *Child Advocacy: Psychological Issues and Interventions* (Chapter 2). New York: Plenum Press.

Mitchell, L. 1984. The clinical/judicial interface in legal representation for children. *Canadian Community Law Journal* 7: 75-108.

Read, A. F. 1987. Minors' ability to participate in the adjudication process: A look at their understanding of court proceedings and legal rights. Unpublished Master's Thesis. University of Toronto.

Roesch R., C. D. Webster, and D. Eaves. 1984. *The Fitness Interview Test: A Method for Examining Fitness to Stand Trial.* Centre of Criminology, University of Toronto and Criminology Research Centre, Simon Fraser University.

Saywitz, K. 1989. Children's conceptions of the legal system: "Court is a place to play basketball". In S. J. Ceci, D. F. Ross, and M. P. Toglia (eds.), *Perspectives on Children's Testimony.* New York: Springer Verlag.

Saywitz, K. and C. Jaenicke. 1987. Children's understanding of legal terminology: Preliminary finding. Presented at the annual meeting of the Society for Research on Child Development, Baltimore, MD.

Warren-Leubecker A., C. Tate, I. Hinton, and N. Ozbek. 1989. What do children know about the legal system and when do they know it? In S. J. Ceci, D. F. Ross, and M. P. Toglia (eds.), *Perspectives on Children's Testimony.* New York: Springer Verlag.

Wilson, J., and M. Tomlinson. 1986. *Children and the Law.* Toronto: Butterworths.

CHAPTER 7
Perspective: Section 22(1), Consent to Treatment Order Under the Young Offenders Act[1]

ALAN W. LESCHIED
CHRISTOPHER W. HYATT

The *Young Offenders Act* (YOA)[32] provides for two new dispositions: open custody and order for treatment in addition to re-naming the *Juvenile Delinquents Act* (JDA) training school committal an "order for secure custody". All three dispositions are served for a pre-determined length of time by the youth. The open and secure custody disposition orders are made by the Court irrespective of the child's wishes. The order for treatment disposition, however, requires the consent of, among other persons, the youth, prior to committal by the court.

Section 22 (1) of the YOA states that:

> "No order may be made under paragraph 20 (1) (i)[2] *unless the youth court has secured the consent of the young person*, the parents of the young person and the hospital or other place where the young person is *to be detained for treatment*."

The implications of this section are far-reaching. In effect, the YOA establishes that the treating hospital, the parents of the young person and the young person, the offender, may refuse an order for treatment even when such an order might be the most desirable intervention for the young person and for the safety of the community.

During the first year of implementation of the YOA, few treatment orders were made by the youth courts in Ontario.[17] Similar results have been noted nationally in the move to a more "correctional" versus rehabilitation model.[13] In the majority of cases, this appears to be caused by the child not consenting to the order. The alternatives which seem to be taking the place of rehabilitative intervention are the use of open and secure custody.

The inclusion of section 22(1) in the YOA appears to be in response to two principles: (1) the emphasis on the individual right of children to protect themselves from what has been seen in the past as "involuntary" intervention, and, (2) the declining confidence in the benefits of rehabilitation as a goal of criminal justice. This latter direction has received considerable impetus from several sources.[20,22,27,5] The dilemma outlined in this article is whether a child, as defined under the YOA, is capable of giving the type of consideration regarding the decision for or against treatment intended by the Act. This article also sets out inconsistencies within the law which indicate how a young person's testimony and/or opinions are to be regarded by the court; and reviews whether the literature in criminology indeed supports rehabilitation as a viable option for a judge determining the most effective intervention for the young person.

CAPICITY TO PROVIDE CONSENT: DEVELOPMENTAL AND THERAPEUTIC CONSIDERATIONS

The fact that the federal government has mandated separate legislation for young persons twelve to seventeen years old for the purposes of the *Criminal Code* reflects the view that adolescents should be considered a special group under the law. In support of this mandate, the declaration of principle in the YOA outlines the need for special accountability and responsibility of young persons. Section 3 (1) (a) states that young persons are to be held accountable and responsible though "not in all instances be held accountable in the same manner or suffer the same consequences for their behaviour as adults", and "young persons who commit offences require supervision, discipline and control, but because of their state of dependency and level of development and maturity, they also have special needs and require guidance and assistance" (section 3 (1) (c)).

These two aspects of the *Declaration of Principle* appear inconsistent with the right instituted under section 22(1), that young persons may refuse orders for treatment. Such refusal assumes that young persons are in a position to understand fully the nature and implications of treatment and to make a decision on the appropriateness of that treatment in their own best interest.

Black's Law Dictionary defines informed consent as "a person's agreement to allow something to happen that is based upon free disclosure of facts needed to make a decision intelligently". It is an act of will. The courts assume the decision is made intelligently, voluntarily and knowingly.

Grisso and Vierling[14] have summarized the empirical evidence regarding the ability of 12 to 17 year old young offenders to provide consent. These authors indicated that young persons of 14 years of age and under were not at a cognitive-development stage (according to Piagetian theory) in their lives to understand in a knowing, intelligent and voluntary manner the meaning behind the issue of consent to treatment. These authors suggested that, though we must be mindful of the potential harm of "coercive treatment", "it is just as important that we not burden them [children] with decisions that may have far-reaching implications for their lives in those cases in which they appear to lack the capacity to address the decisions meaningfully". Given that Grisso and Vierling's conclusions are based on "normal" development in childhood, we can assume that the developmental difficulties which many young offenders incur[15,26] would make the meaningful comprehension of the consent issue extremely onerous, if not impossible, for the majority of young offenders before the court.

The second important issue to consider in regard to consent is the nature of the emotional disorder of the young person who is being recommended for treatment. Recent evidence has indicated that the factors in a young person's adjustment, which pose the greatest concern for a judge, relate to general coping difficulties (i.e. school behaviour, relationship with peers) rather than to the more traditional forensic issues such as insanity and fitness to stand trial.[16] Therefore, in the vast majority of cases, provincial legislation such as Ontario's *Mental Health Act* does not pertain to the issues of treatment for young offenders before the court. Presenting problems of young offenders recommended for treatment tend to be characterized be depressive disorders and social alienation.[7]

A recent study has indicated that, in assessing a younger person's attitude to consent to treatment, juveniles, who were more disturbed as indicated by their responses on a personality inventory, were less likely to consent to treatment than those who were considered "normal" on personality assessment.[28]

THE LAW AS IT RELATES TO A YOUNG PERSON'S OPPORTUNITY TO CONSENT

The YOA provides no opportunity for the court to inquire or comment upon the ability of a young offender to make a reasoned decision about treatment. Concerns regarding the credibility of a young witness have long been recognized by legal writers such as Wigmore.[31] The supreme court of Canada, in *Kendal v. R.* (1962) SCR 49, CCC 216, has ruled on the requirements to be met by young persons before weight can be given to their testimony.[29] Canadian rules of practice require a judge to be given their testimony.[29] Canadian rules of practice require a judge to warn the jury of the danger of convicting on the evidence of a child, even when sworn as a witness. The basis for the rule is the mental immaturity of the child. According to Wigmore, and relied upon by Mr. Justice Judson, four factors are to be considered in a judge's acceptance of a young person's testimony. These are based on a child's: (a) observation (b) recollection; (c) capacity to understand questions and form intelligent answers, and (d) capacity to show "moral responsibility".

The court has recognized in other matters the difficulties regarding acceptance of testimony by a young person. These situations include eye-witness testimony and capacity to be sworn, choice of parental custody, and consent to medical treatment.

The management of the consent issue, under YOA, appears to be inconsistent with the recognized principles of other legislation related to a young person's testimony in court. In criminal and civil matters, a youth can and frequently appear as a witness. Section 19 of the *Ontario Evidence Act*[24] and section 16 of the *Canada Evidence Act* 10 outline specific factors to be used by the court in weighing a young person's evidence. Under both Acts, "a child of tender years" may give evidence under oath only if he in fact understands the nature of the oath. If the youth does not understand the oath, unsworn evidence may still be taken if it can be demonstrated: (1) that the youth is possessed of sufficient intelligence to justify the reception of the evidence; and (2) that the youth understands the duty of speaking the truth.

It is the combination of the long-standing *Bannerman*[30] case and federal and provincial Evidence Acts that creates the incongruity with the YOA. The Acts do not define the phrase "a child of tender years". In common law, a child over the age of 14 years is not considered a witness of tender years and is presumed to be competent to give sworn testimony. A youth under 14 years must, therefore, be questioned by the court as to the child's understanding of the nature of the oath before being sworn. The YOA operates between the ages of 12 and 18 years. A young witness under 14, in any legal proceeding other than youth court, must be scrutinized by the court first before he can be heard. The scrutiny takes place in open court and on the record. A young person in youth court of any age can refuse consent giving reasons; judicial scrutiny is entirely absent.

Examination of a youth for the protection of the litigants is mandated in the proceeding in which the youth is asked to testify. Justice and fairness are clearly seen to be done. In youth court, however, refusal of consent to treatment serves only the interests of the young person and potentially those of his counsel whose fortunes ride on the number of young persons "gotten off".[3] If the stated philosophy of the YOA is to place responsibility for actions of youths in their own hands, section 21 (1) is a way to avoid that burden. Justice is not fairly administered. Neither the youth in need of the treatment, which has been carefully and not arbitrarily designed to fit the young person's needs (as required under a Section 13),[4] nor the community at large can benefit. The authority to administer justice is taken from the control of the presiding judge and given to the young offender.

A youth of 17, who is convicted of an offence but refuses treatment, can then complete whatever other terms of disposition which have been imposed and then be "free" to act out again with behaviour unaltered. Ironically, however, the moment the same youth of 17 turns 18 and finds his way to adult criminal court, no similar choice exists. A term of probation can be made for an adult which requires the probationer to seek counseling or obtain psychiatric or other medical treatment. Failure to comply with this term of probation results in a new offence under section 663(2)(h) of the *Criminal Code* and the adult probationer is returned to court. A young person is given "adult" freedom and choices; but once 18 and truly an adult there is no such freedom. In fact, the judicial system is permitted to take the adult offender by the hand and compel him to treatment.

Capacity to consent under the YOA reflects inconsistency with other legislation. A youth of 12 years is accused of break and enter. The Crown produces a witness to the crime. The witness is 13 years old. Before the Crown witness can be heard, the trial judge must first be satisfied of the child's intelligence and understanding of the duty to speak the truth. No similar right and protection is afforded the court when it asks the accused, after conviction, to consent to treatment, if such recommendation exists. No examination of the intelligence or the capacity or the competence of the convicted youth is possible. A witness in the same case must pass a two pronged test before being heard; the young offender does not.

Unsworn evidence of a young person must be corroborated. Two other checks and balances exist when receiving unsworn evidence of a youth. First, the witness is liable to be prosecuted for willfully giving false testimony and, secondly, the witness is liable to be cross-examined. The YOA provides no mechanism for anyone, even the judge, to cross-examine the youth or even inquire as to how the youth arrived at the decision to refuse treatment. Such inquiry, if made, could be said to be an infringement of the right to freedom of choice under the *Charter of Rights*.

With respect to medical treatment, the Ontario *Public Hospitals Act Regulations*[25] provides that young persons under the age of 16 do not have the right to refuse surgical procedures, that the burden of consent rests solely on parents for this age group.

EFFECTIVENESS OF REHABILITATION

An additional reason for including the consent provision in the YOA is the lack of confidence in treatment efficacy. The popular opinion of criminal justice regarding rehabilitation is, simply put, that it does not work. This perception is based on Martinson's "nothing works" dictum made over a decade ago and, periodically, has been supported by additional reviews of the rehabilitation literature.[6,27] As Gendreau and Ross[12] have aptly observed, however, the "nothing works doctrine" encourages the correctional system to avoid responsibility. by labeling the offender as untreatable, it is apparent to one and all that the system cannot be held responsible for improvement or deterioration. Gendreau and Ross cited over one hundred "efficacy" studies which showed that, when specific conditions are met with respect to program evaluation, benefits from treatment for offenders do emerge. A recent study on young offenders, reported by Leschied and Thomas[18] indicated that, when individual differences among young offenders are accounted for and treatment programs meet these needs through differential programming, positive results can be observed. Over-simplifying the complex issues related to offender treatment has not only meant a disservice to the young person and to the judicial system, but has eroded the influence of rehabilitation in the larger context.

Custody disputes, as an alternative to treatment, with their determinate sentences, also appear to do a disservice to young people. Placing a 14-year-old in custody on a 3 month order maintains an external dependency within the young person and takes away the motivation to change behaviour. Custody orders may supplement a "doing one's time" mentality into the adolescent's psyche. "Doing time" is counter-productive to the need for the young offenders to develop greater independence and an internalized drive to change. Additionally, placing a seriously depressed young person in a custody placement does little to assist that young person in resolving the underlying disorder which may be a major contributor to acting out. In fact, a custody placement may worsen some symptoms of a depressive disorder such as pessimism, hopelessness, and the feeling of personal inadequacy.

The final question to be addressed regarding rehabilitation relates to the advisability of placing young persons in treatment against their will. The popular notion here is that a young persons' resistance to treatment predicts failure and, arguably, is not in the person's interest. In this regard, we must again examine the conditions under which the young person is before the court. The young person has committed an anti-social act and has been found guilty by a judge. Research has indicated that delinquents who are recommended for treatment tend to be suffering from some form of depressive disorder.[11], [19],[21] Young persons may refuse treatment since it reflects a belief in the *hopelessness of change* and the absence of belief in one's own self-efficacy. Based on these two factors, the etiology of the young person's delinquency provides the basis for maintaining an anti-social response to authority (the court) and continuing a pattern of avoidance behaviour in the face of potential threat or conflict (the treatment)

SUMMARY

Under the YOA (s. 21), young persons must provide consent for the court to make a treatment disposition. It is argued, however, that this section is inappropriate within the YOA since: (1) it disregards the developmental issues which preclude a young person from responding meaningfully, (2) it does not take into account the psychopathology as a meditating factor in a young person's ability to consent to treatment, (3) it is inconsistent with precedent and other forms of legislation pertaining to a young person's participation in court process where a "test" of capacity is required, (4) it ignores the evidence of potential benefits from treatment which young offenders can receive.

The major recommendation which follows from these points is that there is need to re-examine the consent to treatment section of the YOA. If the Declaration of Principle in the YOA is to be taken seriously, young persons must be held accountable and responsible. Part of that responsibility must be to accept the direction of the court to deal with the factors which underly the person's delinquency. Section 13 (b) allows the court to request a medical/psychological assessment for the purpose of addressing underlying disorders of the young offender. It is suggested, therefore, that *the court not the young person* be allowed to use that information in acting in the best interests of both the young person and the community.

The authors of the YOA have no doubt included the consent section in an effort to protect the rights of young persons against coercive treatment. The points outlined in this article suggest that, rather than protecting a person's rights, the consent section may be overly exclusive in not providing the best intervention for young offenders.

ENDNOTES

1.   The authors are indebted to Mr. Wayne Willis for his comments on earlier drafts.

2.   Section 20 (I)(i) states that: "Subject to section 22, by order directs that the young person be detained for treatment, subject to such conditions as the court considers appropriate, in a hospital or other place where treatment is available, where a report has been made in respect of the young person pursuant to subsection 13(1) that recommends that the young person undergo treatment for a condition referred to in paragraph 13(1)(e)."

3.   His Honour Judge J. Bennett[8] of the youth court has indicated that the principles of the YOA are heavily dependent on the ability of counsel to show caring as well as to be able to represent the rights of the young person before the court. In this regard, it would appear that there is a need for counsel in YOA matters to act in a non-traditional manner in youth court that follows the requirements for "caring counsel" in the legal representation of young children,

4.   Section 13(c) of the YOA allows a judge to request a medical/psychological report where the court has reasonable grounds to believe that the young person may be suffering from a physical or mental illness or disorder, a psychological disorder, an emotional disturbance, a learning disability or mental retardation and where the court believes a medical, psychological or psychiatric report in respect of the young person might be helpful in making any decision pursuant to this Act.

5.   Allen, F.A. *The decline of the rehabilitative ideal: Penal policy and social purpose.* New Haven: Yale University Press, 1981.

6.   Annis, H.M. "Treatment in corrections: Martinson was right." *Canadian Psychology*, 22, 321-326. 1981.

7.   Austin, G.W., A.W. Leschied, P.G. Jaffe, and L. Sas. "Factor structure and construct validity of the Basix Personality Inventory with young offenders." Submitted for publication, 1985.

8.   Bennett, J. "Concerns about the Young Offenders Act." *Provincal Judges Journal*, 8. 4. 17-18. 1985.

9.   Black, H.C. *Black's law dictionary*, 4th ed., St. Paul: West Publishing Co. 1968.

10. *Canada Evidence Act* R.S.C. 1970, C.E.-10, s. 19.

11. Cole, E. "The CIP battery: Identification of depression in a juvenile delinquent population." *Journal of Clinical Psychology, 37*, 4, 880-884. 1981.

12. Gendreau, P. and R. Ross, "Effective correctional treatment: Bibliotheraphy for cynics." *Crime and Delinquency, 25*. 463-489, 1979.

13. *Globe and Mail*. "Trends in juvenile justice examined" August 6, 1985.

14. Grisso, T. and L. Vierling. "Minor's consent to treatment: A developmental perspective." *Professional Psychology, 9*. 412-427, 1978.

15. Hunt, DE. and R.H. Hardt. "Developmental stage, delinquency and differential treatment." *Journal of Research in Crime and Delinquency, 2*. 20-31, 1965.

16. Jaffe, P.G., A.W. Leschied, L. Sas and G.W. Austin. "A model for the provision of clinical assessments and service brokerage for young offenders: The London Family Court Clinic." *Canadian Psychology, 26*. 54-61, 1985.

17. Leschied, A.W. and P.G. Jaffe. "Implications of the Young Offenders Act in modifying the juvenile justice system." In N. Bala and H. Lilles (eds.) *The Young Offenders Act Update*. Toronto: Butterworths. 1985.

18. Leschied, A.W. and K.E. Thomas. "Effective residential programming for hard-to-serve young offenders." *Canadian Journal of Criminology, 27*. 161-177, 1985.

19. Lesses, S. "Behavioural problems masking depression: Cultural and clinical survey," *American Journal of Psychotherapy, 33*. 41-53. 1979.

20. Martinson, R. "What works? Questions and Answers about prison reform." *The Public Interest, 35*. 22-54, 1974.

21. McConville, B. "Depression and suicide in children and adolescents." In P.D. Steinhauer and Q. Rae-Grant (eds.) *Psychological problems of the child and the family*. New York: Basic Books, 1983.

22. Miller, K.S. *The criminal justice and mental health systems: Conflict and collusion*. Cambridge: Oelgeschlager, Gunn & Harris Publications, 1980.

Chapter 8
Impact of the Young Offenders Act on Court Dispositions: A Comparative Analysis[1]

Alan W. Leschied
Peter G. Jaffe

Proclamation of the *Young Offenders Act* in April, 1984 has meant a new system of justice for Canada's adolescents. No longer can Canada's juveniles expect to be dealt with as children in a state of need thereby requiring guidance and direction as outlined in the *Juvenile Delinquents Act*. Rather, the 'parens patriae' approach has given way to a system of justice that, while acknowledging the special needs of young offenders, emphasizes principles which differ considerably from previous juvenile justice legislation.

Reid and Reitsma-Street[18] have stated that the "Declaration of Principle" of the *Young Offenders Act* focuses on several aspects of the cause and amelioration of juvenile crime. These authors suggest that the Declaration outines four models of criminonlogy: the *justice model*, emphasizing the importance of due process; the *crime control model*, emphasizing accountability/responsibility; the *welfare model* which addresses the special needs of young persons and the best interests of their families; and the *community change model* which addresses the need of society to take reasonable measures to prevent young people's misconduct.

Despite the fact that the *Young Offenders Act* Declaration makes an attempt to be all things to all people, Leschied and Gendreau[14] have argued that an analysis of the *Young Offenders Act's Declaration* points to the fact that the overall theme of the legislation seeks to create an 'equitable' system of justice where dispositions are meant to 'fit the crime.' In this context, discretion is seen as undesirable, particularly as the courts attempt to address special needs within what is arguably meant to be a 'mini criminal code for children'.[4]

"Impact of the Young Offenders Act on Court Disposition: A Comparative Analysis" was reproduced by permission of the *Canadian Journal of Criminology*, Vol. 29 (4), pages 421-429. Copyright by the Canadian Criminal Justice Association.

Perhaps more to the point, Thomson[21] noted that the *Declaration of the Young Offenders Act* betrays, "if not consistency, then at least ambivalence about what approaches should be taken with young offenders."

In the midst of what one distinguished youth court judge noted was an approach to youth crime which was "confusing at best",[8] little data has been provided to disentangle the web of confusion. Data on dispositions which has been generated under the *Young Offenders Act* shows the increased use of custody in response to juvenile crime.[13,15] If this trend towards an increased use of custody were to be confirmed, then it would provide support for the belief that, despite the fact that there is a range of philosophies present within the *Young Offenders Act,* the deterrence 'through punishment' model of controlling juvenile crime may be reigning supreme.

In the present review, two studies examined court outcomes with respect to dispositions. The first study focused on court dispositions across an area of south west and central west Ontario which encompasses forty per cent of the province's juvenile population. Data was collected for a five-month period (April 1-November 30) during the first two years of implementation of the *Young Offenders Act* (1984; 1985). Similar data was collected for the same period for 1983 during which the Juvenile Delinquents Act was in operation.

The second study examined dispositions of young persons who were referred to the London Family Court Clinic during 1983—*Juvenile Delinquents Act* period—and 1984 and 1985—*Young Offenders Act* period. The Clinic sample comprises a select group of young offenders who have been considered by a youth court judge as possessing some special need due to presenting circumstances or offence history. If the hypothesis is correct, i.e. that deterrence through punishment is the model of choice under the *Young Offenders Act,* then even young offenders with special needs will be given dispositions related to crime control (i.e. custody) rather than dispositions related to their special needs.

STUDY 1

Leschied and Jaffe[14] previously investigated dispositions made under the *Juvenile Delinquents Act* and *Young Offenders Act* on a group of young offenders, under 16 years of age, in south west and central west Ontario. This geographical area encompasses nine countries in a heavily urbanized part of the province. Forty per cent of the province's young persons inhabit this area. Primary results from this previous investigation indicated that twice as many custody committals were being made under the *Young Offenders Act* as compared to the *Juvenile Delinquents Act* and needs-based psychological assessments were being made at a considerably lower rate under new legislation. The authors concluded that the results should be seen as preliminary, and that it was difficult to note whether the data reported were signs of a trend or merely reflecting *Young Offenders Act* "growing pains."

The present study examined the same-aged population as noted for the same calender period during 1985—the second year of the *Young Offenders Act*. Data was not included on 16 and 17-year-olds since comparable data for this age group pre *Young Offenders Act* was not available. Results are reported in Table 1 for dispositions across two *Young Offenders Act* time periods and one Juvenile Delinquents Act time period. These results indicate that the preliminary results reported by Leschied and Jaffe seem to be signs of a consistent trend. Committals to custody (open or secure) continue to be high in comparison to committals to training school under the *Juvenile Delinquents Act* though there is a slight decrease when compared to committals to custody during 1984. Requests for needs-based psychological assessment under Section 13 remain low. Noteworthy, orders for victim reconciliation or community service orders became a popular disposition in 1985 comprising almost 20% of dispositions compared to less than 3% under the Juvenile Delinquents Act in 1983.

Table 1
Court Dispositions made under
the *Juvenile Delinquents Act* (1983)
and *Young Offenders Act* (1984/1985)

	JDA (April 1/83- Nov. 30/83)		YOA (April 1/84- Nov. 30/84)		(April 1/85- Nov. 30/85)	
Charges	3,944		3,989		3,404	
Dispositions	2,750		2,585		3,178	
Probation	1,178	(42.8%)	1,203	(46.5%)	1,196	(37.6%)
C.A.S.	121	(4.4%)	-		-	
Open Custody	-		149	(5.8%)	159	(5.0%)
Training School/ Secure Custody	138	(5.0%)	134	(5.2%)	106	(3.3%)
Psychological/ Psychiatric Reports (S.13)	325	(11.8%)	143	(5.5%)	146	(4.6%)

STUDY 2

The second examination of data focused on dispositions made on young offenders referred for assessment to the London Family Court Clinic. Young offenders are referred for assessment when a youth court judge feels the young person has some form of special need. Section 13 of the *Young Offenders Act* outlines, in some specificity, the criterion a judge may use to refer a young offender for assessment. These reasons may include consideration of an emotional or psychological disorder, learning disability, mental retardation or other factors which a judge may consider as important in understanding the needs of a young offender. In general, judges request an assessment of a young offender arising from concerns regarding the length or nature of their court involvement, or as a result of behaviour stemming from an emotional disorder.

Comparative data with Clinic clients examined dispositions regarding custody orders (training school under the *Juvenile Delinquents Act*) and placement on probation. The total sample was comprised of 284 young offenders with 137 (48.2%) youths under the *Juvenile Delinquents Act* from April 1982 to March 1984 and 147 (51.8%) youths under the *Young Offenders Act* from April 1984 to March 1986.[11] No selection criterion was used for inclusion in the study other than the availability of court outcome data on the juveniles. To assess potential between-group differences, two court-related social history variables were examined; previously adjudicated delinquency and type of charge (person or property). In both cases, using chi square analysis, no between-group differences were noted for either previously adjudicated delinquency (X^2 (1) = .00, p.n.s.) or charge type (X^2(1) = 42, p.n.s.) for young persons referred under the *Juvenile Delinquents Act* or *Young Offenders Act*. The one area where there was a difference on presentation between *Juvenile Delinquents Act* and *Young Offenders Act* clinic referrals was in the area of judges' reasons for referral. Chi square analysis on judges' referral concern yielded a significant result (X^2(5) = 69.12, p<.001). Judges are required, upon making a referral for assessment, to indicate which of five specific areas are of major concern to the court. Although there is some interdependency within the categories, judges' concerns are an indication of areas for focus for clinical investigation. Table 2 outlines the different areas of concern judges considered in making a referral. These results indicate that, under the *Juvenile Delinquents Act,* judges expressed greater concern for family problems whereas, under the *Young Offenders Act,* judges expressed more concern for possible emotional disorders with the young offender.

Court outcome data indicate that orders for custody differed under legislation. Whereas 4.2% of Clinic clients were committed to a custodial centre under the *Juvenile Delinquents Act,* this number more than tripled (14.3%) under the *Young Offenders Act* yielding a significant chi square ($X^2(1)$ = 6.72, p<.01).

DISCUSSION

The present findings reinforce earlier data pertaining to the increased use of custody as a disposition under the *Young Offenders Act.* These findings would seem to give added credence to previous reports that, in the midst of competing philosophies in the *Young Offenders Act,* deterrence through punishment as a means of crime control for young offenders has now become a popular concept. This trend holds not only for a broad group of young offenders, but also for special needs young offenders as well. These findings have several implications.

The first implication is that punishment as deterrence has emerged as a major response to youth crime. Though this is understandable given society's frustration with the criminal activity of our youth, empirically its application is without support in reducing criminal activity in the long term. Cullen and Gilbert,[7] in a review of American states using a punishment as deterrence model of crime control, have concluded that "there are no discernable changes in crime rates in those states where the justice/crime control model has become popularized." In other words, though the use of custody may hold appeal to those whose enthusiasm had wanted for the Juvenile Delinquents Act's child welfare model, the ultimate impact of custody in controlling youth crime is still an outstanding question.

Table 2
Judge's Reasons for Referral Under
the *Juvenile Delinquent's Act* and the *Young*
Offenders Act to the Family Court Clinic[1]

	JDA (N=232)		YOA (N=247)	
Placement	24	(45.5)	30	(54.5)
Violence	41	(58.6)	29	(41.4)
Education	29	(51.8)	27	(48.2)
Family Concerns*	85	(74.6)	29	(25.4)
Emotional Disorder*	45	(26.2)	127	(73.8)
Other	7	(58.3)	5	(41.7)

*p<.001
(1) *Percentages exceed 100% since judges may endorse more than one reason for referrals.*

The second implication is that judges seem to be embracing the accountability provisions of the *Young Offenders Act*. This trend is most clearly demonstrated in the seven-fold increase in the use of victim reconciliation orders and community service orders under the *Young Offenders Act* during 1985 as compared to the number of orders made under the *Juvenile Delinquents Act*. This attempt to draw clearer connections for youths between their offending behaviour and their responsibility to the community has been embraced throughout North America.[20] Bartollas[5] has suggested that the broad use of such orders is popular since community service/restitution satisfies both the 'hard-liners' who want a tougher stance taken toward juvenile crime and officials in the juvenile justice system who acknowledge the lack of punishment meted out to juveniles who seem to commit multiple property crimes.

The third implication of these findings is that requests for psychiatric/psychological reports have decreased by half and the trend through the second year of the *Young Offenders Act* 1985 seems to be towards fewer assess-

Young Offenders Act implementation, but other changes in juvenile justice practice have emerged as well. Most notable is the impact from due process under the Act. Felstiner [8] has reported data indicating that judicial process has become more time-consuming with youths. Numerous delays through adjournment in one jurisdiction are increasing the median number of days for completion of a youth's case from 18 to 76 days with a fourfold increase in the number of trials set. Felstiner's conclusion is that, "compared to time spent on legal procedures, proportionally less money, expertise, and concern are spent on the child's needs, whether for help, correction or punishment". Somewhat ironically, Hackler[10] has pointed out that many of the procedural "weaknesses" of due process provisions for Canada's juveniles may have already been rectified through training of defense counsels and prosecutors during the decade leading up to the *Young Offenders Act* proclamation. The ultimate impact on youths of this increased use of custody and proceduralism, both through evaluation of recidivism and youth's perception of the justice system, awaits comprehensive analysis.

Finally, it is difficult to consider the degree of generalizability of the present findings since many factors enter into the court process related to dispositions. Indeed, since it is up to each province to implement the Young Offenders Act, it is likely that there would be many inter-provincial differences in the pattern of dispositions being made under the *Young Offenders Act.* The present findings suggest that there is an emerging trend of *Young Offenders Act* dispositions affecting almost half of the youths in Canada's largest province. It would be important to discover whether the broad philosophical intent of the *Young Offenders Act,* with its emphasis on deterrence, encouraging personal responsibility and application of due process, is more potent than whatever provincial idiosyncracies may be extant in implementation. For the young offenders in the geographical area under study, it is apparent that the youth court has become more formal and restrictive with a greater orientation towards punishment. It may be that, with replication of these findings, a more general statement can be made regarding the impact of the *Young Offenders Act*. Ultimately, the overall effectiveness of the measures contained in the Young Offenders Act will only be justified through data-based findings that examine delinquency rates following the proclamation of the *Young Offenders Act.*

ENDNOTES

1.   Reprint requests should be addressed to Alan Leschied, London Family Court Clinic, Box 5600, Court House, Station 'A', London, Ontario, N6A 2P3. The second author is seconded to the Department of Justice, Wellington, New Zealand. Portions of this paper have been presented by one or both authors at Toronto, and Chaffey's Locks in Ontario. Halifax, Nova Scotia, Cincinnati, Ohio, and Wellington. New Zealand.

2.   Allen, F.A. 1981. *The decline of the rehabilitative ideal: Penal policy and social purpose.* New Haven: Yale University Press.

3.   Bala, N. 1985. "The young offender's act: Why a new era in juvenile justice?" Presented at the Canadian Psychological Association annual meeting. Halifax. Nova Scotia.

4.   Carney, L.P. 1980. *Corrections: Treatment and philosophy.* Englewood Cliffs, N.J.: Prentice-Hall.

5.   Conrad, J.P. 1981. "Can juvenile justice survive?" *Crime and Delinquency.* 544-554.

6.   Cullen, F.T. 1985. "Does rehabilitation work? The origins and meaning of a troublesome question." Reprinted at the University of Ottawa, Department of Psychology, Ottawa, Ontario.

7.   Cullen, F.T. and K.E. Gilbert. 1982. *Reaffirming Rehabilitation.* Cincinnati: Anderson Publishing.

8.   Empey, L.T. 1982. *American delinquency: Its meaning and construction.* Homewood, IL: Dorsey.

9.   Garber, L. 1985. "Panel discussion of the effects of the Y.O.A. on the Nova Scotia juvenile justice system." Presented to Canadian Court Administrators Conference, Halifax, Nova Scotia.

10. Goodstein, L., and J. Hudack. "Importance to prisoners of predictability of release: A test of a presumed benefit of the determinate sentence." *Criminal Justice and Behaviour 9.* 217-228. 1982.

11. Goodstein, L., J.H. Kramer and L. Nuss. 1984. "Defining determinacy:

Components of the sentencing process ensuring equity and release certainty." *Justice Quarterly. 1.* 47-73.

12. Grisso, T. and L. Vierling. 1978. "Minor's Consent to treatment: A developmental perspective." *Professional Psychology. 9.* 412-427.

13. Leschied, A.W. and C. Hyatt. 1985. "Perspective: Section 21(1) of the Young Offender's Act and the consent to treatment." *Canadian Journal of Criminology. 28.* 69-78.

14. Leschied, A.W. and P.G. Jaffe. 1985. "Implications of the Young Offender's Act in Modifying the juvenile justice system." In N. Bala and H. Lilles(eds.) *The young offender's act update.* Toronto: Butterworths.

15. Leschied, A.W. and P.G. Jaffe. "Consent to treatment under the young offender's act: a case study." *Canadian Psychology.* In Press.

16. *London Free Press.* 1985. "Mom failed to read son his rights: Charges dumped because she became 'authority'." August 7, 1985.

17. Martinson, R. "California research at the crossrads". *Crime and Delinquency. 22.* 180-191. 1976.

18. McNally, R.B. 1984. "The juvenile justice system: A legacy of failure." *Federal Probation. 48.* 29-33.

19. Sane-Dubow. S. 1984. "Sentencing reform in the United States: history, content, and effect." Presented at the National Conference on Sentencing. Baltimore, MD.

20. *Toronto Star.* 1985. "Young Offenders jailed longer under new law, Ontario official says." August 6, 1985.

21. Travis, L.F. and F.T. Cullen. 1984. "Radical non-intervention: The myth of doing no harm." *Federal Probation. 48.* 29-32.

CHAPTER 9
Trends in the Use of Custodial Dispositions for Young Offenders[1]

ANTHONY N. DOOB

The *Young Offenders Act* (YOA), which came into effect in 1984, received all party support when it was finally voted on by Parliament. However, a number of criminal justice professionals were critical of the bill. Some of their concern was focussed on the disposition section of the Act in that they saw it as being punitive rather than treatment oriented.

Recently, this concern has focused on the use of custody under the *Young Offenders Act*. For example, Markwart and Corrado (1989) have presented compelling evidence of increased use of custody under the YOA. In British Columbia, for example, there was a 73% increase in admissions of youths under 17 years of age to secure and open custody between fiscal year 1984/5 and 1987/8. For Ontario, the data are equally startling. Between 1984/5 (the first year of the YOA) and 1987/8, the number of offenders sentenced to custody went from 1476 to 2644, an increase of 79%.

When they looked province-by-province at the proportion of cases committed under the YOA to custody for those ages previously governed by the JDA, they found changes during the first three years that varied from a small decrease in the proportion of cases committed to custody of 9% (Saskatchewan) to a dramatic increase of 88% (Alberta). There was little doubt that there was an overall increase in the proportion of cases committed to custody in Canada. It is important to emphasize that these changes relate to *sentencing* data, and do not necessarily relate to "counts" of the number of young persons in custody at any given point.

It would be nice if comparisons could be made (across time and across province) on the use of the different levels of custody (open vs. secure). However, as Markwart and Corrado (1989: 22-25) point out, there are important variations within and across provinces that make such comparisons problematic at best and deceptive at worst. Although a detailed analysis of this variation would, itself, be interesting, it is beyond the scope of this brief note.

Markwart and Corrado (1989; Corrado and Markwart 1988) are not the only observers of the YOA to express concern about the apparent increase in the use of custody. Concern has been expressed that the *Young Offenders Act* is generally more punitive than its predecessor, the *Juvenile Delinquents Act* (JDA). Leschied and Jaffe (1988) present data which, they suggest, support the view that young people are treated more harshly now than they were under the JDA (and, by implication, more harshly than they would have been if we were still operating under the JDA).

As has been pointed out by numerous commentators (Trépanier 1989; Brodeur 1989; Doob 1989), the YOA does not have clear principles for determining dispositions. Thus trends in dispositions across time and across provinces reported by Markwart and Corrado may reflect variation in interpretations of the Act by youth court judges. Data presented by Doob and Beaulieu (1990) suggest that different judges emphasize different principles when faced with similar cases and hand down different dispositions as well. In that study, 43 youth court judges were given identical written descriptions of young offenders cases and were asked to indicate the disposition they would impose and the principles that would guide their decision. In the case of one particular offender, for example, the recommended disposition ranged from a period of secure custody to various forms of non-custodial dispositions (community service order, fine, or simple probation). In this same case, at least one judge indicated that each of the traditional purposes of sentencing (punishment, individual or general deterrence, rehabilitation, or incapacitation) was the most important purpose guiding the choice of disposition.

Different views of the principles that should guide dispositions are but one reason for variation in treatment under the YOA. We know that there are other differences in the manner in which young people are dealt with by the juvenile justice system. In trying to understand "dispositions" under S.20(1) of the YOA, this other variation cannot be ignored.

First, there may be variation in the behaviour of youth from community to community and province to province. Second, there may be differences across communities and provinces in the availability of less formal ways of handling troublesome youth. For example, the Quebec youth protection legislation involves an alternative method of handling troublesome youth outside of the YOA. As Trépanier (1983) has noted, the Quebec *Youth Protection Act* creates a form of institutionalized diversion of troublesome youth from the court system. Ontario's decision to fight, legally and administratively, the spirit and letter of the YOA's goal of using "alternative measures" for some offenders is another example. It is known from other research (Doob and Chan 1982; Hackler 1981) that pre-court discretion in the handling of young offenders can be an important determinant of the mix of young people who end up in court.

Many years ago, data were published on police discretion in the decision to charge young persons under the JDA. Conly (1978) studied 12 metropolitan areas across Canada and found that the percent of apprehended juveniles actually charged ranged from a high of 96% (Calgary) to a low of 17% (Hamilton) in the month that was sampled (December, 1976). Although there is no necessary reason to believe that the same pattern of screening of juveniles exists now, there is every reason to believe that there is still enormous variation in the proportion of apprehended juveniles who are taken to youth court.

The effect of different rates of charging or apprehended youth has important implications for understanding variation in dispositions. If only the most serious cases are taken to court in one location, one might expect that the proportion of severe dispositions would be larger than in a location where many minor cases are also taken to court. Similarly, if the proportion of cases (or the type of cases) going to court changes within one location over time, variation in dispositions may reflect no more than variation in the type of cases going to court.

Most of the analyses of the use of custodial dispositions for young offenders have focused simply on the "rate" of the use of custody—the proportion of cases receiving some form of disposition that receive a custodial disposition. Almost completely ignored is any serious analysis or the length of such a disposition. This is not surprising for one simple—and very important—reason. It is only since the implementation of the YOA that judges have been able to put limits on the length of all custodial dispositions. Under the JDA, the timing of the release of a youth sent to training school was outside of the control of the judge. Indeed, under the JDA there was no easy way that a judge could hand down a short custodial sentence. Even under the YOA, a definite sentence may not be as definite as it might first appear. The review provisions of the YOA allow custodial dispositions to be modified if it is deemed appropriate to do so.

In an attempt to understand what appears to have happened with custodial dispositions, this paper examines the use of custodial dispositions in six provinces. (Ontario, a distinct society in terms of its cooperation with the rest of Canada on youth court statistics, is not included in this analysis since, thus far, it has been unwilling to provide—or it is incapable of providing—information in a form found to be useful in all of the other nine provinces and two territories.) Only one Atlantic province, Newfoundland, is included. My purpose is not to try to describe the pattern of custodial sentences in each province and territory. Instead, it is to suggest that the variation that exists cannot be ignored when trying to assess the impact of the YOA. For this purpose, six provinces' data were sufficient. Because the focus here is largely on those previously under the jurisdiction of the juvenile delinquency legislation in place prior to the YOA, I have limited the analysis to those under the maximum age in place in each province prior to the implementation of the YOA.

Presenting data on young offenders in a manner that is both clear and informative is not easy. Some of the relatively recent issues of *Juristat* have done an admirable job of summarizing some data on young offenders. The problem, however, is that these data are typically pooled across provinces for ease of presentation. Unfortunately, pooling across provinces makes it impossible to examine some of the issues related to dispositions. In addition, in terms of the apparent dispute about whether dispositions under the YOA are more harsh than they would have been had we continued sentencing young people under the JDA, such data, though very useful for other purposes, include dispositions for some ages that were not captured by the JDA.

There were suggestions, in the published data, of some increases in the use of custody immediately before the advent of the YOA (Canadian Centre for Justice Statistics 1984). But more importantly, that same paper presented data showing considerable province to province variation in the use of institutional dispositions under the JDA, ranging from 9.5% of charges resulting in a disposition involving institutional care in British Columbia, to a high of 30.3% institutional dispositions being used in Prince Edward Island and Quebec (Table 2). These comparisons, of course, are difficult to interpret because of the varying maximum ages.

This paper focuses on data from an arbitrary subset of provinces and focuses on those ages that were within the jurisdiction of the JDA for each province. The proportion of cases which included a custodial disposition (of those receiving any disposition) are shown in Table 1. I have attempted to present data from only the ages covered by the JDA in each province. I use the word "attempted" because this is not completely possible to do. For example, some of those who appear to be outside of the age of jurisdiction are there because of such offences as failure to comply with a disposition handed down under the YOA.

Table 1
Proportion of cases receiving custodial sentences

	Nfld.	Que.	Man.	Sask.	Alta.	B.C.
1984/5 YOA (cases)	14.3%	29.5%	14.0%	25.2%	10.4%	11.4%
1985/6 YOA (cases)	19.0%	27.7%	20.5%	26.3%	13.9%	16.1%
1986/7 YOA (cases)	24.2%	29.8%	25.2%	22.8%	19.5%	20.5%
1987/8 YOA (cases)	20.7%	31.3%	22.7%	26.4%	18.5%	22.2%
1988/9 YOA (cases)	21.3%	31.0%	27.9%	24.8%	18.1%	21.6%

Note: Data include only those ages that were under the jurisdiction of the JDA in each province. Secure and open custody as well as detention for treatment are considered custodial dispositions. The number of cases receiving custodial sentences are shown in the last column of Table 2. Data for this table and for Table 2 derive from Canadian Centre for Justice Statistics, Youth Court Statistics, 1984-85 through 1988-89.

These data are presented in detail to illustrate a number of points. First of all, the general trends showing an increased use of custodial sanctions that various people, including Corrado and Markwart. have reported are replicated in these data—a fact which is hardly surprising since we used the same data source. Very sight differences between these numbers and those of Markwart and Corrado reflect largely our decision to include "detention for treatment" in our custody group.

Second, it is clear that in the first five years of experience with the YOA, there are dramatic differences across provinces in the proportion of cases where the offender is put in custody and in the trends across the five years. In 1988/9, for example, 18% of the cases in Alberta involved a custodial disposition as compared to 31% of the cases in Quebec. In some provinces, there is a dramatic increase in the proportion of cases involving a custodial sanction since the implementation of the YOA (e.g., B.C. or Manitoba), whereas in others (e.g., Quebec or Saskatchewan) there is, essentially, no real increase.

Simply on the basis of these data, then, it is clear that no simple "effects" can be attributed to the YOA. To blame the increasing use of custody during the early YOA years in B.C. or Manitoba on the YOA is to ignore the fact that Saskatchewan and Quebec did not show such increases. Nevertheless, there are certainly large increases in the numbers of young persons receiving custodial sentences in some provinces and these increases deserve more study.

At the risk of making a complicated story even more complicated, it should be pointed out that there is also enormous variation from province to province on the proportion of its youth who are in custody on a given day. Kenewell, Bala, and Colfer (1991) present data suggesting that overall, in Canada, we have between 18 per ten thousand youths aged 12-17 (in 1986-7) and 19 per ten thousand youths aged 12-17 (in 1989-90) in custody and detention on an average day. Once again, however, this national figure obscures the provincial variation that they also report. Looking only at the 1989-90 data, the average number of youths in custody and detention (per ten thousand youths 12-17 years old) varies from a low of 10.3 for Quebec and 12.7 for British Columbia, to a high of 27.8 for New Brunswick and 26.7 for Manitoba (Kenewell, Bala, and Colfer 1991, Table 8.5).

It is hard to argue from this array of data that the YOA systematically induces judges to act in a more punitive fashion than they would have done under the previous legislation. There have been changes, but the same Act seems to be creating different effects in various parts of the country. On the other hand, the Act certainly appeared to have done little to limit effectively the number of custodial sentences being handed down.

Markwart and Corrado (1989) entitle their paper "Is the Young Offenders Act more punitive?" and, given the data that they present in the paper, one can assume that the reader is expected to answer the question in the affirmative. The problem is that the data they largely rely on (and those in Table 1 of this paper) demonstrate only an increase in the number of young people going into custody; they tell us nothing about the length of time people are spending in custody. The data on the length of the custodial sentence are shown in Table 2.

Table 2
Length of custodial dispositions

	≤ 3 months		4-12 months		≥ 13 months		Total	
Newfoundland								
1984/5	103	(58%)	61	(34%)	15	(8%)	179	(100%)
1985/6	144	(56%)	82	(32%)	33	(13%)	259	(100%)
1986/7	259	(63%)	139	(34%)	14	(3%)	412	(100%)
1987/8	218	(71%)	71	(23%)	16	(5%)	305	(100%)
1988/9	202	(71%)	81	(28%)	3	(1%)	286	(100%)
Quebec								
1984/5	491	(29%)	919	(54%)	290	(17%)	1700	(100%)
1985/6	692	(36%)	1032	(54%)	172	(9%)	1896	(100%)
1986/7	902	(44%)	1032	(50%)	110	(5%)	2044	(100%)
1987/8	916	(45%)	986	(49%)	114	(6%)	2016	(100%)
1988/9	985	(51%)	861	(45%)	74	(4%)	1920	(100%)
Manitoba								
1984/5	82	(16%)	311	(62%)	110	(22%)	503	(100%)
1985/6	233	(34%)	400	(58%)	59	(9%)	692	(100%)
1986/7	396	(44%)	463	(51%)	50	(6%)	909	(100%)
1987/8	406	(44%)	480	(52%)	34	(4%)	920	(100%)
1988/9	418	(42%)	523	(53%)	45	(5%)	986	(100%)
Saskatchewan								
1984/5	97	(45%)	107	(50%)	10	(5%)	214	(100%)
1985/6	182	(51%)	156	(43%)	21	(6%)	359	(100%)
1986/7	210	(55%)	164	(43%)	6	(2%)	380	(100%)
1987/8	315	(64%)	169	(34%)	6	(1%)	490	(100%)
1988/9	332	(68%)	144	(29%)	14	(3%)	490	(100%)
Alberta								
1984/5	130	(25%)	355	(68%)	40	(8%)	525	(100%)
1985/6	363	(52%)	315	(45%)	15	(2%)	693	(100%)
1986/7	621	(65%)	319	(34%)	10	(1%)	950	(100%)
1987/8	549	(63%)	311	(36%)	7	(1%)	867	(100%)
1988/9	620	(66%)	302	(32%)	13	(1%)	935	(100%)
British Columbia								
1984/5	237	(44%)	249	(46%)	50	(9%)	536	(100%)
1985/6	468	(58%)	313	(39%)	31	(4%)	812	(100%)
1986/7	722	(61%)	425	(36%)	35	(3%)	1182	(100%)
1987/8	870	(68%)	353	(28%)	48	(4%)	1271	(100%)
1988/9	821	(71%)	306	(26%)	29	(3%)	1156	(100%)

Note: Data include only those years under the jurisdiction of the JDA in each province. Secure and open custody as well as detention for treatment are considered custodial dispositions.

Unlike the data in Table 1, these data are very consistent. In each of the six provinces, the proportion of custodial sentences of three months or less has increased dramatically during the first five years of the YOA. The complementary effect—the decrease in the proportion of very long sentence (those of more than a year)—is equally dramatic and consistent. Indeed, this last effect is so dramatic there is a decrease in the number of young offenders receiving long sentences even though the overall number of young offenders receiving some kind of custodial sentence has increased. For these six provinces, 443 more young persons received long sentences (over a year) in the first two years of the YOA than in the last two years for which data were available. Put differently, in these six provinces, fewer than half as many young persons received long sentences (over a year) in the most recent two years of available data as compared to the first two years of the YOA.

The data on the use of custody, then, are relatively easy to summarize. In many, but not all, provinces there has been an increase in the proportion of those cases going to court that are receiving custodial sentences. However, judges appear to be giving many more short sentences and many fewer very long sentences. These results are consistent with the suggestion made by Markwart and Corrado where they report, for Ontario, an increase in committals but note "that the average daily population in custody has not changed substantially since the first YOA year" (1989; footnote 2, page 12).

Does the increase in numbers and decrease in length add up to "increasing rates of use of custody" (Markwart and Corrado 1989:25) in at least some provinces? It clearly depends on one's perspective. What is clear, however, is that the overall pattern of dispositions varies across provinces and across time. By looking only at the type of dispositions, we cannot make any meaningful inferences about whether there would be variation across provinces in how a particular case was disposed of. Thus, although the proportion of young persons receiving a custodial sentence varies in these six provinces, this variation may well reflect only the variation in mix of cases going to the youth court. Across time (but within province) similar factors may account for apparent change in dispositions. For example, during the YOA years, for all ages, there are data that suggest an increase in the proportion of cases arriving at youth court which include a charge involving violence (Canadian Centre for Justice Statistics, January and April 1990).

It does seem that judges are making a large number of very short custodial dispositions. Although not presented in Table 2, many of these are for less than a month. Indeed, in B.C. for 1988/89, 33% of all custodial dispositions were for periods of time of less than a month. In 1984/5, only 14% of custodial dispositions were for this period of time. Clearly, it is these dispositions that are on the rise in at least these six provinces.

It is not the purpose or this paper to assess the appropriateness or the increased use of short sentences for young offenders. In order to do so, one would first need to know much more than is available from the Youth Court Statistics series. Critical issues, such as the primary purpose of dispositions, would have to be settled before dispositions could be evaluated against some abstract standard.

Judges appear, during the first few years of the YOA, to have changed their pattern of use of custodial sanctions. A more detailed analysis and a clearer statement of purpose of dispositions under the present legislation are necessary in order to evaluate these trends.

ENDNOTES

1.   The preparation of this paper was indirectly supported by contributions
      funds from the Solicitor General, Canada, to the Centre of Criminology,
      University of Toronto. I would like to thank Andrew Kohut, Dianne
      Hendrick, and Tracy Leesti of the Canadian Centre for Justice Statistics
      for the careful readings that they have of an earlier draft of the paper. In
      particular, I would like to thank them for the help that they gave me in
      ensuring that the data in Tables 1 and 2 are as accurate as they can be.

REFERENCES

Brodeur, Jean-Paul. 1989. "Some comments on sentencing guidelines." In Lucien A Beaulieu, (ed.), *Young Offender Dispositions Perspectives on Principles and Practice.* Toronto: Wall and Thompson.

Canadian Centre for Justice Statistics, Statistics Canada. 1984-89. "Youth Court Statistics. Preliminary Data. 1984-85 (December 1988.) 1985-86 (December 1988). 1986-87 (April 1989). 1987-88 (April 1989). 1988-89 (August 1989)."

Canadian Centre for Justice Statistics, Statistics Canada. 1984. "Data from Juvenile Courts -1983." *Juristat Service Bulletin* 4(7) November.

Canadian Centre for Justice Statistics, Statistics Canada. 1990. "Sentencing in Youth Courts, 1984-85 to 1988-89". *Juristat Service Bulletin* 10(1) January.

Canadian Centre for Justice Statistics, Statistics Canada. 1990. "Violent offences by young offenders, 1986-87 to 1988-89." *Juristat Service Bulletin* 10(5): April.

Conly, Dennis. 1978. "Patterns of Delinquency and Police Action in the Major Metropolitan Areas of Canada During the Month of December, 1976." Ottawa: Solicitor General, Canada.

Corrado, Raymond R. and Alan E. Markwart. 1988. "The prices of rights and responsibilities: An examination of the impact of the Young Offenders Act in British Columbia." *Canadian Journal of Family Law* 7:93-115.

Doob, Anthony N. 1989. "Dispositions under the Young Offenders Act: Issues without answers?" In Lucien A. Beaulieu (ed.), *Young Offender Dispositions: Perspectives on Principles and Practice.* Toronto: Wall and Thompson.

Doob, Anthony N. and Lucien A. Beaulieu. 1991. "Variation in the exercise of judicial discretion with young offenders." *Canadian Journal of Criminology* 34(1): 35-50.

Doob, Anthony N. and Janet B.L. Chan. 1982. "Factors affecting police decisions to take juveniles to court." *Canadian Journal of Criminology* 24: 25-37.

Hackler, Jim. 1981. "Comparing delinquency statistics in two cities: Indicators of agency involvement." *Canadian Police College Journal* 5: 117-128.

Kenewell, J. N. Bala, and P. Colfer. 1991. "Young offenders" In F. Richard Barnhost and Laura Johnson (eds.), *The State of the Child in Ontario.* Toronto: Oxford.

Leschied, Alan W. and Peter G. Jaffe. 1988. "Implementing the Young Offenders Act in Ontario." In Joe Hudson, Joseph P. Hornick, and Barbara A. Burrows, (eds.), *Justice and the Young Offender in Canada.* Toronto: Wall and Thompson.

Markwart, Alan E. and Raymond R. Corrado. 1989. "Is the Young Offenders Act more punitive?" In Lucien A Beaulieu (ed.), *Young Offender Dispositions: Perspectives on Principles and Practice.* Toronto: Wall and Thompson.

Trépanier, Jean. 1983. "The Quebec Youth Protection Act: Institutionalized diversion." In R Raymond Corrado, Marc LeBlanc, and Jean Trépanier (eds.), *Current Issues in Juvenile Justice.* Toronto: Butterworths.

_____. 1989. "Principles and goals guiding the choice of dispositions under the YOA." In Lucien A. Beaulieu (ed.), *Young Offender Dispositions: Perspectives on Principles and Practice.* Toronto: Wall and Thompson.

CHAPTER 10
Alternative Measures and Services for Young Offenders in Ontario

PREPARED BY THE SUB-COMMITTEE
ON YOUNG OFFENDERS OF THE
JUSTICE, REFORM, AND GOVERNMENT
AFFAIRS COMMITTEE
JOHN HOWARD SOCIETY OF TORONTO
CHAIRPERSON: MARGE REITSMA-STREET
STAFF: GRAHAM STEWART

Executive Summary

This discussion paper presents information and perspectives which are intended to assist the John Howard Society of Ontario to understand some of the social policy and practical problems associated with young offenders. The paper was prepared to encourage discussion within the Society as a basis for the development of John Howard Society policy positions and service strategies.

In the first part of the paper we outline the history of the interest of the John Howard Society in matters relating to youth. The paper also traces briefly the extensive development and breadth of service which we now provide. Clearly, our work with young people has become a major focus of activity for the Society generally in Ontario and in the case of a some of our branches it has become *the* major service component.

The major part of the paper examines the specific "Alternative Measures" as legislated in the 1984 *Young Offenders Act,* and alternatives defined more

"Alternative Measures and Services for Young Offenders in Ontario" was reproduced by permission of the John Howard Society, Toronto.

broadly.

"Alternative measures" is a term defined in the *Young Offenders Act* in the narrow sense of being alternatives to judicial proceedings. The paper describes the *YOA* Alternative Measures and looks at the way in which the Act has been implemented in Ontario and in other provinces. It appears that the implementation of Alternative Measures deserves careful scrutiny because of the implication for youth of a badly planned or implemented concept.

The Alternative Measures program in Ontario begun in April 1988 is different from programs in other provinces in that the young person must appear in court before being considered for Alternative Measures. While the program appears to be intended to be used with restraint, which is good, it may well be targeted to the wrong group of offenders. The research suggests that focusing services on minor offenders may actually increase the rate of criminal activity while focusing intensive services on serious offenders reduces future criminal activity. The Alternative Measures program in Ontario, however, is restricted to minor offenders and appears to have few services available that would be necessary to make it effective even if more serious offenders were admitted to it.

There are a variety of services ranging from pure prevention programs, to diversion programs, and programs designed as alternatives to custody which are often referred to as "alternatives". Whereas all of the programs have positive objectives, research and experience points out that in practice many programs have unintended consequence which negate their value and might actually make things worse. This paper looks at various "alternatives" and analyses them on the basis of which programs hold greater promise of positive benefits and have the least potential for destructive unintended consequences. It appears that prevention programs meet these criteria best, but might be the most difficult to find funding for. Diversion and alternatives to custody programs have the greatest risk attached to them but, ironically, may be the easiest to find financial support for. This situation creates some difficult problems for the Society to address in planning its future service development.

There are, however, two tasks that the Society can undertake which meet our mission statement and definitely help young offenders. The first activity is to assist young offenders who are in detention or custody to secure early release, as well as to find community services. The second task is to advocate generally for youth throughout the juvenile justice system as well as youth in the community who have not been identified as offenders. The need for carefully considered social policy relating to youth and young offenders is necessary. Perhaps the Society at both the provincial and the branch level should engage in effective advocacy for controls and evaluations of initiatives for youth which ensures that the programs meet their objectives as planned.

INTRODUCTION

This paper is intended to help focus discussions within the John Howard Society of Ontario regarding:

1. the advantages and effectiveness of various forms of alternative measures;

2. the directions, if any, that the John Howard Society should take in the promotion and/or delivery of alternative measures services.

Coherent policies supported by complimentary service activities are necessary if the John Howard Society is to have a credible voice in influencing the direction of social policy relating to alternative measures for juveniles. It is hoped the discussion which evolves from this paper will become the basis on which the Society develops policy respecting alternative measures, and guidance for our work with young people in general.

This paper reviews:

a) the background of interest which the John Howard Society has had in young offenders;

b) the formal Alternative Measures programs specified in the *Young Offenders Act;*

c) the various types of services and programs which are often described as "alternative measures";

d) the rationale for priorities of the Society in its service to young offenders;

e) possible courses of action for the Society.

The sources for this discussion paper include:

1) responses of eight branches to "An Alternative Measures

Questionnaire" sent to all branches;

2) conversations with persons working in John Howard Society
    agencies, other agencies, and various government officials;[1]

3) published and unpublished manuscripts dealing with the *Young
    Offenders Act* generally and alternative measures in particular.

This discussion paper will be reviewed by four critics, selected for their variety
of opinion and expertise (Gordon West, John Gandy, Gordon Hay and Bernie
Kroeker) and will be discussed at the fall Couchiching Conference. After this
consultation process is complete, a position paper will be prepared which will
be sent to branches for further comment. Finally, the provincial board will
decide which positions to accept, revise, or reject.

John Howard Society and Young Offenders

The mission of the John Howard Society of Ontario is "the prevention of
crime through service, community education, advocacy and reform. " A theme
of our work is the development of alternatives to punitive, inhumane practices
towards those who commit crimes.[2]

Over the years the John Howard Society in Ontario has been expanding
its interest beyond the aftercare of adults leaving prisons, to the experience of
all offenders and their families within the criminal justice system as well as the
prevention of crime .

In 1908, the *Juvenile Delinquents Act* introduced the juvenile court as
an alternative to the adult court for youth, and probation as an alternative to
incarceration. Over the years, John Howard has acted on behalf of youth to
develop the spirit of alternatives sparked by the J.D.A. For instance, in 1974,
the Hamilton branch developed an attendance centre as an alternative for
those youth who otherwise would be sent to training schools. The Kitchener
branch also developed an attendance program for youth referred to it by the
police. Various community programs of the John Howard Society such as the
employment training programs in Kingston, or Durham and Kitchener's short
anti-shoplifting courses, attempt to divert young people from engaging in
criminal activity .

Among those branches which responded to our questionnaire, budgeted
amounts for youth services, including programs for those aged 16 to 24, varied between $75,000, and almost $500,000. The John Howard Society has
been concerned with youth, and has obtained substantial financial resources
for youth programs .

In 1984 the *Young Offenders Act* replaced the J.D.A. *This* new act was intended to reform perceived shortcomings of the J.D.A. The new justice system for young people was intended to increase opportunities for less coercive interventions for youth ages 12 to 18, while emphasising the responsibility of the young offender and the attention to due process by all participants.

Although the John Howard Society of Canada supported the introduction of the YOA, it wanted to: "help monitor the implementation of all the YOA principles and to increase the quality and quantity of community based services available to young people in conflict with the law."[3]

For instance, in 1986 with the help of funding from the Solicitor General, John Walker of the John Howard Society Canada prepared an inventory of program intiatives for young offenders across Canada. The John Howard Society of Alberta, in conjunction with the Canadian Mental Health Association, prepared an extensive report on the *YOA* implementation (1987). The John Howard Society of Alberta and various other John Howard Society branches across the country have become involved in "court watching" studies, using a format prepared in 1987 by the Church Council on Justice and Corrections. The John Howard Society of Canada also participates with other agencies on a National YOA Table, to monitor implementation of the YOA. Currently, a position paper on young offenders is being debated by the John Howard Society of Canada.

The John Howard Society and other agencies have been very concerned about the *YOA* implementation in Ontario. The provincial government has delayed planning, resisted raising the age level to 18, refused to implement alternative measures, and spit the jurisdiction for those under 16 from those over. The development of consistent policy objectives is hampered by the fact that those aged 12 to 15, those aged 15 and 16, and those aged 17 and 18, are subject to distinct police, court, agency, and correctional procedures. Those under age 12 are dealt with under child welfare legislation rather than the authority of the Young Offenders Act.

Various specific concerns have been addressed by the John Howard Society branches. For example, in Niagara the John Howard Society expressed concern that some open custody facilities were being run below a reasonable standard. Their concern, expressed in concert with those of a local politician, helped to close one open custody institution in Niagara in 1987.

As another example, in a study of local court dispositions in Hamilton, the John Howard Society found that youth in both the under 16 group and the over 16-year-old group received custody dispositions more often in 1986 than 1984 and 1985. The use of probation, community service orders, and discharge also appear to have *decreased* over time. For instance, in the 12 months prior to the implementation of the YOA 1,476 youth under age 16 were sent to open or secure custody, while over a period of only 8 months in 1986 1,915 youth were placed in custody. The use of open custody increased but the use of secure custody remained approximately the same.[4]

The findings of the John Howard Society branches echo the confusions and concerns in various conferences, the media, the research literature, and the various ministries in Ontario and elsewhere. The intent of the YOA, and its principles are being met only in part: the rights of the youth are better protected and participants are more accountable to each other, but the use of coercion is increasing while attention to youth needs is not.[5] Unfortunately no Ontario group has been able to co-ordinate efforts to implement the YOA principles or to monitor problems and effect change. Even basic data are often unavailable. For example, the Canadian Centre for Justice Statistics published its reports in 1986-1987 on youth crime and outcomes without data from Ontario being available to them.

Alternative Measures in the Young Offenders Act

Alternative Measures in Other Provinces

Increasingly, concerns about the Young Offenders Act have prompted the John Howard Society to review issues relating to the implementation of the Act in Ontario. There are many concerns, but we are currently facing pressure to respond to one: alternative measures.

According to the *Young Offenders Act;*

> "Alternative measures may be used to deal with a young person alleged to have committed an offence *instead of judicial proceedings.*"[6] (our emphasis)

Although the term "alternative measure" has been used to mean all forms of intervention and service for youth, the very specific meaning of the term in the YOA can lead to confusion during public discussion. For purposes of clarity we will first discuss the formal Alternative Measures (with capitals) program provisions of the YOA, and later in this discussion paper deal with other alternative services often referred to generically as alternative measures .

Alternative Measures, under the YOA is a post-offence, pre-trial level of diversion directed by a crown prosecutor or provincial director. Referral to an Alternative Measures program requires that the evidence must be sufficient for a possible conviction and the youth must have admitted responsibility and voluntarily consented to participate after explicit instruction on the meaning of Alternative Measures. The young people are referred to nonjudicial personnel, (either community volunteers or government employees) who try to work out what is considered a "creative disposition" with the young person. Dispositions typically agreed to include: reparation to the victim, an apology to the victim, the preparation of a particular assignment such as an essay, community service, attendance at a treatment or a social service program, or some combination of these. If the young person fails to abide by the agreed disposition, then he or she is brought back to court for trial and sentencing.

Quebec has the most extensive system of Alternative Measures since It introduced provincial legislation in 1979 formalizing its system. In Quebec police bring youth to the Director of Youth Protection who diverts almost half of the youth into voluntary programs while those remaining go to court.[7] Manitoba has revamped its older community non-judicial programs into Alternative Measures administered by 22 Community Justice Committees. In 1985, 2,489 youth were sent by Crown Prosecutors to one of these committees. During the same period 948 youths were placed on probation and 358 placed in open or secure custody.[8]

Alternative Measures in Ontario

All provinces except PEI and Ontario have implemented a version of this type of Alternative Measures. Before the YOA, four demonstration diversion programs of this type had been introduced in Ontario, including the experimentally researched Frontenac Diversion Committee.[9] No officially recognized programs exist now.

The Ontario government resisted pressure to introduce an Alternative Measures program until forced to do so by the courts in April 1988. As noted by Professor Bala of Queens University;

> "The failure of Ontario to implement s.4 of the YOA has been
> successfully challenged in an Ontario Youth Court as a violation
> of the Equality Rights guaranteed by s. 15 of the Canadian
> Charter of Rights. In R. v. Sheldon S. it was held that the
> absence of such programs in Ontario constituted a 'denial of
> equal benefit and protection of law' on the basis of residence,
> and hence was a violation of s. 15 of the Charter ".[10]

Pending the outcome of an appeal, the Attorney General for Ontario has announced the immediate introduction of an Alternative Measures program which minimally meets the requirements of the *Young Offenders Act*. The important distinction between the Alternative Measures program in Ontario and most other provinces is that *the young person must appear in court for a hearing*. If the young person has applied for Alternative Measures, and if the Crown considers that the young person is appropriate for referral to the Alternative Measures program, the crown will request a four month adjournment for the young person to complete the program. Cases eligible for Alternative Measures are those which involve minor, non-violent offences committed by youths who have a minimal or no criminal record. In brief, the Ontario Alternative Measures program pays attention to the rights of the young person, and aims to avoid widening the net and expanding services.

The advantages of Alternative Measures over a formal trial are described by Professor Bala as including:

a) an expidicious and informal process;

b) avoidance of a formal record of conviction;

c) avoidance of the potentially harmful impact of being "labelled" a "young offender";

d) consistency with the principle of "least possible interference" which is articulated in S.3(1)(f)C of the YOA;

e) the increased scope for the involvement of parents, victims and the community;

f) the reduction in expense compared to the formal court system.[11]

There are, however major problems with Alternative Measures. According to the research evidence, the minor, first offender is best left to police discretion.[12] The alternative measure might easily become an alternative to the police warning rather than an alternative to court proceedings. Also, there is evidence the net widens in the sense that youth, especially girls and first offenders previously left alone to family and school programs, are now subjected to some formal process.[13] Furthermore, there is definite concern that the due process protection for youth is short-changed and the "voluntary" nature of the informal proceedings is not perceived that way by the youth.

Furthermore, because very little money has been provided for Alternative

Measures related services in Ontario, It will be difficult to implement adequate services. Palmer & Lewis found that better performance was associated with high quality, intensive services. Less than three hours of service over six weeks did not help anyone.[14]

There is also the concern that a properly adjudicated hearing in court presided over by a properly trained judge ensures best that the young person is not punished for an act for which he or she is not responsible or an act which is not criminal. Young people may well accept responsibility for an act which causes harm but for which they are not legally guilty. A person may take something which he or she does not own without committing a theft. It is the proper judicial hearing with the presentation of fair evidence and the opportunity for rebuttal by the defence counsel during the trial that gives some protection to the young person. Some people fear that the opportunity to circumvent the trial might induce some innocent young people into "accepting responsibility" for acts which either they have not committed or for which there might be a reasonable legal defence. Other people fear that young people who do not complete their agreements will be sent to court subject to another sentence, or a double punishment that young people who go directly to court are not subject to.[15]

Other Alternative Services and Programs

In practice the term "alternative measures" has been used to describe a variety of programs and initiatives from education efforts oriented towards prevention to open custody prisons. The John Howard Society in Ontario is already heavily involved in programs which are often described as "alternatives".

Not every program that is referred to as an alternative is a program which we would endorse or be involved in. *It is very likely that the John Howard Society may be in favour of one type of alternative measure, but advocate against another type.* It is necessary, therefore, that discussion of alternatives be defined in more specific terms so that the relative strengths and weaknesses of various alternative programs can be considered. In this section of the discussion paper we will describe three broad groupings of services and programs and provide examples from our current branch activity where possible.

The path young people take who progress through community services to the criminal justice system and back to the community has many points where discretion can be used to stop or reduce the penetration of the young person into the system. The availability of services or programs for young people who have reached these various discretion points may make the difference as to whether or not the discretion is used. The information in *Figure 1* attempts to show the continuum of discretion available in the juvenile justice system and identify programs which are intended to be used as an alternative to further progression along the continuum.

Prevention
Primary Prevention

These are services and programs which are oriented towards eliminating a general problem within the community which is believed to contribute to juvenile delinquency and crime. These programs are directed at the community as a whole or at young people within the community rather than individuals who are "identified" as being delinquents. Frequently these programs are educational or recreational activities. Participation is voluntary. An example of a primary prevention service is The John Howard Society of Oshawa's extensive educational program in schools. Directed primarily at school children in grades 7 and 8 in their area, the program focuses on information relating to shoplifting, vandalism and substance abuse. In response to the questionnaire the Peterborough branch discussed an innovative prevention service: a one stop resource centre in a housing project providing a nursery school, youth recreation and counselling, adult coffee clutches, wellness counselling, parenting and employment programs.

Figure 1:
Points of Discretion and Alternative Programs

Discretion Point   **Program Example**

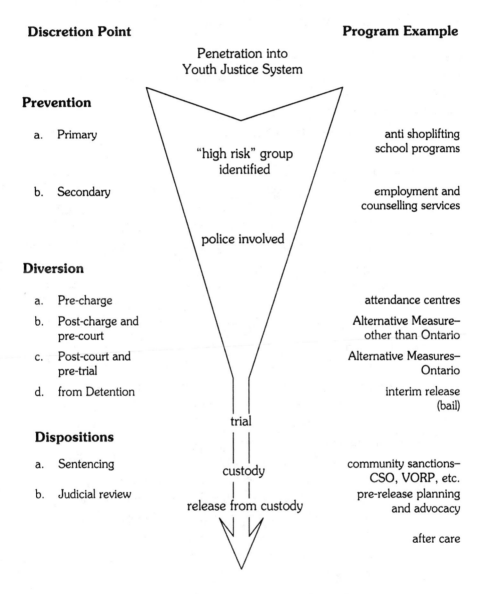

Penetration into
Youth Justice System

Prevention

a. Primary   anti shoplifting
                                                               school programs
           "high risk" group
           identified

b. Secondary   employment and
                                                               counselling services

           police involved

Diversion

a. Pre-charge   attendance centres

b. Post-charge and   Alternative Measure–
    pre-court   other than Ontario

c. Post-court and   Alternative Measures–
    pre-trial   Ontario

d. from Detention   interim release
                                                               (bail)

           trial

Dispositions

a. Sentencing   custody   community sanctions–
                                                               CSO, VORP, etc.

b. Judicial review   pre-release planning
           release from custody   and advocacy

                                                               after care

Discussion Paper – *Alternative Measures and Services for Young Offenders*
John Howard Society of Ontario   revised: October 17, 1988

Secondary Prevention

These services are directed at young people who have not been convicted of an offence but have been identified by police, schools or community groups as being "at risk". Several branches including Kingston, Windsor, and Kitchener provide employment services for young people who have left school and might be considered at risk if they are unable to become self-sufficient. Windsor and Peterborough provide special counselling and group services. Important characteristic of these programs are that they are voluntary but the resources are targeted to identified youth considered to be at risk. Many of the John Howard Society branches made suggestions to expand these services.

Discussion of Prevention

There are various good reasons for the Society to be active in prevention programs.

- The mandate of the John Howard Society is to prevent crime. Our boards, staff, and members are already committed to prevention. In responses to the questionnaires, *all* respondents indicated that they would like to increase prevention programs.

- They can reduce crime. There is some evidence that well-designed and adequately implemented programs focused on increasing the skills, hope, and resources of high-risk communities and groups of youth and also focused on reducing opportunities for committing crimes are most effective in reducing crime as well as the many attendant social and emotional problems of youth.[16] For example, a three year skills development project in one Ottawa public housing complex was shown to reduce vandalism, false fire alarms, calls to the police, and school drop-outs compared to another similar housing complex which did not have the program.[17]

- They may reduce the fear of crime. Education campaigns which reduce public fear also reduce the perceived need for more punitive sanctions such as longer custody sentences. Despite the intention of the *YOA* to restrict the use of custody, sentences to custody have increased in all provinces without corresponding increases in crime rates or the number of young people. There is concern that judges are responding to a *perceived* public wish for tougher sentencing for youth. When the John Howard Society of Hamilton completed its review of pre- and post-*YOA* statistics and held a public forum, several judges called with regrets, but wanted to go over the data since they were concerned with the trends.

The evidence is not conclusive regarding effectiveness of programs to reduce the fear of crime and the impact of this fear on attitudes towards sentencing. What has been well documented is that in those societies where criminal justice and public officials have a higher tolerance for rehabilitation and leniency, the rates of custody are definitely lower without any difference in crime rates than in places where the predisposition is towards severity.[18]

- Participation in prevention programs are largely voluntary. The services tend to be mutually contracted, with minimal infringement on the rights of the youth. *It is unlikely that these programs will harm the participants.*

- The funding sources for prevention services are usually separate from the criminal justice system. This means that the John Howard Society can remain more independent to advocate in relation to criminal justice issues.

- There may be funding available. For instance, given the September 1988 commitment in the Ontario Ministry of Education to drug education beginning in grade 4, there are opportunities and money for cooperative new programs. Housing, job-skill, and literacy projects are other areas to which our government and interested groups are currently committing money, and around which the John Howard Society could cooperate with other agencies to develop. For example, several of the John Howard Society respondents spoke of the need to build affordable housing for youth with multi-services incorporated into the building.

There are problems with prevention programs. Although there is money for preventing crime in high-risk groups, a lot of money is needed for good programs and it has to be shared with other groups. There is little money for public education campaigns. Another problem with prevention programs is that their impact in terms of reducing criminality or changing attitudes towards sentencing at a later date is difficult to establish on a continuing basis by those operating the service. Because the benefits are not clear, It is difficult to identify government structures or educational structures which will assume responsibility to support and fund prevention programs. Similarly, it is difficult for organizations which are carrying out prevention programs to justify funding on the basis of impact alone .

Diversion

These are programs and services which avoid entirely or reduce the degree to which youth are dealt with through judicial procedures. In *Figure 1,* three levels of diversion are described.

Pre-charge Diversion

In the case of pre-charge diversion the young person has been identified by the police as having committed an offence, but the police officer decides not to lay charges. The police may simply warn the young person or take the young person home to explain his or her activity to their parents. The police will sometimes refer the young person to community social programs, when available, rather than proceed immediately with formal charges in court. Kitchener's anti-shoplifting program or Hamilton's proposed "Community reconciliation program" are examples of programs offered by branches to young people at this level.

Generally speaking, if a young person accepts a referral to a community program, whether it be to an attendance centre, family counselling, or recreational program, his or her participation in that program is viewed as being entirely voluntary. If the young person fails to participate in the program there is no immediate action taken by criminal justice officials to bring the young person into court. One must consider, however, that there may be a specific or implied threat that failure to participate in the programs will lead to formal charges for any subsequent activity which would involves criminal activity.

Post-charge Diversion

As described earlier in this paper, Alternative Measures programs which operate under the YOA constitute post-charge diversion. Few post-charge programs divert young people out of the juvenile justice system entirely. Most programs divert the young person *conditionally*. If the conditions are not met the young person is returned to face charges in court.

Diversion from Detention

Release from detention while awaiting trial used to be called "bail" but under the YOA is called "interim release". The YOA provides particular instructions and opportunities for this tyre of diversion, including persons or agencies, such as John Howard, taking responsibility for supervising the terms of release and ensuring the youth gets to court. The degree of involvement of the John Howard Society branches in this type of diversion is not known since It was not on the questionnaire but we know that at least one branch, Hamilton, does run an interim release program.

Discussion of Diversion

Should the John Howard Society become more involved in the various types of diversion? Should the John Howard Society support, protest, or revise the new Ontario Alternative Measures? The pros and cons are diverse, and the research evidence problematic.[19] Even, the Ontario Supreme Court *Sheldon S.* decision was not based on the research evidence for or against diversion but on the basis of fairness across Canada and the intent of the YOA legislation.

Diversion from detention through bail and judicial interim release is an area about which the society should be concerned. There is evidence that we need to become more involved particularly as advocates. There is very little data to suggest stays in detention are good for anyone and custody is costly, although appearance at trial is assured. The evidence is strong, however, that the John Howard Society needs to press strongly for more diversion from detention. For instance, in following 1,568 youth court appearances in Edmonton, Caputo and the John Howard Society reported that 75% of those held in detention before trial did not receive custody sentences.[20] The Hamilton John Howard Society was very concerned that youth had to be double or triple bunked in detention due to lack of space and the increased use of detention. Whether or not we actually offer the programs to divert from custody must be discussed since sanctions and coercion are definitely involved.

We must also be cautious not to rush into programs such as bail supervision, which based on the experience of the adult system, often expands the controls over those who would have received bail anyway rather than serve to release those who would have otherwise stayed in custody. In a discussion paper prepared on young offenders for the John Howard Society of Canada, the authors strongly recommend that the Society look at diversion from detention.

As for the other types of diversion, Palmer & Lewis found that 51% of the 2,500 youth in 15 selected diversion projects in California were truly diverted, and would have been processed within the traditional justice system.[21] If programs are well-designed, professionally staffed, carefully implemented, and provide substantial service to moderate high-risk young offenders, the outcomes are positive.

On the negative side, most programs are not well-designed, adequately financed and staffed, and too often the focus is on minor offenders. For instance, research indicates that for minor first offenses, the simple warning is the best course of action. Too much programming for first-time minor offenders actually seems to *increase* recidivism. The complicated problem for us to consider is how programs of this type can be focused on serious offenders without also including minor offenders in them.

Research by Selke on Youth Service Bureaus in the United States found that the programs were unsuccessful in reducing crime. Noting that the programs set lofty goals in order to secure funding, Selke notes that "Over advocacy of a program necessarily results in failure."[22] Selke attributes the failure of the programs partly to the fact that;

> "...there was neither understanding nor consensus regarding system modification goals. individuals in the Youth Service Bureaus...were much more comfortable with the notion of counselling and individual treatment than they were with concepts like advocacy, coordination, resource development and service brokerage."[23]

Diversion provides opportunities for community participation and education, and the expansion of agencies such as the John Howard Society to obtain money, staff, and new programs. Services in this area are more easily funded than prevention services partly because success, as measured by the completion of the disposition, is high. Evaluations focus on completion rates rather than longer-term recidivism. Funding is often easier to obtain for diversion programs than prevention programs because It is clear which specific government ministries have responsibility for the development of alternative dispositions.

On the negative side, diversion has helped to insert another level of bureaucracy and a new arena for competition among agencies, to expand jobs for professionals and increase the supply of clients to fill up programs.[24] For example, Rappaport launched a successful diversion program which reduced recidivism for a two year period and did not widen the net. But five years later, the program had changed for organizational reasons—to keep the caseload up, to provide student placements, to allay probation officers' concerns that they would lose jobs—and now the program was widening the net to "divert" youth who previously would not have had any contact with the judicial system.[25]

Rojek and Erickson's research did not support the assumptions on which many diversion programs are founded—particularly the theory that left without intervention minor young offenders will become more serious offenders. They caution that "diversion is neither new nor inherently benign. Ill-founded innovations may well become sources of serious abuse."[26]

In sum, the evidence is contradictory over whether to support programs which claim to divert young people from the criminal justice system. Even if some programs *might* be effective in reducing recidivism without expanding the net or threatening rights, should we promote programs when there is no system in place which *ensures* that they will be effective and minimizes the risk that they will be detrimental?

In brief, It may be wisest for the John Howard Society Ontario and branches to encourage program development in prevention and after-care, but to participate minimally, if at all, in providing either pre- or post-charge diversion services and dispositions. A decision not to operate programs in these latter areas would leave us with the obligation to be critical of false diversion and to advocate for reduced use of custody through shorter and fewer sentences to custody. We might also be in a position to propose a system of controls and evaluation which ensures that alternative programs to custody are actually used for that purpose.

ALTERNATIVES SANCTIONS

This section will be brief since we have not yet fully explored the area. However, traditionally the John Howard Society is committed to developing less punitive and more humane sanctions, as well as has taken strong positions on reducing the use of, and length of custodial sanctions.

There are two variations of alternative sanctions. The first variation is where incarceration is *not* a likely disposition. The youth has been found guilty and faces sentencing in court. The offence is not particularly serious and/or the young offender has little if any criminal record. The various programs which might be available to this young person are intended to provide choices to the court so that the sentence can be "tailored" to the needs of the young person and the circumstances. Community Service Orders, orders to stay in school, victim offender reconciliation and many other programs fit into this category and are operated by several branches of the society.

The second variation is where the sanction is an alternative to a sentence of custody. In this situation a young person who has been convicted and would normally be sentenced to custody, is placed *instead* into a community program. Although these services are customarily thought of as having a different objective to those in the previous category, often the programs in these two categories are indistinguishable. Although programs such as the Community Service Order programs operated by the John Howard Society in Kingston, Kitchener and Hamilton were intended to be used as an alternative to custody, it is clear that many, if not most young offenders, would not likely have been sentenced to custody had the program not been available.

There is evidence, as mentioned previously, that the use of custody is increasing. Some of our efforts can be directed to monitoring and protesting the increased use of custody and thinking about how "true" alternatives to custody might be achieved. Several of the John Howard Society branches have recently started to visit institutions and to help reduce time in custody by helping young persons plan for early release. The YOA promotes reviews of time in custody *upon request* (or automatically for longer sentences), but unfortunately there is no mandated discharge planning or remission of time.

CONCLUSION AND POSSIBLE ACTIONS

Understanding and appraising the role of the John Howard Society in relation to various alternative services is not possible without a broader focus on the history, programs, experiences, and perceptions of the Society. Three broad categories of alternative services have been described and illustrated with reference to existing programs in branches. If we are to develop priorities and guidelines for the development of our services with youth we need to analyze the categories according to criteria that are meaningful to us.

The following section lists possible options for action which the John Howard Society of Ontario might consider:

1) At the provincial and branch level we could increase our advocacy for, and actually develop, prevention programs. The programs could focus on changing attitudes through reduced fear of crime, as well as programs geared to personal needs of youth such as work, social skill-building, housing etc., rather than system needs such as sanction administration.

2) At the provincial level we could research and advocate for effective methods to divert young people from detention and custody. We might propose the conditions under which consistently effective service programs could develop.

3) At the provincial and branch level, we could respond to the Attorney General's Alternative Measures program. We may applaud the intent of the Attorney General's Alternative Measures not to widen the net and attend to the youth rights but we could strongly protest the focus on minor, first offenders, the complicated process, and the minimal support for adequate funding and programming. The program is not substantial enough to meet its objective. We could advocate for a more courageous Alternative Measures program that truly diverts real offenders into substantial programs.

4) At the branch level we should encourage cautious and minimal development of alternatives as diversion, with very careful attention to the issues of rights, net widening, and adequate implementation.

5) At the provincial and branch level we could advocate and propose demonstration programs for alternatives to custody. To maximize our effectiveness as an advocacy agency, attention must be given at the branch level to the proportion of the budget going to sanctioned programs and the degree of voluntary participa-

tion by clients.

6)   At the branch level we should increase discharge planning and aftercare, on a voluntary level, for young people in custody.

ENDNOTES

1. See appendix A for list of persons consulted.

2. See Appendix B - John Howard Society of Ontario Mission Statement.

3. Walker (1986).

4. Gillespie & Franken, Table 2, (1987).

5. Leschied & Jaffe (1985); MacDonald (1985); Gabor et al. (1986); Trépanier (1986).

6. Canada. *Young Offenders Act 4(1)* It should be noted that the Alternative Measures in the YOA are not intended specifically to be alternatives to custody.

7. Trépanier (1983 :197); Trépanier (1986). The use of police discretion to not charge youth dropped dramatically with the introduction of Alternative Measures in Quebec. Many of the Children now being dealt with under Alternative Measures were previously dealt with by the police alone.

8. Under the J.D.A. Manitoba had in place a Judicial Measures programme which served a very similar function to the Alternative measures programme which replaced it after the introduction of the Y.O.A. The number of referrals to the Alternative Measures programme has remained the same as the referrals to the Judicial Measures programme. Manitoba Community Services, The Young Offenders Act—The First Year 1985, (unpublished).

9. Morton & West (1983).

10. Bala (1988:22).

11. (1988).

12. Palmer & Lewis (1980).

13. Chesney-Lind (1988).

14. Palmer & Lewis (1980:220).

15. O'Brlen (1984:221) Most youth complete their Alternative Measures agreements. Of 2,387 cases handled by four Atlantic Provinces Projects, only 26 were returned to court for non-completion of the agreement.

16. Weissman (1969); Schlossman & Sedlak (1983).

17. Offord & Jones (1983).

18. Krlsberg et al. (1984).

19. Wrlght & Dixon, (1977); Palmer & Lewis, (1980); Moyer (1980); Gendreau & Ross, (1987).

20 . Caputo et al. (1987:48).

21. Palmer & Lewis (1980:212).

22. Selke (1982: 404).

23. Selke (1982: 405).

24. Lemert (1981).

25. Rappaport (1983:185).

26. Rojek & Erickson (1981-82:2531).

REFERENCES

Attorney General of Ontario (1988) *Alternative Measures: Policy and Procedures,* April, 1988, (unpublished).

Bala, N. The Young Offenders Act: a legal framework. In *Justice and the Young Offender in Canada,* Hudson, J., Hirnick, J. and Burrows, B., (Eds.) Canadian Research Institute for Law and the Family, Calgary, 1988.

B.C. Corrections Branch, *Manual of Operations: Youth Programs,* December 6, 1985, (Unpublished).

Canadian Council on Children and Youth Young Offenders Act, *Third Annual Survey of Programs in the Voluntary Sector: 1987-88,* Submitted to: The YOA Directorate. Dept. of Justice, 1988, (unpublished).

Caputo, T., Sapers, H., and Boles, B., *Justice for Young Offenders,* Paper presented at the 39th Annual meeting of the American Society of Criminology, Montreal, November, 1987.

Chesney-Lind, M. Girls and status offenses: Is Juvenile Justice still sexist? *Criminal Justice Abstracts,* March 1988:144-165.

Gabor, T., Green, I., and McCormick, P., The Young Offenders Act: The Alberta youth court experience in the first year, *Canadian Journal of Family Law,* 5, 1986:301-319.

Gendreau, P. & Ross, R. Revivication of rehabilitation: Evidence from the 1980's, *Justice Quarterly* 4(3), 1987.

Gillespie, D. & Franken, A. *Preliminary trends in response to the YOA in Hamilton,* John Howard Society of Hamilton, June, 1987.

John Howard Society of Alberta, *1987 Edmonton Youth Court Study,* July, 1988, (Unpublished).

Krisberg, B., Litsky, P., & Schwartz, I. Youth in confinement: Justice by geography, *Journal of Research in Crime and Delinquency,* 21(2), 1984:153-181.

LeFebvre, John. *Alternative Dispositions Under the YOA: A Background Paper,* 12 November, 1985, Ontario Social Development Council, 1985 (unpublished).

Lemert, E. Diversion in Juvenile Justice: What hath been wrought? *Journal of Research in Crime and Delinquency,* 18(1), 1981:34-46.

Leschied, A. & Jaffe, P. Implications of the YOA in modifying the juvenile system, In Bala & Lillies (Eds.) *Young Offenders Update*, Butterworths, 1985.

Leschied, A. & Gendreau P.A declining role of rehabilitation in Canadian juvenile justice, *Canadian Journal of Criminology*, 28(3), 1986:303-314.

MacDonald, J. Justice for young persons and the Young Offenders Act, *Canadian Social Work Review*, 1985:64-82.

MacDonald, R. and Bala, N. *Watching Youth in Court: An Invitation to Community Involvement Under the Young Offenders Act*, Ottawa: Church Council on Justice and Corrections with the assistance of the Ministry of the Solicitor General of Canada, March, 1987, (unpublished).

Manitoba Community Services, *Young Offenders Act: The First Year 1985*, (unpublished).

Manitoba Community Services, *Young Offenders Act:The Second Year: April 1985 May 1986*, (unpublished).

Manitoba Community Services (1985 1986), *Working Together: A Manitoba Proposal for Province Wide Community Involvement in the Youth Justice System,* June 19, 1984, (unpublished).

Morton, M.E. & West, G. An experiment in diversion by a citizen committee, In Corrado et al (Eds), *Current Issues in Juvenile Justice*, Butterworths, 1983.

Moyer, S. *Diversion from the juvenile justice system and its impact on children: A review of the literature*, Solicitor General Of Canada, Research Division, Ottawa, 1980.

O'Brien, D. Juvenile diversion: An issues perspective from the Atlantic provinces, *Canadian Journal of Criminology*, 26(2), 1984:217-230.

Offord D. & Jones, M. Skill development: A community intervention program for the prevention of antisocial behaviour, In Guze et al. (Eds.) *Childhood Psychopathology and Development*, Raven Press, 1983.

Palmer, T. & Lewis, R. A differentiated approach to juvenile diversion, *Journal of Research in Crime and Delinquency*, July 1980:209-224.

Rappaport, J. Public policy and the dilemma of diversion, In R.R. Corroda et al. (Eds.) *Current Issues in Juvenile Justice*, Butterworths, 1983.

Rojek, D. & Erickson, M., Reforming the Juvenile justice system: The diversion of status offenders, *Law and Society Review*, 16(2), 1981-82:241-264.

Selke, W., Diversion and crime prevention: A time-series analysis, *Criminology*, 20(3), 1982:395-406.

Schlossman, S. & Sedlak, M., The Chicago Area project revisited, *Crime and Delinquency*, 29(3), 1983:398-462.

Trépanier, J., The Quebec Youth Protection Act: Institutionalized diversion, In Corrado et al. (Eds), *Current Issues in Juvenile Justice*, Butterworths, 1983.

_____, La justice des mineurs au Quebec: 25 ans de transformations (1969-1985), *Criminologie*, XIX(l), 1986:189-214.

Wright, W. & Dixon, M., Community prevention and treatment of juvenile delinquency, *Journal of Research in Crime and Delinquency*, 14, 1977:35-67.

Walker, J., (1986) *Report on YOA Development Activities*, John Howard Society of Canada 1985-1986 submitted: June 23, 1986 John Walker YOA Co-ordinator, (unpublished).

Weissman, H., *Justice and the Law in the Mobilization for Youth Experience*, New York, Association Press, 1969.

Young Offenders Act Implementation Study Group (1987), *Recommendations regarding young offenders: A joint report to the John Howard Society of Alberta and The Canadian Mental Health Association Alberta Division*, November, 1987 (unpublished).

APPENDIX A:
LIST OF PERSONS CONTACTED

1. John Howard Societies

   All Ontario branches
   Jim MacLatchie - Canada
   Howard Sapers - Alberta
   Len Sawatsky - Saskatchewan / Canada
   All provincial societies through JHS Canada
   Issues Committee

2. Department of Justice Canada - Young Offenders Directorate
   - Michel Vallee
   - Barbara Morrison
   - Bruno Marceau
   - Kathy Kulesek

3. Ministry of Community and Social Services Children's
   Services Division
   - Anne Sheffield
   - Pat Coffer
   - Jane Rogers
   - Carol Appathurai
   - Roma Scott

4. Statistics Canada
   - Holly Johnson
   - Tony Dillenhoffer

5. Heather Morrison, Assistant to Brian Ward, Director of Canadian
   Council of Children and Youth

6. Mr. Marie Irvine, Director and Lawyer, Justice for Children, Toronto

7. Dr. John Gandy, Prof. Emeritus, Faculty of Social Work,
   University of Toronto

8. Dr. Alan Leschied, Psychologist, London Family Court Clinic;
   Lecturer, Univ. of Western Ontario

9. Dr. Gordon West, Associate Professor, O.I.S.E.

10. Dr. Ian Greene, Assistant Professor of Political Science, York University

11. John Walker, Consultant, Ottawa

Appendix B:

MISSION STATEMENT

The John Howard Society of Ontario is an organization of citizens who accept responsibility for understanding and dealing with the problems of crime and the criminal justice system.

MANDATE

The mandate of the John Howard Society of Ontario is

1. to provide for the effective integration into the community of those in conflict with the law, and to provide, or encourage others to provide, services to those in contact with, or affected by, the Criminal Justice System;

2. to promote changes in the law and the administration of justice which will lead to the more human and effective treatment of individual;

3. to promote citizen awareness of and acceptance of responsibility for the problems of crime and the Criminal Justice System; and to ensure that citizens may become involved in the delivery and management of justice-related programmes.

The Society's mandate is the prevention of crime through service, community education, advocacy and reform.

CHAPTER 11
Self-Help Network and Community-Based Diversion[1]

DON FUCHS
DENIS C. BRACKEN

INTRODUCTION

The participation of an entity described simply as "the community" is frequently put forth as essential at various stages of the criminal justice process. In particular, intense involvement by "the community" in juvenile justice has become an accepted factor if anything is "to be done" about juvenile delinquency. Some criticism of both the assumptions underlying "community corrections"[5, 6] and the operations of community corrections programs[7, 8] have appeared, although they do not seem to have diminished the acceptance of the concept. However, such criticism have for the most part concentrated on what might be termed the "recipient" role of the community. In this sense, the community is seen as the receiver of persons potentially, officially, or unofficially-but-not-formally charged as delinquent. The recipient role is supported by the assumption that by and large anything "the community" does (assuming also that comunities do things for people) is better for the delinquent than anything the juvenile justice system could do. Organizations, programmes, agencies, etc. are fostered and established within the private sector as representative of "the community". Such organizations can become directly dependent on the formal system for referral and financial support. Juveniles (and sometimes adults) are then returned to, or to use the more common terminology, diverted back into the community. Much of the aforementioned criticism has suggested that such a process simply expands the arena of social control beyond the formal justice system into the community. Such expansion, it is argued, really is antithetical to the original ideas in favour of community

"Self-Help Network and Community-Based Diversion" was reproduced by permission of the *Canadian Journal of Criminology*, Vol. 26 (3), pages 343-355. Copyright by the Canadian Criminal Justice Association.

involvement.[8]

A different role for the community may, however, be suggested. The community, or more likely some organization with a commitment to community action and perhaps change, may take an active role in working with juveniles around the problems of delinquency. Working at "diverting" delinquents from the street life contributory to delinquency as well as from their involvement with the juvenile justice system, the more activist, community-based group does not become dependent on the formal system for its raison d'etre. While not an inevitability, it may be able to avoid the trap of becoming simply a part of the existing social control system. Such a community-based group may be involved with delinquents already formally a part of the juvenile justice system, yet still on the street. Alternatively, or at the same time, it could work with others not necessarily officially labeled delinquent or enmeshed in the juvenile justice process, yet who are considered by some to be at serious risk.

This activist community role, particularly with those young people considered at risk is not always easy to categorize, theoretically speaking. The terms diversion and prevention have been used quite loosely to label and describe a variety of community-based programs. Those programs or groups which emerge or restructure themselves in response to the juvenile justice system request for an alternative to some stage of the formal process, fall quite clearly into line with popular definitions of diversion.[3,17] Groups responding more directly to perceived community needs and not systems' requests are more difficult to categorize. The literature does not appear to provide clear answers. Some authors consider that diversion implies that a delinquent activity has occurred, and, but for some formal diverting along the way, the individual would proceed through the juvenile justice process.[16] Others [11,12,2] suggest that the term should also include community action by "individuals or particular interest groups dealing with trouble in their area."[12] One definition thus sees diversion as a direct action to move identified delinquents away from the traditional system they are about to, or already have entered. The other suggests a much broader range of activity subsumed under the term, ultimately implying that much if not all contact with the formal system can be avoided. Presumably, a variety of definitions of the term "diversion" could fall somewhere in between the two. Underlying both prevention and diversion is the assumption that delinquency and resultant involvement with juvenile justice is to be avoided. What distinguishes the two is their approach to avoiding delinquency and system contact. Preventing might entail broad-based community, or even societal change. It might also suggest a method of deterring or preventing individuals from committing delinquent acts. Diversion, however, implies an alternative to something. As has been proposed by two authors:

> Diversion has no real meaning in relationship to the criminal justice system in the absence of a context that tells us[1] what the process is by which diversion takes place;[2] what the person is diverted from— i.e., what is diversion instead of?—and[3] what he is diverted to.

Rossbrook House Program

The remainder of this paper describes an organization developed at a community level. It is designed to take an activist role in diverting juveniles away from both delinquent activity and involvement with the juvenile justice system. The philosophy of the organizations presumes that it will not act as a recipient of juveniles. Rather, it will promote activity to deal with problems of youth existent within its community. Previous or current involvement in the juvenile justice system is not a major factor in terms of the organizational orientation to those who come to it. The organization, Rossbrook House, can be considered a community-based diversion program. Its goals and objectives, methods of referral, its community-base, all are indicative of diversion in the wider sense of the term as described above. For the organization, diversion means providing an alternative to life on the street, and the resulting patterns of delinquency, alcohol and drug abuse, social service intervention and juvenile justice system involvement.

The operation of Rossbrook House is governed by a board of directors which represents the agency's broad community support base. Membership is representative of staff, users, parents, representatives of the neighboring community, police, and interested professionals from a wide variety of disciplines. Board members are encouraged to take an active role in agency functioning and, in turn, staff members and volunteers are encouraged to take an active role in board functioning.

The agency has a diversified funding base. It is funded by the United Way of Winnipeg, the Province of Manitoba (Department of Community Service and Corrections), the City of Winnipeg, and the Winnipeg Foundation.

A crucial factor in any diversion program (broadly or narrowly defined) relates to what the individual is being diverted. The Rossbrook House organization is decidedly both community based and activist. Hence, the individual is in a sense diverted into an organization very much a part of the local community—both a geographic and ethnic community. In establishing itself as a "neighbourhood diversion" program, Rossbrook is quite clear on what it seeks to divert juveniles from: those aspects of society which are inclined to promote, encourage or maintain delinquent behaviour. As well, it suggests that this be done outside of the traditional social services-juvenile justice system. While not promoting that the traditional systems be ignored, Rossbrook House sees itself as an alternative to life on the street, and the inevitable and not necessarily beneficial involvement with social services and/or juvenile justice which follows. The reaction to Rossbrook House among various segments of the social service system ranges from support and referral by some to strong and open hostility by others.

Rossbrook House operates in a run-down neighbourhood of central Winnipeg, characterized by high unemployment, delinquency, crime, alcoholism and drug abuse among many residents. There is widespread involvement on the part of many residents with social services, the police, and the criminal justice system. Ethnically, the area is made up of largely native and recent immigrants, although some residents have lived in the area for many years. It was begun by a small group of Catholic nuns who were living and working in this area. They had learned of the problems faced by youth in their neighbourhood from a small group of juveniles who came regularly to the nuns' house as an alternative to being "on the street." Primarily through the efforts of these nuns a building was obtained, funding tentatively secured, and an organizational structure established.

It operates on the principles of self-help and self-referral, which will be discussed in detail below. The program and program objectives reflect a commitment to these principles, as well as a commitment to access and availability. The building is open from 9:00 a.m. to 1:00 a.m. during weekdays and on a 24-hour basis on weekends and during times when school is not in session. The suggestion here is that to operate truly as an alternative to both street life and the juvenile justice system, such alternatives must be available during times of greatest need-after school and on weekends.

The objectives of the program of Rossbrook House are quite simple: stabilization, socialization, personal development and crisis intervention when necessary. Stabilization is attempted through the constant availability of a place to go and people to talk to. Few formal activities take place in terms of a regular schedule of events. Those with problems developed on the street are given encouragement and support to deal with them. The goal of stabilization is to eliminate the delinquent behaviour of those who come to Rossbrook House, and to break if possible the alcohol and chemical abuse patterns of these same people. As such, the organization makes clear that it is a supportive alternative to those who wish to change from such life styles.

Socialization involves an attempt to provide some of those experiences, perceived as beneficial in later life, which life on the street or the atmosphere of juvenile group homes and training schools does not provide. In this sense, the programmatic aspects of Rossbrook concentrate on informal group recreational activities, athletic competitions, as well as irregular special events such as trips, craft exhibitions, etc.[15] Rossbrook House seeks to bring about personal development through an educational program and limited employment activities. The Winnipeg School Board operates a limited enrollment alternative school on Rossbrook premises. It aims at taking in those juveniles of junior high age who, finding participation in a regular school program impossible to maintain, seek an alternative to dropping out and living on the street. The majority of those involved in the educational program have been regular attenders at Rossbrook. Employment is a more difficult problem. Short-term government grants have provided some employment but not of any lasting nature. The most successful area of employment has emerged through the hiring of those who have lengthy experience at Rossbrook to act as part-time staff.

Finally, Rossbrook House provides help in times of crisis. Those in direct conflict with the law will find people ready to assist them in dealing with, but not avoiding, legal problems. Similarly, for those in need of informal detoxication of a medically non-serious nature, Rossbrook is a place of support in "coming down" from, and eventually breaking from alcohol or drug use. During periods of 24-hour operation, Rossbrook is used by some as a shelter when family life deteriorates (particularly on Friday and Saturday nights) and a night on the street is the only alternative.

These objectives form the underlying goals of the operation of Rossbrook House. The implementation of these goals through programming occurs by an adherence to the principles of self-help and self-referral, principles consistent with an activist, community-based approach.

SELF-HELP NETWORKS

Increasingly the notions of social networks, social support and self-help have been applied by professionals to the examination of the dynamic linkages between individuals and their social environment.[25] These notions are being used by many professionals to assess and intervene more effectively with populations who generally are not well served by the traditional help giving agencies (i.e. adolescents, post-mentally ill, ex-offenders and alcohol and drug addicts.)[18,14,13]

One of the major terms used is the notion of self-help groups. The most widely accepted definition of self-help group is that which is put forward by Alfred Katz and Eugene Bender[10] who see self-help groups as:

> Voluntary, small group structures for mutual aid and the accomplishment of a special purpose. They are usually formed by peers who have come together for mutual assistance in satisfying a common need, overcoming a common handicap or life-disrupting problem, and bringing about a desired social and/or personal change.

Katz suggests that the initiators and members of such groups perceive that their needs are not, or cannot be met by or through existing social institutions. He maintains that: self-help groups emphasize face to face social interactions and the assumption of personal responsibility by members; they often provide material assistance, as well as emotional support, they are frequently cause oriented, and promulgate an ideology or values through which members may attain an enhanced sense of personal identity.[9]

Katz's definition outlines five key variables which determine differences in self-help group organizations: that is purpose, origin and sanction, source of help, composition, and control.

Social networks, the second key term used in this discussion, refers to those sets of linkages teenagers have with other social units (individuals, families, groups, organizations, neighborhood community). Network Analysis helps researchers and practitioners conceptualize more accurately the structural, functional and content dimensions of the individual's ties to his/her neighborhood or communities.[20,21] In addition, it assists in understanding the flow of resources across network ties.

For the purposes of this paper, we have combined the notion of self-help group with that of social network to form the third major concept used in this paper: self-help networks. Self-help network refers to those linkages established by the teenagers and/or the community based diversion agency which were established to help the teenagers with their day to day problems in living and to help keep them from becoming involved with the criminal justice system.

The notion assumes that the teenagers and their families develop socially supportive ties in their social networks. Caplan defined this social support as an enduring pattern of continuous or intermittent ties that play a significant part in maintaining the psychological and physical integrity of the individual over time.[4] Such support may be of a continuous nature or intermittent and short, and may be utilized from time to time by the individual in the event of an acute need or crisis. Both enduring and short term support are likely to consist of three elements:

a)   the significant others help the individual mobilize his psychological resources and master his emotional burden;

b)   they share his tasks;

c)   they provide him with extra supplies of money, material, tools, skills, cognitive guidance to improve his handling of his situation.[4]

The authors argue that the use of the notion of self-help network enables practitioners to examine and intervene in these networks to stimulate or enhance the flow of these resources over the teens' social support networks. This type of intervention was used by Rossbrook House to keep teens in the community and out of the criminal justice system.

SELF-HELP AND SELF-REFERRAL AS PRINCIPLES OF SERVICE DELIVERY

Overshadowing the four main objectives of Rossbrook House previously mentioned (i.e. stabilization, socialization, personal development and crisis intervention) there are two principles which form the basis for all the programming (i.e. self-referral and self-help).

The principle of self-referral suggests that those who attend Rossbrook House do so on the basis of self-referral (i.e. on their own initiative). Often teens find support in taking this initiative from family members, friends, teachers, or work mates. Rossbrook House offers a number of potential inducements for teenagers to become attenders, i.e. protection, fun, possible work experience and income. Once the teenagers begin to attend there is a great

YOUTH INJUSTICE: CANADIAN PERSPECTIVES

deal of encouragement from the staff and other teens to become involved in the programs, the planning and the work of the agency. Referral means involvement and commitment similar to many other self-help groups e.g. A.A., Recovery, and X-Kalay.

The agency is structured in such a way so that the facilities are available when the local teens feel they are in need of its programs and services. The availability of the agency resources is a key factor in promoting self-referral.

Self-Help, the second major principle, is incorporated in almost all aspects of the agency. This is done in a variety of ways.

The agency attempts to incorporate teenagers in all aspects of its functioning. Teenagers are involved as board members, paid staff, volunteers and program planners as well as consumers. Through this involvement, teens develop a sense of ownership, loyalty and concern for the centre itself.

Teens are involved in bringing other teens to the centre, working with teens with similar backgrounds of poverty, alcoholism, drug abuse and other forms of delinquency. In addition, the centre provides a place for many teens to stabilize their often confusing life situations.

At the time of the authors' study a number of norms were developed and maintained by staff and attenders. One norm was that of involvement in programs, agency maintenance and decision-making. A second norm was that of a common sense of collective ownership. The third norm was that of no use of alcohol or drugs on the premises. These norms served to form the basis for a common organizational ideology which fostered a strong sense of cohesion amongst agency staff, volunteers and attenders. The strong cohesive ties within the agency facilitated the development of self-help and socially supportive activities.

The activities at the drop-in centre were interrelated so that it was difficult to isolate an activity as belonging to one distinct program only. However, three very rough categorizations could be made, under the titles of refuge or shelter, recreational, and education. The interrelated nature of the centre activities can be made clearer by considering that attenders may be taking part in a recreational activity while at the same time seeking refuge from a potentially dangerous home situation.

It is important to note that in all aspects of the drop-in centre, with the exception of crisis intervention, the attenders themselves determine in which activities they wish to take part at any given time. The role of the staff, in this area, became one of suggesting, facilitating, or perhaps supervising the activity chosen by the attenders. Things only became formalized when separate facilities outside of Rossbrook House were required (e.g., ice hockey or floor hockey).

The educational component of the agency emphasized helping the teens develop a greater understanding of their own abilities and their social situation. It consisted of an alternative classroom during the day time. This was a decentralized resource of one of the local schools. In addition it consisted of agency sponsorship of outside speakers (e.g., native awareness activities, health concerns like VD and nutrition) and field trips to educational resources.

On a few occasions, Rossbrook House has agreed to provide limited probation supervision, as well as to act as a resource for the completion of a community service order. However, this has occurred only when the juveniles concerned had had extensive and continuous involvement with Rossbrook House, and it was voluntarily agreed to by all parties concerned. In those instances where this has taken place, the Agency received no financial remuneration, and it does not actively promote such arrangements.

Staff played an important role in maintaining support between teens and their families. In addition to encouraging the involvement of parents and other family members in the agency, extensive care was taken by staff to ensure that only those who were known (and whose home situation was known to be less than ideal) stayed late in the evening. On more than one occasion it was observed by the authors that those in no need of the refuge facilities were driven home at night by staff. Further, it was observed by the authors that there existed a good knowledge about the social situation of most of the attenders by staff, thus providing a measure of awareness concerning who was and was not likely to need refuge on any given evening. This knowledge was useful in assisting staff to link attenders and their families to appropriate informal (other attenders, families, church groups) and formal helpers (police, child welfare, and public assistance agencies).

PROMOTING SELF-HELP THROUGH STAFFING AND STAFF TRAINING

The self-help process at Rossbrook House was facilitated through the recruitment, training and deployment of staff. The 15 staff members include one volunteer executive director; one office manager (bookkeeper/secretary); one program director, and thirteen program staff. All professional staff and volunteers of the agency were required to be knowledgeable about and sensitive to the self-help emphasis of the agency. The director, in consultation with other staff and attenders, screened new staff and volunteers to ensure their orientation was compatible with that of the agency.

Program staff were generally recruited from the regular attenders at the centre and occasionally from direct service volunteers. Recruitment and hiring of staff was primarily the responsibility of the executive director. Regular attenders were from time to time hired on a short term basis to fill in for or supplement existing staff.

Training was carried out by a volunteer community worker. It was focused on helping staff deal with the problems as they presented themselves in the centre. More important, the trainer focused on assisting staff from the neighborhood to use knowledge from their own experience to help deal with situations in the centre.

Staff were clear about their function and role within the agency. They felt they brought a certain level of expertise from their personal experiences which enabled them to understand and work with inner city kids. Staff training assisted them to use their own experiences to help others in the area. As well, staff indicated satisfaction with their own level of input into policy and programming.

The authors maintain that this combination of indigenous expertise, staff training and direct supervision is a vital part of the agency's efforts to promote self-help activities and supportive linkages between teens in the neighborhood.

Consumer Impact of Community Based Self-Help Program

Rossbrook House works mainly with family networks of juveniles and young adults, most of whom have:

- limited formal education;

- few marketable skills;

- little job experience in the permanent labour force;

- problematic home situation;

- juvenile and/or adult criminal records;

- personal abuse pattern relating to solvents, soft drugs or alcohol.

Approximately 45-60 teenagers attended Rossbrook House during peak periods in evenings during weekends. The demographic data for the area indicated the delinquency rate for the agency catchment area was two to three times the rates of other parts of the city. Participant observations by the authors indicated that the potential for delinquency among youth in the area of the agency was high, and that, were it not for the Rossbrook facility (or something similar), some attenders would likely have engaged in criminal activity. A case in point involved the observation by one researcher of a group of youths at Rossbrook. They had expressed an interest in vandalism in the neighborhood, yet remained at Rossbrook and became quite involved in several of the evening's activities.

Informal discussion with attenders took place during observations of the weekend evening shifts. The most common comments on how Rossbrook House helps "kids" were statements like: "It keeps them (kids) out of trouble" or "it keeps them off the streets." Perhaps a better indication of the effects of Rossbrook on individual attenders was the sense of ownership they felt towards the centre. It was observed that norms of conduct and agency rules were reinforced simultaneously by staff and attenders alike. Acts of vandalism were rare and the limits of acceptable behaviour, which were quite broad, seemed well understood by all. Many of the teens came to Rossbrook House because another family member or friend attended. This collective reinforcement of norms, coupled with the family and friendship referral network, appeared to increase the cohesion and sense of identification with the agency. Involvement in the agency meant mitigation of delinquent behaviour and cessation of drugs and alcohol use. Self-help networks provided support necessary to reinforce behavioural change.

The major deficiency was generated because of the nature of the self-help group representation; there was limited involvement of native girls and other ethnic groups in the programming of the agency.

Local Neighborhood Impact

In order to ascertain the impact of Rossbrook House on the local community, the authors interviewed 22 randomly selected residents. Perhaps the most significant finding of the survey was that 17 local residents who knew about Rossbrook House thought it was helpful to kids in the neighborhood. Equally important was that those who thought Rossbrook was helpful, believed it did this by keeping kids off the street and out of trouble, largely by providing them with a place to go and things to do. One might take this as a rudimentary indication that the Rossbrook organization is achieving some of its desired ends.

In additions, the survey provided some evidence of local community involvement. Among those who know about Rossbrook House, 9 (52.9%) had been there and 11 (69.7%) had some family member who had been there. The median length of residents among those who knew of Rossbrook was ten years. This suggests that those interviewed were long term residents of the neighborhood and should be in a position to comment on it both before and after Rossbrook was established.

Staff and attenders were enlisted by the director to help elderly and other community members in need. This strengthened the social support available in the community and helped the teens help themselves. This also served to strengthen agency ties with the community.

CONCLUSION

Rossbrook House differs from traditional diversion programs for juveniles in a number of ways: goals, objectives, method of referrals, to name a few. Yet it remains consistent with several notions of what diversion perhaps ought to be about. It is an active, community-based organization designed to present an alternative to life on the street for juveniles, and the frequently resulting involvement in the juvenile justice system. It presents these alternatives at any stage of juvenile development, including involvement with juvenile justice. The adherence of the Agency to the broader conceptualization of diversion as involving active community participation in dealing with juvenile delinquency is reflected in both its goals and operating principles. Hence Rossbrook House is viewed as separate and distinct from the criminal justice and social service system. Teens view the agency as an informal social support resource which supplements the assistance provided by their family and other primary group structures.

Adherence to the principles of self-help and self-referral in its operation permits Rossbrook House to maintain important links with the community it serves. At the same time, they have assisted the agency in avoiding the development of a dependent relationship—in terms of referral and financial support—with the juvenile justice system. Because of the agency's commitment to self-referral, the agency programming was structured in such a way as to facilitate active choice of agency's services. Once an individual chose the agency, there was an extension of involvement of services to other family members and members of teens' informal helping networks. These networks were used to induct new members and to provide resources to many of the teens and their families in need.

The principle of self-referral provided the basis for the principle of self-help and the norm of involvement or inclusion. Involvement in the agency meant staff became aware of the social networks of the attenders (i.e. family, friends, linkages with social agencies). Involvement in the agency meant that teens were involved in helping themselves through helping other people. The indigenous resources of the group were identified and used in all aspects of the agency.

Agency services are designed in such a way as to facilitate involvement. However, involvement in the agency meant individuals had to change patterns of deviant behaviour. This change was supported by peers and staff and the milieu of the agency. The agency attempted to strengthen individual supportive ties with other with similar problems as well as with formal helping agencies where necessary. The agency provided a supportive setting for attenders to attend school, to learn social and job skills. It extended the resource networks available to them for solving their day to day problems of living. As such it formed a comprehensive community-based program for dealing with teenagers outside the criminal justice system.

ENDNOTES

1.   This paper is a revised version of a paper presented at the American Society of Criminology Annual Meetings in Toronto, Ontario on 6 November, 1982.

2.   Canagarayar, J. "Diversion: A New Perspective in Criminal Justice." *Canadian Journal of Criminology. 22*(2). 1980.

3.   Carter, R. and M. Klein, (eds.). *Back on the Street: The Diversion of Juvenile Offenders.* Englewood Cliffs: Prentice-Hall. 1976.

4.   Caplan, G. and M. Killilea. *Support Systems and Mutual Help.* New York: Grune and Stratton. 1976.

5.   Cohen, S. "Prisons and the Future of Control Systems." In Fitzgerald, M. et al. (eds.). *Welfare in Action.* London: Routledge & Kegan Paul. 1977.

6.   Cohen, S. "Community Control—A New Utopia." *New Society.* 15 March 1979.

7.   Gottlieb, B. (ed.). *Social Networks and Social Support.* Beverly Hills: Sage Publications. 1981.

8.   Hylton, J. "Rhetoric and Reality: A Critical Appraisal of Community Correctional Programs." *Crime and Delinquency. 28*(3). 1982.

9.   Katz, A. "Self-Help Groups and the Professional Community." In Alissi, A. (ed.). *Perspectives on Social Group Work Practice.* New York: The Free Press. 1980.

10. Katz, A. and E. Bender. *The Strength In Us.* New York: New View Points. 1980.

11. Law Reform Commission of Canada. *Studies on Diversion.* Ottawa: Information Canada. 1975.

12. Law Reform Commission of Canada. *Diversion: Working Paper #7.* Ottawa: Information Canada. 1975.

13. Levy, L. "Self-Help Groups: Types and Psychological Processes." *Journal of Applied Behavioural Science. 12*(3) 1976.

14. Lieberman, M. and L. Borman. *Self-Help Groups for Coping with Crisis.* San Francisco: Jossey-Bass. 1979.

15. MacNamara, G. *Rossbrook House: An Experience/Experiment in Neighbourhood Diversion.* Winnipeg: (mimeo) n.d.

16. Moyer, S. *Diversion from the Juvenile Justice System and its Impact on Children: A Review of the Literature.* Ottawa: Solicitor General of Canada. 1980.

17. Scull, A. *Decarceration.* Englewood Cliffs: Prentice-Hall. 1977.

18. Speigal, D. "The Recent Literature: Self-Help and Mutual Support Groups." *Community Mental Health Review.* 5(4). 1980.

19. Vorenberg, E. and J. Vorenberg. "Early Diversion from the Criminal Justice System." In Ohlin, L. (ed.). *Prisoners in America.* Englewood Cliffs: Prentice-Hall. 1973.

20. Wellman, B. "What is Network Analysis?" *Working Paper 1A.* Structural Analysis Programme. Toronto: Department of Sociology. University of Toronto. 1980.

21. Wellman, B. "Applying Network Analysis to the Study of Social Support." In Gottlieb, B. (ed.). *Social Networks and Social Support.* Beverly Hills: Sage Publications. 1981.

CHAPTER 12
From Care to Punishment: Rehabilitating Young Offender Programming in Ontario

BARRY CLARK
THOMAS O'REILLY-FLEMING

FROM WELFARE TO PUNISHMENT

On April 2, 1984 and April 1, 1985, the *Young Offender's Act* (YOA) was introduced to the Canadian Justice toolbox. The Canadian legal system had originally dealt with juvenile delinquency via the much criticized, yet long lasting, *Juvenile Delinquent's Act* (JDA). The JDA was introduced in 1908 and emphasized the doctrine of *parens patriae*, (Platt, 1969) essentially placing the state via the person of the family court judge in the position of parent (Hagan and Leon, 1977, Housten, 1978, Leon 1977). The JDA focused upon the needs of the youthful offender rather than on the aims of punishment. The ambiguities of the act, as a number of observers have concluded, and the lack of due progress safeguards meant that many young offenders suffered the ministrations of the criminal justice system who should not have been the subject of the law in the first place (Hudson *et al* 1988; Caputo 1991). "Crimes" of a moral nature (promiscuity, truancy), what have been referred to as status offenses, were a major component of the court's work under the JDA (Currie, 1986: 65, Hudson *et al* 1988: 5). There was little involvement of legal counsel, and due process was relegated to a secondary position in favour of intervention "in the best interests" of the accused. Judges were accorded wide discretionary powers with regard to disposition (Caputo, 1987). The 1970's were an era in which a rehabilitative approach to juvenile justice mirrored other social movements stressing an emphasis on human

---

rights, womens' rights, prisoners' rights, civil rights'. These included variously children's rights to counsel, an issue which began to be increasingly important in the 1970's which precursored the movement towards a new legislative vehicle (Reid and Reitsma-Street, 1984). Family court judges who had been appointed almost exclusively from the ranks of social workers were ill-equipped to adjudicate technical legal cases raised by increasing numbers of juveniles with lawyers arguing specific points of law and procedure (Bala, 1988).

The YOA was viewed by many as a piece of compromise legislation which reflected a growing disillusionment with the seeming paucity of rehabilitative successes which occurred under JDA programs (Coflin, 1988; Caputo, 1991). Soliciter General Bob Kaplan (1981: 9307) in introducing the legislation reflected the disillusionment many parliamentarians felt with the juvenile justice system that focused on the needs of youth, "...many are now of the opinion that treatment and rehabilitation can no longer stand on their own." Kaplan's speech was, in fact, a direct attack against rehabilitation. The new emphasis was on punishment, he asserted, noting, "society insists more and more on responsibility." A Howard Crosby, one of the few dissenting voices (1981: 9223) called for more emphasis upon the structural conditions which cause delinquency remarking that, "It is only through a competent and effective social justice that we can remedy these kinds of defects." The YOA was born at a politically significant juncture in Britain, Canada and America when conservative governments were, or had recently gained, ascendancy riding the wave of various forms of "law and order" campaigns (Ratner and McMullan, 1985; Caputo, 1991). The YOA was interpreted by judges within the framework of a "justice as fairness" model of justice essentially emphasizing a crime-responsibility-punishment dichotomy (Leschied and Jaffe, 1985; 1988). Cohen (1985: 66-76) argues that juvenile justice systems almost invariably translate themselves into more punative practices when the rhetoric is dropped into this model of control. Whereas the needs of young persons in conflict with the law had been, at least in principle, the thrust of the JDa and YOA centered its focus upon the last of these directives as we clearly argue later in this chapter. The YOA offered a number of empty promises regarding the treatment to be accorded young people. This is particularly true of Ontario, Canada's most populous province which refused to cooperate with the spirit of the uniform national legislation either in terms of compliance with the rehabilitative measures envisaged to be an integral part of the act nor with even simple data collection on youthful offending. Ontario's non-participation in the YOA reveals that custody measures have prevailed at the expense of alternative measures programmes creating a doppelganger of the adult correctional system for young people.

Consultations between government, private and public sector agencies pressed the implementation of the YOA, but it became evident during the first six years of its operation that the YOA in Ontario has suffered directly due to lack of detailed, logistical planning, a paucity of moral consideration, and as a consequence of considerable inter-ministerial wrangling that has characterized the implementation of the act. Earlier attempts to introduce young offenders' legislation in 1970 (bill C-192) failed Caputo (1991: 132-134) since it did not reflect any kind of consultative process. The House of Commons condemned these attempts as punitive and draconian in that they took away many of the rights of children and would punish them more severely that adult counterparts. The introduction of the new YOA failed in several arenas but no more so than in the manner in which its implementation was characterized by ministerial disorder which has left Ontario, at every level of service, with a caricature of the legislation's original spirit.

The resultant shortcomings are neither few nor are they insignificant. Overall they cover the programmatic spectrum from primary to tertiary interventions as well as impacting upon the entire range of Ontario's criminal justice budget. The absence of a sound, comprehensive policy and the gross misapplication of correctional dollars are dialectically and inextricably enmeshed. Therefore it is logical that any attempt effectively to alter the present trend in young offender treatment by the criminal justice system will require a complex, concerted and longitudinal effort on the part of the governmental and private agencies. This chapter goes on to outline some of the major impediments to an optimal implementation of the YOA in Ontario. Further, it explores the interrelationships between these impediments suggesting alternative directions in policy and programmes. Finally, an existing program, the C.O.P.S. approach with some potential to redirect future efforts, is examined in some depth to provide a model for services and to suggest some possible, new directions for efforts in Ontario's juvenile justice system.

PRINCIPLES AND POLICIES

The absence of uniform policy and effective service provision underscores the fundamental chaos that has resulted from Ontario's piecemeal and reluctant phasing in of the YOA. The primary pieces of legislation which mandate services to children and young persons in Ontario are both specific and clear in the declaration of goals. Together, the principles of the acts mutually reinforce and purposefully provide a structural/ethical framework for decision making in both the policy and service arenas. The intent of these acts is clear; both policy and service are to be functionally indivisible. But clearly principles, no matter haw noble their intent, when left unanimated by programmes represent merely broken promises, which have impacted directly to produce the current disarray in service provision to the young in Ontario. Certainly, a brief examination of the relevant principles proclaimed in each of the Acts which govern the care of young persons in trouble with the law reveals that they have the *potential* to provide powerful directions for policy and programme decisions:

Child and Family Service Act	Young Offenders Act
*the best interests, protection and well-being of children	*to acknowledge the state of dependency and level of development and maturity
*to support and to strengthen the family unit	*to recognize special needs which require guidance and assistance
*the least amount of interference	*special rights and freedoms
*mutual consent	*the right to the least possible interference with freedom
*services tailored to needs and differences (cultural, religious, physical and mental)	*taking no measures or taking measures other than judicial proceedings
*children require stability	*giving priority to continued parental supervision when appropriate
*the *least* restrictive alternative	*these principles are to be *liberally construed*

To underscore the functional importance of these statements of basic principles that are to guide the application of both acts, it is crucial to recognize that the principles of the YOA are intended to be "liberally construed". The principles are not apparently presented as an exercise in rhetorical idealism. Their purpose, rather, is to provide a functional integrity and moral order for policy decisions, the application of law, and the conduct of agents and agencies of social control. The current gap between these stated principles and existing programmes provides a lamentable testimony as to exactly how far Ontario has deviated from these primary safeguards.

Certainly, the most salient and disturbing deviation in this area is the dramatic increase in custody that has occurred since the implementation of the YOA. As early as 1985, Peter Jaffe (1985) writing in *The Ontario Lawyers Weekly* was to observe that, "the incarceration rate has *tripled* and that the length of sentence has *doubled* under the YOA for 16 and 17-year-old youths." Similarly, Leschied and Jaffe (1985:2) found that while under the JDA 5% of the youths received custodial sentences, under the YOA 11% of offenders received this form of sentence. Jaffe (1985) also discovered a substantial increase in custody dispositions for 12 to 15-year-olds of 120% under the new act, as well as longer stays recorded in secure custody in his sample. Juristat (1991), a publication of the federal government's Statistics Canada, provides ample evidence of the trends nationally over the period 1986 to 1991. During this period charges against youths rose by 21%. Of 11,223 cases nationally which resulted in custodial dispositions in 1989, 46% involved secure custody. The number of young persons charged with violent offenses has increased considerably since 1984-85 when 3, 559 youths were charged. By 1988-89, 7,256 charges were recorded in this category.

During 1989-90, 16 and 17-year-old young offenders under the jurisdiction of the provincial Ministry of Correctional Services admitted to secure facilities reached a total of 4,029 (Ministry of Correctional Services, Ontario, 1990). Of this number, 3, 576 were males while 453 were females. This represented a 5.8% increase over admissions from the previous year. A further 1,757 young offenders were sentenced to open facilities (859 males and 88 females) during the same period. The John Howard Society of Ontario (1989: 1) found in reviewing custodial decisions in Ontario that "...under the YOA youths are being sentenced to significantly longer periods of probation or imprisonment than was the case with the JDA." This was all the more disturbing since the authors found that "there has been no upward trend in youth crime." Jaffe and Leschied (1989) concluded after an extensive review of the treatment of youths under the YOA versus the JDA that increasingly harsher conditions were being created in the courts and correctional apparatus for the handling of offenders:

> "Many have held the belief that the YOA has been "soft" on adoles-
> cent offenders. This is definitely not the case if one looks at rates for
> committal to custody under the YOA when compared to a similar
> disposition under the Juvenile Delinquents Act. Since April 1, 1984
> when the YOA was implemented for twelve to fifteen-year-old
> offenders, the rate and length of custody sentences has increased
> dramatically. When sixteen and seventeen-year-old youths came
> under the YOA as of April 1, 1985, this group too met the same
> fate....This radical shift in custody placements represents a national
> trend. Nine out of ten provinces have more young offenders in cus-
> tody."

The research of Markwart and Corrado (1989) further corroborates this trend.
They found that for youths under 17 there was a 73% increase admissions to
open and secure custody between 1984/85 and 1987/88 in the province of
British Columbia. Similarly they found for the same period in Ontario an
increase of 79%. Doob (1992:82) concluded that, "...there has been an
increase in the proportion of those cases getting to court that are receiving
custodial sentences." Doob also found that judges appear to be using a large
number of *short* sentences (of 1 month to 12 months) and a far fewer *long*
sentences (of over one year).

The definition of short and long sentences requires some adaptation of
their impact and effect upon youngsters as opposed to applying measures
more appropriate for adult offenders.

The extent of this investment is inprisoning youngsters while ignoring
treatment needs and alternatives is further signified by the amount of funding
expended on custody. By 1989, up to ninety percent of all federal YOA
monies were being channeled to custody beds. Despite the fact that custody
has always been a cost-inefficient and counter-productive intervention, dating
from the records of the first colonial Houses of Refuge, and the later reform
school movement in the second half of the nineteenth century, Ontario has
ambitiously set upon the predestinately futile path of a carceral response to
youth criminality and misbehaviour. During the busy consultative years that
preceded the implementation of the YOA (1980-85), it was already abundant-
ly and unarguably clear from the carceral experience of the United States that
an unbridled reliance on institutionalization was a socially and financially disas-
trous course. As Canada's Paul Gendreau (1987) succinctly states the prob-

lem, the effect created is exactly the opposite of that desired, 'When do you find a correlation between severe punishment and criminal recidivism it is usually in the opposite direction."

His assertion finds a sobering resonance in Conrad's (1985) work in Columbus, Ohio. This study reconfirmed the fact that frequent incarcerations actually accelerate recidivism. There was a consistently positive correlation discovered by Conrad, between increased incarcerations and increased and more serious subsequent criminal behavior amongst his sample. More disturbingly, in terms of Ontario's current "lock em up" policy, was the finding that the younger the person at the first incarceration, the higher the recidivism rate subsequently recorded. One might assert that while adults *adapt* to the custodial system, children and young persons are *adopted* by it. The general failure of Ontario's over-reliance on custody and its associated sequelae, has been substantially documented. The financial burden generated by this drastic imbalance has impoverished the province to the point where it is unable and arguably unwilling to respond proactively and adequately through other less restrictive alternatives. It is not at all surprising that the Province bemoans the lack of dollars for alternatives to custody, which are considerably less costly than custody, when up to ninety percent of its young offender dollars are spent on warehousing young persons—a troubling number of these in adult jails.

This unacceptable reality is further exacerbated by the absence of consistent and thoughtful application of the review procedures provided for under the legislation (Sections 28-34).

As well, the inaccessibility of treatment and the province's resistance to amend Sections 20 (1) and 22 (1) concerning consent to treatment further eclipse the therapeutic/rehabilitative ideal of the YOA. Under 22 (1) treatment may only be ordered by the court if i) the parents or guardians of the offender, ii) the treatment facility, and iii) the young offender all agree to a course of treatment. Without access to liberally funded alternatives to custody, the urban poor as well as status Indian youth are considerably less likely to receive the benefits of consideration for judicial interim release (Section 7 and 8). The reparative ethic at the heart of the principles outlined in the YOA is yet further weakened by the punitive inflexibility of determinate sentencing (Section 24). This effectively demoralizes the incarcerated young offender and diminishes any incentive for change through an earned, early release mechanism (Sections 28-34). Since adolescence is a critical and pivotal period of developmental change, opportunities for healthy, optimal growth must be consistently and liberally accessible, as integral parts of a structured continuum of interventions.

A lack of policy resolve and programme innovation is perhaps nowhere more evident than in Ontario's refusal to implement an effective system of alternative measures. A substantial provision for alternative measures is an indispensable ingredient in a healthy and balanced implementation of the YOA

The entitlements to these alternatives as outlined in Section 4 of the YOA are intended to ensure that critical and delicate equipoise—between indeality and ideology, thesis and praxis, principles and programmes—the dynamic essence of the legislation, is achieved.

Without a liberally and innovatively funded spectrum of alternative measures the moral authority and service potential of the legislation are severely undermined. This absence of minimal intervention has eventuated, invariably, in a reliance on maximal intrusion in the form of increased incarceration, which in turn financially depletes the possibility of developing preventative and early intervention services. To add to the confusion, Ontario has created what has come to be known as the "split jurisdiction" model in which the Ontario Ministry of Correctional Services retains jurisdiction over the 16 and 17-year-old offenders, while The Ontario Ministry of Community and Social Services is responsible for the fate of 12 to 15-year-olds. Under the YOA children under the age of 12 may not be held criminally accountable for their acts. Previously, under the JDA, those under seven years of age were governed by the English common law principles of *doli incapax*, that is, the incapacity to do wrong (Archambault, 1983). In application, split jurisdiction is an ill-conceived inter-ministerial compromise which has created an unhealthy disjunction -an age and service differential based more on convenience than philosophical and practical realities. Nova Scotia, one of Canada's poorest and smallest provinces also adopted the split jurisdiction model. Split jurisdiction provides, yet another example of how a provincial anomaly can erode the pristine spirit of federal legislation. Indeed, to be faithful to the primary rehabilitative spirit of the YOA, the jurisdiction for sixteen and seventeen year olds, at least within the present ministerial context of the Community and Social Services. Their approach, it can be argued, is somewhat more attuned to the spirit and practice envisaged by the original principles which pervade the YOA. If we accept Doob's (1992) argument that there is an increasing use of violence by juveniles wither as criminal acts or in the commission of criminal acts it simply accentuates the need for treatment approaches which recognize wider societal structural problems including the breakdown of the nuclear family, woman and child abuse, widespread unemployment in Canada, and youth disenfranchisement for meaningful employment (West, 1984).

One final issue which, like split jurisdiction, has had significant differential impact on Ontario, is the province's myopic inability to address the needs of the "under-12" population. In Ontario, the implementation of the YOA entailed raising the age of jurisdictional accountability from seven to twelve years. This change resulted in a vacuum of mandate and service to the under 12 person in conflict with society. Ontario's *Child and Family Services Act* does not adequately and specifically respond to this deficit, for it is not a piece of legislation which was intended to deal with lawbreaking behaviours and responses to such deviant acts. Childrens Aid Societies, already beleaguered by spiraling protection cases, have been unable to mount a meaningful service response. Similarly, law enforcement, unaided by sensible legislation, has taken a "wait and charge" position on the under twelve group. Officers file occurrence reports on all such events and when a juvenile comes before the court at the age of 12 they already have in effect, a long "record" of involvement with the police. As a result, the burgeoning under twelve offender, like his or her twelve to eighteen year old counterpart, has negligible or no access to a structured, early intervention system. Boyle and Offord (1988: 19) have argued that our social policy options have been short circuited by funding trends and service provisions which leave "high risk" children without essential treatment services. Further, they see dispositions under the YOA as "...time-limited, offence-based sentences which may be unrelated to a young person's needs." Without the institution of a number of resources they point out, as we are in this article, that "...overspending on custody beds may offer little hope for rehabilitation or accountability and responsibility of offenders." The impact of the repeal of the Juvenile Delinquents Act on the "under twelve" population is yet to be adequately assessed in Ontario. Certainly, there was no paucity of criticism against the establishment of the minimum age at twelve years, even prior to 1984. Conservatives and "get tough" proponents were especially vocal in their opposition. Former Toronto Police Chief Jack Marks, for example, perceived the new minimum age as a harbinger of a children's municipal crime wave. His concern was echoed by the Vancouver and Halifax Police Departments, fearing that children under 12, with their new immunity to criminal prosecution, would be induced by older criminals to commit their crimes. Some critics pointed to a likely parallel between Charles Dickens's *Oliver Twist* and his character Fagin, an exploited child thief. The Windsor Police Department added substance to this concern by illustrating the Detroit situation in which children continue to be recruited as "mules" or couriers in that city's industrious drug trade—citing an organized and lucrative network of child traffickers such as Young Boys Incorporated, Pony Down and Campbell Boys Incorporated.

Also opposing the new, elevated age jurisdiction were more liberal critics who anticipated a vacuum in services and treatment for the "under twelves". Interestingly, while conservatives and liberals share a parallel degree of concerns over the plight of the "under twelves", their diagnostic and prescriptive agendas are radically polarized. The liberal concern laments the withdrawal of child welfare support systems and interventions for the "under twelve" age group. The liberal proponents would argue that this absence of treatment opportunity occurs at considerable risk to child and community. Unlike the conservative, the liberal would argue that considerable preemptive energies and resources should be directed at this early phase—while children may be emotionally troubled but not yet criminally troublesome. Indeed, the "under twelves" would appear to warrant substantive and intensive assistance in the areas of school remediation, drug/alcohol interventions as well as services to address "chronic familial difficulties such as exposure to spousal violence, parental separation/divorce, and being victimized through child abuse". It would appear, in fact, that there exists a narrow but critical window of opportunity for selective intervention and treatment for "under twelves". Studies by Wolfgang, Figlio and Sellin as well as Palmer and Lewis (1980) substantiate the need for appropriate, community-based, intervention. Gendreau and Ross cite three key ingredients in successful primary prevention initiatives: 1) the intervention must begin early, 2) it must involve the family and 3) it should involve problem-solving cognitive skill building. As Palmer and Lewis (1980) further suggest, a differential approach to early intervention is recommended—reflecting a balanced continuum of policy and programme. They write, "some combinations of youths and objectives might best be served by short-term, voluntary programs operated by non-justice system personnel; other combinations might best be served by longer-term, nonvoluntary, justice system-operated programs; and still others might best be served by a combination of the two types of program." Rationally, a broader definition of prevention is required to encompass and to legitimate a wholistic intervention continuum. Such a definition is helpfully provided by Thomas Phelps: (1982, cited in Thornton *et al*) "Delinquency prevention occurs when community services meet the current needs of youth; ideally, non coercive social services are made available to the youngster not yet adjudged delinquent by the police or the courts."

We shall present, in some detail, one programme, the Community Options Programme, which, we propose, represents a flexible, cost-effective service response to an intensive risk/need assessment of children and young persons both at early risk for law-breaking and criminal behavior as well as throughout the spectrum of our formal, law-breaking and criminal behaviour as well as throughout the spectrum of our formal, youth justice system. The Attendance Centre component in particular, is sufficiently and inherently adaptable to respond to a constellation of diagnosed risk/need: familial, social, educational, cultural, psychological, sexual and spiritual issues are capably addressed through its broad, internal curriculum or its parallel and adjunctive referral mechanisms. While this service offers particular promise for early assessment and intervention with "under twelves", the international precursors of the Ontario model were reserved for persons already well enmeshed in the formal criminal justice system. In England, for instance, Attendance Centres originated in 1948 as a response to a critical institutional overcrowding. Young offenders, aged 12 to 21, were ordered to attend Centres for periods of work and training during their leisure time, typically on weekends. Later legislative provisions, introduced in 1972, designated attendance as a condition of a probation order, the hours of attendance, number of days, nature of the work etc. specified by court order. These Day Training Centers, as they are called, programmatically address broader, underlying problems such as social skills, life skills, education and employment. Similarly, Periodic Detention Work Centres were developed in Australia in 1962, reflecting a strong penchant for intensive, less expensive non-residential programming. New Zealand's adult Non-residential Periodic Detention Weekend work projects are enriched by lifeskills/communications lectures and group discussions held on weekday evenings. As we see, intensive, non-residential programmes are remarkably and functionally adaptable to the need/risk, age and lifestyle schedules of their participants. Internationally, they have been successfully employed to reduce institutional overcrowding—a pressing problem in Canada's young offender and adult correctional systems. Demographically, of course, the problems are greatest in Canada's most populated provinces. The category between the ages of 15 to 24, a statistically crime prone group, currently includes one in six Canadians, one out of four residing in Ontario. One is three Canadians live in our three major cities, Montreal, Toronto or Vancouver. These demographics pose obvious logistical and financial problems (and opportunities) for crime prevention practitioners. Ominously, there has been no concerted or substantive effort to develop a uniform policy and programme to address youthful urban crime and the overcrowding of youth institutions in our most populous areas. Toronto, for instance, does not have a single Attendance Centre programme, having failed to support the short-lived Metro Attendance Centre Programme (M.A.C.) in the mid-1980's. Paradoxically, the argument espoused by the provincial Attorney General's office, especially as it relates to their opposition to Alternative Measures, is that preventative/diversionary mechanisms "widen the correctional net" and are too costly. This position, of course, is patently nonsensical - reflecting a narrow, reactive understanding of corrections and based more on ignorance than in fact. The alternative, of course, is, as Irwin Waller succinctly puts it, to continue to expand our unbridled efforts in the arenas of "cops, courts and corrections". These energies, however, over the past quarter century "have left us with twice as many police, twice as many prison guards, more prisons and 50 per cent more prisoners". Daniel Koenig (1991), in analyzing Canadian crime rates over the same 25-year period, between 1962 and 1988, writes, "police effectiveness at containing violent crime has been found wanting over the past quarter century in Canada. Simply increasing police strength has been an unimaginative and demonstrably unsuccessful strategy at reducing rates of violent reported crime". Yet, according to Koenig, Canadian police departments in 1988, on average, spent $82,334. per police officer, amounting to $169. for every Canadian. If one per cent of the Metropolitan Toronto Police Department's annual gross operating budget were withheld and transferred to a municipal Attendance Centre services, 4 such Centres would be operational in one year. Over a five year period, this process could potentially result in the creation of 20 Attendance Centres in the city of Toronto. Given the dubious and costly relationship between increased policing and crime prevention, such a simple rechannelling of dollars and common sense would appear to warrant serious consideration. We have argued that primary prevention initiatives, based upon social welfare and social development concepts, are ultimately and invariably less costly and more efficacious than the traditional, reactive "cops, courts and corrections" syndrome. We have clearly demonstrated that such a reorientation of present policy and practice is not foreign or contradictory to the prevailing legislation; but, rather, would usher in a desirable return to original principles, reaffirming a primary integrity of purpose. This can be achieved at no additional financial cost. In fact, an intelligently planned and coordinated effort would result in a considerable reduction in current financial and social encumbrances.

The weary, unimaginative lament of government, that there are "no new dollars" available for preventative or alternative services, is both specious and tautological. Self-impoverishment is at the heart of Ontario's dominant youth justice system. Heightened policing, expanded judiciary and increased incapac-itation of offenders all conspire to perpetuate this sorry state of corrections. This malignant trinity, of "cops, courts and corrections", is internally capacity driven - continuously bloating itself on its own systemic dysfunction. This "system", however, is not without its own set of internal checks and balances. For instance, a proliferation of informal Alternative Measures and Youth Justice Committees would lessen the need for traditional policing and a costly and protracted court process. Review of custody mechanisms would, by truncating total days in custody, further free up dollars for more proactive services. In Ontario, for instance, the 1986-87 total number of secure facility days for phase II, or 16 and 17 year old young offenders, amounted to about 230,000 days stay, up 72% over the previous year. If one third of this time were spent in post-release, reintegrative Attendance Centres, the province would free up 76,666 days, or 10.7 million dollars annually, for more humane and preventative initiatives. (Of the 4,277 offenses committed by phase II offenders in secure custody, only 132, or 3.08% were violent crimes, 3 of which, or .07% were homicide.) This reallocated amount of "no new dollars" would, for example, provide funding for approximately 100 Attendance Centres in the province. This simple cost efficiency does not begin to reflect the additional dollars saved by diverting young persons from the criminal justice process as well as a reduction of an unacceptably high post-release recidivism through a planned and structured reintegration model. These modifications of the traditional correctional paradigm will also have the immediate and long term palliative impact of moderating the current contagion of prison building that has come to dominate the past quarter century of Canadian corrections. Attendance Centres have been recommended, in Ontario as well as across Canada, by private and public sector task forces as viable options to incarceration. Clearly, however, a reduction and strict reallocation of conventional "cops, courts and corrections" dollars will be required to achieve this desired result.

NATIVE PROGRAMMES

One of the values of the Community Options Programme, next to be presented in some detail, is its versatility. Somewhat chimerical in nature, its curriculum can be adapted to a variety of dissimilar situations. A promising example of this flexibility is found in its application to the aboriginal context, even isolated native reserves. The North Caribou Lake Band model, for instance, is a regional/cultural modification of the Southwestern Ontario programme. Both the content and the process of the programme have been adapted to meet the needs and requirements of the isolated, northern Ontario reserve. During the past decade many sequestered reserves have undergone a

McLuhanesque upheaval of their traditional religio-cultural patterns. Satellite television, while introducing a new and immediate access to world events, has widened the knowledge gap between native elders and youth and between traditional values and modern norms. High rates of alcoholism, family violence and school dropout rates, as high as 80% in some reserves, dramatize the particular plight of the aboriginal condition. An external justice system, from policing to a visitant circuit court, reflect the hegemony of a dominant, white power structure. Lengthy delays between the commission of offenses and their disposition through court—many of the dispositions are virtually unenforceable—dilute the authority of the formal justice system. While the Community Options Programme is not a panacea for the hybrid and entrenched problems experienced on the remote, native reserves, it is, in its adapted form, a highly responsive agent of prevention at a variety of levels. For instance, the standard basic curriculum, developed for native reserves, reflects a cultural and geopolitical sensitivity to a range of endemic problems. Fundamental units of the curriculum, incorporating elements of community and personal service, include: sports nights, remedial homework programmes, community work options, junior firefighters programme, firearm safety (hunting/trapping), fire safety, skidoo/outboard motor maintenance and repair, first aid and household safety programmes, native artist programme, quilt making/beadwork/soapstone carving/woodwork, music, native spirituality, babysitting/parenting programmes, drug/alcohol health promotion, understanding the media, anger management/family violence, teen dances, teen radio programmes and more.

Part of the broader socio-political process is to establish and to work closely with a native policing and native counseling component. Youth Justice Committees, comprised of band elders, provide leadership and ensure aboriginal ownership and empowerment over the system. Ideally, the Community Options Programme, in the native setting, manifests the principles of the Young Offenders Act through a continuum of applications from the precharge voluntary (under 12s), the Alternative Measure intake (A.M.I.), Intensive Probation Supervision and, importantly, a post-custodial function. These measures are particularly helpful when used as either an alternative or a follow-up to custody, since incarceration, for natives, primarily entails removal from the community.

THE COMMUNITY OPTIONS PROGRAMME

The Community Options Programme (COPS) was conceived in 1979 under the initiative and supervision of Herbert O. Kennedy, Senior Probation Officer in the Waterloo Area Office of the Ministry of Community and Social Services, Waterloo, Ontario. The model was developed and expanded to Waterloo, Wellington and Grey/Bruce Counties as a contracted service to the John Howard society of Waterloo Region. This COPS model will be briefly examined, in the context of the preceding issues, since this programme addresses many of the problems that plague the implementation of the Young Offenders Act in Ontario. The COPS model contains the following positive features: (1) it faithfully reflects the principles of both the YOA and the CFSA, (2) the programme curriculum is adaptable to the age and developmental needs of both children and young persons, (3) programme units can be tailored for cultural, ethnic and gender differences, (4) the programme can respond to a continuum of judicial/correctional need (ie, pre-charge voluntary, post-charge/pre-dispositional, post-dispositional and post-custodial models), (5) COPS is cost-efficient, (6) overall the programme has been endorsed by both private and governmental sectors and reduces the problem of overcrowding in young offender institutions.

COPS comprises three service areas; (a) community service orders wherein the offender works within a community agency to fulfill his sentence; (b) attendance centre programmes which permit the offender to benefit from counseling, and (c) primary prevention services (Clark, 1988). This final component includes an array of offense specific programmes including anti-shoplifting, family violence and drug/alcohol abuse prevention units. The curriculum includes workbooks, videos, overheads and board games and was developed by The John Howard Society. The units are presented in elementary schools, generally at a grade six level, and as part of the province's Values, Influences and Peers (V.I.P.) initiative. As well as being directed at a general school population, a more intensive curriculum can be introduced into high risk schools and linkages created between complementary programmes such as Student Watch (school anti-vandalism) or S.A.D.D. (Students Against Driving Drunk). As well, individual referrals can be made from the community, schools and law enforcement, usually at a voluntary level, with a special focus on the "under twelves".

The Attendance Centre model is the most intensive and adaptable component of the COPS programme repertoire. Its application, with appropriate curricular modifications, can be pre-charge/voluntary (usually for the under twelves), post-charge/pre-dispositional (perhaps as a formal Alternative Measures), post-dispositional (usually as a term of regular probation and, finally, post-custodial (as an early release or standard reintegrative follow-up to custody). The Attendance Centre is essentially a highly structured and intensively supervised correctional intervention. Children and young persons attend an evening programme, voluntarily or mandated, up to five evenings a week. Normally, they are transported to and from the programme by staff, between the hours of six p.m. and nine p.m. On occasion, post-programme curfews and weekend activities are added to extend the programmes supervisory strictures. On the average, ten participants attend each evening; however, the average nightly programme count may be double the number since many participants will be in a part-time phase-in or phase-out stage or in a Community Placement Programme. This placement programme arranges for the community activities (hockey, swimming, guides, leader-in-training etc.) as a monitored part of the regular Attendance Centre programme. It is also used to extend the realm and duration of regular programme involvement after participants graduate from the Attendance Centre. The average programme involvement is six months, although, based on individual progress, this duration can be shorter or longer. An Attendance Centre is usually staffed by two full-time and one part-time professional, normally a combination of one accredited teacher, and graduates in the social sciences and recreation. Referrals come from parents, youth agencies, the schools, the police and the courts, depending upon the formal or informal nature of the referral process. An intensive assessment period always commences programme involvement and will dictate the length, intensity and nature of the individual's programme curriculum. The Attendance Centre, which operates nightly out of schools and community recreational facilities and parks, offers a broad and attractive programme menu for participants. While some curricular units are mandatory, there is a heavy emphasis on voluntary, participant-selected options. A typical Attendance Centre programme curriculum, developed and delivered by the professional staff, would include: offense specific modules (anti-shoplifting, anti-vandalism), family violence, anger management, self-esteem, respect for authority, racial/cultural appreciation, nutrition, hygiene, study skills/homework completion and employment/job placement. A full range of less formal units are also standard programme fare: recreation, crafts, computers, woodworking, welding, as well as certification in baby-sitting, bicycle safety as well as tours of community sites. Many students, who are placed on daily homework journals, receive individualized tutorial assistance at the Attendance Centre where time is set aside for homework completion and exam preparation. The homework journal is received and signed daily by the participant's regular teacher.

Participants may also be placed on individualized behaviour contracts in the home and/or at school which are monitored by the Attendance Centre staff daily or weekly. It is highly recommended that, in some instances, a family therapist, attached to the COPS programme, be assigned to high risk, multi-problem youth and their families, and should include an assessment referral component. As earlier mentioned, all participants are encouraged to join community activities and organizations such as formal swim classes, volleyball, baseball etc. Attendance at these placements are monitored and are arranged through the Attendance Centre with funding often coming from local service clubs. The placement programme continues and often intensifies once a participant graduates from the Attendance Centre. It is not surprising that, with such varied curricula scaled to the needs and interests of the participants, that regular attendance is greater for the younger participants. Admittedly, both attendance and success are greater for the younger participants, ranging from the high 90th percentile to the mid 70th percentile for the twelve through fifteen age group respectively. Success is measured by police/court records, regular and formal feedback from probation, schools and the family. Also, most of the curricular modules have pre and post-tests to measure retention of key content. The programme is highly transportable to all communities and has been culturally adapted to isolated Northern Native reserves. Most facilities are accessed free of charge by agreement with city corporations and boards of education and volunteers are use extensively for one-to one assistance in programme delivery.

One rather obvious and salutary application of the Attendance Centre Model, conspicuously unavailable in the Ontario correctional armament, is the post-custodial model. This utilization of the model would provide the necessary and missing link between custody and the community. Assuming that most of the precipitating factors of an offense are neither addressed nor ameliorated by incarceration, the heightened structure and supervision of a post-release Attendance Centre would clearly provide a palpable mechanism to reduce the length of custody for young persons for whom continued committal would be of no further benefit and, coincidentally, would realize this hollow provision of the Young Offenders Act (Section 28 (4)). This option would further alleviate the morale problem created into the custodial arena. The process enriches the post-custodial reintegrative potential; decreases carceral over-crowding through unnecessarily long custodial terms. This latter benefit would translate into considerable financial savings and, for that reason alone, should be appealing to correctional bureaucrats.

The third major component of the COPS program is the Community Service Order (C.S.O.) programme. This programme again reflects the ideals of minimal yet appropriate intervention—skill building, self-esteem enhancing and community participation and responsibility. Participants, often referred by the youth courts as a separate item of disposition (Section 20 (1) (g)) or as a term of probation, are required to perform community service for charitable organizations, churches, retirement homes etc. All participants are individually and formally assessed and placements are made to reflect the strengths, interests and needs of each person. Intransigent youths may complete their community services as part of the Attendance Center programme. In these instances, difficult youth, under supervision of the regular Attendance Center staff, will complete woodworking, welding or craft projects for later donation to charitable services. Most participants, however, fully benefit from their regular community service placement and may continue on, as voluntary or salaried workers, when their court-ordered requirements are satisfied. With more adequate funding and a more sensible interpretation of the Young Offenders Act, the C.S.O. programme could be expanded to include a Personal Service (Section 20 (1) (f)) and a Fine Option component and could assume a pre-charge/voluntary or Alternative Measures format. These latter adaptions would reduce court costs and delays (responding to the Askov decision) and would better reflect the ideals of the Young Offenders Act. Since the Young Offenders Act increased the amount a young person may be fined by the court from $25.00 under the Juvenile Delinquent's Act to $1,000.00, the need for Fine Option Programmes, inflation notwithstanding, would appear to have increased commensurably.

TOWARDS SOCIAL JUSTICE AND COMMUNITY ALTERNATIVES

Ontario's implementation of the YOA, while uninspired and increasingly problematic, is not beyond saving at this juncture. Unquestionably, provincial authorities have placed their faith and finances into a reactive, uni-dimensional and traditionally "correctionalist" approach, eschewing a proactive, multi-dimensional and community-based approach. Bill C-12 (formerly Bill C-58) which represents a knee jerk response to public pressures, like much of the criminal justice legislation put forward by the Mulroney government, will have the effect of further increasing punishments especially facilitating waivers to adult court and increasing the length of custodial sentences. At the heart, if there is one in this sorry espisode in our "treatment" of youth, is a blatant disregard for the needs of youth and a further confirmation of the centrality of the prison as the central means of social control in our society (Foucault, 1977; O'Reilly-Fleming, 1992). Rather than reducing the criminality of the young, our current approach in Ontario contributes to the problem. Ontario is facing a critical point in its correctional history where massive investment in secure beds will not be fiscally possible, and reasonable alternatives such as the COPS programme will have to be developed. What is required, is no less than a complete reversal of the customary approach to child and youth corrections. The current system reflects Foucault's (1977: 255) view of delinquency, "The penitentiary and the delinquent are in a sense twin brothers." What then, are the chief changes that must underly a sensible revamping of the system?

First, "corrections" can no longer operate as a system separate and immune from other co-existing paradigms including mental health, education, medical and social services with which there is a considerable amount of overlap. Greater inter-ministerial collaboration is required to grapple with fundamental policy and practice issues. We suggest that a central independent body similar to the Ombudsmen's Office would provide the opportunity for the development of coordinated approaches. While a scaling down of custodial facilities is urgently needed, it must be accompanied by a parallel, preceding growth in community based alternatives to avoid the bailing out experience in mental health services in the wake of deinstitutionalization (Scull, 1970). These alternative services should provide a logical and sequential concatenation of interventions on a promotional, preventative, early interventionist, treatment and reintegrative continuum. A broader, macrosocial and collaborative concept of child and youth justice will invariably result in a less retributive and more properly "corrective" system. A narrow and vengeful ideology of retributive justice must be tempered by broader and more humane notions of a distributive and contributive ideal of justice—concepts which acknowledge and address basic economic and social inequalities and the need for children and youth to enjoy a sense of common identity with and belonging to the opportunities and entitlements of mainstream society. At the very least the foregoing discussion underscores the need for the establishment of an independently coordinated body with the vested authority to effect inter-ministerial collaboration. Others have argued that a new ministry should be created to deal exclusively with the welfare of youth and children.

In the final analysis, should common sense and social justice prevail, change towards more rational, needs oriented practice will not likely be the result of a well-considered, ethical reversal of policy and programmes. Rather, any significant change will more likely reflect the hard financial realities of a system that can no longer afford the consequences of a retributive ideology. A "system" which spends over ninety percent of its budget on institutionalizing young persons, a cost-inefficient and largely ineffective intervention, is itself dysfunctional. The longer the present course of the YOA is permitted to continue, the more the relationship between "corrections" and its etymology become circumstantial. Ontario has embarked upon a course of action which is, at once, ethically and financially irresponsible. In this regard, it would appear that the province's policy specialists are more dangerous than those young people to whom they impute this characteristic.

REFERENCES

Archambault, O. 1983. "Young Offenders Act: Philosophy and Principles" *Provincial Judges Journal*, 7 (2), 1-7, 20.

Bata, N. 1988. "The Young Offenders Act: A Legal Framework" in Hudson *et al* (eds.) *Justice and the Young Offender in Canada*. Toronto: Wall and Thompson, 11-37.

Ball, N. and Lilles, H. 1982. *The Young Offenders Act Annotated*. Don Mill, Ontario: Richard DeBoo.

Boyle, M. and Offord, D. 1988) "Prevalence of childhood disorders and resource allocation for child welfare and children's mental health services in Ontario." *Ontario Journal of Behavioral Science*, 20, 4, 374-388.

Canada, Department of Justice 1989. *Report of the Workshop on Alternatives to Custody*. Ottawa: Department of Justice.

Canadian Centre for Justice Statistics, Statistics Canada. 1984-89. *Youth Court Statistics. Preliminary Data*. 1984-85 (December 1988). 1985-86 (December 1988). 1986-87 (April 1989). 1987-88 (April 1989). 1988-89 (August 1989).

Canadian Centre for Justice Statistics, Statistics Canada. 1990. "Sentencing in Youth Courts, 1984-85 to 1988-89." *Juristat Service Bulletin* 10 (1): January.

Caputo, T. 1987. "The Young Offenders Act: Children's' Rights, Children's' Wrongs" in *Canadian Public Policy*, XIII: 2: 125-143.

Caputo, T. and Brakcen, D. 1988. "Custodial Dispositions and the Young Offenders Act." in J. Hudson et al (eds.) *Justice and the Young Offender in Canada*. Toronto: Wall and Thompson.

Caputo, T. 1991. "Pleasing Everybody Pleased Nobody: Changing the Juvenile Justice System in Canada" in L. Samualson and B. Schissel, (eds.) *Criminal Justice: Sentencing Issues and Reform*. Toronto: Garamond, 130-146.

Clark, B.M. 1985. *Diversion: A Less Restrictive Alternative*. Toronto: Metro Children's Advisory Group.

Clark, B.M. 1987. *Post-Release Attendance Centres: The Missing Link Between Custody and Community*. Project Description to The Ontario Ministry of Community and Social Services.

Clark, B.M. 1988. *Making It or Breaking It: The Community and Alternatives.* Toronto: Ontario Social Development Council.

Clark, B.M. and Clark, D.H. *Crime Prevention Services for Indian Youth: The Native Options Programme.* 1987. Paper presented to the 13th Annual Canadian Indian Teacher's Education Programme. Walpole Island, Ontario.

Clark, D.H. 1986. *The North Caribou Lake Band Juvenile Attendance Centre Programme: A Project Proposal and Description.* Ottawa: Ministry of the Solicitor General.

Clark, D.H. *North Caribou Lake Band Juvenile Attendance Centre Programme* Ministry of Solgen, 1986.

Coflin, J. 1988. "The Federal Government's Role in Implementing the Young Offenders Act." in J. Hudson *et al* (eds.) *Justice and the Young Offender in Canada.* Toronto: Wall and Thompson, 37-51.

Cohen, S. 1985. *Visions of Social Control.* London: Polity Press.

Conrad, J. 1985. *The Dangerous and the Endangered.* Toronto: Lexington Books.

Corrado, R. and Markwart, A.E. 1988. "The Prices of Rights and Responsibilities: An Examination of the Impacts of the Young Offender Act in British Columbia. *Canadian Journal of Family Law* 7: 93-115.

Currie, D. 1986. "The Transformation of Juvenile Justice in Canada: A Study of Bill C-61" in B. MacLean (ed.) *The Political Economy of Crime.* Scarborough: Prentice-Hall.

Davis, S. *Attendance Centres: An Old Concept, A New Idea.* Ontario Ministry of Correctional Services, Community Programmes Support Services, 1981.

Doob, A. and Beaulieu, L. 1991. "Variation in the exercise of judicial discretion with young offenders."*The Canadian Journal of Criminology* 34 (1): 35-50.

Doob, T. 1992. "Trends in the use of custodial dispositions for young offenders" in *The Canadian Journal of Criminology,* 34, 1: 75-84.

Foucault, M. 1977. *Discipline and Punish: The Birth of the Prison.* New York: Random House.

Hackler, J. "The Impact of the Young Offenders Act" in *The Canadian Journal of Criminology* 29, 2: 205-209.

Gendreau, P. 1987. "Revivification of Rehabilitation: Evidence from the 1980s" *Justice Quarterly,* Vol. 4, 3.

Hagan, J. and Leon, J. 1977. "Rediscovering delinquency: Social history, history, political ideology and the sociology of law" in *American Sociological Review*, 42, 587-598.

Havemann, P. 1986. "From Child to Child Blaming: The Political Economy of the Young Offenders Act" in S. Brickey and E. Comack (eds.) *The social Basis of Law.* Toronto: Garamond.

House of Commons Debates. 1981. 1st Session, 32 Parliament, March 13-April 21, 9307-9323.

Hudson, J., Hornick, J. and Burrows, B. (eds.) 1988) *Justice and the Young Offender in Canada.* Toronto: Wall and Thompson.

Jaffe, P.G. 1985. "Misconceptions About the Young Offenders Act: The Truth Behind the "Leniency Hype." *Ontario Lawyers Weekly.* October 1985.

John Howard Society of Ontario. 1989. *Reform Bulletin.* Ontario: John Howard Society.

Kenewell, J *et al* 1991. "Young offenders" in F.R. Barnhorst and Johnson, L. (eds.) *The State of the Child in Ontario.* Toronto: Oxford.

Koenig, D.J. *Do Police Cause Crime? Police Activity, Police Strength and Crime Rates.* Published by Canadian Police College, P.O. Box 8900, Ottawa, Canada, Ministry of Supply and Services Canada, 1991.

Leon, J.S. "The development of Canadian juvenile justice: A background for reform." *Osgoode Hall Law Journal*, 15 (1), 71-106.

Leschied, A.W. and Gendreau, P. 1986. "The Declining Role of Rehabilitation in Canadian Juvenile Justice: Implication of the Underlying theory in the Young Offenders Act." *The Canadian Journal of Criminology* 28, 3: 315-322.

Leschied, A.W. and Jaffe, P.G. 1985. *Implications of the Young Offenders Act in Modifying the Juvenile Justice System: Some Early Trends.* London: Family Court Clinic.

Leschied, A.W. and Jaffe, P.G. 1987. "Impact of the Young Offenders Act on Court Dispositions: A Comparative Analysis." *Canadian Journal of Criminology* 29, 4: 421-430.

Leschied, A.W. and Wilson, S.K. 1988. "Criminal Liability of Children Under Twelve: A Concern for Child Welfare, Juvenile Justice, or Both?" *The Canadian Journal of Criminology*, 30 (1), 17-29.

Leschied, A. and Jaffe, P.G. 1989. "Implementing the Young Offenders Act in Ontario" in J. Hudson *et al* (eds.) *Justice and the Young Offender in Canada*. Toronto: Wall and Thompson, 65-79.

Leschied, A., Austin, G. and Jaffe, P.G. 1989. *Toward the Development of Risk Assessment in Young Offender Recidivism: A Necessary Concept in Juvenile Justice Policy*. London: Family Court Clinic.

Lundmann, R.J. 1984. *Prevention and Control of Juvenile Delinquency*. New York: Oxford University Press.

MacLean's Article Law: "The Criminally Young" May 13, 1985.

Markwart, A.E. and Corrado, R. 1989. "Is the Young Offenders Act More Punitive?" in L.A. Beaulieu (ed.) *Young Offender Dispositions: Perspectives on Principles and Practices*. Toronto: Wall and Thompson.

Matza, D. 1964. *Delinquency and Drift*. New York: John Wiley and sons.

Ministry of Correctional Services Ontario. 1990. *Annual Report*. Toronto: Ministry of Correctional Services.

O'Brien, D. 1984. "Juvenile Diversion: An Issues Perspective from the Atlantic Provinces" *Canadian Journal of Criminology* 26, 2: 217-230.

O'Reilly-Fleming 1992. "The Dark Factory": Prison Conditions, Life Imprisonment and The Politics of Release" in K. McCormick and L. Visano (eds.) *Canadian Penology: Advanced Perspectives and Research*. Toronto: Canadian Scholar's Press.

Palmer, T., and Lewis, R. "A Differential Approach to Juvenile Diversion" in *Journal of Research in Crime and Delinquency*, July, 1980, p. 209.

Platt, P. 1989. *Young Offenders Law in Canada*. Toronto: Butterworths.

Platt, T. 1969. *The Child Savers*. Chicago: Chicago University Press.

Ratner, R. and McMullan, J. 1985. "Social Control and the Rise of the Exceptional State in Britain, the United States and Canada" in T. Fleming (ed.) *The New Criminology's in Canada: State, Crime and Control*. Toronto: Oxford University Press, 185-206.

Reid, S and Reitsma-Street, M. 1984. "Assumptions and implication of the new Canadian legislation for young offenders" *Canadian Criminology Forum*, 7: 1-19.

Report of the Workshop of Alternatives to Custody, Department of Justice, Canada Ottawa (Workshop held June 18-21, 1991, Winnipeg, Manitoba).

Scull, A. 1970. *Decarceration*. Englewood Cliffs: Prentice Hall.

Smith-Gadacz, T. 1983. "Speak No Evil, Hear No Evil?: Juveniles and the Language of the Law" in T. Fleming and L. Visano (eds.) *Deviant Designation: Crime, Law and Deviance in Canada*. Toronto: Butterworths, 351-374.

Thornton, W.E., Voight, L. and Doerner, W. *Delinquency and Justice*. Random House, 1982. p. 432. (Reference to Definition of Prevention by Thomas Phelps.)

Trepanier, J. 1989. "Principles and Goals Guiding the Choice of Dispositions Under the YOA." in L.A. Beaulieu (ed.) *Young Offender Dispositions: Perspectives on Principles and Practices*. Toronto: Wall and Thompson.

Wardell, W. 1986. "The Young Offenders Act: A Report Card 1984-1986" in D. Currie and B. MacLean (eds.) *The Administration of Justice*. Saskatoon: Social Science Research Unit.

West, G. 1984. *Young Offenders and the State: A Canadian Perspective*. Toronto: Butterworths.

Legislation

An Act to Amend the Young Offenders Act, the Criminal code, the Penitentiary Act and the Prisons and Reformatories Act (Bill C-106), Statutes of Canada 1984-85-86, c. 32.

Child and Family Services Act, Statutes of Ontatio 1984, c. 55.

Bill C-61, Juvenile Delinquents Act Revised Statutes of Canada, 1970, c.J-3.

Bill C-192, an Act Respecting Young Offenders and to Repeal the Juvenile Delinquents Act, 3d Sess., 28th Parliament., 1970-71-72.

Cases Cited

R. v. Askov *et al*. 1988. Canadian Criminal Cases 37 (3d), 289.

R. v. Brian P. 1987. 2 Weekly Criminal Bulletin (2d), 121 (Ont. Prov. Ct. Fam. Div.).

R. v. Sheldon S. 1986. 17 Weekly Criminal Bulletin 399 (Ont. Prov. Ct.), Bean, J.

CHAPTER 13
A Wilderness Experiential Program As An Alternative For Probationers: An Evaluation

JOHN WINTERDYK[1]
RONALD ROESCH

While a considerable amount of literature has been published about experiential education programs such as Outward Bound,[38] several issues remain ambiguous. In particular, the efficiency and effectiveness of such programs are not clear, and more specifically, the factors, components and/or tasks which are possibly causally related to any positive benefits which might be experienced are unknown. This situation may exist because the theories and techniques employed in the area have been as varied and vague as the dependent measures used to determine program "success". An additional problem involved the fact that the research has been primarily problem oriented rather than concerned with identifying positive outcome factors.[13] This orientation has been very evident in experiential programs employed in juvenile corrections.[4,8,9,11,18,21,24]

This article presents the results of an evaluation of an experiential wilderness program, based on the Outward Bound philosophy, employed for a group of juvenile male probationers, in eastern Canada.

Because there are now an estimated 100 plus adaptive wilderness programs for "treating" delinquent youths in North America.[6,7,8,19,27,29,43] but less than a dozen official evaluations available in Canada.[6,7,8,19] and even fewer adequate ones,[43] it is felt that a well controlled study of the effects of these programs was important.

While the formal and impressionistic evaluations of adapted Outward

Bound programs collectively suggest that empirically and observationally the goals of such programs offer a "viable" therapeutic environment for an assortment of clientele, the majority were plagued with design and measures, limited or no follow-ups for psychological and/or, sociological variables such as recidivism, and a lack of clear definition of independent and dependent variables. As Arthur[4] noted, however, there is an intuitive appeal about wilderness programs—fresh air, situated away from trouble and good clean fun—and since the majority of reports still suggest that the outdoor wilderness experience can serve as a potential milieu[35] for youths (and adults) of various types, we must attempt to improve our evaluation designs and procedures before we make any decisions about the true status of the alternative.

The evaluation of the 21-day A.C.T.I.O.N. (Accepting Challenge Through Interaction with Others and Nature) program was developed with many of the above criticisms in mind. While the present evaluation does not purport to be the definitive work in its field it has attempted to address a number of the above shortcomings.

LITERATURE OVERVIEW[2]

As previously noted, evaluative literature pertaining specifically to adaptive wilderness programs for delinquency intervention is very limited in quality.[21,43,45] Nevertheless wilderness programs adapted for treating special populations have received considerable recognition and coverage in the media, both in terms of sensational wilderness experiences, and more important, in terms of their psychological and behavioral benefits. Some of the benefits have included promoting social acceptance,[39] improving self-concept,[27] reducing recidivism,[21,24,29] and for some, improving a number of interpersonal skills.[5,6,35]

The programs, in general, contribute their course effects to the type of environmental setting provided which: (a) offers both physical and mental challenges as well as adventure, and (b) offers an experiential education process which is directed to promoting personal growth and identity.[16] Individual growth is attempted by impelling (willing) participants to overcome a series of unique problem-solving tasks, with few artifacts, in a natural environment, in a struggle for survival. Uniquely, the programs tend to emphasize high impact and stress-directed involvement which demands that the individual excel beyond what they believed they were capable.[11] This would appear appropriate for juveniles, as one of the underlying assumptions of the present study, and similar programs, was that by participating, the delinquents' self-concept and self-esteem would improve and they would adopt more socially acceptable mode of behavior, such as keeping out of further trouble.[30]

Since 1968, some of the different adaptive programs that have been instituted have been for juvenile offenders:[21,24,30,33,44] while others have been used for drug users:[41] as an alternative for young adult offenders:[10,12,40] as an alternative to traditional education:[9] as a therapeutic modality for physically and mentally handicapped,[7,35] and for other assorted groups which have a need to learn through experience and co-operation with others.[36]

A.C.T.I.O.N. 1979

The objectives of the A.C.T.I.O.N. project, operating out of Ontario and supported jointly by Experience '79 for summer students and the Kitchener, Ontario, Probation Office, as presented in the 1979 proposal by Mazur[31] were as follows:

1. The main purpose was to improve the probationers' self-esteem and self-concept by providing innovative, challenging and adventurous activities (i.e. backpacking, canoeing, rockclimbing, etc.). In developing a pride in the youths' new abilities it was hoped that he might carry them back into the community.

2. To develop an improved relationship with his peers based on the major philosophy of the program—teamwork.

3. To help the boys accept and understand the role of authority figures. During the twenty-one day program, the probationers would be interacting with their instructors on a 24-hour basis.

4. To help delinquent adolescents be more self-reliant. The youths were required to participate in all activities, and throughout the session were taught various survival and technical skills.

5. To offer a recreation program for youths living in an urban environment.

As can be observed from the literature review, the objectives are not that much different from those expressed by similar programs for similar populations.[16, 21, 24, 26]

General Purpose of the Evaluation

Based on previous research and theories,[4,23,24,35] dealing with adapted wilderness adventure-therapeutic programs for adjudicated juveniles, ten stochastic and contingent propositions were formulated. In general, the propositions stated that both groups, the experimental and control, would be relatively homogeneous on the pre-measures. Following exposure of the experimental group to the A.C.T.I.O.N. program, however, there would be significant differences between the two groups on the dependent measures used at the post data collection period and at the 4 to 6 month follow-up interval.

The main theorem tested was that, other things being equal, the A.C.T.I.O.N. program would serve to show that it is a viable alternative to placing juveniles on probation.

METHOD

Participants

The participants were sixty adjudicated males and between the ages 13-16, who were placed on juvenile probation for minor first (official) offenses. They were randomly divided into two equal groups of thirty. This was done after they had expressed a willingness to participate and had been initially screened to control for age, sex, type of prior offense(s), school and family background, as well as for general emotional and physical stability.

The experimental group was, in turn, subdivided into three groups of ten boys, according to which session was most convenient for them to attend. All participants were required to complete a number of forms including medical, parental consent, as well as a document expressing their knowledge of requirements and willingness to participate for the complete session.

Staff

The four male staff were hired jointly through Experience '79 and the probation office as outdoor recreation officers. They were all university or college students ranging in age from 21 to 25.

Before the actual sessions began, all staff were required to undergo a strenuous two-week training period at DARE, the location site for the project. The training sessions allowed the staff to become familiar with their responsibilities, sharpen their skills, learn how to efficiently conduct the evaluation reports, as well as provide them an opportunity to become acquainted with one another.

Measures

Table 1 contains a summary of the dependent measures. Selection of the measures was based on previous literature[17,24,35,39] and on the limitations noted in the studies reviewed. They included two psychometric measures (Jesness Inventory—JI and an adapted Peirs-Harris Self-Esteem Measure— (SEM), a number of self-report inventories completed by the staff, probation officers, participants' parents, and the juveniles themselves. Two of the more unique measures introduced were the multi-level recidivism indicators and the program evaluation forms completed by the A.C.T.I.O.N. participants. The decision for using a multi-level recidivism indicator was primarily based on the work of Waldo and Chircos[42] and Moberg and Ericson.[32] The participant evaluation was considered unique because it has never knowingly been employed in such programs before and is considered to be an interesting positive outcome measure.

Table 1
Research Design for Program A.C.T.I.O.N. 1979

	Pre		Experimental Conditions				Post	Follow-up
Experimental:	O_1	O_2	O_3	O_4	O_5	O_6	O_7	O_8
Control:	O_1						O_7	O_8

Measurement(s)			Observation(s)	
1. Self-esteem measure		O_1	O_7	O_8
2. Jesness Inventory		O_1	O_7	O_8
3. Background Information Probationer	O_1			
4. Instructors' Rating Form	O_2	O_3	O_4	O_5
5. A.C.T.I.O.N. self-report questionnaire	O_6			
6. Probation Officer's Response Inventory	O_7			
7. Parent/Guardian Life Domain Survey	O_8			
8. Participant's follow-up questionnaire	O_8			

Design and Data Analyses

The design for analysis represents a pretest-posttest control group design with a 4 to 6 months follow-up period. For a graphic illustration of the design and testing procedures refer to Table 1.

While no design is ever fault-proof, the present design was considered to be methodologically and theoretically more sound than the majority of previous studies in the field. The statistical breakdown of the data involved two modes of emphasis: 1) to aid in making reliable inferences from any significant observations. The standardized measures were subjected to various statistical techniques such as analysis of variance, analysis of covariance, t-tests and factor analysis as were deemed appropriate. The self-report data were meant to provide a new perspective for program evaluation—a look at identifying positive outcome factors. Therefore, the self-report data were meant to possibly: 1) identify certain variables/factors both for participants and the wilderness program which would account for the success/failure of the youths, and 2) identify variables that might be considered in the future evaluations for similar alternative programs.

RESULTS

The statistical analyses in the post and follow-up periods on the standardized personality measures did not lend conclusive support to the primary proposition that the A.C.T.I.O.N. program could serve as a viable alternative to probation. Conversely, however, the descriptive reports and self-report questionnaires along with the narrative comments received from the parents, and staff as well as the positive changes on two of the Jesness Inventory subscales in the post data, do lend support to the proposition that the A.C.T.I.O.N. program did have a short term impact on the probationers in a number of areas identified in the program's objectives. As indicated in Table 2, there were improved changes in peer relationships, self-confidence, and relationships with authority figures and parents.

Table 2
Incidence of Problems and Change
During Probation Period

Experimental/Control Group

Problem Areas	Some Improvement	No Consistent Trend or Change	Some Deterioration	Not a Problem
Peer Relationship	60/43	27/47	0/7	13/3
Self-confidence	57/20	17/35	5/10	19/35
Relationship with Authority	40/23	40/53	7/13	13/10

Table 3 shows that three sub-scales of the JI (alienation, social anxiety, and immaturity) showed significant variation (analysis of covariance. $p < .05$) at the post testing: but all differences disappeared at the follow-up period. The adapted Self-Esteem Measure by Peirs and Harris showed no significant variations on any of the scales at any of the testing periods.

Table 3
Analysis of Covariance on Jesness Inventory
for Pre-post Data: Main Effect Explained

Scale	Mean Square	F Value (df=1)	Signif. Level of F
Social-Maladjustment	6.96	.22	.63
Value Orientation	9.52	.49	.48
Immaturity	21.03	1.75	.19
Autism	0.42	.04	.82
Alienation	114.74	9.55	.003
Manifest Aggression	17.47	2.15	.14
Withdrawal	3.45	.60	.44
Social Anxiety	53.42	6.63	.01
Repression	0.82	.22	.63
Denial	6.46	.87	.35

The detailed descriptive analyses presented in Table 2 combined with the results in Table 3 strongly suggest that the experimental group's initial perception of the wilderness program was very positive. In addition, the staff felt that given the areas of evaluation the boys, in general, improved significantly (p < .01) throughout the program. The areas evaluated by the staff included effort, maturity, leadership, competence, physical ability, initiative, environmental awareness, determination, and peer and staff relationships. Similar support of the program's effectiveness also came from the parents and to a lesser degree from the supporting probation officers. These results, however, were not statistically significant.

The results suggest that those involved in the wilderness experience were experiencing something more positive and beneficial than the controls.

The Student Rating Form completed by the A.C.T.I.O.N. staff lends further objective support to the main theorem, in that the staff were able to predict with 90% accuracy whether a student would recidivate (be legally apprehended) within a short period of leaving the program (before the follow-up).

Finally, while the personality inventories provided inconclusive results, the recidivism date provided some very interesting observations that lend support to the self-report questionnaires. As indicated in Table 4, both groups had a reconviction rate of approximately 20 percent. The types of offenses committed, however, by each group varied substantially from a subjective perspective. A qualitative examination reveals that the experimental group, although not significantly (perhaps because of the small sample size), committed less "severe" offenses, and given the number of offenses committed by either group had fewer charges completed (5 vs. 7).[3]

DISCUSSION

This study was intended to provide a controlled systematic evaluation and comparison of the therapeutic effect of a wilderness adventure experience as compared to probation for adjudicated male juveniles. Results from the study were very mixed. The psychometric measures provided inconclusive support for program effectiveness. This was in contradiction to similar studies using the similar measures which observed distinctive changes at the post periods.[21, 24] The self-report questionnaires, recidivism data and field behavior reports by the A.C.T.I.O.N. staff suggest, however, that the program accomplished some of its primary objectives such as improvement in self-confidence, better peer relationships and a reduction in the severity and frequency of delinquency. In addition, the participants in the wilderness program clearly found their course exciting, educational and challenging in terms of their immediate and follow-up evaluation of it. However, it was observed that any initial changes observed at the post period appeared to "wear off" at the 4 to 6 month follow-up period. While most articles reviewed failed to include any substantial follow-ups, or use of control groups, and few of them used more than one dependent measure, support for the present results have come from Kaplan[23] and Kelly.[25]

Table 4
Kendall Correlation Coefficient for Instructors' Rating Forms between Testing Interval Scores

Scale	Time Intervals	Scale	Time Intervals
Effort	1-2** 1-3** 1-4** 2-3** 2-4** 3-4**	Initiative	1-2** 1-3** 1-4** 2-3** 2-4** 3-4**
Maturity	1-2** 1-3** 1-4** 2-3** 2-4** 3-4**	Environmental Awareness	1-2** 1-3** 1-4** 2-3** 2-4** 3-4**
Physical Ability	1-2** 1-3** 1-4** 2-3** 2-4** 3-4**	Staff Relationship	1-2** 1-3** 1-4** 2-3** 2-4** 3-4**

Note: Kendall Correlation Coefficient is best for N< 30 and when many have tied scores.

Note: Time intervls
1. day five of program
2. day ten of program
3. day fifteen of program
4. day twenty (final evaluation)

**p < .001
*p < .01

Both articles note that the effects "eroded before the onslaught of negative environmental pressure...."[23] Based on the observations of the present study the results concur with those of Kaplan and Kelly in that "perhaps some of the youngsters might have been helped by community based Outward Bound adaptive programs serving to reinforce and consolidate the gains achieved...."[25] This observation also suggests that perhaps similar single programs should consider comparable or other community follow-up programs, as most appear ineffective by themselves.[37]

Success in our lives depends on the ability to make appropriate choices. Yet (adolescents) make few decisions of any importance and receive no training in decision making or in the implementation and reassessment cycle which constitutes the basic growth pattern.[15]

The above quote complements a further inference drawn from the results. While it may be granted that a wilderness experiential program may be an interesting and viable alternative in and of itself, it is necessary to go one step further if field behavior reports, for example, are going to serve as a reliable evaluative tool. There is a strong need for process evaluations of programs. It is important to understand whether a program succeeds or fails, and why. In the case of the A.C.T.I.O.N. program, it may have been the level of staff competency,[16] the activities, program length and/or stress level,[26] type of clientele,[24] general administration,[34] or the careful matching of participants.[21] As noted at the beginning of this paper there is a need for accountability and an emphasis on the process components is a positive move in that direction.

Finally, the results endorse the need for multi-level measures and the need for the use of a range of measures.[17,31] As Golins[17] points out, contrary to Hackler's[20] and Partington's[34] skepticisms about evaluations and wilderness programs, "we need not join the legions of skeptics who are given over a priori to pessimism when it comes to finding solutions to criminality (delinquency). Education represents a partial, tenable solution."

ENDNOTES

1. This paper is based on the first author's Masters thesis completed at Simon Fraser University. Requests for reprints should be directed to Mr. Winterdyk, the senior author.

2. For readers who are not familiar with the origin and history of experiential wilderness programs the author recommends Hogen,[22] Kelly and Baer,[24] Lingle[28] or Rice[16] for a brief capsulization.

3. The decision for a subjective assessment of the degree of severity was based, in part, on the reports by Gendreau and Leipciger,[14] and Moberg and Ericson[32] who note that to date an objective index of delinquency recidivism is stll very crude and of dubious utility.

4. Arthur, M. "The survival experience as therapy: An appraisal". *Journal of Leisurability. 2.* 1975.

5. Baer, D.J., P.T. Jacobs, and F.E. Carr. "Instructors' rating of delinquents after Outward Bound survival training and their subsequent recidivism." *Psychological Reports. 36.* 1975.

6. Behar, L. and D. Stephens. "Wilderness camping: An evaluation of a residential training program for emotionally disturbed children." *American Journal of Orthopsychiatry. 48* (4). 1978.

7. Berube, P. "Survival camping: A therapeutic modality". *Journal of Leisurability. 2* (1). 1975

8. Birkenmayer, A. and M. Polonoski. *The community adjustment of DARE graduates: 1971-1972.* Ontario Ministry of Correctional Services, 1973.

9. Brown, W.K. and B.F. Simpson. "Group and individual growth through the out-of-doors." *American Journal of Corrections. 39* (6). 1977.

10. Casapari, P. and B. Rotts. *Adventure programming in an adult prison setting.* Unpublished paper presented at the Eighth Annual Conference for the Association of Experiential Education. Glorieta. New Mexico. 1980.

11. Cave, S. and E. Rapoport. *Wilderness Experiences: Preventive Techniques and crises intervention.* Unpublished doctoral dissertation

presented at the Eighth Annual Conference for the Association for Experiential Education. Glorieta. New Mexico. Oct. 22, 1980.

12. Dewdney, M.S. and M.H. Miner. "Evaluating correctional programs: Methodology in theory and in practice. *Australian and New Zealand Journal of Criminology.* 8 (3) 1975.

13. Gable, R.J. and W.K. Brown. "Positive outcomes: A new approach to delinquency." *Juvenile and Family Court Journal.* Aug. 1978.

14. Gendreau, P. and M. Leipeiger. "The development of a recidivism measure and its application in Ontario." *Canadian Journal of Corrections.* 1978.

15. Gibbons, M. "Walkabout: Searching for the right passage from childhood and school." *Phi Delta Kappan.* May 1974.

16. Golins, G.L. "A resource document on design and managing Outward Bound courses for delinquent populations." In *Outward Bound in corrections: A compilation.* Colorado Outward Bound School. 1975.

17. Golins, G.L. *Utilizing adventure education to rehabilitate juvenile delinquents.* Colorado Outward Bound School. Denver, Colorado, 1979.

18. Gonzales, M.R. "Organized camping: A therapeutic tool for the juvenile delinquent." *Therapeutic Recreation Journal.* 6. 1972.

19. Grant, R.J. *An assessment of a juvenile wilderness correction program.* M.A. Thesis. Dept. of Physical Education. Edmonton, Alberta. Spring, 1979.

20. Hackler, J.C. *The prevention of youthful crime: The great stumble forward.* Toronto. Methuen Publications. 1978.

21. Hileman, M.A. *An evaluation of an environmental stress challenge program on the social attitudes and recidivism behavior of male delinquent youth.* Unpublished M.A. Thesis. Southern Illinois University-C. 1979.

22. Hogan, J.M. *Impelled into experience.* Wakefield. Yorkshire: Educational Productions Ltd. 1968.

23. Kaplan, L. "Outward Bound: A treatment modality unexplored by the social work profession." *Child Welfare. 1.* 1979.

24. Kelly, F.J. and D.J. Baer. *Outward Bound Schools as an alternative to institutionalization for adolescent delinquent boys.* U.S. Dept. of

Health. Education and Welfare. Office of Education. Massachusetts. 1968.

25. Kelly, F.J. *Outward Bound and delinquency: A ten year experience.* Unpublished paper presneted at the Conference on Experiential Education. Estes Park. Colorado. Oct. 1974.

26. Kimball, R.O. *Wilderness experience program: Final evaluation report.* Santa Fe: State of New Mexico Forensic System. 1979.

27. Lemire, Jean-Marc, "Changes in self-concept and perception of others among participants of an Outward Bound program." *Journal of Leisurability. 4* (2). 1975.

28. Lingel, K.I. "Alternatives for youth-at-risk." *Camp Magazine.* May 1980.

29. Matheson, M.A. "Search and leadership training for young offenders at Lakeview forest camp." *Canadian Journal of Corrections, 8.* 1966.

30. Mazur, R.S. *Evaluation of the summer wilderness adventure program A.C.T.I.O.N. 1978.* Unpublished report for the Ontario Probation and Aftercare Services. 1978.

31. Mazur, R.S. *Proposal for summer wilderness adventure program A.C.T.I.O.N.* Kitchener Probation and Aftercare Services. 1979.

32. Moberg, D.O. and Ericson, R.C. "A new recidivism outcome index." *Federal Probation 36.* 50-57. 1972.

33. Oates, M.L.B. Jr. *Project Sea Adventure: 1980-1981.* Unpublished manual and evaluation. Prince Rupert Juvenile Probation Service.

34. Partington, J. "Project WILD: A wilderness learning experience for high delinquent risk youth." *Journal of Leisurability. 4* (2). 1977.

35. Porter, W. *The development and evaluation of a therapeutic wilderness program for problem youth.* Unpublished M.S. Thesis. University of Denver. 1975.

36. Rice, B. "Going to the mountain." *Psychology Today. 13* (7). 1979.

37. Schmidt, P. and A.D. Witte. "Evaluating correctional programs: Models of criminal recidivism and an illustration of their use." *Evaluation Review. 4* (5). 1980.

38. Shore, A. *Outward Bound.* Outward Bound Inc., New York, New York. 1977.

39. Smith, M.L., R. Gabriel, J. Schott, and W.L. Padia. *Evaluation of the effects of Outward Bound.* Unpublished report. School of Education. University of Colorado. Boulder. 1975.

40. Thorvaldson, S.A. and M.A. Matheson. *The Boulder Bay Experiment.* Criminal Justice Planning and Research Unit. Dept. of the Attorney-General. B.C. 1978.

41. Ventura, M.A. and Dundon, M. "A challenging experience in canoeing and camping as a tool in approaching the drug problem." *Journal of Drug Education. 4.* 1974.

42. Waldo, G.P. and T.G. Chiricos. "Work release and recidivism." *Evaluation Quarterly. 1* (1). 1977.

43. Wichmann, T.F. *Evaluation of the Outward Bound model as delinquency intervention.* Unpublished paper. Southern Illinois University C. 1979.

44. Willman, J.R. Jr. and R.Y.F. Chun. "Homeward Bound: An alternative to the institutionalization of adjudicated juvenile offenders." *Federal Probation.* 1973.

45. Winterdyk, J.A. *A wilderness adventure program as an alternative for juvenile probationers: An evaluation.* Unpublished M.A. Thesis. Depts. of Criminology. Simon Fraser University. 1980.

CHAPTER 14
Variation in the Exercise of Judicial Discretion with Young Offenders[1]

ANTHONY N. DOOB
LUCIEN A. BEAULIEU

Forty-three judges from across Canada each of whom was experienced in hearing Young Offenders Act cases read and responded to two written descriptions of cases involving a total of four young offenders After reading each case each judge recommended sentences under S 20(1) of the YOA for each of the four offenders They also indicated what purposes they were trying to accomplish with their disposition as well as what aspects of the case they found to be important in making their decision regarding disposition.

There was a good deal of variability in the dispositions recommended for each of the four young persons Judges prioritized the purposes they were trying to accomplish with the disposition in quite different ways. Most judges indicated that most of the purposes or factors of the case were important for each offender

The variability shown by the judges in how they approached the question of disposition reflects, we think variability inherent in the Young Offenders Act but not necessarily envisaged by its framers. Though judges appeared to have been thoughtful and principled in the manner in which they arrived at their dispositions—each of which individually could probably be justified under the Act—the results as a whole suggest that the lack of overall policy for dispositions under the Young Offenders Act leads inevitably to widely disparate treatment of similar young offenders convicted of the identical offence.

In recent years, it seems that much of the focus on the *Young Offenders Act* (YOA) has been on the question of the severity of dispositions. As a result of a very small number of cases, a substantial amount of public concern and legislative energy has focused on the maximum penalty for those convicted of murder. Quite different concerns have been expressed by another group of observers: that there may be an increasing number or proportion of young offenders receiving custodial sentences (see, for example, Corrado and Markwart 1988; Markwart and Corrado 1989; Leschied and Jaffe 1987).

Recently, the nature of the concern about young offender dispositions seems to have shifted somewhat In 1987, a conference on the *Young Offenders Act* was held (Ontario Social Development Council 1988). Although some of those attending the conference reported "substantial increases in the absolute number and duration of custodial dispositions since the proclamation of the Act" (Ontario Social Development Council 1988:25), considerable emphasis in various parts of the conference report was put on policies or principles. For example, the report notes that "There remain a number of... questions fundamental to sentencing policy [including]... whether adult sentencing principles... are being applied in the sentencing of young people and if so, whether this is appropriate? What is the major purpose behind the sentencing of young offenders? Are youth court judges in need of specific sentencing principles?" (Ontario Social Development Council 1988:95).

A book published in 1989 (Beaulieu 1989) focused largely on principles in dealing with dispositions (bail, sentencing, transfer, etc.) for young offenders. A number of the individual papers in that volume identified issues which, when translated into practice, might be seen as matters of concern with respect to *principles* for determining dispositions.

Trépanier, for example, notes that judges must choose which of a number of different goals to emphasize in a given case. However, he points out that "There is no restricting rule" on the matter of how a judge chooses "to assign one or several goals to a given decision" (Trépanier 1989:63). In choosing goals, Trépanier suggests that "a judge is not likely to resort to the same goals in all cases" (1989:64). Finally, he notes the importance of ensuring "that the goals selected must be attainable in a realistic way." Such an analysis, however, emphasizes the manner in which decisions are individually tailored to the case: where different tailors may well select different materials (perhaps from different sets of choices) to arrive at quite different end results. The decision process in each case may be defensible in terms of the application of a set of principles to the case. However, different judges might well arrive at equally defensible, but dramatically different, dispositions.

The idea of giving judges more complete guidance on principles and actual sentences has, of course, been raised with respect to adults in the Report of the Canadian Sentencing Commission (Canada 1987). That report recommended an explicit set of principles be established by Parliament to guide the sentencing of adult offenders. In addition, judges would have presumptive guidelines available for all offences—where a presumptive range of appropriate sentences would be offered and within which judges would be expected to sentence unless there were some principled and defensible reason to do otherwise.

One of the reasons that the Canadian Sentencing Commission offered for moving in this direction was that courts of appeal had not (and, it suggested, could not and should not) taken a more active legislative role in developing explicit guidance to judges. With the advent of the *Young Offenders Act*, some expected that courts of appeal in Canada would fill the breach left by an Act which gives judges relatively little guidance. Unfortunately, thus far, careful analysis of court of appeal decisions suggests that this has not happened. As Alan Young points out,

> (It is) difficult to distinguish between our treatment of adult and young offenders except on the basis that the duration of sentence is usually less in the case of the youth. However, the manner of arriving at the applicable sentence appears no different in youth and adult court, as the judges appear to be guided by the same considerations and principles. The appellate courts have not successfully developed sentencing principles that promote a unique identity for juvenile justice. The special needs of young people are constantly alluded to but the courts appear uncertain as to what exactly these special needs are and how it is that these special needs can be translated into a distinct penal philosophy (Young 1989: 104).

This is not a position held only by observers of the court of appeal. Doob (1989) quotes an anonymous member of one provincial court of appeal as saying that he doesn't believe that

> "courts of appeal are able to prioritize the principles (of dispositions), without making some probably unwarranted assumptions about legislative purpose. The philosophical ambivalence seems to have been a choice of Parliament which might indicate an intention to leave

> flexibility for the individual case, or, a cynic might say (an intention)
> to dump the problems on the courts. At the moment, the courts
> seem to have assumed the former. (Doob 1989:203)"

Such a situation—where a clear set of principles designed to guide decision makers does not exist and where appeal courts have not adequately filled the policy gap—appears, then, to be the same for youth as it is for adults. Under the *Criminal Code*, then, we know what the impact of this problem is for adults: two offenders whose relevant characteristics are similar and who have committed similar offences under similar circumstances often get dramatically different sentences. The difference occurs not because of the perversity of judges, but rather because judges weigh the different goals of sentencing differently and go about attempting to achieve these goals in different ways (Palys 1982; Palys and Divorski 1984).

The data on unwarranted disparity in adult sentencing has been summarized elsewhere (Canada 1987) and need not be repeated here. However, studies such as that of Palys and Divorski (1984), where judges are asked to indicate the dispositions they would give in hypothetical cases, have not been reported for youth under the *Young Offenders Act*. This study is designed to fill this gap. It represents an attempt to understand more fully how different judges would sentence the same young offenders. It also attempts to contribute to an understanding of the purposes judges are trying to fill in handing down dispositions to young offenders.

METHOD

Approximately sixty youth court judges from all regions of Canada were sent a booklet (in the apparently more appropriate of the two official languages) containing four hypothetical cases—two involving dispositions under S. 20(1) of the Young Offenders Act, one involving bail, and one involving transfer to adult court.[2] All judges in the sample heard Young Offenders Act cases, though, depending on the province, some also heard cases involving adults. Judges were asked to answer a number of questions concerning each accused in each case and to return the completed questionnaire by mail. They understood that they would never be personally identified in the reporting of the results and that they would have an opportunity at a conference held shortly after the data were sent in to discuss the results. Forty-three judges returned completed questionnaires.

The Cases

The first case involved two young offenders—"SS" (a 17-year-old) and "DS" (age 15)—convicted of theft under $1000 as a result of shoplifting at a department store. SS had taken a small tape recorder and a belt. DS had taken a cassette tape. SS had no record of offending; his parents (a teacher and a part-time librarian) had appeared in court and indicated they had restricted his activities immediately after they found out he had been charged; SS was described as a better-than-average student who had not been in trouble before and typically associated with others who also did not cause trouble. He offered no explanation for the offence.

On his first appearance, DS appeared alone, but on his second appearance, his mother (a secretary) appeared with him. DS's father lived in another city, gave no financial support to his former wife and child, and rarely saw his son. DS's performance in school was described as "much improved such that he is now doing average work." When he was 12, he had been caught shoplifting; at 14 he was in court on two separate occasions for mischief to private property. On the first of those occasions, he had been given fifty hours of community service, and, on the second, he had been fined and compensation had been ordered. The year prior to the current offence had been trouble free. He offered no explanation for the theft of the cassette other than to suggest that he had been planning on buying it but SS had said to him that only a fool would pay for something that could so easily be stolen.

The second case involved JS (age 16) and GH (age 15) who were convicted of assault causing bodily harm. The assault was racially motivated in that the victim, a Canadian born boy of parents who had immigrated from India 23 years previously, had been first verbally and then physically assaulted for going out with a white girl. The victim lost one tooth and had a badly cut lip requiring stitches. Although both boys participated in the assault, JS clearly took the major role.

The older accused, JS, had been apprehended when 12 for shoplifting but had not been brought to court for that offence. He had apparently never been in any other legal trouble. He lived with his mother (a sales clerk) and two sisters. The father had abandoned the family shortly after JS was born A psy chologist's report suggested that, with help, JS could learn to control his emotions.

The second offender, GH, had appeared in court on three previous occasions—on two separate occasions for break, enter, and theft and once for an assault on a younger child when a disagreement broke out about who was first in a queue at a fast food restaurant. His most recent sentence had been 150 hours of community service. He was described as being a poor and uncooperative student. He lived with his mother (a clerk) and father (a mechanic). An assessment by a psychologist had been suggested but not done.

After reading each case, the judges were asked to indicate what sentence they would give to each offender. They then answered fourteen questions relating to each case. Twelve of these questions concerned the importance of various factors in determining the disposition. An additional question asked for the relative importance of each goal of sentencing (punishment or denunciation, rehabilitation, general deterrence, individual deterrence, and incapacitation). The final question asked for the judge's view on whether the youth should have been brought to court.

RESULTS

Most of the judges thought that each of the four accused should have been brought to court. The only accused for whom there was significant variability was "SS" who was a first-time offender whose (middle class) parents seemed to have attempted to take control of their child. Thirty-five percent of those judges who expressed an opinion thought that he (probably or definitely) should not have been brought to court. For the other three offenders, the vast majority (95-100%) thought that the youth should have been charged and brought to court.

It is clear that there is a fair amount of variability in the dispositions handed down in these cases. Table 2 lists the "most severe" type of disposition recommended by each judge for each of the four offenders. We defined severity in terms of the likely degree of constraint on the young person's freedom (with a scale ranging from "secure custody" to "discharge"). Clearly this is an arbitrary ordering of disposition types, especially when one considers that low levels of a more severe disposition (e.g., 10 days in secure custody) is likely to be seen as less severe than a more severe instance of a lower-ranked disposition (e.g., a year of open custody). Furthermore, it should be emphasized that only the most severe disposition is included in this table. Many judges gave a combination of dispositions (e.g., a fine and a term of probation); in cases such as these, only the more severe would be contained in this table (e.g., the fine).

Table 1
Recommended disposition

Offence: Youth	Shoplifting				Assault			
Most severe disposition:	SS		DS		JS		GH	
Secure custody	—		—		2	(5%)	3	(8%)
Open custody	—		4	(11%)	14	(37%)	21	(57%)
CSO	20	(54%)	26	(68%)	15	(40%)	6	(16%)
Fine	7	(19%)	4	(11%)	1	(3%)	1	(3%)
Probation	8	(22%)	3	(8%)	6	(16%)	6	(16%)
Discharge	2	(5%)	1	(3%)	—		—	
Total	37	(100%)	38	(100%)	38	(100%)	37	(100%)

There is little consensus about the dispositions that are seen by judges as appropriate for any of these young people. For each youth, the range of dispositions recommended by different judges is wide. Thus, for example, for "GH", judges indicated that they would hand down dispositions ranging from 12 months in secure custody to a term of probation.

There did seem to be a certain amount of consistency within judges across the different youths. In other words, judges who tended to me the severe end of the disposition scale for one youth tended to use it for other youths as well.[3] The correlations among the dispositions given to the four youth are shown in Table 2. The possible exception to this generalization is "GH" where the dispositions appeared not to be significantly related to those given the other three offenders.

Table 2
Correlations (and 1-tailed "p") among most severe
dispositions given to the four offenders

	DS	JS	GH
SS	.37	•33	•17
	(p = .01)	(p = .03)	(Not sig.)
DS		.28	.27
		(p=.04)	(p=.06)
JS			.17
			(Not sig.)

The YOA lists a number of different principles that are to guide decisions under the Act, but does not give precedence to any single principle, nor does it indicate how much weight should be.given to any one principle. Thus one should not be surprised to find that the relative importance of the different principles or purposes guiding dispositions differed across judges and across cases.

The goal that each judge indicated was the most important for each of the cases is shown in Table 3.

Table 3
Number of judges listing each "goal" as being the most important in guiding the choice of disposition

Purpose:	SS		DS		JS		GH	
				Offender				
Punishment	5	(12%)	4	(10%)	8	(19%)	7	(17%)
Rehabilitation	18	(43%)	21	(50%)	14	(33%)	13	(32%)
General deterrence	3	(7%)	2	(5%)	—		2	(5%)
Individual deterrence	16	(38%)	15	(36%)	20	(48%)	18	(44%)
Incapacitation	—		—		—		1	(2%)
Total	42	(100%)	42	(100%)	42	(100%)	41	(100%)

There does not exist a consensus on the goals to be emphasized in determining the sentence for any of the four young people. The split seems to be, for the most part, between those favouring individual deterrence and those giving precedence to rehabilitation. However, at least 15% of the judges thought that one of the other three goals should be given precedence in each of the four cases.

Judges tended to be fairly consistent across offenders in the goal that they thought should be given prime importance (See Table 4).

Table 4
Percent of judges who indicated primary goal guiding dispositions should be the same for the two accused

Offender 1:	Offender 2: DS	JS	GH
SS	83%	54%	49%
DS	—	51%	54%
JS	—	—	80%

Levels of consistency across youth are higher when the youths were involved in the same offence (SS and DS; JS and GH). Because of the limited data, we do not know whether this relates to the fact that the offences were the same or that the two were co-accused.

Of the 41 cases for which we have complete data, 16 judges (39%) listed the same purpose as being paramount for all four young offenders. Three of these chose "punishment"; four chose "rehabilitation"; and nine chose "individual deterrence."

There is a large amount of variation in the recommended disposition even among judges who thought the same sentencing purpose should be paramount for a given case. The numbers of cases are too small to determine whether there was, overall, a relationship between the primary purpose chosen and the most serious component of the disposition. However, it is clear that even when trying to accomplish the same purpose, judges went about it in quite different ways. These data are shown, for each offender in Table 5.

Table 5
Primary purpose in sentencing and disposition

Disposition for "SS" (Most severe component):

	Fine/ CSO	Probation	Discharge
Primary purpose:			
Punishment	5	0	0
Rehabilitation	12	4	0
General deterrence	1	0	0
Individual deterrence	10	4	1

Disposition for "DS" (Most severe component):

	Open custody	Fine/ CSO	Probation
Primary purpose:			
Punishment	0	4	0
Rehabilitation	2	15	3
General deterrence	O	1	0
Individual deterrence	2	10	O

Table 5 (continued)

Disposition for "JS" (Most severe component):

	Secure custody	Open custody	Fine/ CSO	Probation
Primary purpose:				
Punishment	2	2	3	1
Rehabilitation	—	5	5	4
Individual deterrence	—	7	8	1

Disposition for "GH" (Most severe component):

	Secure custody	Open custody	Fine/ CSO	Probation
Primary purpose:				
Punishment	1	4	1	1
Rehabilitation	1	8	1	3
General deterrence	—	1	—	—
Individual deterrence	1	8	4	1
Incapacitation	—	—	—	1

By concentrating on the primary purpose of the disposition, it could be argued that we are putting undue weight on this single purpose in trying to understand how the judge determined the disposition. For each of the four offenders, over half of the judges indicated that rehabilitation was either the first or second most important goal of sentencing.

The next set of comparisons examines the dispositions recommended by judges who indicated that *rehabilitation* was either the first or the second most important purpose and compares them to judges who did not give rehabilitation so high a ranking (See Table 6).

Table 6
Disposition for each offender
(most severe component):

Offender:	Rehabilitation given high priority:	Secure custody	Open custody	Fine/ CSO	Probation	Discharge
SS	Yes	—	—	16	6	—
	No	—	—	11	2	1
DS	Yes	—	3	20	3	—
	No	—	1	10	—	—
JS	Yes	1	10	12	4	—
	No	1	4	4	2	—
GH	Yes	2	11	4	5	—
	No	1	10	2	1	—

There was considerable variability across judges as to whether they chose rehabilitation as one of the primary purposes of the disposition. This choice did not appear to be related to the disposition handed down.

Under the YOA, there is no single "standard" against which to assess an individual case. Judges may, therefore, begin with different purposes, look at different information and arrive at different outcomes. Alternatively, of course, they could look to other trial courts and their own (or other provinces') court of appeal for guidance. As can be seen in Table 7, the importance of these other sources of guidance was seen to be higher in the more serious case (involving "JS" and "GH") than in the less serious, but more common, shoplifting case.

Table 7
Importance of information from other courts in determining the disposition for each offender. Percent seeing information as "very" or "somewhat" important

| | Offence and offender: | | | |
| | Shoplifting | | Assault | |
Information	SS	DS	JS	GH
Trial decisions for similar cases, own province	37%	40%	65%	61%
Court of appeal judgement, own province	47%	54%	67%	68%
Court of appeal judgement, other provinces	19%	19%	28%	29%

There was a fair amount of consistency within judges on the use of information. Each judge indicated the usefulness of three types of "case" information for each of the four offenders. There are 66 correlations among these twelve measures. A high positive correlation in this setting suggests that a judge who indicated that one type of information was important would also rate another type as being important. All of the 66 correlations were positive, and most were relatively high, ranging from .22 to .95 with an average of .52; most (52 of 66) were statistically significant at the 0.01 level. Thus it is *not* the case that judges would tend to look to one type of information (e.g., court of appeal decisions from their own province) and ignore others (e.g., trial decisions in their own province). Rather, it seemed that judges who thought *any* kind of YOA decisions to be helpful, would tend to think *all* types of YOA decisions to be helpful in handing down decisions for all four offenders.

DISCUSSION

There is substantial variation both in the dispositions these judges indicated they would hand down and in the priority of the goals that they were trying to achieve with the dispositions. Part of the problem for the judges in arriving at a disposition may have been that they were trying to accomplish too much in sentencing the young offender. It will be recalled that we asked judges a number of specific questions about the importance of various factors in determining the disposition. A simple summary of these findings for all four accused would be that most judges found most goals or purposes to be either very important or somewhat important in determining the disposition. The data are shown in Table 8.

Table 8
Percent indicating each factor was very or somewhat important

	SS	DS	IS	GH
Offence seriousness	72	74	100	100
Level of involvement	93	91	100	98
Making him accountable	98	98	100	100
Show him act not to be tolerated	81	81	100	100
Protecting society	84	79	95	98
Deterring others	47	54	70	79
Providing help: offender/family to stop him offending	61	86	95	95
Ability of family to control	93	84	84	83
Providing help: offender/family to make him useful citizen	61	84	91	88

These data are notable for one simple reason: they suggest that judges, within the context of a single disposition, are attempting to accomplish an enormous amount. Indeed, when choosing which of the five traditional goals of sentencing (e.g., rehabilitation, deterrence, etc.) were relevant, judges chose on the average about 3.5 of the five as being relevant for *every* offender. It suggests that judges have set themselves an almost impossible task: combining sometimes contradictory goals to arrive at a disposition. The only factors that fewer than two thirds of judges indicated were important in determining the disposition were general deterrence in the case of the two shoplifters and helping the family of the middle class shoplifter that, on the surface, did not appear to be in need of much help.

Priorities of purpose, then, probably reflect priorities among a set of purposes most of which are seen as relevant. It is little wonder, then, that judges, when trying to accomplish these multiple purposes do not arrive at similar dispositions.

It should be remembered, of course, that the *Young Offenders Act* itself *requires* judges to weigh, individually, without legislative guidance, contradictory goals. judges are required, under the act to respond simultaneously to all of the following:

> "while young persons should not in all instances be held accountable in the same manner or suffer the same consequences for their behaviour as adults, young persons who commit offences should nonetheless bear responsibility for their contraventions." Section 3(1)(a)

> "society must, although it has the responsibility to take reasonable measures to prevent criminal conduct by young persons, be afforded the necessary protection from illegal behaviour." [YOA Section 3(1)(b)]

> "young persons who commit offences require supervision, discipline, and control, but, because of their state of dependency and level of development and maturity, they also have special needs and require guidance and assistance." [YOA Section 3 (I) (c)]

It is not difficult to read the five traditional goals or purposes of sentencing into these three subsections of the "Declaration of Principle" of the *Young Offenders Act*. When the "Declaration of Principle" is looked on as a potential guide for sentencing, it is clear that no guidance is given on how, for example, to weigh prevention, protection of society, the special needs of the young person which require assistance, and the principle of making young persons accountable for the offences when each of these principles taken by itself would lead to vastly different dispositions.

The data presented in this paper support the view, we believe, that the variation in dispositions for young offenders reflects, at least in part, variation in the way in which judges weigh purposes and goals. Traditionally, judges have been encouraged to think of each case as being unique. As a truism, one cannot argue with this position. The difficulty is that judges have their own *different* individual approaches to the *identical* case. Hence, similar cases are being dealt with in dramatically different ways, though each of those ways may well be thoughtfully arrived at. The variation in dispositions that we have shown in Table 1, therefore, can be understood as being a direct result of the *Young Offenders Act* itself. Though judges are responsible for their individual decisions, the Act itself is responsible for the fact that very different sentences can legitimately be given to the same case. Individualized decision making by individual judges acting without much guidance is not compatible with a high degree of consistency in sentencing.

Brodeur (1989:117) has noted that increased guidance for judges can come in a variety of different forms. In addition, he points out that guidelines generally are not designed to constrain judges "in cases where particular circumstances demand a special effort to individualize the sentence". Thus, guidelines of the sort recommended in the report of Ontario Social Development Council (1988) explicitly note the importance of individualizing sentences for special needs youth.

Guidelines, Brodeur (1989:117) points out, are the product of "rational choice and are the expression of a concerted policy". Clearly *individual* sentences handed down under the *Young Offenders Act* are a product of rational choice. The data presented in this paper, however, suggest that sentences handed down to young offenders cannot be described as being the expression of a concerted policy.

ENDNOTES

1. The research reported in this paper was supported, in part, by a contribution from the Department of Justice, Canada, to the Advanced Judicial Seminar (Montreal, 30 November to 3 December 1988) sponsored and organized by the Canadian Association of Provincial Court Judges. Other costs were defrayed, in part, by contributions funds from the Solicitor General, Canada, to the Centre of Criminology, University of Toronto. We wish to thank the forty-three participants in this study for their contribution to our attempt to understand, more fully, the *Young Offenders Act*. Finally, we wish to thank Dorothy Marcil for her extensive help with the arrangements that allowed this study to be done.

2. The data from the latter two cases will be reported in a subsequent paper.

3. For purposes of these correlations:; a complete scale, which included treatment (3) and confusion/restitution (6) was included The effect of including these empty categories is only to emphasize three distinct categories Custody (1 and 2); intermediate sanctions, CSO and fine (4 and 5); and the less punishing sanctions, probation and discharge (7 and 8).

REFERENCES

Beaulieu, Lucien A. (ed.). 1989. *Young Offender Dispositions Perspectives on Principle and Practice.* Toronto: Wall and Thompson.

Brodeur, Jean-Paul. 1989. Some comments on sentencing guidelines In Lucien A Beaulieu (ed.), *Young Offender Dispositions Perspectives on Principles and Practice.* Toronto: Wall and Thompson.

Canada. 1987. *Sentencing Reform: A Canadian Approach. Report of the Canadian Sentencing Commission.* Ottawa: Minister of Supply and Services.

Corrado, Raymond R. and Alan E. Markwart. 1988. The prices of rights and responsibilities: An examination of the impacts of the Young Offenders Act in British Columbia. *Canadian Journal of Family Law 7* (1): 93-115.

Doob, Anthony N. 1989. Dispositions under the Young Offenders Act: Issues without answers. In Lucien A. Beaulieu (ed), *Young Offender Dispositions Perspectives on Principles and Practice.* Toronto: Wall and Thompson.

Leschied, Alan and Peter G Jaffe. 1987. Impact of the Young Offenders Act on court dispositions: A comparative analysis. *Canadian Journal of Criminology.* 29(4):421-430.

Markwart, Alan E. (ed.), and Raymond R. Corrado. 1989. Is the Young Offenders Act more punitive? In Lucien A Beaulieu (ed.), *Young Offender Dispositions Perspectives on Principles and Practice.* Toronto: Wall and Thompson.

Ontario Social Development Council. 1988. *Y.O.A. Dispositions: Challenges and Choices (A report of the conference on the Young Offenders Act in Ontario).* Toronto: Ontario Social Development Council.

Palys,T.S. 1982. *Beyond the Black Box: A Study in Judicial Decision Making.* Ottawa: Solicitor General, Canada.

_____. and Stanley Divorski. 1984. In D C Muller, P.E. Blackman, and A. J. Chapman (eds..), *Psychology and the Law.* Toronto: Wiley

Trépanier, Jean. 1989. Principles and goals guiding the choice of dispositions under the Y.O.A. In Lucien A. Beaulieu (ed.), *Young Offender Dispositions Perspectives and Principles and Practice.* Toronto: Wall and Thompson.

Young, Alan. 1989. Appelate court sentencing principles for young offenders. In Lucien A Beaulieu (ed.), *Young Offender Dispositions Perspectives on Principles and Practice.* Toronto: Wall and Thompson.

CHAPTER 15
Children's Understanding of the Juvenile Justice System: A Cognitive-Developmental Perspective[1]

MICHELE PETERSON[2]

The development of children's understanding of crime, and of the justice considerations embodied in law, has been little studied until recently. This is, however, an important topic for investigation, first because the concept of "crime" presumes understanding and intent, and second, because in order for juvenile justice legislation to be most effective, children should have some basic knowledge of how it affects them. The present study attempted a preliminary exploration of these issues, with the Young Offenders Act (YOA) as its focus. 144 children from Grades 5 through 8 were interviewed and their knowledge assessed, both by questioning them on specific critical aspects of the YOA, and indirectly, through the presentation of hypothetical crime scenarios in which a child of varying age and gender committed a crime, either "petty" or "serious". The results indicated that although all the children possessed a basic knowledge of what constitutes a crime, they showed a progressively more sophisticated understanding with age in a number of areas related to criminal behaviour. Their overall knowledge of the YOA areas questioned was quite poor, however. Recommendation was made for a program designed to educate children on some of the most important aspects of the law, with the suggestion that if children have a better understanding of the consequences of criminal behaviour, they may be less likely to participate.

INTRODUCTION

One of the most interesting and important, and yet unstudied, areas of developmental psychology involves the cognitive capacities and development of children as they relate to public policy, which in its ultimate form is often embodied in law. Policy makers, politicians and other leaders have recognized for over a century that children have a special status in our society by virtue of their developmental immaturity, and that this status must be recognized and protected by the law. In framing policy and legislation, efforts have been made to implement modifications which reflect a developmental perspective by setting age boundaries and by dealing with children in a manner consistent with their juvenile status. These efforts necessarily involve many assumptions regarding childhood—what children are capable of and what they need in terms of nurturance and care. For the most part, these assumptions are made and incorporated into policy and law without clear reference to the theory and research in psychology which deals with developmental issues. Developmental psychologists, in turn, have not addressed themselves explicitly to the implications of their theory and data on the framing of policy designed to deal with children despite the fact that the effects of this policy on the lives of children can be enormous.

Although there were a number of provincial and federal acts in the 19th century which dealt specifically with children, it is convenient to date formal federal acknowledgment of the implications of the cognitive immaturity of children from 1908, with the passage of the *Juvenile Delinquents Act* (JDA). The JDA established a separate legal system to deal with people under the age of 16 (17 or 18, depending on the province). No minimum age was set in the Act, but the *Criminal Code* of Canada contained a minimum age of 7 for a child to be dealt with by criminal law. The scope of the JDA was very broad—children who committed an offense contrary to the *Criminal Code,* or to any provincial or municipal legislation, or who were guilty of "sexual immorality" or any similar form of vice, or who were likely to be put in a juvenile reformatory for some other reason were labelled delinquent and dealt with under this law. The basic intent of the Act was to treat the young person not as a criminal but as a misdirected child requiring help and guidance and proper supervision".[5] In the 1960s and 1970s the JDA was criticized for neglecting legal rights of children.

The *Young Offenders Act* (YOA), which has now replaced the JDA, was designed to bring into balance welfare and justice orientations, thus improving the method for dealing with young people who come into conflict with the law. The Act now encompasses children from 12 through 17 years of age, a change which presumably reflects a changed view of children's cognitive and emotional capacities and development. In his comments on this change in age limits, the Solicitor General stated that "consideration has been given to the stage of development of the child in physiological, mental and emotional terms, particularly as these factors apply to the formulation of a criminal intent. The setting of a precise age is necessarily arbitrary as children vary greatly in their rate of development but it is assumed that deviant behaviour by children under the age of twelve is better and more effectively dealt with under provincial legislation pertaining to child welfare or youth protection.[5]

Explicit reference has thus been made to the importance of developmental psychological factors with respect to juvenile criminal behaviour and the impact that these factors must have on the way in which the law handles young offenders. It appears, however, that no study has systematically examined the relevance of the ages set out in our juvenile legislation to the issues in development as they have been studied by psychologists. The classic cognitive-developmental work of Piaget serves to focus attention on the changes in cognitive processing which occur at about 12 years of age, one of the critical ages in the new legislation. Prior to this age children are likely still in the concrete operational period, in which logical thinking has developed, but is rooted in the immediate world. These children have not yet developed the ability for *abstract* reasoning, according to Piaget, and thus cannot consider a number of possible or hypothetical alternatives in a problem-solving situation. This progression from concrete to formal operations (the hallmark of which is abstract reasoning) has implications for the juvenile justice system. The YOA established a due process model for children 12 years and older, which assumes that these children are capable of criminal intent and criminal behaviour. If the youngest children to whom the Act applies have not yet reached the stage where they can reason out the possible elements or outcomes of a given situation, then it could be argued that they should not yet be held fully accountable for their actions. As the Solicitor General noted, the developmental rate of children is varied, and children of the same chronological age are not necessarily homogeneous with respect to their cognitive level. It would be valuable, however, to attempt to determine whether the majority of 12-year-olds possess the cognitive capacities (such as the reasoning process characteristic of formal operations) which could be prerequisite to the establishment of criminal intent.

One of the aims of this study was to examine children's reasoning, and its development in order to lay the groundwork for providing an answer to this question. Children ranging in age from 10 to 14 were interviewed in order to explore the development of the understanding of several aspects of criminal behaviour, the court process, and especially the significance of a child's age as it relates to the disposition of a case. Subjects were presented with two hypothetical scenarios, each of which portrayed a young offender's case. In a partially structured interview, each child was asked questions about the case, and was asked about specific aspects of the YOA.

METHOD

Subjects

Subjects were 18 boys and 18 girls from each of Grades 5, 6, 7 and 8 drawn from three different schools in two school boards. Subjects in each grade were drawn from at least two of the three schools so that grade level was never completely confounded with school.

Procedure

Each subject met individually with the experimenter in a quiet room. The experimenter explained briefly that the subject would hear two short stories about a boy or girl who got into trouble with the law, followed by some questions relating to the scenarios.

Each subject was then presented with two brief stories which depicted a child committing a crime and subsequently being picked up by the, police. The stories indicated the gender and age of the child, and the fact that he or she had never been in trouble with the law before. They described the crime committed (either a petty theft or a break and enter plus theft) as neutrally as possible in order not to bias the subject before the interview questions were asked.

The stories were presented orally and each subject was also given an index card on which the story was printed, so that he or she could follow along. Because the subsequent questions were not designed to test the subject's memory, the cards were also provided for reference during the interview if necessary. After reading each story, the subject was asked the interview questions and the experimenter noted the responses on an interview form.

Subjects were debriefed together in their classroom after all interviews had been completed. The experimenter explained the purpose of the study—to examine the changes with age in children's understanding of the law—and briefly described some of the most relevant points of the YOA. Questions were solicited and answered.

Design

The present study followed a 2 x 2 x 4 x 3 x 2 design. Gender of subject, gender of story character and grade level of subject were between subjects factors. The age of the story character (11, 13 or 15 years) was nested within gender-grade combinations. The gravity of the crime (petty vs. serious) was a within subjects factor.

To summarize, each subject received two stories depicting a crime (one petty and one serious) and both story characters were of the same sex. Since each subject heard only two stories, he or she could not receive all three age levels of the age of story character factor. Stories were therefore combined in the following manner: first, each of the three age levels was paired with each type of crime (petty and serious), yielding six scenarios. Then, these scenarios were combined pairwise to yield all possible combinations of the six versions, with the constraint that one story portray the serious crime and the other the petty crime. This yielded nine story pairs. These pairs were then crossed with the gender of the story character, yielding 18 different story pair combinations. Each combination was given to one male subject and one female subject. Order of presentation of the two stories was determined randomly for each subject.

RESULTS

Culpability of the Story Character

The first question that subjects were asked in the interview was whether they felt that the story character had done something wrong, and if so, why this was wrong. All of the subjects replied that a wrong had been done. With respect to the petty crime, all of the subjects appeared to understand what was wrong about the character's action; they all gave an explanation which involved the concept of theft. The serious crime was more complex, as it actually involved two offenses: break and enter plus theft. It was of interest to see whether the subjects differed in terms of their recognition of the dual nature of this crime. For this purpose, the explanations were divided into theft only, break and enter only and both theft and break and enter (dual). There were no differences with grade in the proportion of each type of explanation given, though there was a jump in the percentage of dual explanations from the Grade 5 to the higher grades (from 25% to roughly 45%), showing a tendency for the explanations to become more accurate after age 10-11.

Consequences to the Story Character

Next, the children were asked what they thought would happen to the culprit. Responses were divided into three categories: criminal sanctions (arrest, court appearance, fines, etc.), civil action (being barred from the store, sued, etc.) and informal action (a lecture, parental punishment, etc.). There was no age difference in the proportion of subjects who suggested a criminal sanction in response to the petty crime (percentages ranged from 50 in Grades 5 and 7 to 61 in Grade 8), but there was a significant increase with age when the serious crime was considered (X^2 (3) = 8.85, p < .05). Specifically, while 78% of the older subjects (Grades 7 and 8) suggested a criminal sanction, 55% of the younger subjects (Grades 5 and 6) did so. With respect to replies indicating civil action, a significant chi square was obtained for the petty but not the serious offense. Only 5% of Grade 5 students mentioned civil action with respect to the petty crime, but a full third of the Grade 6 children included this type of explanation in their answer. The mention of civil action decreased again for Grades 7 and 8, however, to 18% and 22%. respectively. The students did not differ by grade in their inclusion of some informal action; the proportion of students who mentioned these consequences was fairly high in all grades (X = 66% for the petty crime and 49% for the serious crime).

When the consequences were analyzed according to the age of the story character (rather than the grade of the subject), the proportions of criminal, civil and informal sanctions were found to be quite similar, regardless of the character's age. There was a nonsignificant trend in both the petty and serious cases for the mention of informal actions to decrease as the age of the character increased.

Gravity of the Offenses

The subjects were also asked how serious they felt each crime was. Because of the nature of the design with respect to the "age of story character variable", it was not possible to run one factorial Analysis of Variance. An overall Anova was therefore performed on the data, collapsed over age of story character. The petty and serious crimes were then analyzed individually in order to assess the effect of age of story character on gravity ratings.

The main effect of grade on gravity ratings was significant, with the Grade

8 students rating the crimes as less serious than the subjects from grades 5, 6 or 7, whose ratings did not differ from one another ($F(3,125) = 2.7$, $p < .05$). Post hoc comparisons, using a Spjotvoll and Stoline[6] test, confirmed this finding. The Grade variable also interacted with sex of subject ($F(3,125) = 3.7$ $p < .025$). Essentially, the Grade 5 males did not consider the crimes as particularly serious, while the Grade 6 boys gave a much higher gravity rating. The ratings dropped off somewhat for the Grade 7 males, and again for the Grade 8s. The pattern for the girls was quite different, however. The females in Grade 5 rated the crimes as quite serious, but in Grade 6 the girls were much more conservative in their ratings. The gravity ratings increased for the Grade 7 girls, but then dropped again in Grade 8, creating a seesaw pattern.

This Grade x Sex of Subject interaction was further dependent upon the Sex of the Story Character, yielding a significant triple interaction ($F(3,125) = 3.3$, $p < .025$). Both the male and female subjects' rating differed markedly with grade when assessing a crime involving a male culprit, but in virtually opposite directions. While for the boys, the mean gravity rating peaked at Grade 6, and then fell off again in grades 7 and 8, the girls rated the crime as fairly serious in Grade 5, but ratings dropped in Grade 6 (to 'somewhat serious'), only to rise again in Grade 7 and dip in Grade 8. While the particulars of the seesawing pattern evidenced in reaction to the male character's crimes are difficult to account for, it is clear that somehow a male character produces far more disagreement and controversy in ratings from grade to grade than does a female character; as they got older, male subjects tended to rate a crime involving a female as progressively more serious, whereas female subjects produced similar (moderate) gravity ratings up to Grade 7, with a drop in the rated gravity shown by the Grade 8 girls.

Aside from the Grade variable, the only other main effect in the Anova was that of Gravity of the crime, with the serious crime rate as significantly more serious than the petty crime ($F(1,125) = 176.5$, $p < .01$). This result essentially confirmed the intended manipulation of the gravity of the crime.

Aside from the interaction of Gravity with Grade, as described above, the Gravity variable also interacted with sex of Story Character ($F(1,125) = 6.5$, $p < .025$). The difference in rated Gravity between the petty and serious crime was larger when a male perpetrator was involved. There was less distinction made between the two types of crime when a female story character was rated. This interaction was also dependent on the sex of the subject, however, as indicated by a significant triple interaction ($F(1,125) = 7.0$, $p. < .01$). In the petty crime case, both male and female subjects rated the crime as more serious when it involved a girl rather than a boy. In the serious crime case, however, males rated the crime as less serious when perpetrated by a female than by a male, whereas female subjects made no distinction between the sex of the perpetrator.

Factors Affecting Disposition of the Offenses

The subjects were also asked to name factors which they felt might influence the decision as to how the culprit's crime would be handled. The responses were divided by grade, and petty and serious crimes were analyzed separately. The factor mentioned most by subjects was prior record, and in both the petty and the serious cases there was a significant increase over grade in the proportion of subjects who made this suggestion (X^2 (3) = 11.03, p < .02 and X^2 (3) = 20.9, p < .001, respectively).

Subjects also frequently mentioned age as a factor, and in the petty case there was an increase with grade in the number of subjects who suggested this variable (X^2 (3) = 23.2, p < .001; there was a similar, though nonsignificant, trend in the serious case.

A third group of factors suggested by the subjects comes under the heading psychological variables—the child's emotional state, home life, peer pressure, intent and attitude. Again, there was a significant tendency in both the petty and serious cases for the percentage of subjects who mentioned this factor to increase with grade (X^2 (3) = 11.4, p < .01 and X^2 (3) = 12.3, p < .01, respectively.

The fourth factor mentioned, gravity of the crime, did not differ according to grade in either the petty or the serious analysis. This factor was mentioned by a lower percentage of the students than the preceding variables.

When these four factors were analyzed according to the age of the story character, few differences were found between the three age groups. In fact, only the prior record in the petty crime analysis reached significance (X^2 (2) = 11.5 p < .01). Here there was a jump, from age 11 to ages 13 and 15, in the percentage of subjects who felt that prior record would be taken into consideration.

Understanding of the Young Offenders Act

The interview was also designed to assess the children's understanding of some of the most salient of the YOA. Of specific interest was whether they would know the age at which one becomes a young offender and the age at which one is considered an adult. As Table 1 shows, there was a definite progression with the child's age in the understanding of under/over 12 distinction, although the chi square just failed to reach significance. Despite this growth in understanding, however, the overall level of knowledge regarding this distinction was not high, with at best less than a third of the students in a class responding correctly. There was no significant developmental trend in the understanding of the under/over 18 distinction, but here the overall level of understanding was better, with a third to a half of the students responding correctly.

Table 1
Percentage of Subjects Who Understood the Age Distinctions Relevant to the *Young Offenders Act* (N in brackets)

	Under/ Over 12		Under/ Over 12		Total N in each cell
Grade 5	5.6	(2)	30.6	(11)	36
Grade 6	19.4	(7)	30.6	(11)	36
Grade 7	11.8	(4)	32.3	(11)	34
Grade 8	27.8	(10)	50.0	(18)	36

$X^2 (3) = 7.4, p < 10$ $X^2(3) = 4.2,.$ N.S.

Sources of Information

Finally, the children were asked where they obtained their information about the juvenile justice system, and Table 2 contains these sources. Many of the students named family as a source of their knowledge, but there was no age trend evident with respect to this variable. Another source given was school, and here there was a significant increase with age in the number of students who mentioned it. This appears to be due to the jump after Grade 5 in the number of children who mentioned school as a source. The students also mentioned friends, police and media as sources of information, but again with no developmental trend.

Table 2
Percentage of Subjects Who Cited Each Source of Information About the Consequences of Juvenile Crime (According to Grade) (N in brackets)

	Family		School		Friends		Police		Media	
Grade 5	69.4	(25)	11.1	(4)	16.7	(6)	27.8	(10)	44.4	(16)
Grade 6	75.0	(27)	36.1	(13)	19.4	(7)	30.6	(11)	50.0	(18)
Grade 7	70.6	(24)	44.1	(15)	23.5	(8)	38.2	(13)	50.0	(17)
Grade 8	58.3	(21)	33.3	(12)	38.9	(14)	27.8	(10)	44.4	(16)
X^2	2.5		10.0		5.7		1.2		.5	
p	N.S.		< .01		N.S.		N.S.		N.S.	

DISCUSSION

The main focus of this study was to examine the developmental changes in children's understanding of the juvenile justice system. Developmental differences were found in some, though not all, of the areas where difference did occur, but also those in which consistency across age was the result.

At the most basic level, it was found that all of the children in grades 5 through 8 knew that the story character had done wrong and further, that they were reasonably accurate at identifying specifically what the transgression was. These results suggest that at least when the offense is relatively straightforward, children are capable of understanding what constitutes a criminal action. This is an important point since comprehension of wrongdoing is a prerequisite to criminal responsibility; it is already acknowledged in our juvenile laws that it does not make sense to hold a child responsible for an action that he or she did not know was wrong. However, this finding is qualified by the fact that the offenses presented to the children were quite straightforward and simplistic. It would be interesting to present children with a number of different types of offense, varying in their degree of complexity and/or "criminality", to ascertain just how refined their knowledge of criminal behaviour is. It may well be that if a wide range of transgressions was presented, developmental differences would appear, with older children grasping more subtle situations which the younger children would simply not see. Perhaps more importantly, no attempt was made here to determine whether children of different ages could differentiate between harms resulting from negligence or accident and harms resulting from criminal intent.

Though there was no dispute as to whether or not a crime had been committed, children did differ in their perceptions of its gravity. Specifically, the Grade 8 students rated the crimes as significantly less serious than the subjects from grades 5 through 7. It would be useful to present children with a wider range of crimes in order to obtain a better picture of how age relates to their understanding of different types of offense.

Developmental differences were also apparent in the children's assessment of what would happen to the culprit. With respect to the serious crime, there was an increased likelihood with age (up to Grade 7) that a subject would mention at least one criminal sanction against the perpetrator. This again seems to reflect an increasing understanding of the realities of juvenile criminal behaviour, since the likelihood is that some type of criminal sanction would follow apprehension for break and enter.

There were also developmental changes in response to the question of which factors the students felt would influence the fate of the culprit. With increasing age, children were more likely to mention prior record, age, and psychological variables as key factors in deciding the fate of the perpetrator. Clearly, children are becoming more attuned to the variables that affect the judicial process as they grow older.

When asked for specific information about important distinctions in the *Young Offenders Act,* the evidence for a developmental progression was mixed. Children were more likely to understand the under/over 12 distinction with increasing age, but the age trend with respect to the understanding of the under/over IX distinction did not reach significance. There was, however, a 20% jump from grades 5, 6 and 7 to Grade 8, in proportion of students who correctly articulated this transition to adulthood at 18 years, which provides at least some evidence for an increase in understanding of this distinction.

Overall, only 16% of subjects correctly identified age 12 as the lower bound for the YOA, indicating a general ignorance which, though not surprising, should be remedied. The children had a better overall understanding of the under/over 18 distinction (36% of subjects), but this too could be greatly improved. These percentages are similar to those reported by Jaffe, Leschied and Farthing,[3] who administered questionnaires concerning the YOA to students between 12 and 18 years of age. The authors found that 22% and 23% of subjects correctly identified the basal and ceiling ages, respectively, for the YOA.

These results are not surprising when one considers the level of legal ignorance within the adult population. In his study of adults' comprehension of,
and knowledge about, various laws Ribordy[4] stated that "most statutes are
unknown to the majority of the population" (p. 29). Knowledge of specific
aspects of several statutes was assessed by presenting statements to which
subjects responded "Yes", "No", or "Don't Know". The percentage of subjects
who responded correctly ranged from 21-62%. However, this multiple choice
question format lends itself to a higher level of correct responses than the
open ended format used in the present study because of the limitation in
response choices as well as the vulnerability to correct guesses. Thus,
Ribordy's results suggest that ignorance of specific legal "facts" may not be
limited to children.

Of all the people and institutions that children cited as sources for their
knowledge, the only one which reflected a developmental trend was school.
As children get older, school appears to become a more important source of
information about criminal activity and juvenile law. There was an interesting
drop, however, from Grade 7 to Grade 8, in the number of students who cited
school as an information source, indicating perhaps that in the upper grades it
no longer plays as important a role in their knowledge base. This is quite
understandable when one considers the increase in the role of peers at this
time, together with the fact that children of this age are starting to become
more involved first hand with the world at large, including criminal activity. It is
interesting to note that there was an increase with age in the number of children who cited friends as a source of knowledge about crime and the law, and
that this trend accelerated after Grade 7, though this relationship was not statistically significant.

The generally poor knowledge of some of the most relevant distinctions in
the *Young Offenders Act,* together with the information regarding the
sources of children's understanding, indicate that some sort of program is necessary to impart these facts and their relevance to children's choices and activities. Further, this program should focus on the school and should start at least
by Grade 5 and perhaps before. The generally large percentage of students
who cited the media as sources of information indicates that they could be
another important vehicle for a program designed to increase children's
awareness of their position vis-à-vis the law.

The study also examined the effects of several other factors on children's
understanding of criminal behaviour and its consequences. It was of interest to
ascertain whether the students' opinions varied according to the age of the
story character, since a child's age is an important factor in determining how

he or she will be dealt with after committing a crime. In general, age of the culprit seemed to have very little effect on the children's responses. Subjects did not modify what they felt would happen to the culprit according to his or her age, and their responses were remarkably similar across age groups. Neither was there a main effect of age in the ratings of gravity of the crime, although there was an interesting interaction between age, sex of the culprit and sex of the subject.

This finding focuses attention on the importance of the interaction between the gender of the subject and culprit. Girls and boys appear to have different responses toward male and female culprits, a finding which may well result from socialized attitudes toward the different sexes and perhaps also from differences in the children's ability to take the perspective of a same-sexed verses opposite-sexed character. When faced with a decision concerning a culprit of their own sex, the subjects uniformly agreed that the crime became more serious with age. With respect to the opposite sex, girls actually rated the crimes as less serious with age, perhaps due to a notion that criminal behaviour is more acceptable, or even simply more prevalent in males, especially as they get older. Boys on the other hand, gave uniformly high gravity ratings in response to a female culprit, irrespective of her age, again suggesting that their opinion reflects the societal notion that crimes involving females are somehow less acceptable than those involving males.

Yet another finding indicates that this study of the relationship between sex and attitudes toward criminal behaviour should be broadened: subjects made less distinction in gravity between the petty and serious crimes when a female perpetrator was involved than when the culprit was a male. It appears that there may be some striking differences in the way that young male and female culprits are viewed by children, and that these differences vary with the child's own gender.

To summarize, it appears that the majority of the children in Grades 5 through 8 possess a relatively basic knowledge of what constitutes criminal behaviour and what its results are likely to entail. If understanding that an act is illegal constitutes the criterion by which criminal intent and responsibility is assessed, then age 12 does appear to be a reasonable minimum for the application of formal criminal sanctions. However, the youngest children lack a more refined understanding of this area, including an acknowledgement of its relativistic nature, and some of the specifics of the law which affect them. This understanding appears to increase with age, but there are still areas in which it is woefully inadequate, especially when one considers that children are already beginning to make choices about criminal activity which could affect them in ways of which they are ignorant.

ENDNOTES

1. Reprint requests may be sent to the author, Department of Applied Psychology, Ontario Institute for Studies in Education, 252 Bloor Street West, 9th floor,Toronto, Ontario, M5S IV6.

2. The author wishes to thank Professor Anthony N. Doob, Director, Centre of Criminology, University of Toronto, for all his assistance and support in the execution of this research project and in the preparation of this manuscript.

3. Jaffe, P., A. Leschied and J. Farthing. 1987. "Youth's knowledge and attitudes about the Young Offenders Act: Does anyone care what they think?" *The Canadian Journal of Criminology. 29* (3), 309-316.

4. Ribordy, F.X. 1986. Legal education and information: An exploratory study. Ottawa: Department of Justice.

5. Solicitor General of Canada. 1977. "Highlights of the proposed new legislation for young offenders." *Criminal Reports. 37,*113-137.

6. Spjotvoll, E.. and M.R. Stoline. 1973 . "An extension of the T-method of multiple comparisons to include the cases with unequal sample sizes." *Journal of the American Statistical Association. 68,* 975-978.

CHAPTER 16
West Indian
Adolescent Offenders[1]

FAY E. MARTIN
GEORGINA WHITE[2]

This is a retrospective file study of all WEST Indian adolescent offenders referred to the Toronto Family Court Clinic compared with a group of Canadian-born offenders matched for age, sex, and date of referral. Twenty-six boys and 12 girls in each group, with a mean age of 14 years, are compared with respect to family background, developmental. social and school history, delinquency history, and clinical interventions. The immigration history of the West Indian subjects is described. A broad spectrum of related literature is discussed. Differences between the two groups are subtle, perhaps obscured by methodological limitations. Results are discussed with a view to modifying conceptual, and intervention frameworks.

Migrating populations are a fact of modern life, and Canada has demonstrated a sustained willingness to welcome them. The process of transition is extremely stressful, however, and immigrants are at increased risk for mental health problems. Effective interventions are required to resolve the difficulties that arise so that individual discomfort can be relieved, and integration proceed.

This study examines, within the confines of a retrospective file study, the experience of one mental health facility, the Toronto Family Court Clinic, in addressing the needs of one group, West Indians. The experience may be helpful to other settings, and applicable to other groups.

"West Indian Adolescent Offenders" was reproduced by permission of the *Canadian Journal of Criminology*, Vol. 30 (4), pages 367-379. Copyright by the Canadian Criminal Justice Association.

In reviewing files, it appeared to us that West Indian cases often elicited frustration from the Court and clinicians because they failed to respond in the usual way to the assessment process. We began to conceptualize two cultures interacting, each without a reciprocal perception of how the other culture operated. Unwarranted assumptions were made by all players, with resulting ineffectiveness and frustration. It seemed useful to gather and present data to increase sensitivity to the cultural environments within which the event of court referral and assessment occurred.

LITERATURE REVIEW

There is very little Canadian research on West Indian adolescents available, so we surveyed the literature broadly, looking at work with younger West Indian children, clinical populations, studies in other countries, and non-research literature that increased our understanding of this population.

Robinson, Christiansen and Thornley-Brown[8] discuss the historical development of West Indian family structures, pointing out that the history of blacks in the western hemisphere is rooted in slavery. The family as a unit had no status within the slave economy, and continuity of the parental role was provided by the development of a matriarchal structure in which a variety of individuals carried the mother role as necessity demanded. The dominance in this role of older women is still evident. Legal marriage was meaningless in the absence of individual rights, but the role of the father, differentiated from the role of the husband, was sustained, even in the prolonged absence of the man himself.

The most extensive research on West Indian families was done by Rutter *et al.*, who conducted an epidemiological study of all 10-year-olds in an inner-city borough of London, England, in the late 1960s. A sub-group of 54 West Indian children, of whom 33 had been born in Great Britain, was compared with a group of children of British parentage. This allowed comparison of West Indian children who had experienced the trauma of immigration with West Indian children who had not, and comparison of children of West Indian parents with children of British parents. The researchers addressed family characteristics, school performance, and psychiatric and behavioral deviance.[10]

Rutter found that the families of West Indian children compared to British families were as nuclear but more self-sufficient, had more children, more often owned their own homes but lived in more crowded conditions, were under-employed relative to their education, had a higher proportion of working mothers and substitute care-givers, did not value play as a pre-educational activity, strongly supported educational attainment, expected their children to demonstrate domestic competence and self-reliance, and exerted more control over how their children spent their leisure time."[11]

Although teachers tended to believe that misbehaving West Indian children had been born abroad, there was in fact no difference in the school behavior of West Indian children born in Great Britain and those born abroad. Rutter found that teachers reported more behavioral deviance from West Indian children than from children of British parents, and that in fact, their behavior differed. West Indian children engaged more often in socially disapproved conduct, but not in behaviors reflecting emotional disturbance. They were less likely to be truant. Parental reports of behavior at home indicated that West Indian children did not misbehave at home, even when they did at school, whereas British children did misbehave at home, even when they did not at school. Rutter concludes that this reflects a real difference in behavior, rather than a difference in reporting, and conjectures that it is attributable to factors such as community reactions to racial differences and reading retardation.[10]

British-born West Indian children scored somewhat higher on intelligence tests than West Indian-born children, but neither group did as well as the children of British parents. Children who immigrated before age 8 scored somewhat better than children who immigrated at a later age, but all did more poorly than non-immigrating children.[14]

West Indian children had the same rate of psychiatric disorder as British children, but West Indian boys and girls with disorders were more likely to have conduct disorders, whereas British girls tended to have emotional disturbances. There was no difference in the rate of disorder between West Indian children born in Britain and born abroad, and disturbance when it existed was often reported to have begun before the child immigrated. Rutter conjectures from clinical experience, however, that children immigrating at adolescence might have more sustained or pronounced migration-related difficulties.[10]

In exploring the relationship between parent-child separation and subsequent disturbance,[9,12] Rutter concludes that the characteristics of the child's living situation—its stability, consistency, adequacy and amiability—are more important determinants of psycho-emotional and. social functioning than the singular factor of parent-child separation, through immigration or otherwise. The number of stressors experienced, rather than their individual nature and severity, was the salient factor in predicting probability and severity of disturbance.

A 1976 Toronto conference on the urban black student described a number of school difficulties. West Indian children arrive academically disadvantaged by non-attendance or poor level of instruction in West Indian schools; their patterns of social interaction with authority figures and peers are at odds with Canadian expectations; their families do not engage collaboratively with the educational process; their dialect is not a second language and therefore confounds the remedial structure.[4] Toronto newspapers report that West Indian children continue to be streamed into vocational courses in sufficient numbers to raise the spectre of racial prejudice.[5,13] The effect of poor academic preparation for employment may be exacerbated by racial prejudice. A 1984 study of Toronto employer hiring patterns found that a white person was three times more likely than a black person to be hired for a job for which they were equally qualified.[6]

METHODOLOGY

This study provides a descriptive analysis of a cohort of West Indian adolescent offenders referred to the Toronto Family Court Clinic for pre-disposition assessment, and compares them with a group of Canadian offenders. The sample included all West Indian-born offenders (n = 38) referred during the years 1981 to 1983, and a selected group of Canadian-born offenders (n = 38) matched for sex, age, and date of referral.

The Toronto Family Court Clinic, which has been described elsewhere,[3,7] is a service of the Clarke Institute of Psychiatry. To be seen at the clinic, a child must commit a delinquent act, be convicted in court, and the judge must make a decision to order a clinical assessment.

The offenders studied and at least one of their parents or guardians took part in a structured intake interview. Information was recorded on the demographic characteristics of the child and the family, previous police and court involvement, and the child's developmental history, social behavior, and school history. In addition, the child and parent separately completed a 64-item checklist of symptoms and problem behaviours. At the end of the assessment, the clinician responsible for the case completed an assessment information checklist, which contained data on the assessment process, including the number of types of contacts with the various family members and other involved service agencies, the recommendations made regarding disposition and treatment, and diagnostic information about the child.

The West Indian and Canadian offenders were compared on all intake and assessment variables using either chi-square tests for qualitative variables, and t-tests for quantitative variables. In addition, the investigators completed a questionnaire from clinical records, that examined the process of immigration for the child and the family. The overall inter-rater reliability on this instrument was .95, with individual item reliabilities ranging from .88 to 1.00.

FINDINGS

A Comparison of Canadian and West Indian Offenders

Family Information

There were 26 boys and 12 girls in each group, with a mean age of 14 years. Most children in both groups were living with both natural parents or with their mothers at the time of referral. The West Indian families were significantly larger than Canadian families. Half of the Canadian children and virtually all of the West Indian children had been separated for a period of at least one month from one or both parents. The average duration of separation from mothers for West Indian children was 4 years, and for Canadian children, 2 years. The separations occurred at a much younger age for the West Indian children.

Table 1
Family Information +

	Canadian	West Indian
Child lives with		
both natural parents	12	9
mother and step-father	2	7
father and step-mother	1	1
mother	15	14
father	2	1
CAS ward	3	4
mother and relatives	1	0
step-father	1	0
relatives	1	1
other	1	2
Number of people living in family home	4.0	4.9*
Number of children in family	3.3	4.5*

Table 1 (continued)

	Canadian	West Indian
Separation from		
mother	19	35****
father	24	37****
both parents	4	12*
other(s)	4	12*
Age at first separation from		
mother	9.2	3.1****
father	6.3	3 .3***
Age at reunion with		
mother	11.4	7 5****
father	8.3	4.1
Affiliated with church	32%	83%

*p < ,.05   ** p < .01   *** p < .005
**** < .001
N.B. Categories < 5 should be cautiously interpreted

More Canadian parents reported previous involvement with Ontario courts, and more Canadian mothers reported that they had physical and emotional problems. West Indian parents rarely reported previous mental health problems or criminal histories.

Mothers and fathers in both groups generally had secondary school educations and worked in skilled or semi-skilled jobs. Canadian mothers were described as homemakers more frequently than West Indian mothers. Eighty-three per cent of West Indian mothers and 67% of West Indian fathers were active church members, primarily in fundamentalist sects, compared with 29% of Canadian mothers and 16% of Canadian fathers.

Developmental, Social and School History

West Indian children were seldom reported to be delinquent or behaviourally difficult prior to immigration (although parental absence during the child's early years makes this finding questionable). Canadian parents were more likely to report that their children were overactive, impulsive, easily frustrated, had difficulty concentrating, and stole during their early years. The

Canadian children were more likely to have had previous contacts with mental health resources. Canadian mothers also more frequently described difficult pregnancies and deliveries and significant family problems in the child's first three years.

Table 2
Developmental, Social and School History

	Canadian	West Indian
Problems during pregnancy or at birth	17	4***
Family problem at birth to 3 years	22	13*
Early symptoms (birth-3 years)		
Overactive	18	7*
Previous psychiatric assistance for child	16	5***
Child has failed a grade	28	13****
Parent knows child's friend		
yes	23	5
no	5	9
some of them	9	22

*p < .05   **p < .01   ***p < .005   ****< .001
N.B. Categories < 5 should be cautiously interpreted

As current symptoms, Canadian parents more often described their children as easily frustrated, touchy, accident prone, small for their age, having difficulty making or keeping friends, having no interest in sports, playing with matches, and having bowel problems. West Indian families described behavior/discipline problems almost exclusively, e.g., stealing, lying, and being overly dependent on peers. Most of the West Indian children were described as being relatively problem-free until the onset of adolescence. West Indian parents more frequently indicated that they did not know their children's friends and described their children, socially, as followers.

Both Canadian and West Indian children did poorly in school. West Indian children were significantly less likely to have failed a grade, and were somewhat less likely to be described as having problems with teachers and being truant.

Delinquency History

The West Indian adolescents were significantly more likely to have previous charges and previous involvement with the juvenile court. Thirty-one percent of the West Indian offenders, compared with 3% of the Canadian offenders, had been charged with offenses against persons, such as common or indecent assault. West Indian and Canadian offenders were equally likely to be placed in detention at the time of the charge; however, the West Indian youngsters were more likely to remain in detention through the clinical assessment.

Table 3
Delinquency History +

	Canadian	West Indian
Present Charge		
Against person	7	13
Against property	21	23
Drugs, truancy	13	5*
Breach of probation, rehearing	1	1
Previous Charges		
Against person	1	12****
Against property	16	25*
Drugs, truancy	3	2
Previous Court Involvement	18	26*
Family Involved with Other Ontario Court	20	6***
Placed in Detention at Apprehension	14	15
In Detention at Time of Assessment	6	13*
Previously on Probation	3	10*

*p c .05　　　**p < .01　　　***p < .005　　　****< .001
N.B. Categories < 5 should be cautiously interpreted

Clinical Interventions

Single or multiple family interviews occurred significantly more frequently in the assessment of Canadian offenders. Treatment recommendations were made more often for Canadian children, and more Canadian children began treatment during the assessment. Recommendations for placement outside the parental home, and for Children's Aid Society involvement occurred with equal frequency in both groups.

Table 4
Assessment Process and Recommendations

	Canadian	West Indian
Entire family interviewed		
no	8	23*
once	12	6
twice or more	14	6
Began treatment during assessment	15	6*
Recommendation		
treatment	22	11*
placement	13	13
probation	11	11

* $p < .05$ ** $p < 01$ *** $p < .005$ **** $< .001$
N.B. Categories < 5 should be cautiously interpreted

DESCRIPTION OF THE IMMIGRATION PROCESS FOR THE WEST INDIAN

Offenders and their Families

Eighty-two per cent of the West Indian children in the group were from Jamaica. Most children were born to families that included both biological parents or extended families, usually maternal. The children tended to remain in this care-giving situation when the first parent emigrated, which occurred when the child was very young, a mean age of 2.7 years. One-third of the children were less than one year of age when the first parent emigrated, and the remainder were between 2 and 5 years of age. For 58% of the children, the care-giving constellation remained in place until they themselves emigrated, at a mean age of 7.5 years.

None of the subjects emigrated with both parents; 10% came with one parent. The family which the child joined in Canada consisted most frequently of both biological parents, or slightly less often, of the biological mother and a step-father not known to the child. Sixteen per cent came to a single mother. One-third of the marriages to which the child emigrated subsequently ended, 13% of the custodial parents remarried, and 24% gained additional children.

DISCUSSION

The following discussion takes into account that similarities between the two groups of subjects exceed the differences, likely reflecting the complex process by which each child was selected for assessment by the Family Court Clinic. They represent a mix of clinical and delinquent concerns, perhaps with other confounding factors operating, such as lack of family cooperation with the court process, or confusion among remedial resources.

The West Indian children and their families were reported as having fewer mental health symptoms, both historically and at the time of assessment, than their Canadian counterparts. In this respect, they resemble Rutter's West Indian sample. Within the limitations of a retrospective file study, we could not address whether this was a real difference that would be supported by objective evaluation, or an artifact of reporting.

If the difference is due to reporting, how should we understand it? The West Indian parents may have been protecting themselves by reporting a rosier picture than existed in fact. They may have received poor information from earlier care-givers, and been unaware of difficulties that really existed. They may not have perceived their child's history in terms of the particular symptoms offered, but may have described precursors to disturbance if presented with a list that captured a more familiar way of seeing children at risk. Or perhaps, as was found in Rutter's sample, the children did not present difficulties in the home, even when misbehaving in the community.

Alternatively, it may be that the West Indian children were not at risk from a young age or as a result of chronic dysfunction, but came to delinquent behavior as a result of sudden difficulties. It is tempting but difficult to draw a connection with the event of migration, since migration occurred on average 7 years earlier than delinquency. It is more plausible to postulate the onset of adolescence as a stressor that overwhelmed coping mechanisms already struggling with a prolonged series of changes. A developing awareness of the consequences of school failure and racial prejudice may have erupted in delinquent behavior. The push of the adolescent towards individuation may have threatened the stability of the family unit, or its progress toward nuclearity or economic success or some other valued goal, and thus created a crisis.

With respect to the differences reported in the kind of delinquency charges, and reactions of the justice system and the psychiatric assessment system to those charges, it is not clear from the data available whether the behavior of the two groups of youngsters differed in fact, or whether the police and/or judicial and/or family systems responded differently to produce the statistically significant differences noted.

For instance, the referral process may have operated more slowly with West Indian children: they had more charges, more charges against person, and had more often been on probation before being referred. Referral for assessment sometimes indicates that the justice system is unsure how to understand a delinquent act and/or how to intervene effectively, and sometimes that mental illness or severe emotional problems are suspected. The slower referral process may indicate that there was initially little question about how to understand the delinquencies, and only when the remedies did not prevent further charges was assistance sought. Alternately, it could be that psychiatric intervention was seen by police, lawyers, or by the court as inappropriate for West Indian children, or was actively opposed by West Indian parents. The latter may be culturally syntonic, since West Indian parents report little historical involvement with such resources, and engaged more sparingly with the assessment when it was ordered. A more helpful resource may not have existed.

The usual reasons that children remain in detention awaiting disposition is to protect society, or because there is no better resource available, as when the family refuses to have the child return home. Anecdotal material suggests that the West Indian family's patience with the delinquent was sometimes exhausted by the time referral was made, or that their frustration with the child was exacerbated by referral to a psychiatric service. Limited involvement with the assessment procedure invites a similar explanation.

It may be that the weakness of the connection between parent and child initiated by early and prolonged separation during serial migration, tentatively bridged during post-migration years, cannot withstand delinquent behavior. Because the culture of the juvenile justice system holds that the parent is part of the problem and part of the solution, further demands are placed on a family that already may be struggling to accommodate many stresses. Their reaction may be to refuse further involvement with the child and focus available energy on protecting that which is successful.

If the family is not able to be part of the solution for the child, what options are available? West Indian children were not recommended for placement, which could be seen as provision of a surrogate family, any more frequently than Canadian children. Treatment (counselling) was recommended only half as often. It appears that the "right" resources to meet the need may not have been available.

What resources might be helpful? In this study, West Indian parents, more than Canadian parents, reported that they did not know their children's friends and saw their children as followers, suggesting that peer relations were seen to be part of the difficulty. It is a skill to relate to adolescents and their friends as they push away from the family in the process of individuation. West Indian parents from a rural extended family situation would have no reason to have developed this skill, since they would naturally know everyone with whom their child could associate and adult surveillance would happen without any effort on their part. Perhaps teaching this skill would prevent the premature rupture of the parent-adolescent tie.

The church is an important institution in the life of the West Indian parents in this study. Perhaps it should be explored as a medium for offering assistance to the family, or to the parents, as they struggle with transitional difficulties, helping them to understand and facilitate the process of accommodating a different culture.

It seems self-evident that serial migration poses massive difficulties for individuals and for the family unit, and any steps to expedite family reunification would be a valuable preventive move. School is the dominant environment for immigrating children, and any changes that improve their ability to be sensitive to each child and provide the resources necessary for that child's successful transition will be preventive of future difficulty. An investment in teaching parents how to be assertive consumers of the educational system for the benefit of their children would also be appropriate to Canadian culture, and preventive of future difficulties.

A study of a normal population of West Indian children who have successfully made the transition into adolescence and Canadian life would produce more answers about preventive measures.

The judicial and psychiatric systems are called into play when prevention has not been successful. The challenge in working with migrating populations continues to be to achieve sensitivity to the world of the client, as much as possible by someone outside that world, in order to create helpful alternatives that will achieve success, mutually defined, in the process of cultural transition.

ENDNOTES

1. The authors gratefully acknowledge the sponsorship and support of the Toronto Family Court Clinic, Clarke Institute of Psychiatry, with special thanks to George Awad, M.D., Director, and Jerome Pauker, Ph.D., Chief Psychologist and Director of Research for their assistance with this project. This research was conducted while the authors were employed at the Family Court Clinic. The opinions expressed are those of the authors and do not necessarily reflect those of the Family Court Clinic, or of their current employers.

2. The authors acknowledge the support of the 1986 Sophie Boyd Award granted by the University of Toronto Faculty of Social Work Alumni Association, in preparing the research for publication, with special thanks to John Gandy Ph.D., for his helpful comments on the manuscript.

3. Chamberlain, C. and G. Awad. 1975. "Psychiatric Service to the Juvenile Court: A Model." *Canadian Psychiatric Association Journal.* 20, 599-605.

4. D'Oyle, Vincent and Harry Silverman (eds.). 1976. *Black Students in Urban Canada.* Toronto: Citizenship Branch. Ontario Ministry of Culture and Recreation.

5. *Globe and Mail.* April 4, 1984.

6. Henry, F. and E. Ginsberg (eds.). 1985. *Who Gets the Work: A Test of Racial Discrimination in Employment.* Toronto: Urban Alliance on Race Relations and the Social Planning Council.

7. Moms, R. and C. Wilks. 1976. "Computerized Data in the Family Court Clinic: An Effective Multidisciplinary Model of Assessment, Treatment and Research Functions." *The Ontario Psychologist. 8.* 27-31.

8. Robinson, J.A., J.M. Christiansen and A. Thornley-Brown. 1980. West *Indians in Toronto: Implications for Helping Professionals.* Toronto: Family Services Association.

9. Rutter, M. 1971. "Parent-Child Separation: Psychological Effects on Children." *Journal of Child Psychology and Psychiatry.* 12, 233-260.

10. Rutter, M., W. Yule, M. Berger, B. Yule, J. Morton and C. Bagley.

1974. "Children of West Indian Immigrants 1: Rates of Behavioral Deviance and of Psychiatric Disorder." *Journal of Child Psychology and Psychiatry. IS,* 241-262.

11. Rutter, M., B. Yule, J. Morton and C. Bagley. 1975. "Children of West Indian Immigrants - III Home Circumstances and Family Patterns." *Journal of Child Psychology and Psychiatry, 6,* 105-123.

12. Rutter, M. "Protective Factors in Children's Responses to Stress and Disadvantages." 1979. In M. Kent and J. Rolf (eds.). *Primary Prevention of Psychopathology. Vol. III. Social Competence of Children.* New England: University of Vermont Press.

13. *Toronto Star.* June 19, 1985.

14. Yule, W., M. Berger, M. Rutter and B. Yule. 1975. "Children of West Indian Immigrants". Intellectual Performance and Reading Attainment. "*Journal of Child Psychology and Psychiatry. 16,* 1-17.

CHAPTER 17
Predictors of Status and Criminal Offences among Male and Female Adolescents in an Ontario Community

IAN M. GOMME

INTRODUCTION

Early analyses of adolescent misconduct based upon official statistics presented a profile of male and female delinquency differences which was consistent in two respects. First, gross rates of juvenile crime for females were observed to be relatively low in comparison to those of males and secondly, female delinquency was found to be concentrated in a small number of offence categories—sexual promiscuity, incorrigibility, and running away from home.[37, 43, 59] From these findings, which suggested that female delinquency is considerably more limited and more specialized than male delinquency, emerged a view of female misconduct as less in need of prevention and control than the misbehavior of males.[3, 63] Consequently, as several investigators have pointed out, the importance of understanding the delinquent behavior of females has been depreciated.[5, 33, 50, 54]

More recent examination of adolescent misconduct using self report delinquency (SRD) data as opposed to official statistics indicate that female participation in delinquency resembles more closely that of males in terms of rates, types, and patterns of deviant behavior.[12, 13, 22, 23, 28, 50] Differences are largely confined to the facts that males more than females 1) are somewhat more frequently involved in delinquency and 2) are more likely to engage in delinquent activities involving physical aggression.

Most self report (SRD) research on sex and delinquency has been aimed at explaining the small but consistent differences in the rates of male and female misconduct. There are very few comparative analyses of the causal structures precipitating male and female involvement in delinquent behavior. In what limited research exists, some studies indicate the existence of distinct differenes in causality, while others find that those differences that do exist are minimal. Hagan, Simpson, and Gillis,[24] for example, note the tendency for the nature of social control mechanisms to differ markedly for males and for females and suggest that these differences influence the opportunity for male and female involvement in delinquency. Alternatively, Johnson[35] and Segrave and Hastad [51] maintain that causal differences are slight while Smith[55] argues that there are no differences at all.

In addition, while the dimensionality of delinquency has been investigated and subdimensions (drugs, theft, violence, etc.) have been theoretically and empirically differentiated, very few assessments of the consistency of etiological roots among subsets of delinquent behaviors have been forthcoming to date.[29] Not only are there questions regarding the extent and nature of causal differences between male and female delinquent behaviors but there are also uncertainties with respect to whether causal inputs vary for each sex by type of misconduct.

In this paper, the nature of differing causal structures of male and female delinquency are explored. Following Johnson's[35] assertion that several of the heretofore competing explanatory perspectives have isolated delinquency generating forces, potentially salient causal variables from differential association, social control, and strain theories are incorporated into the analysis and their relative contributions to male and female delinquency are assessed. Predictor variables are (1) associations with other delinquents (differential associations), (2) belief in the law (social control theory), (3) school performance (social control theory, strain theory), (4) socioeconomic status (SES) (strain theory), and (5) age. In past research, the effects of these variables have most frequently been examined separately or have been assessed in mutually exclusive theoretical clusters. Rarely have their impacts been evaluated simultaneously and their effects compared across samples of male and female adolescents on a variety of types of misconduct. This integration is designed not only to add to the amounts of variance explained in the illegal conduct of male and female youth, but also to permit identification of any systematic differences in the causal structures of a variety of types of male and female delinquency.

THEORIES AND PREDICTORS

Differential Association Theory

The emphasis in this orientation is placed upon socialization in a group context. Delinquency is viewed as the product of group influences through which individuals learn, by way of interaction in intimate personal groups, the skills and the rationalizations supportive of misconduct. Definitions of the situation are learned which encourage the individual, depending upon the norms of the particular group, either to observe or to break the rules of society. "A person becomes delinquent because of an excess of definitions favourable to violation of law over definitions unfavourable to violation of law."[44]

Definitions both favourable and unfavourable to law violation are viewed as affected by frequency, duration, priority, and intensity. Thus, definitions promoted more frequently, for a longer time, earlier in life, and which are espoused by a more prestigious source have greater impact in the process of producing delinquent or conforming behavior.[40]

A number of researchers have pointed out that empirical tests of this perspective have tended to employ an operationalization of differential association which has not directly measured ties to the normative definitions of a particular group. Rather, what has been assessed are ties to persons who represent the medium through which normative definitions are learned. As Linden and Fillmore note, such tests of differential association treat the perspective as a form of reference group theory, which places more emphasis upon who is taken into account in making personal choices with respect to behavior, rather than upon attachments to definitions favourable or unfavourable to rule breaking.[38] What is measured specifically is the number of ties to significant others who themselves either approve or disapprove of the violation of norms.

A central finding in much delinquency research is that the possession of delinquent friends is a factor strongly predisposing youth to participation in delinquent activity.[19, 30, 39]

Social Control Theory

Social control theory operates under the premise that individuals are naturally inclined to break the rules and will refrain from doing so only where special barriers to deviance exist.[30] These barriers are composed of ties or bonds to the conventional system which serve to inhibit engagement in delinquent activity. Where ties to the conventional normative order are weakened or broken, the individual is freed to engage in non-conforming behavior. Where bonds to society are intact and strong, the teenager does not possess the time required for misconduct, does not wish to jeopardize future opportunities with present transgressions, or simply views delinquent action as incompatible with accepted moral standards.

The bonds most commonly identified by social control theorists are conceptualized as four distinguishable but interwoven strands which tie the individual to the larger society.[40] They are attachment, commitment, involvement, and belief. The attachment dimension refers to a person's sensitivity to the feelings and opinions of significant others—parents and teachers, for example. Commitment relates to the time and energy invested in conforming activity. Those teenagers who have devoted a great deal of effort to conventional undertakings (e.g. acquiring an education) calculate carefully the high risks involved in travelling along delinquent paths and refrain from doing so. Involvement comprises that which an individual does with time. It is suggested that those heavily involved in lawful endeavors have little time remaining to become entangled in illegal enterprise. Finally, belief is a construct which represents the degree of acceptance of the rightness of the normative order. The greater a person's belief in society's norms, the less likely the individual will engage in delinquent acts.[40]

In this study, the impacts of two social control dimensions, commitment and belief, are assessed employing 1) school performance and 2) attitudes toward law and the moral order respectively as operationalizations. Social control theory maintains that fortuitous negotiation of the various obstacles presented by the school requires a commitment to the values of industry, achievement, and deferred gratification. Failure to "pass" through the system is viewed as negatively affecting the individual's future prospects while satisfactory performance is seen as resulting in the individual being suitably rewarded for the invested effort. Thus, inadequate school performance and the attendant losses of both currently rewarding experiences and future educational and occupational opportunities is taken as generating a relatively lower degree of commitment to the social order. With little to lose at present or in the future, the adolescent is freed to become delinquent.[30, 38]

A large number of research studies indicate a strong relationship between unsuccessful school performance and delinquency.[10, 18, 19, 27, 36, 48] This association is found to hold even where such potentially confounding variables as I.Q., sex, age, socioeconomic status (SES), race, school neighbourhood, and parental aspirations are controlled.[49, 62]

Belief in the validity of the law and the moral order is a variable central to the social control formulation. Bonds to such conventional institutions and figures as the law and the police are regularly used in social control research as indicators of a respondent's stake in conformity.[32] Belief in the legitimacy of institutions of law and order and positive attitudes toward social control agents are frequently cited as "breaks" on delinquent behavior.[26, 27, 30] As Jensen[32] contends, a positive evaluation of the law and its agents is indicative of a strong social bond the existence of which results in lower rates of delinquency.

Strain Theory

Where social control theory presents the notion that delinquents are innately non-conformists whose delinquency has been facilitated by the absence of barriers, strain theory suggest that youth are inherently conformists who are propelled into deviance by structural forces. The most important etiological force, from this perspective. is the teenager's socioeconomic status (SES). The strain approach asserts that all youth, regardless of their class positions, are enticed to pursue similar culturally defined success goals. While goal aspirations are constant across lower, middle, and upper class groupings, ease of access to those goals is not. For lower class youth, avenues to goal attainment are more restricted if not entirely blocked. Thus, lower class youth possess inadequate resources to enable effective competition for status rewards through legitimate routes. In the face of this structurally based pressure, the young of the lower classes are more or less driven to delinquency either as a mode of adaption to achieve ends inaccessible through legitimate means,[14, 42] or as a reaction to the problems of adjustment which ensue as a consequence of the frustration experienced.[15]

In an early application of self report delinquency (SRD) measures. Short and Nye[52] reported no relationship between socioeconomic status (SES) and delinquency. In subsequent SRD research, the lack of any link between socioeconomic status (SES) and delinquent behavior[30, 57] has been a frequent finding. Some research, however, has indicated that an association between these variables exists but that the strength of the relationship is weak.[16, 17, 21] Also, in the rare instance, the direction of the relationship has been found to be reversed.[60] Thus, it is hardly surprising that Tittle and Villemez[58] conclude, in their review of the literature, that the findings with respect to the relationship between social class and delinquency are "inconsistent". An enlarged survey of the literature on the class-crime issue, conducted more recently by Braithwaite, reports similar inconsistencies. Of the 47 studies employing self report delinquency scales, 38% reported delinquency concentrated in the lower classes and 15% provided some indication of this pattern. The remaining 47%, however, reported no significant differences in delinquency activity by class.[8]

Age

Age is not typically incorporated into any of the differential association, social control, or strain theories as a causal variable because, as Hirschi and Gottfredson argue, the central causal variables in these perspectives have no effect upon the shape of the distribution of crime related to age.[31] As Nettler notes, in this regard, "if the relation between age and proclivity to crime is invariant, whatever causes crime at one age may also cause it at another."[44] Age does, however, have an impact upon delinquency independent of the theories discussed above.

SRD research reveals the existence of a curvilinear relationship between and the frequency of delinquent activity.[10, 19, 61] Frequency and seriousness of delinquency generally increase into mid-adolescence and then decline. Both status and criminal offences of lesser seriousness, in particular minor property crimes, are found to peak during adolescence.[34]

METHODOLOGY

Sample

An anonymous survey was conducted in the spring of 1978 in ten elementary and junior high schools in a smaller urban center in southern Ontario. The self report questionnaire was completed in regularly scheduled classes by 429 students in grades 7-10. Participation in the study was voluntary.

Table 1
Multiple Repression of Self Report
Male and Female Delinquency

	DEL				STAT				CRIM			
	M		F		M		F		M		F	
	B	Beta	B	Beta	B	Beta	B	Beta	B	Beta	B	Beta
AGE	.797	.189*	.470	.156*	.496	.283*	.357	.246*	.300	.108*	.136	.074
ACH	-1.685	-.155*	-.082	-.008	-.714	-.157*	-.092	-.020	-1.074	-.150*	-.129	-.023
SES	-.525	-.045	.974	.119*	-.318		.214	.054	-.423	-.056	.620	.125
DAS	-2.316	-.220*	-3.132	-.370*	-.851	-.194*	-1.418	-.348*	-1.360	-.196*	-1.715	-.335*
BEL	-.860	-.459*	-.527	-.299*	-.274	-.350*	-.241	-.284*	-.609	-.493	-.277	-.261
	$R^2 = .50$		$R^2 = .36$		$R^2 = .43$		$R^2 = .35$		$R^2 = .46$		$R^2 = .27$	

Table 1 (continued)

| | THEFT | | | | DRUGS | | | | B & E | | | |
| | M | | F | | M | | F | | M | | F | |
	B	Beta	B	Beta	B	Beta	B	Beta	B	Beta	B	Beta
AGE	.042	.037	.096	.113	.157	.222*	.117*	.212*	.023	.155*	.000	.002
ACH	-.295	-.099	-.0113	-.043	-.240		.075	.044	-.145	-.131	-.018	-.022
SES	.086	.027	.358	.153*	-.173		.005	.003	-.151	-.130	-.052	-.072
DAS	-.214	-.417*	-.483	-.201*	-.313	-.178*	-.565	-.365*	-.164	-.153	-.176	-.234*
BEL	-.214	-.417*	-.118	-.235*	-.118	-.375*	-.069	-.216*	-.069	-.363*	-.035	-.335*
	R2 = .28		R2 = .18		R2 = .38		R2 = .29		R2 = .26		R2 = .14	

| | VANDALISM | | | | INTER-CON | | | |
| | M | | F | | M | | F | |
	B	Beta	B	Beta	B	Beta	B	Beta
AGE	.038	.069	.004	.010	.008	.014	-.079	-.236*
ACH	-.110	-.078	-.002	-.002	-.135	-.089	-.156	-.151*
SES	-.152	-.101	.081	.071	-.029	.018	.090	.099
DAS	-.094	-.068	-.280	-.238*	-.137	-.093	-.178	-.189
BEL	-.114	-.470*	-.044	-.182*	-.062	-.239	-.017	-.086
	R2 = .29		R2 = .12		R2 = .10		R2 = .14	

LEGEND

Dependent

DEL - gen delinquency

STAT - status offences

CRIM - criminal offences

B & E - break and enter

INTER-CON - interpersonal conflict

Independent

ACH - school achievement

DAS - deliquent friends

BEL - belief in law

*p = <.05

OPERATIONALIZATION OF DEPENDENT VARIABLES

Self Reported Delinquency

Delinquency was measured by a scale developed from items designed to tap a variety of dimensions of deviant behavior. These items include status offences; (1) skipping school, (2) staying out all night without permission from parents, (3) running away from home, (4) buying or drinking liquor or beer, and (5) criminal offences; (1) selling or using drugs, (2) theft under $5, (3) theft $5-50, (4) theft over $50, (5) taking a car without the owner's permission, (6) breaking into a building or house, (7) damaging or destroying private property, and (8) hurting or beating up another person on purpose. Participants were asked whether, the last year, they had committed these acts: (1) "never" (2) "once or twice", (3) "several times", or (4) "very often". Scales were created by summing the items in the fashion commonly adopted with SRD measures.[30, 52]

In SRD research, innocuous delinquent acts tend to be reported much more frequently than more serious acts of deviance and hence, where correlates of non-serious and serious delinquency differ, the scales reflect the correlates of the relatively inconsequential criminal activity. Also, where the correlates of certain types of delinquency differ, global scales may serve to mask these differences.[16] By creating subscales, grouping items according to offence type (status, criminal, violence, etc.), clarification of relationships between predictors and dependent variables is permitted. Subscales included status, criminal, and theft offences. Drug offences, break and enter, vandalism, and interpersonal conflict were measured by single items.

OPERATIONALIZATION OF INDEPENDENT VARIABLES

Delinquent Associations

Respondents were asked to indicate whether or not they had any close friends charged during the year prior to the study.

Belief in the Law

Adolescent evaluations of belief in the law are measured by scores on a scale devised from questions concerning attitudes toward and expressions of willingness to cooperate with the police in a variety of circumstances. The pool of items was originally selected from a study of the attitudes of adolescents toward law enforcement agents in the United States.[7] These items were subjected to a factor analytic procedure designed to isolate principal components. A subset of items tapping a single dimension, belief in the law, was identified and a scale was constructed using the standard procedure for factor scale variable creation outlined by Nie et al.[45]

School Performance

School performance is assessed by asking respondents whether or not they had failed a course of study in the past two years.

SES

Father's occupation, coded using the Blishen scale, was used to establish each respondent's class position.[64]

Age

Age was determined on the basis of respondents' birth dates.

REGRESSION ANALYSIS

The results of a standard regression analysis are presented in Table 1 which contains unstandardized (b) and standardized (beta) regression coefficients and R^2s for male and female subsamples on a variety of delinquency offences. In the discussion which follows, subsamples of males and females are compared and relative effects are rank ordered for each. Unstandardized coefficients indicating the change in unit on the dependent variable due to a change in unit on each independent variable when other independent variables are controlled are discussed when comparing between male and female subsamples. When rank ordering the independent variables in terms of their relative contributions to variance explained in a dependent variable, the appropriate statistics to examine are the standardized regression coefficients. The R^2s indicate the proportion of variance in a dependent variable explained by all of the independent variables. The discussion is confined mainly to status and criminal offence groupings except where notable differences occur on specific subdimensions.

FINDINGS

COMPARISON OF EFFECTS BETWEEN
MALE AND FEMALE SUBSAMPLES

Delinquent Associations

While association with delinquent friends affects delinquency for both males and females, females are consistently more strongly predisposed toward a variety of delinquent acts than are males. The notion that females are just as likely or more likely than males to conform to the anticipations of their friends is supported in social psychological research which indicates that females actually conform to peer expectations more than males.[46, 56] Similar empirical support exists in delinquency research. Giordano and Cemkovich,[20] for example, note a tendency for girls to commit crimes in the company of other boys and girls and argue that it is this mixed "company" that provides social support for delinquent activity while also supplying the opportunities to learn and to participate in illegal activity. An investigation by Cameron (11) of the shoplifting practices of juvenile girls also disclosed that females frequently engage in this activity in a supportive group context. Gender role research in the field of criminology has revealed that female criminal roles are frequently performed in such a way as to render "support" for the illegal conduct of their male associates. From this perspective, females are seen as "going along with" the actions of their male companions. The idea that females are socialized to more compliant and conforming forms of behavior and that subsequently they are more dependent upon peer support[53] is emphasized in this explanation. Males, conversely, are viewed as being socialized to more assertive, more independent, and more individualistic behaviors and hence are comparatively less affected in their delinquent activities by associations with delinquent peers.

Belief in the Law

Belief in the law reduces involvement in status and criminal offences for both males and females. This finding is consistent with those of previous researchers who observe that such bonds to the moral order act as "brakes" on delinquent conduct.[26, 27] However, the effects of this predictor, for all delinquency subdimensions with the exception of drug offences, are consistently greater for males than for females.

A tentative explanation for the greater power of belief in the law and the moral order to predict male delinquency is found in the recent work of Donald Black.[6] Black suggests that the more informal control to which individuals are subject, the fewer formal controls or the less law to which they will be subject. Black maintains that there is a shifting balance between informal and formal controls with the relative lack of one being compensated for by the relative presence of the other.

It is suggested that females more than males are not only socialized to compliant conforming behavior but are subject to greater degrees of informal supervision in the family setting. Conversely, males more than females are taught to be more self assertive, more independent, and more aggressive. At the same time, males are informally supervised in the family context to a lesser extent. The relative lack of informal control experienced by males is balanced by their more frequent subjection to more formal mechanisms of social control. As a consequence of their socialization to be more self assertive and as a result of their reduced subjection to informal social controls, males more than females are more likely to confront agents of formal authority—first teachers and then other such figures including the police. A number of psychologists have argued that increasingly critical attitudes toward impersonal authority is a function of increased contacts with agents of formal control.[41] There is evidence as well to suggest that attitudes toward one figure of authority, the teacher, are often generalized to other such figures, especially the police.[4]

Recent sociological research assessing Black's formulation indicates that males are indeed more subject to and affected by formal social controls (law, police, courts) while females are more subject to and influenced by informal social controls (family, peers).[24] It seems quite probable, given these findings, that low levels of belief in the law and a lack of support for its agents might prove to be more salient precursors of delinquency for males that for females.

School Performance

While the relationship between school performance and all types of delinquency is non-existent for females, this is not the case for males. For boys, lower levels of academic performance prefigure both status and criminal offences. That the degree of delinquent involvement of males is more affected by school performance than that of females is a finding which has some support in previous research.[5, 35] The greater influence of school failure on male as opposed to female delinquency is explained by noting the more intense pressures for success in society which are faced by males. Given the crucial role of the school in paving the way to future occupational success and given the added importance for males of later securing a favourable position in the occupational structure, school failure is viewed as a more salient contributing factor to their disenchantment and disengagement. The "failure" in school has little to lose by engaging in delinquent conduct and hence is encouraged to do so while the "success" has too much at stake to risk involvement in delinquency.[30] Poor school performance is typically considered to have less of an impact upon females in these respects in that their future social status is more frequently established in later life, not by their own performance, but by the occupational statuses of their husbands.

Socioeconomic Status

The data reveal, consistent with much of the research conducted using SRD measures,[30, 57] that there is not direct causal relationship between SES and participation in delinquent behavior. Theories suggesting that the disjunction between the aspirations and expectations of the lower class produces strain which, in turn, results in delinquency are not supported by the data.

While delinquent conduct appears evenly distributed by class in this sample, some caveats are necessary. In self report delinquency surveys, measures of SES based upon occupational categories frequently fail to include in samples of students, representatives of what might truly be thought of as a lower, or as Johnson[35] terms it, and "underclass". SES, it is argued from Johnson's perspective, may simply be inadequately operationalized in studies of this nature. In addition, other researchers have argued that self report scales tend to include only minor offences of which all youth are guilty. They have argued that the inclusion of more serious offences would, in fact, yield class differences more similar to those observed in the analysis of official statistics.[16, 28]

Age

Age is a significant predictor of status offences for both sexes but particularly for males. Reasons for this general increase in status offence commission with age, particularly for boys, include (1) the growing rebelliousness of youth through their adolescent years, (2) the increased opportunity for older teenagers to engage in delinquent behavior, (3) the decreased supervision of older adolescents by adult authority figures (parents, teachers, etc.), and (4) the anticipation, on the part of "maturing" adolescents, of soon assuming adult status and hence being able to legitimately engage in activities such as driving, travelling, and drinking alcohol. That age predicts status offences in a finding for which there is much support in the literature.[47]

That age is not a significant predictor of criminal offences is probably a function of the limited age range of this sample. Respondents (under the age of 16) were not representative of that age group (later teens) more likely to be involved in more serious forms of delinquency.

COMPARISON OF EFFECTS WITHIN MALE AND FEMALE SUBSAMPLES

An examination of the betas in Table 1 permits the assessment of the relative strengths of independent variables in explaining variance in male and female delinquency and its subdimensions. For both status and criminal offences, the major explanatory variable for males is belief in the law. Conversely, the most powerful predictor of female delinquency is the possession of delinquent peers. Of the remaining independent variables, age is generally a less powerful predictor ranking, with the exception of male status offences, below both belief in the law and possession of delinquent friends in its explanatory power. School achievement too is consistently less powerful as a predictor and exerts a significant effect on delinquent behavior only for males. SES has no predictive power for either males or females on any type of delinquency.

SUMMARY AND CONCLUSION

The analysis of official statistics has indicated that the deviant conduct of females is infrequent, innocuous, and specialized. This profile of female deviant behavior has provided little justification for viewing female crime as a significant social problem in need of remedy and hence has resulted in insufficient attention being directed toward women in sociological theories of deviance. While self report delinquency studies have found female delinquent behavior to be considerably more similar to that of males in terms of rates, types, and patterns of deviant behavior, theoretical efforts have either centered upon accounting for the small but consistent differences in male and female self report frequencies or have concentrated upon the creation of models of deviance designed to specify the nature of causes of male delinquency. These emphasis have caused some sociologists to maintain that general theories of deviance are in reality theories of male deviance[24] and, consequently, to assert that a balance must be achieved if the etiology of female crime is to be more clearly understood.

Results of the regression analysis suggest that the causal structures of deviance for males and females differ from one another. Association with delinquent peers better predicts female than male delinquency while attitudes toward the law and its enforcement agents provides a better predictor of male and female delinquent behavior. These findings are consistent across a variety of offence types.

More of the variance in male and female delinquencies is explained by the integration of variables drawn from these major theoretical orientations. This unequal explanation of variance lends some support to the assertion that a sexist bias is inherent in the sociological theories of deviance developed to date. The necessity of constructing and testing more adequate theoretical models which are sufficiently sensitive to the complexities of the causal forces precipitating female deviance is understood.

ENDNOTES

1. The data on which this analysis is based were collected by Mary Morton and Gordon West as part of the study of a Diversion program in an Ontario county.

2. Due to the lack of sophistication of the teenager's answering, however, it proved impossible to determine fine gradations of difference on father's occupational status on the basis of Blishen scale readings. Also, as Broom *et al.* have demonstrated with respect to children reporting on parental occupation, such tests are not direct and consequently "one cannot confidently claim that what they say about daddy is true."

3. Adler, F. *Sisters in Crime.* New York: McGraw-Hill. 1975.

4. Amorso, D.M., and E.E. Ware. "Youth's Perception of Police as a Function of Attitudes Toward Parents, Teachers, and Self." *Canadian Journal of Criminology. 25.* 1983.

5. Biron, L., R. Gagnon, and M. LeBlanc. *La Delinquance des Filles.* Montreal. Group de Recherche sur l'Inadaption Juvenile. 1980.

6. Black, D. *The Behavior of Law.* New York: Academic Press. 1976.

7. Bouma, D.H. *Kids and Cops.* Grand Rapids: Eerdman. 1969.

8. Braithwaite, J. "The Myth of Social Class and Criminality Reconsidered." *American Sociological Review. 46.* 1981.

9. Broom, L., F. Jones, P. McDonnell, and P. Duncan Jones. "Is it True What They Say About Daddy?" *American Journal of Sociology. 84.* 1978.

10. Byles, J. *Alienation, Deviance and Social Control.* Toronto: Interim Research Project on Unreached Youth. 1969.

11. Cameron, M.O. *The Booster and the Switch.* New York: Free Press. 1964.

12. Canter, R.J. "Sex Differences in Self-reported Delinquency." *Criminology. 20.* 1982.

13. Cernkovich, S.A. and P.C. Giordano. "A Comparative Analysis of Male and Female Delinquency." *Sociological Quarterly. 20.* 1979.

14. Cloward, R. and L. Ohlin. *Delinquency and Opportunity.* New York: Free Press. 1955.

15. Cohen, A.K. *Delinquent Boys: The Culture of the Gang.* New York: Free Press. 1955.

16. Elliott, D. and S. Ageton. "Reconciling Differences in Estimates of Delinquency." *American Sociological Review. 45.* 1980.

17. Empey, L. and M. Erickson. "Hidden Delinquency and Social Status." *Social Forces. 44.* 1966.

18. Empey, L. and S. Lubeck. *Explaining Delinquency.* Lexington: Heath/Lexington. 1971.

19. Frechette, M. and M. LeBlanc. *La Delinquance Cachee des Adolescents Montrealais.* Montreal: Group de Recherche sur l'Inadaption Juvenile. 1978.

20. Giordano, P. and S. Cernkovich. "On Complicating the Relationship Between Liberation and Delinquency." *Social Problems. 26.* 1979.

21. Gold, M. *Delinquent Behavior in an American City.* Belmont, C.A.: Wadsworth, 1970.

22. Gomme, I.M. *A Multivariate Analysis of Juvenile Delinquency Among Ontario Public and Separate School Students.* Unpublished Ed.D. dissertation: University of Toronto. 1983.

23. Gomme, I.M., M. Morton, and W.G. West. "Rates, Types, and Patterns of Male and Female Delinquency in an Ontario County." *Canadian Journal of Criminology. 26. 3.* 1984.

24. Hagan, J.J. Simpson, and A. Gillis. "The Sexual Stratification of Social Control: A Gender Based Perspective on Crime and Delinquency." *British Journal of Sociology. 30.* 1979.

25. Harris, A. "Sex and Theories of Deviance: Toward a Functional Theory of Deviant Typescripts." *American Sociological Review. 42.* 1977.

26. Hepburn, J.R. "Testing Alternative Models of Delinquency Causation." *Journal of Criminal Law and Criminology. 67.* 1976.

27. Hindelang, M. "Causes of Delinquency: A Partial Replication and Extension." *Social Problems. 21.* 1973.

28. Hindelang, M., T. Hirschi, and J. Weis. "Correlates of Delinquency: The Illusion of Discrepancy Between Self-report and Official Measures." *American Sociology Review. 44.* 1979.

29. Hindelang, M., T. Hirschi, and J. Weis. *Measuring Delinquency.* Beverly Hills: Sage Publications. 1981.

30. Hirchi, T. *Causes of Delinquency.* Berkeley: University of California Press. 1969.

31. Hirschi, T. and M.R. Gottfredson. "Age and the Explanation of Crime." *American Journal of Sociology. 89.* 1983.

32. Jensen, G. "Inner Containment and Delinquency." *Journal of Criminal Law and Criminology. 64.* 1973.

33. Jensen, G. and R. Eve. "Sex Differences in Delinquency: An Examination of Popular Sociological Explanations." *Criminology. 13.* 1976.

34. Jensen, G. and Rojek. *Delinquency: A Sociological View.* Lexington, Mass: D.C. Heath. 1980.

35. Johnson, R.E. *Juvenile Delinquency and its Origins: An Integrated Theoretical Approach.* Cambridge: Cambridge University Press. 1979.

36. Kelly, D.H. "School Failure, Academic Self Evaluation, and School Avoidance and Deviant Behavior." *Youth and Society. 2.* 1971.

37. Langelier-Biron, L. "The Delinquent Young Girl a Non-Entity?" In R. Corrado, M. LeBlanc, and J. Trepanier (Eds.). *Current Issues in Juvenile Justice.* Toronto: Butterworths. 1983.

38. Linden, R. and C. Fillmore. "A Comparative Study of Delinquency Involvement." *Canadian Review of Sociology and Anthropology. 28.* 1981.

39. Mathews, V.M. "Differential Identification." *Social Problems. 15.* 1968.

40. Matsueda, R.I. "Testing Control Theory and Differential Association. A Causal Modelling Approach." *American Sociological Review. 47.* 1982.

41. Matteson, D.R. *Adolescence Today: Sex Roles and the Search for Identity.* Homewood Dorsey Press. 1975.

42. Merton, R.K. "Social Structure and Anomie." *American Sociological Review. 3.* 1938.

43. Morris, R.R. "Female Delinquency and Relational Problems." *Social Forces. 43.* 1964.

44. Nettler, G. *Explaining Crime* (3rd ed.). New York: McGraw-Hill. 1984.

45. Nie, N., C. Steinbrenner, and D. Brent. *Statistical Package for the Social Sciences* (2nd ed.). New York: McGraw-Hill. 1975.

46. Nord, W.R. "Social Exchange Theory: An Integrative Approach to Social Conformity." *Psychological Bulletin. 71.* 1969.

47. Palmore, E. and P. Hammond. "Interacting Factors in Juvenile Delinquency." *American Sociological Review. 29.* 1964.

48. Polk, K. and W. Schafer. *Schools and Delinquency.* Englewood Cliffs: Prentice-Hall. 1972.

49. Rhodes, A. and A. Reiss. "Apathy, Truancy and Delinquency as Adaptations to School Failure." *Social Forces. 48.* 1969.

50. Richads, P. "Quantitative and Qualitative Sex Differences in Middle Class Delinquency." *Criminology. 19.* 1981.

51. Segrave, J. and D. Hastad. "Evaluating Structural and Control Models of Delinquency Causation: A Replication and Extension." *Youth and Society. 14.* 1983.

52. Short, J. and E. Nye. "Reported Behavior as a Criterion of Deviant Behavior." *Social Problems 5.* 1957.

53. Shower, N., S. Norland, J. James, and W. Thornton. "Gender Roles and Delinquency." *Social Forces. 58.* 1979.

54. Smart, C. *Women, Crime and Criminology: A Feminist Critique.* London: Routledge and Kagan Paul. 1976.

55. Smith, D.A. "Sex and Deviance: An Assessment of Major Sociological Variables." *Sociological Quarterly. 20.* 1979.

56. Thomas, D.L. and A. Weigart. "Socialization and Adolescent Conformity to Significant Others: A Cross-Cultural Analysis." *American Sociological Review. 36.* 1971.

57. Tittle, C.R. "The Myth of Social Class and Criminality: An Empirical Assessment of the Empirical Evidence." *American Sociological Review. 43.* 1978.

58. Tittle, C.W. Villemez, and D.A. Smith. "Social Class and Criminality." *Social Forces. 56.* 1977.

59. Vedder, C. and D. Sommerville. *The Delinquent Girl.* Springfield. Il: Charles C. Thomas. 1970.

60. Voss, H. "Differential Association and Reported Delinquent Behavior: A Replication." *Social Problems. 12.* 1964.

61. Wallerstein, J. and C. Wyle. "Our Law-Abiding Lawbreakers." *Probation. 25.* 1947.

62. West, W.G. "Adolescent Deviance and the School." *Interchange. 5.* 1975.

63. Wise, N.B. "Juvenile Delinquency Among Middle Class Girls." In Vaz. E.W. (Ed.). *Middle Class Delinquency.* New York: Harper and Row. 1967.

CHAPTER 18
Criminal Liability In Children

J. THOMAS DALBY

INTRODUCTION

Traditional legal views of criminal responsibility generally require two elements to be present in establishing liability. A physical element (actus reus), a voluntary act of commission (or in limited cases, omission) that contravenes a legally defined prohibition, is obligatory. In addition, a mental component (mens rea) is imposed for some offences, necessitating personal fault or intention for the violation. Specific applications and interpretations of these legal concepts have consumed much legal energy.[29] Unfortunately, the examination of children's conpetence in regard to these views has been scant and establishment of laws for young offenders has been detailed almost exclusively by prevalent social forces. This paper will outline findings from scientific research on human behavioral development and suggest possible applications to legal questions of competence.

The difficulty presented in deciding the age at which children may be considered responsibile for legal violations has been with us since the first attempt at codifying societal law in the Hammurabic Code in 2270 B.C. Ancient Chinese societies often made parents responsible for their children's public offence and this idea can also be found in the Old Testament. The Hebrew Codes opposed this view and asserted personal liability should be imposed on children.[27] In early Roman times, biological markers of puberty were used to separate children on this question, with perpubertal children not held responsible. After the Middle Ages, German Law concluded that twelve years was the appropriate age of responsibility but a lesser degree of responsibility could be assigned to younger children. In Sweden in 1721, the age of fifteen was chosen while in Ireland age 12 was decided upon. Following the Norman conquest, early England common law specified seven as the age under which children could be exempt from prosecution but this was largely left to the judge's discretion.[8] In the seventeenth century, French law held that the age of seven was the lower bound of liability with only partial responsibility until the age of twenty-five.

Since the first Criminal Code in Canada in 1892, the English common law has been applied, holding children under the age of seven to be doli incapax or incapable of crime. Between the ages of seven and thirteen (inclusive), incapacity was presumed but was open to challenges. No incapacity exemptions on the basis of age were allowed upon reaching the age of 14 (Sections 12 and 13, Criminal Code). The Young Offenders Act, which received Royal Assent by the federal government of Canada in July 1982, raises the minimum age considered for criminal responsibility from seven years to 12 years. Inconsistency still remains among Western countries regarding the minimum age of responsibility, with England having opted for the age of ten and, within the United States, different states having settled on different age guidelines.

It is instructive to review the historical backdrop against which these age limits are drawn, particularly the changing social circumstances in Canada. Berkeley, Gaffield and West[2] point out that in medieval society children upon reaching the age of seven were included in the adult world largely because of their importance in the economic health of the family. They, for example, were engaged as servants and farm laborers. Important also was the fact that the Church recognized children as responsible adults at the age of seven. The 1700 and 1800s brought the commercial and industrial revolutions which reduced the financial power of youth. Canadian farms began to replace child labor with adult wage-labor and children increased their formal educations involvement. Children then, moved from economic and social parity with adults to a state of dependence. This shift was accompanied by changes in the attitudes towards their misdeeds. Before this era, children were subjected to the same harsh corporal punishment meted out to adults and were incarcerated together with adults. The Victorian period, however, heralded a different view of young offenders.

Juvenile delinquency was a term coined to demark a state separate from the trait of "criminal behavior". The scope of offences was broadened to include "moral" misbehavior and this focus on moral pathology reflected the determinist view that poverty (93% of "juvenile delinquents" of the era were from poor, working class families)[5] led to delinquent behavior. Children, however, were not responsible for being born into deprived circumstances. The child-saving movement of the time lobbied governments to assume the role of the parent (parens patriae) when the best interests of poor children were not met.[13] An acceptance of this philosophy led to the creation of the informality in juvenile courts that has persisted to the present day. Procedural rights and standards of evidence were set aside in favour of a supposed benevolent authoritarianism. The adoption of the parens patriae view also had the unfortunate result of muting the distinction between youth who were neglected and dependent and those who were antisocial. The doctrine of parens patriae emphasized treatment, and minimized accountability. Punishment was viewed as vengeful rather than corrective. Informal systems of control (social welfare) replaced legal control.

In Canada, the child-saving movement had a direct impact on the drafting of the Juvenile Delinquent Act (JDA) which was enacted in 1908.[19] The general philosophy of the act remained unchallenged until the early 1960s when the federal Department of Justice established a committee on Juvenile Delinquency which published its report in 1965.[7] The 100 recommendations of the committee anticipated many more recent proposals but a change in government and the less restrictive social atmosphere allowed these proposals to lapse. In 1975, redrafting efforts were resurrected and these labors eventually produced the new Young Offenders Act.

The philosophical change with regard to the legal liability of young persons is clearly seen in comparing the Juvenile Delinquents Act and the Young Offenders Act. The JDA directed that "where a child is adjudged to have committed a delinquency he shall be dealt with, not as an offender, but as one in a conditions of delinquency and thereby requiring help and guidance and proper supervision."[15] The Young Offenders Act, however, now declares the principle that "while young persons should not in all instances be held accountable in the same manner or suffer the same consequences for their behavior as adults, young persons who commit offences should nonetheless bear responsibility for their contraventions."[33] This increased level of responsibility is accompanied by some appropriate increases in rights and protections for the young offender. The setting of the minimum age limit at twelve years, however, appears to have been reached on an arbitrary basis. One can agree with Stuart[29] that this arbitrariness seems preferable to the impracticality of not setting any age, but total arbitrariness is not necessary in face of the vast amount of data available on developmental factors relating to competence.

Three areas of developmental psychology research which relate to the question of criminal competence are cognitive development, moral development and conative development.

Cognitive Development

Cognitive development refers to a host of mental processes including learning, using and understanding language, memory, thinking and perceiving.[10, 11] Insufficient development of these faculties may compromise an individual's ability to be aware of the wrongfulness of an illegal act (mens rea) and, therefore, release the individual from personal fault. A substantial amount of developmental psychological research has been produced which could be applied to legal questions about children's cognitive competence. While many theories abound in this area, the most widely accepted approach is Piaget's[12] general theory. This theory represents an interactionist view that cognitive development occurs as an interplay between the active internal forces and the environment in which the individual lives. The child does not just passively receive information from the external world but actually marshals resources to act upon it to gain understanding. Piaget outlined four basic stage of cognitive development:

1. **Sensorimotor Stage (Birth of 2 years)**
   The child is in physical contact with objects around him and is actively discovering their operations.

2. **Preoperational Stage (2 years to 7 years)**
   Knowledge advances from simple actions to the use of representations such as images, language and symbols.

3. **Concrete Operations (7 years to 11 years)**
   Children develop logical thinking and concepts. Many aspects of a situation, rather than just one, may be taken into account when drawing conclusions.

4. **Formal Operations (after 11 years)**
   Children become able to form abstract and hypothetical thought which is not bound to physical reality.

In cognitive development, the age of seven is a significant plateau. In Piaget's scheme, most children at this age shift from an egocentric view to a comprehension of concepts and fundamental laws of nature (cause and effect). Our society recognizes that by this age large vocabularies have been developed, memory processes are in operation and children are considered able to participate in formalized education. With these skills, they are typically able to fulfill the criterion of knowing the wrongfulness of most illegal acts.[1, 24]

Related to cognitive development and the concept of mens rea is a line of research that has examined children's views of motives and intentionality in wrong-doing. Berndt and Berndt (4) reported that children as young, as five years understood the concepts of motive and intentionality. Additionally, it has been found that when children are given stories where a character causes a large amount of damage by accident and another character causes a small amount of damage through malice, greed or carelessness, they place more emphasis on the intention of the character even when they are as young as six.[3] Therefore, children at about the age of seven not only possess the cognitive capacity for a "guilty mind", they are able to make judgements about this intent in others.

MORAL DEVELOPMENT

The development of moral values often has been thought to underline lawful behavior in society. Much of our scientific knowledge in regard to the development of moral thinking is owed to Piaget[23] and Kohlberg[16]. According to Piaget, children begin to make moral judgements when they shed their egocentric view of life. Thus moral development is closely linked with cognitive growth. Moral development then is based partly on the maturational process and also results from experience in interacting with adults and peers. Like cognitive development, moral development in this perspective follows in distinct qualitatively different stages. The sequence of development is presumably universal but age attainment may vary. Building on Piaget's work, Kohlberg describes six stages of moral development embedded in three levels:

> Level 1—Preconventional Morality
>
>> External control is recognized and behavior becomes dependent upon the motive to avoid punishment and reap rewards.
>
> Level 2—Convention Morality
>
>> Moral behavior becomes living up to the expectations of existing social order and, in particular, of important figures such as parents and teachers.
>
> Level 3—Postconventional Morality
>
>> Self-accepted moral principles are asserted. Control is internalized and there is independence from the authority of social groups.

Research on this developmental sequence has resulted in much debate over the mean ages which separate these levels. Kohlberg recently[17] suggested ages four to ten years for level 1, age ten to thirteen for level 2 and thirteen and above for level 3. Stage 3 however, often would not be reached until young adulthood if at all. Like cognitive development, more recent research documents a trend to find children at younger ages responding at higher levels of development. Peisach and Hardeman,[22] for example, recently reported that 75% of their samples of six and seven year olds were responding at a postconventional level of moral development. Preconventional stage is considered by most researchers to be characteristic of the child below the age of seven. When "juvenile delinquents" are examined on measures designed to evaluate these stages of moral development, some evidence partially supports Kohlberg's initial suggestion that delinquents are functioning at a preconventional level;[9] although some findings indicate no association between moral reasoning and delinquency.[21] Regardless of this debate, the relationship between moral reasoning and lawful behavior is not close. Indeed, it could be argued that children at the preconventional level may behave more lawfully than children at the postconventional stage. The postconventional reasoning child, while acknowledging the general need for social laws, may in particular instances contravene these laws if they conflict with internalized standards. The problem in relaying these ideas to the legal context is that young offenders may display well developed knowledge of moral values and reasoning, yet their behavior may be contrary to these verbalizations. As Bartol[1] points out, the affective or emotional component of morality may be the most crucial aspect; for without feelings of anxiety, shame or guilt to accompany moral knowledge, moral training would be inadequate. Even if knowledge and feeling of moral issues is intact, behavior still may contradict these.

Glanville Williams[31] in 1954 argued that any moral test of responsibility should be regarded as obsolete in children's offences. In adult insanity cases, he pointed out, courts had settled that "wrong" means exclusively legal wrong and could not enter into the question of morals. In Canada, the Supreme Court has agreed that in the interpretation of Section 16 of the Criminal Code "knowing that an act or omission is wrong" refers to wrong according to the law and not morally wrong.[25] A section of the Criminal Code (Section 13) which deals with the ages of children and responsibility has been interpreted by Canadian courts[32] as meaning that children[7, 8, 9, 10, 11, 12, 13] must, in addition to knowing that an act is legally wrong, comprehend the moral implications of their act. The repeal of Section 13 with the implementation of the Young Offenders Act should resolve this inconsistency. The issue of moral development then will not have a direct bearing on the issue of criminal responsibility of children or adults.

CONATIVE DEVELOPMENT

Conative development in children also relates closely to judgements of criminal responsibility. It refers to the growth of free-will, self-control and the ability to resist impulses. For persons to considered criminally culpable, they must have conscious and voluntary control over their behavior (actus reus). For example, Holland[14] portrays a scene where X, while driving his car, has a sudden and unexpected "blackout" and the car goes out of control, he would have a defence against a charge of careless or dangerous driving. While the concept of voluntariness had been explored in depth with adult offenders, even the law Reform Commission of Canada (18) had little information to guide specific recommendations for children. They noted that "it is arguable that children under fourteen who know what they are doing and know that is wrong, may still be unable to resist temptation to the same degree as adults". When do children change from organisms who react involuntarily, to individuals who have control over their behavior?

One line of research directly confronts the question of impulse control — the delay of gratification paradigms. In these situations, a child is placed in a position where he must choose between an immediate reward and a delayed reward of higher value. A recent study[26] has concluded that children as young as 3 years choose to delay gratification and, like adults, are sensitive to the anticipated length of delay. While delay of gratification increase as the child ages,[20] there is no well defined limit where a child reaches the adult level of delay. This would be a difficult cross-sectional task; for the value of a particular reward would vary across ages. The more appropriate question would ask, when does a child develop sufficient self-control abilities in a legal context? Typical inhibitory mechanisms are clearly evident in most seven years olds and this is closely tied to the development of cognitive and moral abilities. In a legal framework, many more adults display poor self-control despite adequate cognitive ability. There are recognized disinhibitory syndromes in children and adults (eg. psychopathology, attention deficit disorders,[6] alcoholism) but these are rarely successful defences for complete dismissal of criminal responsibility. Debates about self-control inevitably becomes mired in confusion.[30]

CONCLUSIONS

The conclusion drawn from a review of developmental competencies is that most children at about the age of seven meet at least minimum criteria for criminal responsibility. In developmental research, it is important to caution that not all children reach the same development level at the same age and some children may not be legally competent at the age of seven. Section 13 of the Criminal Code made it possible for competency in criminal matters to be examined on an individual basis between the ages of seven and thirteen inclusive. In light of our knowledge of child development, this was an inherently sensible approach. By the age of fourteen, the vast majority of children would clearly have the requisites for liability. The Young Offenders Act, by setting the age of responsibility at 12, has actually lowered the unquestioned age limit. It has marked a clear dividing line rather than supporting an age-graded approach.

Changes in the age of responsibility do not appear dependent upon political or administrative convenience. In the highlights of the proposed legislation, it was purported that "deviant behavior by children under the age of 12 is better and more effectively dealt with under provincial legislation pertaining to child welfare or youth protection."[28] This is certainly an uncritical and nonspecific evaluation of provincial law and current thinking among provincial governments. As Stuart[29] suggest, we should be cautious about raising the age of criminal responsibility if this dilutes the legal rights of the child to protection from state intervention.

The Young Offenders Act defines an age zone (12 to 17 inclusive) where reduced responsibility is assumed. It is unlikely that many young offenders would be found not responsible for their behavior using the typical legal criteria reviewed here. Despite this, it is argued that the sentencing process should not be a reflection of adult practices and that alternatives to court action should continue to play a key role with young offenders. Adult privileges and legal consequences cannot be extended to children, for their circumstances in modern society are significantly different from those of adults. Children have temporary status and therefore are not organized. They are disadvantaged by their physical size which makes them vulnerable to adult threats or use of force.[2] They are dependent and controlled by the adult world and are uninformed about the working of society and particularly about recourse to judicial responsibility. Without equal protections and rights, equal consequences would be unfairly conferred. The Young Offenders Act does increase the legal protections to young people but it is uncertain how these protections will be interpreted and implemented.

Full and partial legal defenses due to mental abnormality in adults have little relevance to the issues of responsibility in children. In adults, mental abnormality challenges both *mens rea* and *actus reus*. The case has been made in this review, that age abilities do not typically challenge either element of criminal responsibility. In cases where children have a condition (eg. mental retardation, attention deficit disorder) that might compromise their legal responsibility, psychological evaluations will play a major role in the issue of determining responsibility but these cases very likely will be small in number. It is more accurate to describe children older than 7 (or 12) not as having reduced legal responsibility but as having decreased consequences for their acts because of their social status. The clear separation of these concepts may assist in the practical administration of justice under the Young Offenders Act.

ENDNOTES

1. Bartol, C.R. *Criminal Behaviour: A Psychosocial Approach.* Englewood Cliffs, New Jersey: Prentice-Hall, 1980.

2. Berkeley, H.C. Gaffield, and G. West, "Children's rights in the Canadian context." *Interchange: A Journal of Educational Studies, 8.* 1-4. 1977-78.

3. Berg-Cross, L.G. "Intentionality, degree of damage, and moral judgements". *Child Development. 46.* 970-974. 1975.

4. Berndt, T.J. and E.G. Berndt. "Children's use of motives and intentionality in person perception and moral judgement." *Child Development. 46.* 904-912. 1975.

5. Conly, D., "A critique of the institutional response to juvenile delinquency in Ontario". *Interchange: A Journal of Educational Studies. 8.* 195-202. 1977-78.

6. Dalby, J.T., R.D. Schneider, and J. Arboleda-Florez. "Learning disorders in offenders". *International Journal of Offender Therapy and Comparative Criminology. 26.* 145-151. 1982.

7. Department of Justice (committee on Juvenile Delinquency). *Juvenile Delinquency in Canada.* Ottawa: Queen's Printer 1965.

8. Eldefonso, E. and W. Hartinger. *Control, Treatment and Rehabilitation of Juvenile Offenders.* Beverly Hills, California: Glenco Press. 1976.

9. Fodor, E.M. "Delinquency and susceptibility to social influences as a function of moral development". *Journal of Social Psychology. 86.* 257-360. 1972.

10. Gleman, R. "Cognitive development". *Annual Review of Psychology. 29.* 297-332. 1978.

11. Ginsburg, H. and B. Koslowski. "Cognitive development". *Annual Review of Psychology. 27.* 29-61. 1976.

12. Ginsbury, H. and S. Opper. *Piaget's Theory of Intellectual Development: An Introduction.* Englewood Cliffs, New Jersey: Prentice-Hall, 1969.

13. Griffiths, C.T., J.F. Klein, and S.N. Verdun-Jones. *Criminal Justice in Canada.* Toronto: Butterworths. 1980.

14. Holland, W.H. "Automatism and criminal responsibility". *Criminal Law Quarterly.* 95-128. 1983.

15. *Juvenile Delinquents Act,* R.S.C. 1970, c. J-3.

16. Kohlberg, L. "Stage in the Development of Moral Thought and Action." New York: Holt, Rinehart and Winston. 1969.

17. Kolberg, L. "Moral stage and moralization". In T. Lickona (Ed.) *Moral Development and Behavior.* New York: Holt, 1976.

18. Law Reform Commission of Canada. *Working Paper No. 29. Criminal Law: The General Part—Liability and Defences.* Ottawa: Minister of Supply and Services Canada. 1982.

19. Leon, J.S. "New and old themes in Canadian juvenile justice: The origins of delinquency legislation and the prospects for recognition of children's rights". *Interchange: A Journal of Educational Studies. 8.* 151-175. 1977-78.

20. Mischel, W. "Processes in delay of gratification". In Berkowitz (Ed.). *Advances in Experimental Social Psychology* (Vol.7). New York: Academic Press. 1974.

21. Morash, M.A. "Cognitive developmental theory: A basis for juvenile correctional reform?" *Criminology. 19.* 360-371. 1981.

22. Piesach, E. and M. Hardeman. "Moral reasoning in early childhood: Lying and stealing". *The Journal of Genetic Psychology. 142.* 107-1120. 1983.

23. Piaget, J. *The Moral Judgement of the Child.* New York: Macmillan. 1955.

24. Sametz, L. "Children, law and child development: The child developmentalists' role in the legal system". *Juvenile and Family Court Journal.* August. 49-67. 1979.

25. *Schwartz, v. The Queen* (1976), 29 C.C.C. (2d) 1 (S.C.C.)

26. Schwarz, J.C., J.B., Schrager, and A.E. Lyons. "Delay of gratification by preschoolers: Evidence for the validity of the choice paradigm". *Child Development. 54.* 620-625. 1983.

27. Simonsen, C.E. and M.S. Gordon. *Juvenile Justice in America.* Encino, California: Glenco Publishing Co. 1979.

28. Solicitor General of Canada *Highlights—The Young Offenders Act.* Ottawa: Supply and Services, 1981.

29. Stuart, D. *Canadian Criminal Law: A Treatise.* Toronto: Carswell Co. 1982.

30. Westcott, M.R. "Free will: An exercise in methaphysical truth or psychological consequences". *Canadian Psychological Review. 18.* 249-263. 1977.

31. Williams, G.L. "The criminal responsibility of children". *Criminal Law Review.* 493-500. 1954.

32. Wilson, J. *Children and the Law.* Toronto: Butterworths. 1978.

33. *Young Offenders Act.* S.C. 1980-81-82. C. 110.

CHAPTER 19
Revivification of Rehabilitation: Evidence from the 1980's

PAUL GENDREAU
ROBERT R. ROSS

We reviewed the offender rehabilitation literature for the period 1981-87 and assessed the following types of interventions: biomedical, diversion, early/family intervention, education, getting tough, individual differences, parole/probation, restitution, and work. We evaluated treatments applied to specific subgroups of offender populations: sexual offenders, substance abusers, and violent offenders. The hypothesis that the "nothing works" credo has had a pervasive influence and has suppressed the rehabilitative agenda was not borne out when we examined the number and variety of successfully reported attempts at reducing delinquent behavior. In fact, the rehabilitative literature is growing at a noticeable rate; moreover, it suggests several strategies for developing more effective programs. Finally, we speculated why the "nothing works" doctrine continues to receive support in spite of empirical evidence to the contrary.

> It is much easier to be critical than correct.
>
> Benjamin Disraeli

It seems that only recently the cynics were in full flower. They said that correctional treatment was impotent, recidivism could not be reduced, and delinquency could not be prevented by treatment programs which focused on individual offenders. They were wrong.

Even Robert Martinson, who argued most often and most persuasively that "almost nothing works," recognized that he was in error. His original condemnation of correctional rehabilitation was published in *Public Interest* in

1974. As Cousineau and Plecas (1982) noted, his article is one of the most frequently quoted and least frequently read in the criminal justice rehabilitation literature. Furthermore, Martinson's conclusions provided support for proponents of other competing criminal justice ideologies, such as deterrence and justice as fairness, and for criminal justice administrators who desired devoutly to repudiate the rehabilitative ideal. The notion that offenders could be rehabilitated successfully quickly became a historical oddity, fit only for study by criminal justice paleontologists.

Subsequently, without any of the fanfare associated with his 1974 pronouncement, Martinson renounced his views. First he reaffirmed the virtues of probation as a rehabilitative method (Martinson and Wilks 1977). Then, two years later, he declared that under various conditions there were many examples of successful rehabilitation efforts…"such startling results are found again and again…. for treatment programs as diverse as individual psychotherapy, group counselling, intensive supervision, and what we have called individual help" (1979: 255). This repentance, published in the *Hofstra Law Review,* is probably the most infrequently read article in the criminal justice debate on rehabilitation.

Just about when Martinson was experiencing a professional conversion a second generation of cynics evolved, but in this case they doubted the empirical validity of the "nothing works" position. The most prescient and courageous was Ted Palmer (1975), who was virtually alone in opposing the conventional wisdom of the time. Palmer focused his attention on the rehabilitation literature (up to 1968) with which Martinson was concerned. Following Palmer, varying degrees of support for rehabilitation came from other sources. In Palmer's (1983) view, the present authors were among those academics and clinicians who advocated rehabilitation most forcefully. Our concerns were motivated in part by the fact that criminal justice pundits were not only overlooking. critical literature, but also seemed not to be concerned that correctional policy was being formulated on the basis of research (no matter how instructive for its time) that was dated by at least a decade! Conceivably some significant advances might have been made in rehabilitation during the intervening years; this, in fact, was the case.

Our reviews of the research literature demonstrated that successful rehabilitation of offenders had been accomplished, and continued to be accomplished quite well. Evidence was presented (Gendreau 1981; Gendreau and Ross 1981a; Gendreau and Ross 1979; Ross and Gendreau 1980) that between 1973 and 1980 reductions in recidivism, sometimes as substantial as 80 percent, had been achieved in a considerable number of well-controlled studies.

Effective programs were conducted in a variety of community and (to a lesser degree) institutional settings, involving predelinquents, hard-core adolescent offenders, and recidivistic adult offenders, including criminal heroin addicts. The results of these programs were not short-lived; follow-up periods of at least two years were not uncommon, and several studies reported even longer follow-ups. One such study included a 15-year post-treatment follow-up. In addition, the claims for effective rehabilitation of offenders far outdistanced those of the major competing ideology, applied deterrence or punishment (Gendreau and Ross 1981b). Finally, the knowledge generated by both the successful and the unsuccessful studies suggested various principles accounting for the success or failure of a program (Gendreau & Ross 1983,1984).

Thereafter it was gratifying to record that these contributions, along with others, were being referenced as supportive evidence in a wide variety of contests: assessments of probation practices (Clear and Gallagher 1985), classification issues (Palmer 1984), work incentive and education programs (Linden & Perry 1982; Orsagh and Marsden 1985), documentation of public support for rehabilitative ideology (Cullen, Skovron, Scott, and Burton in press), widely publicized conferences such as that organized by Jerome Miller on reaffirming rehabilitation (*Criminal Justice Newsletter* 1986), program implementation issues (Van Voorhis 1987), conditional rights to rehabilitation (Rotman 1986), and various treatises on criminal justice theory and practice (Bartollas 1985; Cullen and Gilbert 1982; Currie 1985b; Gibbons 1986). Scholars have even assessed the assessors of rehabilitation efficacy (Garrett 1985; Gendreau 1985; Palmer 1983). At the very least, the recent trends in the literature support a grudging acceptance of the renewed possibilities of a potent rehabilitation agenda.

Sanctimony, however, particularly among those advocating a minority opinion, is an easily acquired virtue. The proponents of rehabilitation would be wise to note the realities proffered by the recent history of the debate. Many criminal justice observers remain convinced that the concept of effective rehabilitation is an oxymoron (Brody 1981; Clarke 1985; Van den Haag 1982). Criminologists continue to exorcise the notion of rehabilitation from their academic agenda (Cullen 1985). In addition, we should not forget that the reviews in the late 70s were based on studies that were conducted before the "nothing works" ideology might have affected much of the funding for rehabilitative programs. As a result, an incubation effect may have occurred, depriving the current treatment literature of persuasive evidence; therefore the present optimism may be based on little substance.

It is difficult, however, to make an assessment in this regard. Recently, two texts have covered a wide range of empirically based literature (Kazdin 1985; Rutter & Giller 1983). Some statistical synthesis, such as meta-analysis (e.g., Garrett 1985; Gensheimer, Mayer, Davidson, and Gottschalk 1986) of the literature has appeared, but these publications referenced primarily pre-1980 literature.

New program directions have been suggested (Greenwood and Zimring 1985) as well as principles underlying effective treatment (Gendreau and Ross 1983, 1984), but, again, these reports have not taken into account the recent literature on treatment outcome. Thorough reviews of select areas of offender rehabilitation have appeared, however (e.g., Apter and Goldstein 1986); Blumstein, Cohen, Roth, and Visher 1986; Lanyon 1986; Ross and Fabiano 1985; Ross and Lightfoot 1985).

To assess the current overall status of programs that "work," we must update our knowledge. We will use a format similar to that of our 1979 publication in *Crime & Delinquency,* in which we reviewed the treatment literature as defined by program structure, such as diversion, and by individual modes of antisocial behavior, such as sexual offending. In compiling the 1981-87 offender rehabilitation literature we made occasional reference to a 1979-1980 study not included in Ross and Gendreau (1980). As before, we relied on personal library search. To be "counted," a study had to undergo the standard academic peer review process and be published in an edited journal or text. Studies were required to have re-arrest, reconviction, re-incarceration, or self-report of illegal behavior as an outcome measure. In the case of the early intervention literature the outcome criteria were applicable to the age group in question—that is, delinquent behaviors predictive of future criminal behavior. Post-treatment follow-up with control group comparisons were necessary. Literature that did not meet these criteria was referenced, however, if it made a contribution to theory development and new program directions.

This review does not include the treatment "fugitive" literature (Sechrest, White, and Brown 1979) of various agency and government documents that have not undergone formal peer review. Deterrence/punishment paradigms are also "treatments" (cf. Gendreau and Ross 1981), but with the exception of "getting tough" approaches, such as shock probation, this topic is left to recent review in this journal by Paternoster, and also by Gendreau, Tweedale, and Kennedy (under review).

In some instances, the classification of an individual study or studies representing a particular line of inquiry was quite arbitrary. Several studies could have been classified easily in two or three other categories. This review has three parts: Part A consists of rehabilitation topics defined by programmatic structure such as biomedical, diversion, early/family intervention, education, getting tough, individual differences, parole/probation, restitution, and work. Part B refers to therapies as applied to distinct classes of offenders: sexual offenders, substance abusers, and violent offenders. Part C concerns meta-analyses of the treatment literature.

PART A

Biomedical

Our conclusions have not changed since 1979 regarding the effectiveness of biomedical methods for delinquent behaviors. The enthusiasm for such procedures is not matched by compelling empirical evidence.

The Grendon psychiatric prison program is representative of a traditional style of medical-model "service" delivery (Gunn and Robertson 1982). After a nine-month follow-up, their sample of 20 neurotic inmates performed significantly better on a general health questionnaire than a comparison group imprisoned elsewhere. Two years after the program, however, the treated group had a 70 percent reconviction rate, similar to the comparison group. The authors argued against control-group studies, which they claimed were inappropriate for the evaluation of institutional care. They preferred descriptive studies and presented two case studies in support of the program.

A growing diagnostic literature concerns itself with the neurological and biochemical basis of youth violence (Lewandowski and Forsstram-Cohen 1986). One of the treatments evolving from such assessments is pharmacological. Supportive evidence for drug therapies includes the biochemical basis of some forms of schizophrenia and their treatment, animal research attesting to the biological underpinnings of aggressive behavior, and the development of medications that control childhood hyperactivity, aggressivity, and depression (Kazdin 1985). Although Kazdin believes that a promising agenda can be derived from these perspectives, the strongest evidence comes from a series of studies by Campbell and her colleagues (Campbell, Small, Green, Jennings, Penny, Bennett and Anderson 1984). The latest study was a random-assignment, double-blind study of hospitalized children age five to 13 with DSM-3-diagnosed conduct disorders who received lithium carbonate and haloperidol. The follow-up lasted only six weeks. The treated children showed improvement on a global measure of clinical judgment, but not on staff and teacher ratings.

Finally, the dramatic claims of orthomolecular physicians (Hippchen 1976) were put to the test by Schoenthaler (1983), who set out to test dietary theories of delinquency prevention, in an extensive series of double-blind studies that used subjects as their own controls. His 1983 paper summarized and reported on the results of data gathered from 5,000 juveniles in ten prisons, who were treated by revisions in their diet. Food high in sucrose and additives were reduced and were replaced by complex-carbohydrate diets featuring fruit juices and vegetables. The results reported were consistent across all settings; misconduct and acts of violence were reduced by 21 to 54 percent. The implications of Schoenthaler's research for delinquency prevention programs are obvious, but to date we are unaware of any well-controlled, and community-based outcome studies. Only anecdotal case histories are reported (Schaus 1980) as supporting evidence.

DIVERSION

If ideology is the permanent hidden agenda of criminal justice (Miller 1973), this fact of life is illustrated best by the diversion literature (Binder and Geis 1984). Diversion was intended as an alternative to further processing by the justice system. Such processing could only lead, it was surmised, to further contamination of the young offender; he or she might become more criminogenic as a result. A "pure" form of diversion would involve no service delivery whatever; it was assumed that people would outgrow or avoid problems if allowed to proceed randomly through life. Actually, however, the diversion process had certain "add-ons," mainly in the form of poorly specified social services (see Gensheimer et al., 1986) provided either directly by the diversion program itself or through brokerage to other social service agencies.

Yet what appeared to be a benign procedure was interpreted by some disciplines, such as criminology and sociology, as having a dark side. Now there was another form of social control; crisis intervention, and family and employment counseling all had the potential for labeling youngsters as deviates and being abusive (Bullington, Sprowls, Katkin, and Phillips 1978). According to Binder and Geis (1984), sociologists, the major figures in this field succumbed to a rhetorical syllogism whereby the traditional view—"Diversion widens the net of social control. Therefore diversion is bad"—became, for all intents and purposes, "Diversion provides services to youngsters and their families where none was provided before. Therefore diversion is bad" (643). Obviously many sociologists and criminologists would argue that Binder and Geis were unduly provocative and may have misrepresented their position, but it is fair to say that the attitude toward diversion as an effective rehabilitative vehicle has been neutral at best. If one sides with the "sociological" perspective, diversion programs should (if anything) support the "nothing works" view. Diversion was not intended to produce marked behavioral changes, as intensive treatment services were not the major concern of many of the classic diversion experiments (e.g., Korbin and Klein 1983). Rather, diversion might have negative consequences.

The recent outcome data on diversion supports the sociologists' gloomy predictions. Almost all diversion evaluations made a valiant attempt at proving the null hypothesis when future criminal behavior was the dependent measure (Erickson 1984; Gensheimer et al 1986; Kobrin and Klein 1983; Lipsey, Cordray, and Breger 1981; Palmer and Lewis 1980; Rojek and Erickson 1982; Selke 1982; Severy and Whitaker 1982; Spergel, Reamer, and Lynch 1981; Webb and Scanlon 1981). Even those who were sympathetic toward diversion could not substantiate earlier promising results (Binder, Schumacher, Lurtz, and Moulson, 1985; Denno 1980; Denno and Clelland 1986).

What may appear on the surface as failure, however, becomes quite another matter when the fine print of the evaluations is scrutinized. At that point one concludes that diversion supports the fact that structure without content is a synonym for "nothing works." The diversion literature parallels precisely the prison counseling literature (see Kassenbaum, Ward, and Wilner 1971), which was condemned as a failure; only to be reported later, however, that the services delivered were of abysmal quality (Quay 1977).

From Kobrin and Klein's (1983) documentation of the quality of the national diversion program in eight sites we learn the following 1) programs were often short-term and low-level, and in various instances it was impossible to develop a satisfactory program; 2) some sites offered programs that were "extraordinarily narrow"; 3) programs often were conducted in an atmosphere of turbulence and uncertainty; 4) type of service was one of the least important considerations; 5) the skill level of the staff was questionable; 6) the treatment philosophies of the staff were not articulated; and 7) some first-time offenders did not need the service.

Rojek and Erickson (1982) tell us the following about the large-scale (N=4982) Arizona diversion program: 1) inappropriate services often were rendered by community agencies—37 percent of cases received service for behaviors different from those for which they were arrested; 2) whether or not they had the resources, community service agencies referred 96 percent of the cases to themselves as they tried to diversify and become bigger, so as to become permanent; 3) some agencies appeared to be less tolerant and more punitive than the courts; and 4) the project did not consider the capacity of the community for rehabilitating offenders in the first place.

Spergel et al.'s (1981) evaluation observed bluntly that one Illinois diversion program did not have reduction of recidivism as a goal. Children received about two weeks of service; no special attention was directed to alleviating the problems of the offenders. Selke (1982) reported on seven youth service bureaus in Michigan and found that 1) staff members were poorly trained; 2) the programs suffered from over-advocacy because of the short-term nature of the funding, and 3) the agencies were too small to achieve their objectives.

Finally, Gensheimer et al.'s (1986) meta-analysis of 44 juvenile diversion projects calculated that on the average, clients received only 15 hours of intervention over four months. Services were nonspecific, and clients were referred frequently to services with no control over what services were provided. The evaluation methods were poor; in two-thirds of the evaluations the investigators had no control over the treatments. This seemingly unrelated information is vital: the meta-analysis section presents evidence that higher-quality evaluations, which also involve the investigation directly, are likely to reflect more therapeutic integrity and (not surprisingly) stronger treatment effects.

Even the dross, nevertheless, contained a few instances of therapeutic integrity. Palmer and Lewis (1980) surveyed 74 diversion projects in California and followed up on 15. Overall they noted a ten percent lower re-arrest rate for diverted offenders. They also studied those projects that "worked" better than others, and discovered reductions in recidivism ranging from 33 to 56 percent for 12 to 18-month follow-ups. In two projects, clients were higher-risk types, and on the average received at least 50 therapeutic contacts by counselors. Better outcome was associated with more services and with individual counseling that exhibited personal concern and internal approaches to problem solving. Effective strategies included civic activities such as community projects, informal exposure to authority via tours of the police and probation departments, and making sure that the youth saw the worker as the main (external) source of decision-making power for problem solving. Kobrin and Klein (1983) remarked that in a few cases where youth services were related to recidivism they noted staff co-operation, a well-functioning local network of community-based services, and staff members' attribution of the causes of delinquency to personal deficiencies and to lack of adequate social controls (e.g., education) in the community.

Indeed, diversion can work if something of substance and integrity is provided to the young offender. We end this section by outlining a very important evaluation by Davidson, Render, Blakely, Mitchell, and Emshoff (1987). This study was an attempt to replicate earlier findings (Davidson, Seidman, Rappaport, Benck, Rapp, Rhodes, and Herring 1977) that diverting young offenders was effective when paraprofessionals applied various therapies based on social learning. Davidson et al. examined the effects of a multifaceted treatment program within a diversion format for juvenile offenders (N=213). Their mean age was 14; 83% were male; in the year before treatment, the average arrest rate was 1.5, primarily for larceny and breaking and entering. The therapists' training was impressive. Paraprofessionals (university students) had to undergo a pre-assessment; they received eight weeks of training, up to 80 hours in total followed by 18 weeks of supervised intervention. Each student worked in the juvenile's community for six to eight hours per week, one-to-one with the client. Psychometrics were administered to assess each student's knowledge of training at the end of training and at the termination of the case. Self-reports and adult and juvenile police records were obtained on the clients two years after the intervention took place. Juveniles were assigned randomly to treatment conditions that had considerable empirical foundation as effective therapies in the delinquency literature (see Ross and Gendreau 1980, for a compilation of reports on some of the therapies by Davidson and colleagues, Douds and Collingwood, and Alexander and Parsons that were employed in this study). The therapies consisted of (a) behavioral contracting and child advocacy, which were conducted both in the community and under the direct auspices of the court system with court personnel as supervisors of treatment; (b) the above-named treatment within the context of family-focused behavioral treatment, directed only at the families of the delinquents; and (c) interpersonal relationship approaches (e.g., Truax and Carkuff 1967).

The community-based therapies produced significant reductions in recidivism rates: up to 29 percent, compared with subjects assigned randomly to the usual court processing and with a group that controlled for nonspecific attention factors. Therapists in this last group relied on their natural skills and on mostly recreational activities. The court-based intervention performed worst of all.

The authors concluded that treatments are effective when they are well grounded theoretically within social-support and social-control propositions, are straightforward, and focus on positive rather than on pathological or punishment processes. Paraprofessionals, contrary to some opinions (cf. Durlack 1981), can be effective when well trained. The authors argue that in view of fiscal shortages in justice systems, paraprofessionals offer the only hope for providing services of therapeutic integrity. Davidson et al. also tentatively support labeling theory in regard to the performance of the court-based group.

EARLY/FAMILY INTERVENTION

The early/family intervention field, unlike other fields in criminal justice such as diversion, has no time for ideological gamesmanship. Scholars speak urgently of taking off their blindfolds and becoming more literate. They speak of increasing their appreciation of the fact that the early antecedents of crime come from all aspects of social science inquiry, such as child clinical and developmental psychology and psychiatry, community psychology, family law, genetics, pediatrics, public health, sociology, and the eclectic literature on family processes. In the words of Gerald Patterson, one of the leading researchers in delinquency prevention, "The prevention field is exploding right now... there is a lot of excitement because we are finding a consensus about the variables that relate to delinquency...ten years ago that did not seem possible" (see Hurley 1985: 64).

As might be expected, the literature in this area would be beyond the scope of the present review even if this were the only topic we intended to cover. We hope that the following summary will provide the reader with the major themes and most of the significant current outcome literature.

The "excitement" that Patterson refers to is not ephemeral, for three reasons. First, a broad social-philosophical constituency supports early intervention. "Just society" philosophers (e.g., Rawls 1971) argue cogently that justice, in contemporary sociopolitical terms, must insist that universal liberties are accessible to all; moreover, society must rectify social and economic inequalities. The application of this social philosophy proceeds naturally into the mandate of those medical and allied professions concerned with public health. The U.S. Surgeon General's (1979) task force has given the highest priority to preventive activities in the most comprehensive sense. From the rehabilitative perspective these constituencies are certainly not ineffectual. As George Albee (1986: 897) commented, "Primary prevention research inevitably will make clear the relationship between social pathology and psychopathology and then will work to change social and political structures in the interests of social justice."

Second, the rapprochement between psychobiological and sociological theories has been a most welcome development. Wilson and Hernnstein's

(1985) text is the signpost publication in this respect. Rowe and Osgood (1984) have presented data and the necessary rationale to illustrate how the sociological theories of Cohen (1955), Elliott, Ageton, and Canter (1979), Gold (1970), and Hirschi (1969) are not inconsistent with developmental theories of delinquent behavior, but support and invigorate them. The result of this type of theory development need not be retrogressive. Two of the foremost genetic researchers, Gabrielli and Mednick (1983: 71) stated, "Understanding the genetic, biological, developmental and social factors...leads to benign and effective intervention strategies." Wilson and Hernnstein (1985) echo the above statement. Wilson, who has never been among the leading supporters of rehabilitation, was quoted recently as being quite "hopeful" (see Hurley 1985) about the prospects of early intervention.

Third, the viability of early prevention has been confirmed in an exceptionally rich clinical process literature documenting the functioning of families at risk with the law (Alexander and Parsons 1982; Patterson 1982, 1986; Wahler and Dumas in press). In addition, two masterful reviews of the delinquency prevention literature (Loeber and Stouthamer-Loeber 1986, 1987) have documented empirically the high degree of consensus in a vast and diverse literature. These bodies of knowledge, along with the ever-growing and influential body of longitudinal delinquency research (e.g., Elliott, Huizinga, and Ageton 1985; Eron and Huesmann 1986) point to specific therapeutic strategies.

Admittedly, one should be cautious in approaching the implications of prediction studies for intervention (Lorion, Tolan, and Wahler 1987; Snyder and Patterson 1987), but the ability to predict delinquency is one step on the road from correlation to causation (Farrington 1985a). Policy makers can be proactive, given the present state of knowledge (Loeber and Stouthamer-Loeber 1986). The implications for intervention strategists are to match the most potent interventions with risk factors (Rolf 1985); that is, that minority group of moderate- to high-risk children with early conduct problems whose behaviors (e.g., aggression, stealing, and drug use) have been replicated reliably time and again with the prediction of serious delinquency and recidivism (Loeber and Stouthamer-Loeber 1987).

A developmental perspective should also guide the interventions. From the ages of one to 12, early school enrichment, such as Head Start and parent training, has been suggested. From ages 12 to 18 the focus should be on peer-group positive reward programs, role modeling for social skills, employment, and alcohol and drug counseling (Farrington 1985 a,b). Patterson's (1986) model, which has some impressive psychometric validities, has identified poor family management practices as prime intervention targets; these practices include inconsistent parental discipline and inadequate parenting skills, which cause the child to fail socially and academically and to act out antisocially.

Some circumspectness is in order, however. The foregoing agenda shows signs of seeking a cure-all (cf. Ross and McKay 1978). Before reviewing the outcome literature we must admit that it is one thing to outline a vitalizing agenda for social action but another to do something about it. Rickel (1986) provides some depressing evidence that the commitment to the prevention of physical and mental disorder among children is far from profound, particularly in the present American sociopolitical context. Disparities of income and wealth have increased over the last few years (Enrenreich 1986); high-risk, resource-poor communities face truly perplexing problems in their attempt to avoid further deterioration (Fagan and Hartstone under review).

As to the intervention literature itself, whether from the perspective of behavioral family therapy, social skills training, or social support systems, gaps in knowledge still remain. Studies with weak methodological criteria and problems in the generalizability and durability of treatment effects have been all too common (Conger and Keane 1981; Fehrenbach and Thelen 1982; Gresham 1985; Griest and Wells 1983; Henderson and Hollin 1983; Hirsch 1985). It is also difficult to ascertain whether some of the interventions (e.g., Feldman, Caplinger, and Wodarski 1983) enacted to date were directed toward runny-nosed brats rather than high-risk predelinquents (see Spergel 1984).

In spite of these reservations, the evidence for effective early intervention programs has been impressive by any standards. The field includes three literatures, which overlap to some degree: training approaches to cognitive problem-solving skills, early prevention, and family intervention.

Cognitive problem-solving therapies have been heralded as a breakthrough in the treatment of high-risk children (see Rickel, Eshelman, and Loigman 1983; Ross and Fabiano 1985), but several detours have occurred along the way. The highly regarded Ottawa skill development program (Kazdin 1985) of Offord and Jones (1983) provided a three-year intervention centering on athletic and cultural skill building, such as guitar and ballet instruction, but after the intervention was terminated the outcome changed for the worse (Jones and Offord under review). A rebound effect occurred for some of the specific skills acquired as well as for unobtrusive measures of antisocial acts.

The cognitive interpersonal problem-solving skills of Spivack, Platt, and Shure (1976) have been adopted by a number of school-based preventive programs, but the promise of this appealing strategy has not been upheld in thorough replications by other investigators (Rickel et al. 1983; Yu, Harris, Soloritz, and Franklin 1986).

One possible reason for the failures was that these programs did not approach the problem directly enough. To effect significant long-term change, more than happenstance modeling must take place (Offord and Jones 1983); children must do more than list alternative solutions and consequences (Rickel et al. 1983). The children must have the opportunity to engage extensively in specific role modeling and pro-social behavioral rehearsal and to practice them repeatedly under supervision. When these procedures were followed, changes did occur among high-risk adolescents (Kazdin, Esveldt-Dawson, French and Unis 1987; Lochman, Lampron, Burch and Curry 1985). Kazdin et al.'s study deserves noting. Their training program in cognitive-behavioral problem-solving skills employed the procedures of Spivack et al. (1976) and Kendal and Braswell (1985). Theirs was a random assignment study; the children were high-risk on all counts; the treatment was intensive (approximately 50 hours of therapy); the therapists were well trained; and procedures were established to sustain the integrity of treatment. In contrast to a relationship therapy group that focused on empathy, unconditional positive regard, and enhancing self-esteem, and a treatment-contact control, the training in problem-solving skills produced significantly greater changes a year after treatment on measures of child behavior at home and school. The poor performance of the relationship group, a therapy often applied to delinquents, confirmed the prognosis of Andrews & Kiessling (1980) about the questionable value of such programs for delinquents.

Our reviews of the next two sections will be brief, as most of the following literature has been summarized already (Blumstein et al. 1986; Farrington 1985a; Gordon and Arbuthnot 1987; Hurley 1985). The early intervention school and community-based literature have demonstrated promise (Berreuta-Clement, Schweinhart, Bennett, Epstein, and Weikart 1984; Bry 1982; Chandler, Weissberg, Cowen, and Guare 1984; Feldman et al. 1983; Johnson and Breckenridge 1982; Jordon, Grallo, Deutsch, and Deutsch 1985; Safer, Heaton, and Parker, 1981). Most of the above studies were random assignment, and reported follow-ups up to four years or more.

Of interest for our purposes were the studies by Berreuta-Clement et al. (1984) and Bry (1982), as they recorded delinquency outcome data. The Perry preschool project, part of the Head Start program, was an enriched group that received services during the ages of three and four years. Eleven years later the randomly assigned experimental group displayed better school achievement and less self-reported delinquency. Berreuta-Clement et al.

(1984) reported that at age 19, 40 percent of the controls (N=65) were charged or re-arrested as adults, compared to 25 percent of the 58 preschool participants. The results from the Perry project were similar to that reported in 11 other Head Start projects, although the other projects did not collect delinquency outcome data. Bry (1982) employed a school-based behaviorally oriented program for high-risk adolescents, and also found significantly less chronic offending (9 percent vs. 27 percent) in the randomly assigned experimental group five years after the intervention. Two important program features of Bry's program were the use of "booster" treatment sessions and training students in self-efficacy techniques thereby enabling them to master difficult situations.

Finally, the family intervention literature offers, in our view, the most convincing demonstration that early intervention programs can be effective. In the 1979 review we described three of the major programs: the behavioral-systems family therapy approach of James Alexander and his colleagues in Salt Lake City, the behavioral-parent and skills training interventions as exemplified by Patterson's Oregon social learning group, and the Achievement Place behavior-oriented teaching family programs in Lawrence, Kansas. Since that time, any number of variations on these program themes have reported some success in reducing at-risk children's antisocial behaviors (Baum and Forehand 1981; Budd, Leibowitz, Rinder, Mindell, and Goldfarb 1981; McPherson, McDonald, and Ryer, 1983; Serna, Schumacher, Hazel, and Sheldon 1986; Strain, Steele, Gillis, and Timm 1982; Webster-Stratton 1984,1985; Wilson 1980).

Among the three approaches the Achievement Place program has met with the least success (Kirigin, Braukmann, Atwater, and Wolf 1982). Kirigin et al. compared the effectiveness of the prototype program and 12 replication programs with the effectiveness of nine programs that did not use the teaching-family model. The teaching-family model produced superior, dramatic reductions in offense rates during treatment, but there were no post-treatment effects. The authors speculated that one reason for long-term failure may have been the lack of adequate training of some of the teaching parents. It is essential that teaching parents communicate effectively with the children a crucial factor in effective family therapy programs (see Alexander and Parsons, 1982). A process evaluation of the program by Skolnick, Brauckmann, Bedlington, Kirigin, and Wolf (1981) showed very high correlations (r>.80) between self-reported delinquency and the frequency of parent-child interactions in some of the homes.

During the last few years Patterson has provided further replications of his training program. Patterson, Chamberlain, and Reid (1982) provided 17 hours of behavioral parent training to ten families of highly aggressive children and compared them to nine families of aggressive children who were referred randomly to community treatment. At termination of treatment, the reduction in a measure of total aversive behavior was 60 percent in the experimental group, in contrast to 15 percent among the controls. As recounted by Gordon and Arbuthnot (1987), Marlowe, Reed, Patterson, and Weinrott (1986) applied their procedures to an older, higher-risk group than they had studied in the past. Subjects were assigned randomly either to the social learning program or to an unspecified community treatment program. Each family received 21 hours of therapist time; booster sessions during the follow-up year were also administered. The results were equivocal; of the two outcome measures reported, the experimental group showed a significant decline in number of days spent in institutions for the one-year period following treatment, but there was no such decline in the number of offenses committed.

The evidence that is quoted most often to attest that early intervention has been effective with delinquents is the series of studies by Alexander and Parsons (1973) and Klein, Alexander, and Parsons (1977). The replication of Alexander's family behavioral systems approach has been truly impressive. Recently Alexander and his colleagues replicated their earlier findings on a much harder-core delinquent sample than they studied in 1973 (Barton, Alexander, Waldron, Turner, and Warburton 1985). Thirty adolescents (each of whom had about 20 adjudicated offenses) received functional family therapy, while 44 yoked, matched adolescents received a comparison treatment which consisted of a variety of combined services, primarily a group home program patterned after Achievement Place. At the end of a 15-month posttreatment follow-up period 60 percent of the experimental group had been charged with committing an offense, while 93 percent of the comparison treatment group had been so charged. The difference was statistically reliable.

Alexander's work was supported again on a poor, rural-based sample by Gordon, Arbuthnot, Gustafson, and McGreen (under review). Their family therapy group (N=27), based on Alexander's principles, was compared to a group (N=28) of probation—only delinquents who were, in fact, lower-risk. There was a 2-1/2 year follow-up period. Court adjudications for the treatment group were 11 percent vs. 67 percent for the controls; in addition, the treated youths showed a decrease in severity of offenses. The authors attribute their greater success rates (as compared to Alexander and Parsons) for several reasons: their families received significantly more therapist contact over a longer period of time, therapists received longer training, and more supervision was given to the therapists. In addition, treatment was terminated only after the youths showed evidence of temporal and situational generalizations of skills learned in therapy sessions. Furthermore, treatment always took place in the home, which may have contributed to reducing family resistance to change. Subsequently, Gordon, Graves, and Arbuthnot (under review) reported on a sub-sample of their original study that were followed up for a period of approximately five years. When criminal offenses and felonies were combined, the recidivism rate was significantly less (10 percent vs. 45 percent) for the treated group.

EDUCATION

The education literature reviewed here is limited to prison programs, with two exceptions. Education strategies with pre or early adolescents are covered in the previous section.

Linden and Perry (1982) provide a useful review of prison education programs. The reports emanating from the 1960-80 period indicate great expectations for the success of education as a means of reforming inmates. Although considerable data attest that inmates benefit academically, well-controlled evaluations of the effect of education on post-prison behaviors are rare. Two well-known contemporary programs, for example, Lorton and Glen Mills (Dubnov 1986; Haber 1983), are described enthusiastically but have not yet reported outcome data on recidivism.

Some optimism remains for continuing to develop education programs, particularly if two conditions are met. First, transitional and post-release services must be part of such programs. Linden and Perry (1982) reviewed the evaluation (Seashore, Haberfield, Irwin, and Baker 1976) of Newgate prison education programs which were carried out in five separate states. The evaluators concluded that Newgate achieved most of its goals but did not influence inmates' post-prison recidivism rates. When programs were examined individually, however, different conclusions were reached. The Pennsylvania program, with the cooperation of Penn State University, insured a smooth transition for prisoners to continue their education in regular academic programs. Pennsylvania participants had lower recidivism rates that those at other sites.

A second condition is derived from the famous University of Victoria (UVIC) program conducted in concert with Canadian federal penitentiaries in British Columbia. UVIC challenged educationalists to de-emphasize instruction in the three R's and to focus on cognitive restructuring, moral development, and problem solving in the interpersonal and social skills necessary for the prisoner to function pro-socially in society (Ayers 1979; Duguid 1981 a,b). These goals were taught in undergraduate humanities courses, a direct but subtle method of teaching social cognitive skills. Professors, employing small groups and Socratic dialogue, served as role models and presented the information not as a "treatment" of personal deficits, but for the purposes of working toward a university degree. This latter strategy was important, as many of the participants were older high-risk offenders with long and serious criminal histories, who might resent a traditional authoritarian approach.

The first evaluation conducted on the UVIC program was not published by Linden and Perry until 1984. Sixty-six inmates with Grade 8 equivalent or higher were assigned randomly to UVIC and normal prison routine at two different penitentiaries. Fifty-six subjects were available for follow-up six to eight years after release from prison. Outcome was defined as having no criminal record, having a steady job, attending school, and avoiding the company of criminal associates. The success rates for experimental and control groups were 35 percent and 21 percent and 31 percent and 26 percent respectively for the two prisons, but the differences were not statistically reliable. The authors claim that the reported differences were underestimates. The time involved in the program was less than optimal (5 1/2 months), and the Parole Board changed its policies. It had been agreed that inmates who completed the program would be released afterward, but unfortunately, some languished several more years in prison (the number was not specified). Any beneficial effects of the program were probably dissipated for these inmates. Finally, the prison producing the poorest results was the least cooperative in implementing the program.

Some of the problems noted by Linden and Perry were rectified when Ayers, Duguid, Montague and Wolowidnyk (1980) conducted their evaluation. Process evaluations indicated that the program was having a positive effect both on inmates and staff and on inmates' behavior in the institution. The experimental group of inmates, who had completed at least two terms of coursework (7 1/2 months minimum), were compared to a matched control group of inmates who had not participated in the education program. After an average follow-up period of 20 months, the recidivism rate for experimentals was 14 percent and for controls was 52 percent. Experimentals also had a very low rate of post-discharge unemployment. The authors recommended that successful education programs must be intensive, and must be carried out so as to provide the inmates with an alternative community within the prison.

Inmates must receive peer support for their activity; support services should be provided upon release to enable inmates to continue their education and to assist them in finding jobs.

Education programs are rarely part of a probation framework. Walsh (1985) analyzed the re-arrest rate of probationers who had to be enrolled in a general equivalency diploma program as a condition of their parole. The control group consisted of probationers matched on age and crime seriousness who were not taking the diploma course; there was a 3 1/2-year follow-up. The re-arrest rates for program completers, non-completers, and controls were 16 percent, 32 percent and 44 percent, respectively.

Last, in a rather innovative study, Mayer, Butterworth, Nafpatktits, and Sulzer-Azaroff (1983) developed a school anti-vandalism program in Los Angeles. The authors endeavored to create an environment for positive behavioral change by using teachers as change agents who employed a variety of operant techniques. Youth clubs and citizen participation were also involved. Periodic training with workshops helped insure therapeutic integrity. Eighteen elementary and junior high schools were involved in a delayed-treatment control design; treatment was delivered after four and after 13 months of baseline. Follow-up periods were nine to 18 months. There was a 79 percent reduction overall in project schools, while vandalism at other schools in Los Angeles increased by 35 to 56 percent.

GETTING TOUGH

With the rehabilitation of deterrence ideology as a practical criminal justice policy, treatment programs that emphasized negative reinforcement or punishment became fashionable (Wilks and Martinson 1976). Typically, the recommended punishment paradigm was incarceration, although in one instance electric shock was advocated as a more humane and more just procedure (Newman 1983). A seminal piece of research, which revitalized the notion that incarceration could be an effective treatment, came from Murray and Cox's (1979) influential text Beyond Probation. The work has been interpreted by many policy makers as indicating that escalated punishments, in this case incarceration, were more effective than community treatments (cf. Empey 1979; Lundman 1986). This is believed to be the case because offenders supposedly fear the further punishment of imprisonment.

Murray and Cox's work already has been the subject of much discussion, but two additional points deserve comment. First, as outlined by Lundman (1986), if Murray and Cox had used the standard outcome measure of percentage of re-arrest or reconviction—as most treatment studies have done—ironically, they would have concluded that "nothing works." The authors, however, considered that standard too stiff for a deterrence study; instead they created a delinquency suppression measure, which was more sensitive and more appropriate for their purposes.

If we assume acceptance of their suppression measure, the second point revolves around "what worked." The suppression effects reported were highest for an intensive care program based in a hospital and in residential settings. The behavior-changing techniques were positive peer programs, individualized counseling, and academic work. The second highest suppression effects were noted in out-of-town residential camps that featured vocational activities, schooling, recreation, counseling, and follow-up services for clients on their return to the community. Next most effective was imprisonment, followed by group homes, nonresidential services, and wilderness programs.

No one seems to have asked whether these data are persuasive evidence that punishment or treatment works. Indeed, Murray and Cox seem to have been demonstrated that the most intensive programs produced the best results; the reader will discover in other parts of this review that this result is now becoming routine in the rehabilitation literature (cf. Andrews, Robinson, and Balla 1986). Furthermore, the program descriptions in Beyond Probation show that some of the effective intervention principles found in the rehabilitation literature (Agee 1986; Andrews and Kiessling 1980; Gendreau and Ross 1984) formed components of the two most efficient programs.

In view of the popular interpretations ascribed to Beyond Probation, it is interesting to note the authors' careful reasoning that the most effective programs may have worked for reasons other than deterrence or punishment. Theoretical conceptualizations from attention and decision-making perspectives were other potent rationales that could have accounted for the results. The programs included many positive elements such as caring, informative counselors who were effective pro-social role models and enforced program contingencies in a realistic, problem-solving manner (Murray & Cox, 1979:182-83). Finally, Lundman (1986) contends that replication of Murray and Cox's results assumes "extraordinary importance"; therefore he re-analyzed two classic delinquency projects, Provo and Silverlake, and reached conclusions contrary to those reported by Murray and Cox. The Provo data revealed that nonresidential services were more effective than institutionalization in suppressing delinquency; the Silverlake data indicated that residential services suppressed delinquency as effectively as incarceration. Lundman also suggested that the inference from Beyond Probation—that fear of punishment explained the suppression effect—could be applied just as well to community-based treatment.

We turn now to three specific deterrence procedures. Two employ incarceration; all have the intended effect of inculcating fear in the offender so that he or she will be unwilling to go or return to prison.

In shock probation, offenders receive a short period of incarceration preceding probation. Vito (1984) provides a review of shock probation programs. Although they were designed initially for specific deterrence, Vito states that any evidence of deterrent effects of shock probation is extremely slight. In comparing the results of shock probationers with similar probation groups, it was found that the shock probation regime produces no better recidivism results and in some cases demonstrably worse results (Vito and Allen 1981). Therefore, Vito states, shock probations should be reexamined in the light of a "reintegration rationale." They have the potential of reducing overcrowding and are applicable to offenders who are not good candidates for regular probation. Recently, Boudouris and Turnbull (1985) reported on a comparison of shock probationers in Iowa with matched comparison groups of offenders placed on parole, on regular probation, and in halfway houses. The period of incarceration before probation ranged anywhere from hours to one year. There were only very slight differences among the groups; nonviolent criminals who had no prior experience with incarceration had a "slightly lower recidivism rate" than parolees over a one-to-four-year follow-up period. These differences dissipated with the longer follow-up.

Another form of incarceration that is supposed to instill dislike, if not fear, of prison life, comes from proponents of "get tough" or "boot camp" prison regimes. These programs received nationwide publicity from an article in Time (Aug. 11, 1985: 15), which reported on boot camps in a southern U.S. jurisdiction. Program designers stated that the boot camps were meant to be a distasteful experience, with constant harassment of offenders for a 90-day period. The time was extended for individuals who were performing inadequately. In addition, there were adjunct therapies labeled "psychocorrectional therapy" and "brain transplant." It was claimed that graduates of the program had 35 percent lower return rates than normal.

An English penal variation on "get tough" regimes was evaluated by Thornton, Curran, Grayson, and Holloway (1984). In two prisons for adolescents 14 to 20 years of age the essential program components were hard and constructive activities, discipline and tidiness, the generation of self-respect, and respect for those in authority. Some of the results were fascinating. Staff did not feel that the program was "tougher" than past efforts. The new regime did seem "busier"; there were more drills and physical education, but fewer work programs and incentives. The adolescents apparently viewed the staff in a more positive light. Older adolescents (17-20) said they were having an easier time, but younger subjects (14-16) showed an increase in minor infractions during the program. One-year follow-up reconviction results from the two prisons were compared with those of offenders from four other centers. The conviction rate for the older group was reduced by 57 percent and for the younger group, 48 percent. The reconviction rates for the comparison institutions were 43 to 52 percent for the same period.

It is somewhat unfair to conceptualize wilderness or outward bound types of programs in this section. On the other hand, the emphasis in outward bound experiences on physical challenge, on demanding that individuals excel beyond what they feel they can do and on increasing self-esteem and respect for authority have something in common with prison "get tough" regimes. According to Winterdyk and Roesch (1981), there have been well over one hundred wilderness programs for treating delinquent youths in North America in the early 1980s. Thorough outcome evaluations, however, have been extremely rare; thus the Winterdyk and Roesch experiment is important in the evaluation literature of such programs. The program that they evaluated assigned juveniles 13 to 16 years of age randomly either to a 21-day outward bound type of program or to juvenile probation. Participants reported improvements in self-confidence and in relationships with peers, authority figures and parents. They also found their course exciting, educational, and challenging. The authors noted, however, that the initial changes observed immediately after the end of the program appeared to "wear off" at the four-to-six month follow-up period. There were no differences between reconviction rates for the experimental and the control groups.

Finally, we come to the controversial "Scared Straight" programs. The two most recent evaluations in the literature are by Buckner and Chesney-Lund (1983) and Lewis (1983). The former program was patterned after "Scared Straight," but no scare tactics were employed. A clear message was given, however, that crime does not pay. The 150 male and female adolescents taking the program were compared one year later to a matched comparison group. A significant effect was reported only for boys attending the program who had a higher re-arrest rate than their control group counterparts. This difference may have been due to exposure to the program or to concurrent involvement in other prevention programs, where the subjects may have been influenced negatively by other peers.

Lewis (1983) evaluated the San Quentin "Scared Straight" program. Subjects were 14 to 18 years of age, and took part in rap sessions, tours of the prisons, films of prison violence, and confrontational one-to-one hot-seat interviews. Subjects were assigned randomly to the program. There was a one-year follow-up, with no reported differences in re-arrest rates. There were some individual differences, however; minority-group adolescents and the older adolescents were arrest-free for a longer period of time than the controls, but these two groups committed more serious crimes. Younger experimental adolescent subjects committed more minor offenses than their control counterparts. The authors also suggested that moderately delinquent youth may have benefited more from the program, while higher-risk delinquents performed the worst.

INDIVIDUAL DIFFERENCES

The research examining the interactions among individual differences, types of treatment, and nature of settings transcends virtually all content areas in the treatment literature. These studies range from single groups of investigators, who assess the relationship of individual-difference variables to treatment outcome, to an organization such as the International Differential Treatment Association (IDTA), an influential group of practitioners and researchers who are committed to developing skills and knowledge about the effectiveness of major classifications of treatments. IDTA has produced numerous documents (e.g., Reitsma-Street and Zager 1986) devoted to the psychometric properties and practical application of Behavioral Categories (Quay 1979), Conceptual Level Matching Model (Harvey, Hunt, and Schroder 1961), Interpersonal Maturity Level or I-level (Warren 1969), the Minnesota Multiphasic Personality Inventory (Megargee and Bohn 1979), and Moral Development (Kohlberg 1969).

Throughout this review we provide ample testimony that individual differences are crucial to our understanding of "what works," but in this section we are concerned only with those reports in which a component of individual difference was the primary concern.

From the IDTA perspective, much of the persuasive outcome literature, most of which comes from I-level programs, was published in the previous decade (cf. Harris, 1983). Since then, Lukin's (1981) study, based on personality types derived from I-level theory, emphasized that personality and change must be taken into account in examining the effects of treatment. Otherwise contradictory effects will obscure the potency of interventions. Lukin found that both increases and decreases in personality change for neurotic acting-out or anxious types during treatment in two California Youth Authority institutions were predictive of recidivism on parole. Recently Hebison (1986) reported on a follow-up of 96 percent (N=200) of their youths two to five years after leaving group homes in Kansas. Successful community adjustment, as defined by structured interview, varied from 55 to 100 percent, depending upon the I-level reached by the clients while enrolled in the program. Comparisons among treatment units revealed few significant differences.

Conceptual level matching, sometimes used in conjunction with I-level, has been the subject of much interest (Leschied, Jaffe, and Stone 1985; Reitsma-Street 1984; Reitsma-Street and Leschied in press), as it appears to be an effective management procedure that matches the clients' abilities with environmental and programmatic structures. Subjects with low conceptual levels, for example, required higher degrees of structures, both environmentally and in counseling strategies, in order to respond best to treatment. Leschied and Thomas (1985) presented a one-year follow-up of 62 Craigwood adolescents, mean age 15, most of whom had had out-of-home placements since the age of 10, including reformatory experiences. Their combined I-level/conceptual level matching program resulted in 32 percent reconviction and 17 percent re-incarceration rates respectively. Re-incarceration rates were 30 to 50 percent for comparable groups of juveniles in other sites. For the year before the Craigwood treatment the average number of charges was 6.2 per resident; a year after treatment, the average was .83.

Jurkovic's (1980) review of the moral development literature suggested that rather than focusing on the content of the offenders' moral orientation (beliefs about moral rules and roles), it would be more fruitful to examine delinquents' reasoning concerning moral "oughts" in various situations.

With this approach in mind, and drawing upon cognitive-developmental theoretical perspectives (Kohlberg 1969; Piaget 1965), Arbuthnot and colleagues (Arbuthnot and Faust 1981; Arbuthnot and Gordon 1986; Arbuthnot, Gordon, and Jurkovic 1981) explored systematically the utility of interventions to develop moral reasoning among high-risk pre-delinquents. Their 1986 publication was one of the first to link the enhancement of cognitive and moral structures with changes in antisocial behavior. Forty-eight Grade 7 to 10 students, nominated by teachers as high-risk for delinquency, participated in a cognitively based moral reasoning development program for 16 to 20 weekly

45-minute sessions. A one-year follow-up found significant increases in moral reasoning, grades, and attendance and decreases in behavioral referrals for the treated group in comparison to a matched randomly assigned nontreatment group of students, who were equated according to the initially rated severity of behavior problems.

The importance of individuation from the perspective of differential association was documented by Wormith (1984). In a prison-based study, in which inmates were assigned randomly to several treatment and control conditions, he found that inmates who received the highest quality prosocial modeling program in attitude change and the best self-management training in behavioral skills demonstrated the greatest positive behavioral changes in prison. Three years after release from prison this treatment group had committed significantly fewer serious crimes, ranging from 12 to 25 percent, than the other groups. Changes in personality during incarceration were also predictive of recidivism. Those offenders whose self-esteem and identification with criminal others increased had higher recidivism rates, while decreases in recidivism were reported for those who experienced increased feelings of inadequacy while imprisoned.

What may prove to be the most potent individual-difference factor has emerged from one of criminal justice's most venerable topics, the literature on risk variables which are predictive of recidivism. The urgency to employ risk assessment as a programmatic aid has been fueled by the emerging crisis in parole and probation regarding unmanageable caseloads and, secondarily, by prison overcrowding (see Federal Probation, June 1986). It is imperative that probation and parole services develop rational, empirically based classification systems (Clear and Gallagher 1985).

An offender's risk level may be defined by only a few social and criminal history items, such as the Wisconsin Risk Scale (Baird, Hemus, and Heinz 1981) and the U.S. Salient Factors score (Hoffman and Stone-Meinhoefer 1979), or by more extensive inventories that also explore offenders' personal needs and deficits, such as the Level of Supervision Inventory (LSI) (Andrews 1983). Risk measures have been effective predictors of recidivism (Andrews 1983; Motiuk 1984), and in some instances have demonstrated more predictive power than some of the standard classification procedures like the MMPI (Motiuk, Bonta, and Andrews 1986). In addition, some of the measures, such as the LSI, have generated an impressive amount of predictive criterion validity in probation, halfway houses, and prisons (Andrews, Kiessling, Mickus, and Robinson 1986; Bonta and Motiuk 1985; Bonta and Motiuk in press).

No matter how risk is measured, the data are beginning to show incontrovertibly that level of risk, either alone or in interaction with the intensity or therapeutic integrity of service delivery, correlates with noticeable shifts in outcome. On the basis of research with adult offenders and high-risk juveniles (Andrews, Kiessling, Robinson, and Mickus 1986; Andrews, Robinson, and Bala 1986) and assessments of the risk literature in social services generally (Andrews, Hoge, Baitz, Robinson, Hollett, and Stewart in press) the point was confirmed many times over. Within the criminal justice field up to a 40 percent difference in recidivism was not an uncommon finding, depending on whether high-risk cases received intensive services. In addition, it has been reported that for some extreme high-risk cases the level of service delivered may be inconsequential (Byles and Maurice 1982), whereas there are lower-risk cases that should receive relatively minimal attention. In this latter regard, some data have attested to increased recidivism as a result of intervention and/or contact with higher-risk clients enrolled in other programs (Andrews et al. in press; Bonta and Motiuk in press; O'Donnell, Lydgate, and Fo 1971; Severy and Whitaker 1982; Shorts 1986). Independently of the Andrews group, Lerner, Arling, and Baird (1986) found significantly lower parole revocation warrants (approximately 10%) in two large-scale studies in Texas and Wisconsin among probationers assigned randomly to intensive rather than regular supervision on the basis of the Wisconsin Risk Measure.

It is of particular interest that the above findings do not appear to be confirmed by preliminary data recorded by the Georgia Intensive Probation Supervision (IPS) project (Erwin 1986). The Georgia IPS program has received considerable attention and acclaim (e.g., Conrad 1985) for its emphasis on punishment (see Erwin 1986: 17). On examining Table 1 of Erwin, however, the IPS group produced no better reconviction or re-incarceration results than regular probation services across four risk categories. In the case of low-risk clients (although the N was only 23), IPS fared worse. These overall results may be explained partly by the fact that the studies cited by Andrews and Lerner et al. employed therapies with much more focus on positive skill building. Possibly the risk-intensive service interaction depends upon the nature of the service delivered. Another explanation might be that the IPS group was not more intensive than regular probation in practice. Erwin's writeup did not make clear the exact differences between the two forms of probation.

Finally, the risk principle has spawned two concepts that can serve only to augment the therapeutic integrity of future treatments when individual differences are matched with the appropriate levels of service delivery. The concepts are those of need and responsivity assessment (Andrews et al. in press; Duffee and Clark 1985). In simple terms, risk assessment tools that stress the measurement of static variables, such as age and previous convictions, are not especially helpful in designing treatment programs. The offender can do little about the past. The targeting of dynamic variables as represented by personal needs, which in themselves can be predictors of risk, such as degree of substance abuse or criminal thinking, is more productive in dealing constructively with the offender's current situation.

The responsivity principle of case classification suggests that higher-risk cases will be able to respond positively only to programs that are tailored to fit their abilities and learning styles. In some instances programs have been at a level beyond the clients' abilities. This principle was illustrated by Arbuthnot and Gordon (1986), who discovered that some of their participants were unresponsive to interventions for developing moral reasoning. They stated that such subjects may have not had the general cognitive skills necessary for taking the program in the first place.

PAROLE/PROBATION

Like the diversion literature, parole/probation evaluations tend to show rather modest results, where it is difficult to ascertain what was done from a therapeutic standpoint (Erwin 1986; Gottfredson, Mitchell-Herzefeld, and Flanagan 1982; Jackson 1983; Lichtman and Smock 1981; Petersilia, Turner, Kahan, and Peterson 1985; Petersilia, Turner, and Peterson 1986). Of these studies the most potent results in favor of parole and probation were described by Erwin (1986). Comparisons were made between regular probations and incarcerates across four risk categories for four different measures of outcome over an 18-month period. As calculated from Table 1 (Erwin 1986: 20), the probation sample averaged a 17 percent lower recidivism rate. Petersilia et al. (1986) reported 72 percent re-arrest rates for released prisoners, compared to 63 percent for probationers, for a two-year follow-up. Gottfredson et al. (1982) found that their parolees had five to eight percent less recidivism on four of six risk measures, excluding technical violations, than conditional-release and mandatory-expiry-of-sentence groups. This study had a five-year follow-up. Both studies found that re-arrest rates varied as a result of individual differences, such as age, property, and drug offenses.

On the other hand, outcome data are more persuasive when it is clear that substantial therapeutic integrity was maintained in probation programs. Some of the data relevant to this argument have been reviewed already in the "individual differences" section. In addition, Andrews and Kiessling (1980), on whose research we commented in 1980, gave precise descriptions of the quality and type of therapeutic process in a probation setting. Differences in recidivism rates of probationers were as high as 80 percent, depending on the matching of type of supervision with the client's characteristics. Robert Lee's CREST program, which was evaluated systematically for several years, has been exemplary in its attention and adherence to the details of an intensive, eclectic service delivery system in probation (e.g., Lee and Haynes 1980). His program contains components of reality, rational-emotive, client-centered therapies, and role playing.

Since our 1980 review, Lee and Olejnik (1981) reported once again on a randomized evaluation of their program with a two-year follow-up. This study also has been one of the rare evaluations to include a sizeable proportion of female offenders. CREST subjects performed significantly better than regular probationers, particularly after the probation period ended for both groups. There were no sex differences in response to treatment. Treatment contributed significantly beyond the suppression effect of probation: just 30 percent of the CREST group's offenses occurred when probation was terminated, whereas the similar figure for the controls was 70 percent.

Shawver, Clanon, Kurdys, and Friedman (1985) found that the quality of prisoners' performance in a prison group therapy program was predictive (N=.47) of parole success a year after release. Recently Ross and Fabiano (personal communication with R. Ross, Aug. 3,1987) disclosed the first preliminary results from their cognitive model of offender rehabilitation (see Ross and Fabiano 1985). The major components of their program were rational selfanalysis, self-control training, means-end reasoning, critical thinking, and interpersonal cognitive problem solving. Judges assigned 62 high-risk adult offenders, as defined by the LSI, randomly to regular intensive probation, to attention control with life skills training, and to the cognitive group. After nine months, reconviction rates for the three groups were 70 percent, 48 percent, and 18 percent respectively. Re-incarceration rates were 30 percent, 11 percent, and 0 percent. A two-year follow-up is now being completed.

Previously we mentioned the Georgia IPS program, which brings us to what Petersilia et al. (1985: 385), in referring to IPS programs in general, hail as "one of the most significant criminal justice experiments in the next decade." It may well be that when this review is published, solid, well-controlled evaluations on IPS will have appeared, making the following comments obsolete.

For the present it is difficult to know exactly what IPS is. The Georgia project makes no apologies for the fact that the idea behind IPS is to "increase the heat on probationers...satisfy the public demand for just punishment... and criminals be punished for their misdeeds" (Erwin 1986: 17). On the other hand, although IPS is often described in terms of reducing overcrowding, intermediate punishment, controlling deviant behavior, and cost savings (e.g., Pearson 1985), much of what has been considered to be traditional treatment in IPS continues. On several occasions, New Jersey officials have told the senior author that they are providing treatment services in addition to surveillance options. Harris (see Byrne 1986) notes IPS has a "garbage can" mentality; new program components have been added willy-nilly, with no evidence that IPS will meet goals of either rehabilitation or deterrence. Target populations vary, and in some cases those probationers who most require intensive supervision are not receiving it (Rosencrance 1986). Only 29 percent of Georgia's maximum-risk cases have been subjected to IPS (Byrne 1986).

As for outcome data, we have only Erwin's data indicating that IPS was no better than regular probation. Most IPS programs have not been evaluated formally; and few have met even elementary design requirements (Burkhart 1987; Byrne 1986). Finally, cynics like Rosencrance (1986) argue that any program that must provide assistance and surveillance is impossible because of bureaucratic and client-related factors. Treatment should be provided by other social service agencies. Some scholars might demur on this point: Andrews and Kiessling (1980) documented that the therapeutic principles of authority and the quality of interpersonal relationships need not be inimical in the effective delivery of probation services.

Restitution

Restitution programs have received considerable support because they appeal to a wide variety of rationales that emanate from deterrence and justice models of corrections. These include punishment, reformation, inexpensive alternatives to jail, and reparation mandating the offender to be accountable to the community and individuals that he or she victimizes (Menzies 1986). As an example of the tremendous growth of these programs, one of the jurisdictions (Ontario) that first developed restitution in the form of community service increased orders for community service from 206 in 1978 to 11,381 in 1983. Another form of restitution, the victim-offender reconciliation program, has also become popular. Several dozen such programs are now operating in

North America, England, and New Zealand (Criminal Justice Digest 1985).

Evaluations of these programs, unfortunately, have been few. Schneider and Schneider (1985) reviewed the literature, but with few exceptions (Bonta, Boyle, Motiuk, and Sonnichsen 1983; Shichor and Binder 1982) it is unpublished. Many of the programs contained scant information to allow for an assessment of their therapeutic integrity. If control groups were employed, there seemed to be little equivalence between them and the experimental groups. When recidivism rates were reported, the differences between restitution and comparison groups were minimal.

Schneider and Schneider's (1985) evaluation of a restitution program in Georgia appears to be the most methodologically impressive to date. Subjects were assigned randomly to a "pure" restitution condition, where community work was done or payment was made. Over 80 per cent completed the restitution program. Clients were involved in the program for three and one-half months on the average. They were followed up for three years. The groups consisted of a restitution group only, a restitution group that also received counseling and recreation, a recreation and counseling group and a group receiving probation or incarceration. Two outcome measures were reported: Percentage of subjects with no reoffending and overall reoffense rates per 100 youths per year. In both comparisons the group that performed best was the restitution group that also received additional counseling services. The group that produced the worst results was the recreation and counseling group. It was unclear from the program descriptions why the counseling group should combine with restitution to produce the most potent treatment effect but on its own was relatively ineffective.

Finally, in a study unique to the area, Van Voorhis (1985) examined the relationship of individual differences to the offenders' ability to carry out a financial restitution program satisfactorily. Individual differences were defined in terms of Kohlberg's stages of moral development. This study was important because it looked beyond the superficial structure of a program to offender's opinions of the services they were receiving, which were related in turn to their performance. Low-maturity offenders were more likely to identify with the deterrent intent of restitution, while high-maturity offenders were oriented toward the reparative and rehabilitative aspects. Specific attitudes among both the high-and low-maturity groups were also related to success. Some low-maturity offenders performed very badly, probably because they viewed restitution as an inconvenience, felt that the sentence was lenient, and believed that they were getting a "good deal." Van Voorhis argued for a differential counseling strategy to enhance the effectiveness of restitution.

In view of the abundant evidence that individual differences interact with a variety of rehabilitation programs, it is crucial that programs based on an ideology of deterrence or justice also take individual differences into account.

WORK

In the current sociopolitical climate, work programming is one of the few avenues of reform capable of providing broad-based political support for rehabilitation (Cressey 1982; Cullen and Travis 1984). Lately more interest has been expressed in this area; in our 1979 review, there were few evaluative studies. These are the latest results on the effectiveness of work programs.

Smith (1980) compared a work-release program with two comparison groups of inmates who met the program criteria but did not participate for various reasons. After an 18-month follow-up the felony convictions were 26 percent for work releases and 40 percent and 47 percent for the control groups.

In 1976 the U.S. Department of Labor, in conjunction with the states of Texas and Georgia, initiated the celebrated Transitional Aid Research Project (TARP) program, which provided a modest income to ex-convicts after their release from prison, thereby facilitating their immediate adjustment to society and providing help in finding employment. As a result, it was reasoned, recidivism should be reduced. Almost 2,000 ex-prisoners were assigned randomly to the six groups, four treatment and two control groups. Duration of payment varied, and payments could be reduced if the ex-convicts engaged in paid employment. The results were reported in Berk, Lenihan, and Rossi (1980) and Rossi, Berk, and Lenihan (1980). The authors concluded that limited financial aid decreases arrests in the year following release by 25 to 50 percent. Jurik (1983) reported similar positive results for female offenders in the same program. The findings, however, have been questioned vigorously (Zeisel 1982). Acceptance of the results depends on which type of statistical analysis is to be believed. The design of the study was ideal for a form of analysis of variance assessment, the most appropriate for a randomized experiment such as TARP. On the basis of this statistical analysis the authors concluded that the number of arrests was not reduced (Berk et al. 1980: 777). Yet if a structural equation statistical technique is used, which Zeisel considers to be less appropriate, positive conclusions are reached.

Beck (1981) reported on the Federal Community Treatment Center (CTC) placement program, which supplemented resources of released inmates on probation by providing short-term support in the form of room and board. The results from this study stand as testimony to an individual difference/risk approach to work programs. First, the program was more successful in helping its subjects find employment than the comparison group of inmates who did not take part in the CTC program. According to the author, however, the quality of the employment (average daily wages) was upgraded only for the minority-group offenders. When the control group was equated statistically to the experimental group by means of the salient factor score, a significant reduction in recidivism was found after 12 months—11 percent for the minority groups. When the authors assessed the level of risk and its relationship to treatment success in the minority group, they found that higher-risk individuals had significantly greater decreases in recidivism, in the range of 16 to 21 percent. Good-risk minority inmates had lower recidivism rates, but only one to ten percent. Beck concluded that minority groups have a much greater disadvantage in gaining employment and thus benefit from such a program.

In a carefully designed and reasoned study that featured random assignment, extensive assessment, vocational training, and an Outward Bound component, Johnson and Goldberg (1983) reported no program effects after a three-year follow-up on youths' employment, schooling, and re-incarceration rate. They noted that a major problem with the program was the high turnover rate among counselors. During one period there was no counselor available, and some counselors had difficulty in motivating youths.

Two other work projects are worth noting, both are comments on the value of maintaining therapeutic integrity in programming. In the Anderson (1985) job training study, the experimental group of probationers was encouraged to learn the value of work and to develop responsible work habits. A one-year recidivism follow-up disclosed no differences between them and a random sample of probationers that did not receive job training. Anderson questioned why the employment of individuals enrolled in the program decreased from 84 to 26 percent while they were in the program.

In summary, if work programs are to be successful in the future, the following principles should be followed (Homant 1984; Katz and Decker 1982; Lightman 1982; Vito 1985). Work programs should be targeted to higher-risk offenders who do not have job skills. All too often work programs are directed toward relatively stable offenders who have adequate employment histories. Empirical support for this notion comes from the Beck (1981) study and from one of the first work programs conducted by Jeffrey and Woopert (1974), which also reported successful results with higher-risk offenders. Support for an individualized approach to work programs has also been forthcoming from the economic sphere. Orsagh and Witte (1981) and Orsagh and Marsden (1985) argue that work programs fail to pay attention to individual differences, but in contrast to the above recommendations they state that work programs should focus on low-risk offenders who are older, who have a history of consistent work patterns, who committed crimes related to monetary gain but who have low economic status, and who have no major alcohol or drug problems. As supporting evidence, Orsagh and Witte (1981) quote the TARP program which, in our opinion, is not the strongest evidence for their position.

Another principle, and one that makes eminent sense, is that work programs must enhance practical skills, develop interpersonal skills, minimize prisonization, and ensure that work is not punishment alone. Various behavioral modification schemes must be established so that inmates are motivated to succeed. General confirmation for this view comes from a recent large scale survey of students reporting their work experiences. Gottfredson (1985) stated that if workers' experiences are to be viable they must include work that is socially reinforcing, personally meaningful, and well supervised. An excellent example, consistent with the thrust of these arguments, comes from the classic Walters and Mills (1980) study reported in our 1980 literature review (cf. Ross and Gendreau 1980). There can be no better example of a rehabilitation program, work or otherwise, that insisted upon therapeutic integrity. In this study jobs were available, employers were motivated, and the offenders were prepared in detail, both in attitude and in specific behavioral skills, to accept and perform the jobs well. The authors also provided detailed guidelines as to how a program should be implemented successfully in the community so that significant others, such as courts, media, employers, and schools, would cooperate to the fullest. Not surprisingly, 70 percent reductions in criminal conduct were reported for the youths in the program, in contrast to members of the control group.

PART B

SEXUAL OFFENDERS

Those who commit sexual crimes are the most visible offenders in the criminal justice system. When a sexual offender, particularly a child molester or a rapist, commits a crime, an outraged public typically demands swift, harsh justice. An increasing number of criminal justice and mental health agencies have responded, and are in the process of providing programs.

Not surprisingly, treatment for sexual offenders has been an unpopular concept (Abel, Mittlemen, and Becker 1985). Lately, however, the recognition that most sexual offenders eventually will be released has generated a demand for prison and hospital treatment services that will insure successful social re-integration. Sex offenders now account for about 10 percent of prison popula-tions; rates are as high as 20 percent in some prisons (Borzecki and Wormith 1987). Borzecki and Wormith's (1987) survey revealed that 21 states have established programs, most of which are prisonbased, and ten are in the process of doing so; In Canada, 12 programs were noted; most are located in hospitals. Another source, the Safer Society Press (Criminal Justice Newsletter 1986), claimed the existence of 650 such treatment programs in North America.

Although these growing resources are encouraging, many jurisdictions still have no services and most programs are in their infancy. As a result, data attesting to their therapeutic integrity and their treatment success are extreme-ly sparse. Furthermore, few agencies have developed a network of community resource centers for vocational and family re-integration after the course of treatment in prison is completed (Borzecki and Wormith 1987). Some of the programs, however, are quite intensive. Many programs employ behavior modification on a one-to-one basis and continue until deviant sexual arousal is negligible as assessed on objective measures. Groups often continue for one to two years, with five to 25 hours of counseling each week.

A considerable number of clinical case studies, combined with a few empirical investigations, has led to some consensus as to what types of treat-ment are effective (Abel, Rouleau, and Cunningham-Rathner 1985; Blair and Lanyon 1981; Lanyon 1986; Quinsey 1984, 1986). Psychoanalytic therapies are considered ineffective. For valid reasons castration is not used in North America, although it has been employed occasionally in Europe with reports of success. The reduction of sexual drive by chemotherapy, such as depo-provera, has some strong advocates (e.g., Liaison 1984), but sexual arousal often returns after the drug is terminated. Drug treatment may be limited to select subjects who have not responded to other treatments.

It is agreed generally that several behavior modification or "conditioning" therapies, such as covert sensitization, aversive conditioning, and satiation therapy, have been effective. Their effectiveness may be augmented when combined with sociosexual education, training in life skills, and assertive and cognitive training procedures. Incest cases apparently respond to family-sys-tem treatment methods.

The empirical justification for such positive therapeutic claims is based on the following evidence. Blair and Lanyon (1981) reviewed 12 studies with follow-up periods of up to one year, which reported treatment success with exhibitionists. Compared to other sexual offenders, exhibitionists have high rates of recidivism. Kelly (1982) examined 32 studies of child molesters; 167 individuals in all were treated. Follow-up periods ranged from two weeks to six years. Success, as defined by reported reductions in urges to molest children, were found for 79 percent of the subjects. Abel et al. (1984) found that between 79 percent and 91 percent of self-referred sex offenders reported no further deviant activities at six and 12-month follow-up periods, respectively. (Abel's research group went to considerable lengths to ensure confidentiality.) The best outcome results were those for incest and heterosexual child molesters; homosexual child molesters performed worst. Davidson (1984) compared the treatment effectiveness of a behaviorally oriented program for 36 incarcerated sexual assaulters with the outcome for a matched sample of 36 prisoners who received no treatment. Five years after release from prison the recidivism rate of the treatment group was one-fifth that of the comparison group.

Romero and Williams (1985) evaluated a project that involved random assignment of sex offenders either to group psychotherapy and probation (N=148) or to an intensive probation supervision program (N=83). A ten-year follow-up was recorded. Recidivism rates were 14 percent and 7 percent respectively for each treated group.

Although incest cases often do not come to the attention of the courts, the Santa Clara child abuse family therapy program (Giarretto 1982) asserts that only one percent of the hundreds of father-daughter incest cases that have undergone treatment have relapsed.

In the authors' opinion, the most impressive data comes from a long-term series of clinical evaluations by Maletzky (1980), beginning in 1974. He treated a total of 155 exhibitionists with follow-ups of one to nine years. His program relied principally on assisted covert sensitization and, to a secondary extent, on counseling for related problems, such as marital therapy. Subjects were treated twice weekly for up to five months. Then, most important, "booster" sessions were provided at home for a further year to these requiring additional treatment. Maletzky reported that 87 percent of his clients eliminated all exhibitionistic behaviors. His work is noteworthy because it testifies to the currently popular idea that relapse prevention treatment models, borrowed from the addictions literature, are relevant to sexual offenders (Pithers, Marques, Gibat, and Marlatt 1983). Pithers et al. outlined how the events promoting relapse among sexual offenders are highly similar to those among alcohol and drug addicts.

Nevertheless, some warnings are in order. To date, the sex offender treatment literature has been curiously isolated from the ongoing "what works" debate. The cautious optimism about treatment effectiveness (Quinsey 1986) is refreshing, particularly in view of the nature of the behaviors and the difficulty of conducting sex offender programs. On the other hand, it is hard to believe the dramatic claims that recidivism among some sex offenders has been reduced to only a few percent, no matter how intensive the treatment. Either sex offenders have peculiar offending patterns or much of their crime goes undetected. It may well be the latter case (Groth, Longo, and McFadin 1982). Abel et al. (1985) reported the startling statistic that on the average, their sample of sex offenders committed 44 crimes per year! Some researchers are well aware of the issue and admit to limited searches for recidivism in their follow-ups (Romero and Williams 1986). In addition, we must remember that few controlled evaluations of treatment efficacy exist. Finally, a host of assessment and treatment-related issues (e.g., Lanyon 1986) still awaits resolution.

SUBSTANCE ABUSE

For reasons outlined previously (Gendreau and Ross 1979; Ross and McKay 1978) the literature on alcohol and drug abuse treatment has been dismissed casually as having little consequence for offender programming. On the other hand, prison and probation caseloads are replete with substance abusers, but programming appropriate for their needs has rarely been provided by corrections agencies (see Ross and Lightfoot 1985). Admittedly, treatment breakthroughs in this field are not imminent, but there is room for some optimism. Alcohol researchers recently have generated concepts of treatment that have potential not only for alcohol offender treatment but for offender programs in general. Drug addiction treatments, on the other hand, are more than suggestive of what might work. The recent evidence indicates that some drug addicts, including those with criminal histories, have benefited from treatment.

Ross and Lightfoot (1985) have reviewed the literature on alcohol treatment outcome for offenders. They concluded that with isolated exceptions (e.g., Annis and Chan 1983), very few well-controlled evaluations, with at least several months' follow-up, attest that alcohol programs for offenders have been effective. On the other hand, not much has been tried with offenders in view of recent developments in alcohol treatment. It is agreed that covert sensitization, behavioral self-control, and broad-spectrum interventions, which include social skills training, stress management, and marital and family therapy, have demonstrated success with some alcoholics (Miller and Hester 1986). It is also generally agreed (see Nathan and Skinstad 1987) that controlled drinking strategies are effective (e.g., Sanchez-Craig, Annis, Bornet, and MacDonald 1984). Controlled drinking appears to be a suitable treatment for young adult heavy drinkers who have not yet become alcoholics; many offenders fit this description. Controlled drinking should have appeal for offender populations from the viewpoint of reintegrating the offender into his or her home setting, where absolute abstinence might not be tolerated by peers.

The notions of relapse prevention (Brownell, Marlatt, Lichtenstein, and Wilson 1986) and self-efficacy theory (Bandura 1977) also enhance the prospects for successful intervention. The general notion is that one should focus interventions on the reasons why individuals fail to maintain positive changes after they demonstrated success during treatment. Therefore, relapse prevention is crucial for any long-term effects of treatment. Self-efficacy refers to judgments that one has the ability to behave in a certain way; the goal is to instill a sense of personal capacity and confidence in the client to help him or her cope with situations that may promote relapse. Annis and Davis (1987) were among the first to demonstrate practically the usefulness of relapse prevention and self-efficacy concepts in the treatment of alcoholics. After a six-month follow-up they reported dramatic reductions in drinking rates per week. In addition, 29 percent of their 45 clients reported total abstinence. Annis and Davis would be the first to admit that these results are very tentative and await replication with longer follow-up periods, but in any case, this type of program cannot be ignored by those interested in designing programs for offenders. Furthermore, when one examines the specific treatment strategies employed by Annis and Davis, it becomes apparent that their procedures may have considerable relevance for modifying problematic offender behaviors other than alcohol abuse.

Our brief comments on drug abuse treatment does disservice to the complexity of this treatment literature, which now numbers several hundred publications. The literature relevant to criminal justice concerns has been summarized elsewhere (Gendreau under review). Granted, the evaluation of drug abuse treatments has been compromised by studies that failed to employ randomized designs or carefully chosen comparison groups. Methadone and therapeutic community treatment studies have also suffered from high dropout rates. Nevertheless, increasing evidence shows that addicts who stay the course of treatment or re-enroll after initial failure can decrease their drug intake and reduce criminal offenses. Anglin and McClothlin (1984) stated that the pertinent question is not whether drug abuse programs work but rather what types of programs work for what types of addicts at different points in their addiction career. The following publications are only a representative sample of the current drug abuse treatment studies.

Dwayne Simpson and his colleagues have assiduously reported follow-up data on the Drug Abuse Reporting Program (DARP) since its inception in 1969. Twenty-five DARP agencies located across the United States involved almost 30,000 addicts in treatment. DARP included methadone maintenance, therapeutic communities, outpatient drug-free programs, and detoxification programs. The latest follow-up was based on 405 black and white opioid addicts 12 years after first entering a DARP facility (Simpson, Joe, Lehman, and Sells 1986). The authors found that in the twelfth year after treatment the reduction in daily heroin use was 74 percent. Forty-two percent of the subjects did not abuse heroin over the entire period. Many of the DARP clients had extensive criminal histories, but arrest rates decreased by 74 percent after they enrolled in DARP.

The California Civil Addict Program reduced daily narcotic use and associated property crime among participants by three times as much as among similar addicts not in the program (Anglin and McGlothlin 1984; McGlothlin, Anglin, and Wilson 1977). Anglin (in press) identified several features that contribute to effective programming: the appropriate use of various support systems that would enhance the addict's personal resources, a behavior modification orientation, administrations that have extensive background in treating addicts, relapse prevention, and aftercare programming.

Stanton (1982) described a family therapy program for heroin abusers, which had several components similar to that employed by effective family therapy studies reviewed in the early intervention section. Stanton assigned subjects randomly to two conditions of family therapy and to two control groups. At the six-month follow-up the experimental groups had 17 to 30 percent more drug-free days than did the control groups.

Platt, Perry, and Metzger (1980) developed a therapeutic community program featuring guided group interactions, interpersonal problem-solving skills, and family therapy for incarcerated substance abusers. Two years after release from prison the treated group had significantly fewer arrests (17 percent) than their matched control group.

DeLeon (1985, 1987) reviewed the therapeutic community (TC) literature.

Several studies demonstrate that immediate and long-term outcome status for addicts improved significantly over pretreatment status; some of the follow-up periods were as long as five years. Drug use and criminality declined, while measures of prosocial behavior increased; at least moderately favorable outcomes occurred in 50 percent of the clients. Positive outcome was reported even among program dropouts, depending on length of stay in treatment.

We conclude with the acclaimed "stay'n out" prison substance abuse treatment program, based on the Phoenix House TC model. The program includes both males and females and has been operating in two New York State prisons for the last ten years. Wexler and Williams (in press) describe the program structure. Critical to the program's success are the maintenance of high standards of therapeutic integrity in prison (the authors provide details on how to achieve this difficult feat), extensive treatment lasting at least six months, and the establishment of a post-prison TC aftercare network.

Parole outcome data were obtained for 1626 males and 398 females who were involved in the evaluation. Outcome results for the TC group were compared to results for two groups of inmates who participated in counseling programs, a group enrolled in a non-TC milieu (male only) program; and a group of inmates who volunteered initially but either changed their minds or did not meet the admission criteria (Wexler, Lipton, and Foster in press). Follow-up periods varied from two to three and one-half years after release from prison. Both male and female TC participants showed significantly lower arrest rates than their respective notreatment and counseling comparison groups. The percentage differences ranged from six to 27 percent, depending on the comparisons. The milieu program, which was ranked second to the TC program in therapeutic intensity, also produced significantly better outcome results, although not as good as those for the TC group. The authors also reported an optimal treatment period of 12 months. If the offender was not paroled after that time, his or her prognosis deteriorated.

Violent Offenders

In the minds of many concerned observers, aggression and violence in North America have increased to alarming proportions. Commonplace forms of violence, such as homicide and assaults, have increased. In addition, much attention has been directed to specialized forms of violence such as child abuse, spouse battery, and television and film violence (Apter and Goldstein

1986; Goldstein 1983),

Defining this topic area for the purposes of a succinct review is virtually impossible. One of the recent texts on "youth violence" (Apter and Goldstein 1986), for example, contained articles on samples of youth in diversion and special education programs, social learning treatments for offenders in several contexts, school vandals, and neurologically impaired acting-out youth.

Depending upon one's perspective, these samples of violent youth were probably no more "violent" than those included in other parts of this review, such as in high-risk probation studies. Actually, the truly violent offender is elusive. They exist, but—contrary to popular belief—in small numbers. Elliott, Huizinga, and Morse (1986) have examined the careers of presumed violent offenders, and found that those involved in repeated violent offending were estimated at just four percent.

The confusion over definitions eventually will be resolved, but in the meantime, social scientists in this field have produced a wealth of valuable information that has added much to our understanding of what is likely to work in the future. The contributions are noted in clinical knowledge and public policy.

The clinical perspective permits marked gains in knowledge. In this regard three major contributions collectively have spawned hundreds of programs in clinical settings across North America.

The first contribution comes from the study of anger and aggression. Two viable models have been proposed; they differ in theoretical emphasis but for all practical purposes have much in common. Novaco's (1975) approach, commonly referred to as stress inoculation training, borrows from the cognitive-behavioral theories of Meichenbaum (see Meichenbaum and Turk 1976) and attempts to restructure the individual's cognitions about anger-arousing events. The structural learning paradigm of Goldstein (1973, 1981) assumes that aggressive behavior is a consequence of poor psychological and social skills. Thus the therapy focuses on teaching appropriate means of expressing anger; it employs modeling, role playing, and transfer training techniques advocated by social learning theories of behavior (Bandura 1973).

The second contribution to clinical knowledge about violence emerged from cognitive models of delinquent behavior that can be traced to research in the early 1950s by Glueck and Glueck (1950) and Sarbin (1952). The view that the offender's thinking has been short-circuited developmentally is central to an eclectic variety of theories: cognitive social learning perspective (Sarason 1978), interpersonal cognitive problem solving (Spivack, Platt, and Shure 1976), I-level (Palmer 1968), moral reasoning (Kohlberg 1969), and neutralization (Sykes and Matza 1957). Variations on these themes have been applied extensively to almost all areas of delinquency prevention (see Ross and Fabiano 1985). Among the recent developments in this regard, by far the most publicized is Yochelson and Samenow's (1976) concept of criminal personality. Their theory evolved from their clinical work with a sample of chronic offenders, some of whom had long histories of violence and related psychiatric disorders.

The third contribution comes from the literature on the institutional treatment of violent offenders. Vicki Agee, the leading authority in the field, who also developed one of the prototype programs (Agee 1979), has summarized the clinical and programming principles necessary to provide effective programming in these settings (Agee 1986; Agee and McWilliams 1984). Therapeutic community and team management concepts that emphasize structured treatment and discipline, peer-culture reinforcement systems, fostering of prosocial relationships, and awareness of victims are crucial to success.

These gains in knowledge are clinical, but little of this compelling clinical lore has been corroborated by post-treatment followup data in community settings. Stress inoculation and structured learning techniques are practiced routinely by clinicians, but one of the few pieces of evidence for the long-term benefits of Novaco's procedures is found in Bistline and Frieden's (1984) case study, which includes a twelve-month follow-up. Goldstein, Apter, and Harootunian (1984) and Goldstein (1986) have reviewed the published treatment literature on psychological skills training programs for aggressive youngsters. They examined 42 experimental studies; most of these were well designed, and employed the required control groups. This data base provides persuasive recommendations for the development of more effective programs (see Goldstein 1986: 103-13). Nonetheless, we note the lack of longterm follow-ups assessing the generalization of the principles learned in the clinical setting to the community. One of the few exceptions is the study by Bornstein, Bellack, and Hersen (1980), a multiple-baseline study of four aggressive hospitalized adolescent inpatients. The authors reported a decrease in aggressiveness six months after treatment.

Yochelson and Samenow's claims for success contain no before-and-after assessments—only doctrinaire statements that the program was effective with 13 of 30 offenders (Samenow 1984). Agee's Closed Adolescent Unit program in Denver reported recidivism rates of only 33 percent for her very high-risk violent adolescents, but the recidivism follow-up was limited in scope and no adequate control-group data were reported. Similarly, other programs treating violent offenders (U.S. Department of Justice 1981) have reported little evaluative data. This lack of evaluation will be rectified, however, as the Rand

Corporation presently is providing a comprehensive assessment of Agee's latest program (P. Greenwood, personal communication, Sept. 9, 1986). Although those "nothing works" cynics who are keenly misanthropic will rejoice in the lack of outcome data, we believe that this field of study will parallel the early intervention literature which was only a vague promise a decade ago.

We hope the Fagan and Hartstone (under review) report will be the first in a series of high-quality outcome evaluations. Fagan and Hartstone's research encompassed programs in four U.S. cities. The essential program elements were social networking, provision of opportunities for youth, social learning techniques, the linking of specific behaviors to each client's needs and abilities, and provision of appropriate therapies. Case management and gradual reentry into the community via multiple-phase residential programs were used to facilitate the program. In our opinion, this study is noteworthy because it addresses the crucial factor of program integrity (cf. Sechrest et al. 1979). The authors took care to assess the quality of implementation and the intensity of the service delivered. Preliminary results (J. Fagan, personal communication, July 16,1987) are as follows: After 12 months' follow-up the rates of re-offending and violent offenses were significantly lower in three of four sites, and in two of four sites the rates of re-incarceration were lower than in comparable groups of adolescents sent to secure care. Most important, those sites that were superior in implementation and service delivery produced the best outcomes.

Lastly we turn our attention to public policy contributions to violent crime. Two of the significant contributions come from Chaiken and Chaiken (1984) and Currie (1985a). Their recommendations are applicable to crime issues in general, (see Currie 1985b), but are included in this section because they address violent crime. On the basis of their analysis of 2,000 male offenders, Chaiken and Chaiken (1984) concluded that those offenders whom they defined as "violent predators" could be managed best by early intervention strategies focused on preventing the behavioral patterns from developing initially. Their recommendations are certainly congruent with the research evidence on early intervention. In addition, their comment that "violent predators" would be the best candidates for rehabilitation is consistent with those like Andrews et al., who argue that middle-to high-risk offenders should be targeted for intensive programming. Chaiken and Chaiken also found little basis for support of control mechanisms, namely selective incapacitation or sentencing, for violent offenders. In their estimation a 3 percent false identification rate is the maximum allowable for selective incapacitation. Their data uncovered false alarm rates above 30 percent for some of their high-risk offenders.

Currie's (1985a) prescriptions for violent crime are more far-reaching At one level he calls passionately for an end to the destruction of inner-city life by the varies of the private market. The lack of public commitment to funding and planning for employment and economic development can only exacerbate the conditions that promote violent crime. Narrowly conceived policies of income supports that promote welfare dependency, community crime prevention, and magical notions of effective punishment for high-risk offenders have been failures. Rather, Currie argues, why not reinforce the notion of selective treatment? Nobody challenges the belief that informal conditions applied by family and community are more effective in bringing about change. Like Chaiken and Chaiken, Currie is convinced that the prediction and treatment data currently being generated from the early prevention literature offer a positive, constructive agenda for combating violent behavior in its earliest stages.

PART C

META-ANALYSIS

The development of statistical syntheses of evaluation literature, particularly the technique known as meta-analysis (Glass, McGraw, and Smith 1981), is considered in some quarters to represent a methodological breakthrough (Fiske 1983). Proponents of meta-analysis argue justifiably that the conventional qualitative approach to literature evaluations is fraught with problems ranging from a failure to account for all the pertinent literature to a lack of specificity and standardization of assessment criteria (Glass et al. 1981). Meta-analysis forces researchers to evaluate literature more carefully in a quantitative mode that is open to replication.

On the other hand, the procedure is not without problems. Wilson and Rachman (1983) point out that biases still occur in the selection of the data base, the classification and coding of studies, and the interpretation of methodologically weak studies as opposed to rigorous designs. Lipsey (1986) notes that the interpretation of the essential statistic produced by meta-analysis—effect size, or the measure of the potency of main-effect study outcomes—is still problematic. Lipsey (1985) recognized the dilemma when he asked when an effect size was too small to detect but too big to neglect.

The growing pains suffered by this new methodology are reflected in the five meta-analyses that have been applied to the offender treatment literature. The meta-analyses come from two sources: Garrett (1985) and the Michigan State group (Davidson, Gottschalk, Gensheimer, and Mayer 1984; Gensheimer, Mayer, Gottschalk, and Davidson, 1986; Gottschalk, Davidson, Gensheimer and Mayer 1987; Mayer, Gensheimer, Davidson, and Gottschalk 1986). The investigators applied their meta-analyses to treatment programs directed toward juvenile offenders in institutions and the community, but the articles reviewed do not overlap substantially. In addition, Garrett, trained by Glass, interpreted her effect sizes at face value, while Davidson et al. applied further methodological criteria derived from Hunter, Schmidt, and Jackson (1982) to the effect sizes reported. Garrett's conclusion was robust: from her review of 111 studies emcompassing over 200 treatment-versus-control comparisons involving 13,000 juveniles, she found the treatment of adjudicated delinquents in institutions and community-based settings worked. The conclusions of Davidson and his colleagues were more cautious, although they also reported positive effect sizes for the literature they reviewed.

Garrett (1985) found that the effect sizes for both rigorously and less rigorously designed studies indicated that behavioral approaches were by far the most potent, in contrast to life skills and psychodynamic techniques. Among specific treatments, the largest effect sizes were found for family therapy, contingency management programs, and cognitive behavioral approaches.These kinds of conclusions are similar to those reported in qualitative reviews of the literature (Gendreau and Ross 1984).

The first meta-analysis produced by Davidson et al. (1984) examined 91 studies that had outcome measures in the general area of treatment/intervention studies with juvenile delinquents. The 1987 publication, identical in format to the 1984 study, incorporated some revisions in the studies (N=90) selected to focus on "community-based" interventions. The remaining two meta-analyses were subsets of the original 1984 and 1987 data bases. In the 1984 document Davidson found that 60 percent of the studies under review provided evidence for the positive effect of the interventions overall, but statistical assessment of the actual effect size led Davidson et al. to conclude that technically the null hypothesis could not be rejected.

Under the rules of analysis employed by Davidson et al., it was suggested that moderator variables existed which were predictive of differential effects. It was found that behavioral interventions were the most effective, followed by academic programs, service brokerage models, and vocational interventions. Group therapy approaches and transactional analysis were more likely to produce negative effects. The professional training of investigators was related to positive results: pyschologists and educators produced the largest effect sizes. Investigators' disciplines associated with the least effective programs were social work, criminal justice, and psychiatry. The authors also found that it was crucial to involve programmers in the design administration and the control of the interventions to ensure systematic manipulation of the critical variables.

Contrary to the belief that the more stringent the design, the less the effectiveness, Davidson et al. reported that random assignment of subjects in the experimental design was predictive of more positive effects. As in Garrett's work, some of the important moderator variables uncovered by Davidson et al. replicated previous findings predictive of factors related to program effectiveness by Andrews and Kiessling (1980) and Gendreau and Andrews (1979). The 1987 report by Gottschalk et al. produced similar conclusions about the effectiveness of moderator variables, with some differences reported in the ordering of effectiveness rates for intervention. Positive reinforcement, token economies, behavioral contracting, probation, and client-centered therapies had effectiveness ratios greater than 50 percent.

The two meta-analyses reported in 1986 examined 34 studies on the juvenile delinquent social-learning treatment literature and 44 studies portraying diversion program practices. These analyses did not reveal any results profoundly different from those reviewed above. The diversion review of Gensheimer et al. (1986) was noted previously in the "diversion" section. The Mayer et al. (1986) analysis found that behavioral social-learning approaches seemed to be at least moderately effective. in contrast to diversionary programs.

Finally, two other statistical syntheses of the literature, although not meta-analyses, are worth noting. Ross and Fabiano (1985) classified juvenile and adult treatment studies operationally according to whether they were cognitive or noncognitive, as determined by descriptions of the program components. Cognitive programs employed modeling, negotiation skills, problem solving, training in interpersonal skills, role playing, and cognitive behavior modification techniques. The total number of programs was small because of the strict criteria for selection. Of 16 cognitively based programs, 15 produced highly significant long-term outcome results, whereas positive outcome data were reported for only ten of the 34 noncognitive programs. The statistical syntheses reported by Genevie, Margolies, and Muhlin (1986) appear to be quite different from those noted above. They undertook to identify the efficacy of intervention programs employing "nonexperimental" data. Curiously, they claimed that although experimental research produces the most reliable form of information, it may not be of immediate value if only the null hypothesis is confirmed. Most of the studies contained in the previous meta-analyses focused on experimental research published in journals, much of which was positive. Genevie et al. compiled a list of 555 documents containing information about the rate of recidivism in 12,000 groups of juvenile and adult released offenders. The documents were prediction studies, reports of evaluation studies, official state reports, and—seemingly contradicting the above— studies that had experimental and quasi-experimental designs.

At the time of this review, we did not have recourse to Genevie et al.'s extended document, which would allow us to inspect their studies and to compare them with those of Garrett and of Davidson et al. Some of their conclusions appear to be at variance with the previous meta-analyses and with the contents of the present publication. They concluded, for example, that promising results for adults were found in short-term resource-oriented programs, such as financial aid and job placement, as well as in social work interventions such as specialized supervision and contract programming. Nonprofessional group counseling was not found to be effective. The data on juveniles were less optimistic, with the exception of job training, work study, and shock probation. Group homes, social work strategies, and special treatment-oriented prisons were associated with higher rates of recidivism.

Finally, the forthcoming meta-analysis of Lipsey (1986) may well-represent a considerable advance in the meta-analysis of the delinquency intervention literature. This will be the most comprehensive work to date; it includes 926 studies on juvenile (age 12 to 20) intervention programs Lipsey deemed to be cited for meta-analysis. According to Lipsey (personal communication, June 20, 1986), the literature seems to display positive effects similar to those reported by Garrett and by Davidson et al. In addition, one of Lipsey's major concerns will be to assess a number of methodological issues pertaining to meta-analysis techniques themselves. This information in itself will represent a major contribution.

CONCLUSIONS

It is easier to be critical than to be correct, and we speculate why this might be the case. (We hope the reader will approach the following comments with a sense of humor.) It is easier to be critical because that is what criminal justice social scientists do quite well, within the limited methodological boundaries imposed on us by our respective disciplines. Beyond that, we have no special exprrtise in being correct; otherwise, many of us would be gainfully employed in Las Vegas and Washington. Like people in many walks of life, we are prone to becoming inextricably bound up in ideologies. All too often, in the face of all contrary empirical evidence, we adhere to theories for political or ideological reasons (see Wilson and Hernnstein 1985) or cavalierly switch ideologies depending upon transient political developments (Kamin 1986).

Ironically, the effective interventions that we recommend so heartily for offenders (i.e., differential association and peer-group counseling) also apply to us. To illustrate this point we refer briefly to our own case histories. In the past we were accused of having far too cheerful a disposition toward offender rehabilitation (Brody 1981), but in recent years, when our professional contacts come to be primarily with prison and probation administrators and criminal justice academics, we began to suffer from the prevalent criminal justice virus of negativitis (Gendreau and Ross 1981). Before embarking upon this review our peer group was beginning to convince us that the "nothing works" credo was having a suppression effect on the current rehabilitation literature.

In summary, it is downright ridiculous to say "Nothing works." This review attests that much is going on to indicate that offender rehabilitation has been, can be, and will be achieved. The principles underlying effective rehabilitation generalize across far too many intervention strategies and offender samples to be dismissed as trivial.

Over the last decade we have mistaken the issue. It is this: how do we translate our ever-developing behavioral technology so that it is readily available to those in need? In North America we proclaim boldly that we are the "experimenting society" (see Campbell 1969; Tavris 1975), but we are absolutely amateurish at implementing and maintaining our successful experimentally demonstrated programs within the social service delivery systems provided routinely by government and private agencies. This is what doesn't work! We have made only very tentative progress in examining the conditions under which the principles of effective intervention can be implemented and maintained successfully in the real world (see Backer, Liberman, and Kuchnel 1986; Fagan and Hartstone under review; Gendreau and Andrews 1979; Shadish 1984). This topic will be the subject of our forthcoming work. Meanwhile, if the last two years have been any indication, another review will be necessary in several years to keep us abreast of the constructive developments in offender rehabilitation.

REFERENCES

Abel, G.G., M.S. Mittelmen, and J.V. Becker. 1985. "Sexual Offenders: Results of Assessment and Recommendations for Treatment." In M.H. BenAron, S.J. Hucker and C.D. Webster (eds.), *Clinical Criminology: The Assessment and Treatment of Criminal Behaviour.* Toronto: Clarke Institute of Psychiatry and University of Toronto.

Agee, V.L. 1986. "Institutional Treatment Programs for the Violent Juvenile." In S. Apter and A. Goldstein (eds.), *Youth Violence: Program and Prospects. New* York: Pergamon Press.

_____, 1979, *Treatment Of the Violent Incorrigible Adolescent.* Lexington: D.C. Heath.

_____, and B. McWilliams. 1984. 'The Role of Group Therapy and the Therapeutic Community in Treating the Violent Juvenile Offender." In R. Mathias (ed.) *Violent Juvenile Offenders. An Anthology.* Newark National Council on Crime and Delinquency.

Albee, G.W. 1986. "Toward a Just Society: Lessons From Observations on the Primary Prevention of Psychopathology." *American Psychologist* 41: 891-898.

Alexander, J.F. and B.V. Parsons. 1983. "Short Term Behavioral Intervention with Delinquent Families: Impact on Family Process and Recidivism." *Journal of Abnormal Psychology* 81: 219.

_____, and B.V. Parsons. 1982. *Functional Family Therapy.* Monterry Brooks/Cole.

Anderson, A. 1985. "Impact of Job Training Program on CETA-Qualified Probationers." *Federal Probation* 49: 17-20.

Andrews, D.A. 1983. "The Assessment of Outcome in Correctional Samples." In M.J. Lambert, G.R. Christensen and S.S. Dejulio (eds.), *The Measurement of Psychotherapy Outcome in Research and Evaluation.* New York: Wiley and Sons.

Anglin, M.D. (in press) "Civil Commitment as a Model for Reducing Drug Demand." *Perspectives on Drug Abuse.*

_____, and W.H. McGlothin. 1984. "Outcome of Narcotic Addict Treatment in California." In F.M. Tims and J.P. Ludford (eds.). *Drug Abuse Treatment Evaluation Strategies. Progress and Prospects.* NIDA Research Monograph 51. Washington: U.S. Government Printing Office.

Annis, H. and D. Chan. 1983. The Differential Treatment Model: Empirical Evidence from a Personality Typology of Adult Offenders." *Criminal Justice and Behavior* 10:159-173.

_____, and C.S. Davis. 1987. "Self-Efficacy and the Treatment Trial." In T.B. Baker and D. Cannon (eds.), *Addictive Disorders: Psychological Research in Assessment and Treatment.* New York: Praeger.

Apter, S., and B. Harootunian. 1984. *School Violence.* Englewood Cliffs: Prentice-Hall.

Apter, S.J. and A.P. Goldstein. 1986. Youth *Violence: Program and Prospects.* New York: Pergamon Press.

Arbuthnot, J. and D. Faust. 1981). *Teaching Moral Reasoning: Theory and Practice.* New York: Harper and Row.

_____and D.A. Cordon. 1986. "Behavioral and Cognitive Effects of a Moral Reasoning Development Intervention for High-Risk Behavior—Disordered Adolescents." *Journal of Consulting and Clinical Psychology 54*: 208-216.

_____, K.E. Gustafson, and P. McGreen. 1987. "Home-Based Behavioral Systems Family Therapy with Disadvantaged Juvenile Delinquents." Manuscript submitted for publication.

Ayers, D.J. 1979. "Education in Prisons: A Developmental and Cultural Perspective." Paper presented at Symposium on Education as a Cultural Alternative for Prisoners and Delinquents. *Canadian Society for Study of Education* (June).

Backer, T.E., R.P. Liberman, and T.G. Kuchnel. 1986. "Dissemination and Adoption of Innovative Psychosocial Interventions." *Journal of Consulting and Clinical Psychology* 54: 111-118.

Baird, S.C., R.C. Heinz and B.J. Bemus. 1979. "The Wisconsin Case Classification and Staff Development Project: A Two-Year Follow-up Report." Madison: Division of Corrections.

Bandura, A. 1973. *Aggression: Social Learning Analysis.* Englewood Cliffs: Prentice-Hall.

_____, 1977. "Self-Efficacy: Toward a Unifying Theory of Behavioral Change." *Psychological Review,* 94:191-215.

Bartollas, C. 1985. *Correctional Treatment: Theory and Practice.* Englewood Cliffs: Prentice-Hall.

Barton, C., J.F. Alexander, H. Waldron, C.W. Turner. and J. Warburton. 1985. "Generalizing Treatment Effects of Functional Family Therapy: Three Replications." *American Journal of Family Therapy* 13:16-26.

Baum, C.G. and R. Forehand. 1981. "Long Term Follow-up Assessment of Parent Training by Use of Multiple Outcome Measures." *Behavior Therapy,* 12:643-552.

Beck, J.L. 1981. "Employment, Community Treatment Placement and Recidivism A Study of Released Federal Offenders." *Federal Probation* 45:3-8.

Berk, R.A., K.J. Lenihan, and P.H. Rossi. 1980. "Crime and Poverty: "Some Experimental Evidence from Ex-Offenders." *American Sociological Review* 45:766-786.

Berrueta-Clement, J.R., L.J. Schweinhart. W.S. Barnett, A.S. Epstein, and D.P. Weikart. 1984. *Changed Lives: the Effects of the Perry Preschool Program Through Age 19.* Ypsilanti: High/Scope Press.

Binder, A. and G. Geis. 1984. "Ad Populum Argumentation in Criminology: Juvenile Diversion as Rhetoric." *Crime and Delinquency* 30:624-647.

Bistline, J.L. and F.P. Frieden. 1984. "Anger Control: A Case Study of Stress Innoculation Treatment for a Chronic Aggressive Patient" *Cognitive Therapy and Research* 8:551-556.

Blair, C.D. and R.I. Lanyon. 1981. "Exhibitionism: Etiology and Treatment." *Psycholgical Bulletin* 49:439-463.

Blumstein, A., J. Cohen, J.A. Roth, and C.A. Visher. 1986. *Criminal Careers and Career Criminals.* 1 Washington D.C.: National Academy Press.

Bonta, J.L., J. Boyle, L. Motiuk, and P. Sonnichsen. 1983. "Correctional Halfway Houses: Victim Satisfaction, Attitudes and Recidivism." *Canadian Journal of Criminology* 25:140-152.

———, and L.L. Motiuk. 1985. "Utilization of an Interview-Based Classification Instrument: A Study of Correctional Halfway Houses." *Criminal Justice and Behavior* 12:333-352.

———, and L.L. Motiuk (in press) "The LSI as a Decision-Making Aid for the Diversion of Incarcerated Offenders to Correctional Halfway Houses." *Journal of Research in Crime and Delinquency.*

Bornstein, M., A.S. Bellack, and M. Hersen. 1980. "Social Skills Training for Highly Aggressive Children." *Behavior Modification* 4:173-186.

Borzecki, M. and J.S. Wormith. 1987. "A Survey of Treatment Programs for Sex Offenders in North America." *Canadian Psychology 28:3044.*

Boudouris, J. and B.W. Turnbull. 1985. "Shock Probation in Iowa." *Journal of offender Counselling Services and Rehabilitation 9:53-67.*

Bowman, P.C. and S.A. Auerbach. 1982. "Impulsive Youthful Offenders: A Multimodel Cognitive Behavioral Treatment Program." *Criminal Justice and Behavior 9:432-454.*

Brody, S.J. 1981. "Review of Effective Correctional Treatment" *British Journal of Criminology 21:279-281.*

Brownell, K.D., G.A. Marlatt, E. Lichtenstein, and G.T. Wilson. 1986. "Understanding and Preventing Relapse." *American Psychologist 41:765-782.*

Bry, B.H. 1982. "Reducing the Incidence of Adolescent Problems Through Preventive Intervention: One and Five-Year Followup." *American Journal of Community Psychology 10:265-275.*

Buckner, J.C. and M. Chesney-Lund. 1983. "Dramatic Cures for Juvenile Crime: An Evaluation of a Prison-Run Delinquency Prevention Program." *Criminal Justice and Behavior 10:227-247.*

Budd, K.S., J.M. Leibowitz, L.S. Riner, C. Mindell, and A.L. Goldfarb. *1981.* "Home-Based Treatment of Severe Disruptive Behaviors: A Reinforcement Package for Preschool and Kindergarten Children." *Behavior Modification 5:273-298.*

Bullington, B., J. Sprowls, D. Katkin, and M. Phillips. *1978.* "A Critique of Diversionary Juvenile Justice." *Crime and Delinquency 24:59-71.*

Burkhart, W.R. 1986. "Intensive Probation Supervision: An Agenda for Research and Evaluation." *Federal Probation 50:75-77.*

Byles, J.A. and A. Maurice. 1982. "The Juvenile Services Project: An Experiment in Delinquency Control." *Canadian Journal of Criminology 24:155-165.*

Byrne, J.M. 1986. "The Control Controversy: A Preliminary Examination of Intensive Probation Supervision Programs in the United States." *Federal Probation 50:4-16.*

Campbell, M., A.M. Small, W.H. Green, S.J. Jennings, R. Perry, W.G. Bennett, and L. Anderson. 1984. "Behavioral Efficacy of Haloperidol and Lithium Carbonate." *Archives of General Psychiatry 41:650-565.*

Campbell, D.T. 1969. "Reforms as Experiments." *American Psychologist 24:409428.*

Chaiken, M.R. and J.M. Chaiken. 1984. "Offender Types and Public Policy." *Crime and Delinquency 30:195-226.*

Chandler, C.L. and R.P. Weissberg, E.L. Cowen, and J. Guare. 1984. "Long-Term Effects of a School-Based Secondary Prevention Program for Young Maladapting Children." *Journal of Consulting and Clinical Psychology.* 52:165-170.

Clarke, R.V.G. 1985. "Jack Tizard Memorial Lecture: Delinquency, Environment and Intervention." *Journal of Child Psychology and Psychiatry* 26:505-523.

Clear, T.R. and K.W. Gallagher. 1985. "Probation and Parole Supervision: A Review of Current Classification."*Crime and Delinquency 31:423-443.*

Cohen, A. 1955. *Delinquency and Opportunity: A Theory of Delinquent Gangs.* New York: Free Press.

Conger, J.C. and S.P. Keane. 1981. "Social Skills Intervention in the Treatment of Isolated or Withdrawn Children." *Psychological Bulletin* 90:478-495.

Conrad, J.P. 1985. "The Penal Dilemma and its Emerging Solution." *Crime and Delinquency* 31:411422.

Cousineau, F.D. and D.B. Plecas. 1982. "Justifying Criminal Justice Policy with Methodologically Inadequate Research." *Canadian Journal of Criminology 24:307-321.*

Cressey, D.R. 1982. "Forward." In F.T. Cullen and K.E. Gilbert *Reaffirming Rehabilitation.* Cincinnati: Anderson.

Cullen, F.T. 1985. "Does Rehabilitation Work? The Origins and Meaning of a Troublesome Question." Invited address presented at the University of Ottawa.

_____, and K.E. Gilbert. 1982. *Reaffirming Rehabilitation.* Cincinnati Anderson.

Currie, E. 1985a. "Crimes of Violence and Public Policy: Changing Directions." In L.A. Curtis (ed.). *American Violence and Public Policy: An Update of our National Commission on The Causes and Prevention of Violencce* New Haven: Yale University Press.

_____, 1985b. *Confrontng Crime: An American Challenge.* Westminster: Pantheon.

Davidson, P.R. 1984. *Behavioral Treatment for Incarcerated Sex Offenders: Postrelease Outcome.* Unpublished manuscript, Kingston Penitentiary, Kingston, Ontario.

Davidson, W.S., R. Gottschalk, L. Gensheimer and J. Mayer. 1984. *Interventions with Juvenile Delinquents: A Meta-Analysis Treatment Efficacy.* Washington: National Institute of Juvenile Justice and Delinquency Prevention.

_____, R. Redner, C. Blakely. C. Mitchell, and J. Emshoff. 1987. "Diversion of Juvenile Offenders: An Experimental Comparison." *Journal of Consulting and Clinical Psychology* 55:68-75.

_____, E. Seidman, J. Rappaport, P. Berck, N. Rapp, W.R. Rhodes, and J. Herring. 1977. "Diversion Programs for Juvenile Offenders." *Social Work Research and Abstracts* 13:40-49.

DeLeon, G. 1985. "The Therapeutic Community: Status and Evolution." *International Journal of* Addictions 20:823-844.

_____, 1987. "Legal Pressure in Therapeutic Communities." Paper presented to NIDA technical review meeting on civil commitment for drug abuse. Rockville.

Denno, D.J. 1980. "Impact of a Youth Service Center: Does Diversion Work?" Criminology 18:347-362.

_____, and R.C. Clelland. 1986. "Longitudinal Evaluation of a Delinquency Prevention Program by Self-Report." *Journal of Offender Counselling Seruces and Rehabilitation* 10:59-82.

Dubnov, W.L. 1986. "The Glen Mills Project: Innovation in Juvenile Corrections." *Journal of Offender Counselling Services and Rchabilitation* 10:87-103.

Duffee, D.E. and D. Clark. 1985. "The Frequency and Classification of the Needs of Offenders in Community Settings." *Journal of Criminal Justice* 13:243-268.

Duguid, S., C. Montague, and S. Wolowidnyk. 1980. "Effects of the University of Victoria Program: A Post-Release Study." Report prepared for the Ministry of the Solicitor General of Canada, Ottawa.

_____, 1981a. "Prison Education and Criminal Choice: The Context of Decision Making." *Canadian Journal of Criminology* 23:421438.

_____, 1981b. "Moral Development, Justice and Democracy in the Prison." *Canadian Journal of Criminology* 23:174-162.

Durlak, J. 1981. "Evaluating Comparative Studies of Paraprofessional and Professional Helpers." *Psychological Bulletin* 89:566-569.

Ehrenreich, B. 1986, September 4. "Is the Middle Class Damned?" New *York Times Sunday Magazine,* p. 44.

Elliott, D.S., S.S. Ageton, and R.J. Canter. 1979. "An Integrated Theoretical Perspective on Delinquent Behavior." *Journal of Research in Crime and Delinquency* 16:3-27.

Empey, L.T. 1982. "From Optimism to Despair: New Directions in Juvenile Justice." In C.A. Murray and L.A. Cox Jr. *Beyond Probation: Juvenile Corrections and the Chronic Delinquent*. Beverly Hills: Sage.

Erikson, P.G. 1984. "Diversion—A Panacea for Delinquency? Lessons from a Scottish Experience." *Youth and Society* 16:29-45.

Eron, L.D. and L.R. Huesmann. 1986. "The Relation of Prosocial Behavior to the Development of Aggression and Psychopathology." *Aggressive Behavior* 10:201-211.

Erwin, B.S. 1986. "Turning up the Heat on Probationers in Georgia." *Federal Probation* 50:17-24.

Esveldt-Dawson, K., N.H. French, and A.S. Unis. 1987. "Problem-Solving Skills Training and Relationship Therapy in the Treatment of Antisocial Child Behavior." *Journal of Consulting and Clinical Psychology* 55:76-85.

Fagan, J. and E. Hartstone. 1987. "Innovation and Experimentation in Juvenile Corrections: Implementing a Community Reintegration Model for Violent Juvenile Offenders." Manuscript submitted for publication.

Farrington, D.P. 1985a. "Delinquency Prevention in the 1980's." *Journal of Adolescence* 8:3-16.

_____, 1985b. "Chairman's Letter." *Division of Criminology and Legal Psychology Newsletter*. 17:2-8.

Fehrenbach, P.A. and M.H. Thelen. 1982. "Behavioral Approaches to the Treatment of Aggressive Disorders." *Behavior Modification* 6:465-497.

Feldman, R.A., T.E. Caplinger, and J.S. Wodarski. 1983. *The St. Louis Conundrum. The Effective Treatment of Antisocial Youths*. Englewood Cliffs: Prentice-Hall.

Fiske, D.W. 1983. "The Meta-Analytic Revolution in Outcome Research." *Journal of Consulting and Clinical Psychology* 51:65-70.

Garrett, C.J. 1985. "Effects of Residential Treatment on Adjudicated Delinquents: A Meta-Analysis." *Journal of Research in Crime and Delinquency* 22:287-308.

Gendreau, P. 1981. "Treatment in Corrections: Martinson was Wrong." *Canadian Psychology* 22:332-338.

_____, 1985. "Critical Comments on the Practice of Clinical Criminology." In M.H. Ben-Aron, S.J. Hucker and C.D. Webster (eds.), *Clinical Criminology: The Assessment and Treatment of Criminal Behavior*. Toronto: Clarke Institute of Psychiatry and University of Toronto.

_____, 1987. "Why the Offender Rehabilitation and Substance Abuse Treatment Literatures Should Become Acquainted." Unpublished manuscript.

_____, and D.A. Andrews. 1979. "Psychological Consultation in Correctional Agencies: Case Studies and General Issues." In J.J. Platt and R. Wicks (eds.), *The Psychological Consultant.* New York: Grune and Stratton.

_____, and R.R. Ross. 1979. "Effective Correctional Treatment Bibliotherapy for Cynics." *Crime and Delinquency* 25:463-489.

_____, and R.R. Ross. 1981a. "Offender Rehabilitation: The Appeal of Success." *Federal* Probation 45:45-48.

_____, and R.R. Ross. 1981b. "Correctional Potency: Treatment and Deterrence on Trial." In R. Roesch and R.R. Corrado (eds.), *Evaluation and Criminal Justice Policy.* Beverly Hills: Sage.

_____, and R.R. Ross. 1983. "Success in Corrections: Programs and Principles." In R. Corrado, M. Leblanc and J. Trepanier (eds.), *Issues in Juvenile Justice* Toronto: Butterworths.

_____, and R.R. Ross. 1984. "Correctional Treatment Some Recommendations for Successful Intervention." *Juvenile and Family Court Journal* 34:31-40.

Genevie, L., E. Margolies, and G.L. Muhlin. 1986. "How Effective is Correctional Intervention?" *Social Policy* 17:52-57.

Gensheimer, L.K., J.P. Mayer, R. Gottschalk and W.S. Davidson. 1986. "Diverting Youth from the Juvenile Justice System: A Meta-Analysis of Intervention Efficacy." In S. Apter and A. Goldstein (eds.), *Youth Violence: Program and Prospects.* New York: Pergamon Press.

Giarretto, M. 1982. "A Comprehensive Child Sexual Abuse Treatment Program." *Child Abuse and Neglect* 6:263-278.

Gibbons, D.C. 1986. "Correctional Treatment and Intervention Theory." *International Journal of Offender Therapy and Comparative Criminology* 30:255-271.

Glass, G.V., B. McGraw, and M.L. Smith. 1981. *Meta-Analysis in Social Research.* Beverly Hills: Sage.

Glueck, S. and I. Glueck. 1950. *Unravelling Juvenile Delinquency. New* York: Commonwealth Fund.

Gold, M. 1970. *Delinquent Behavior in an American City.* Belmont: Brooks/Cole.

Goldstein A.P. 1973. *Structured Learning Therapy: Toward a Psychotherapy for the Poor.* New York: Academic Press.

_____, 1981. *Psychological Skills Training*. New York Pergamon.

_____, 1986. "Psychological Skill Training and the Aggressive Adolescent." In S. Apter and A. Goldstein (eds.). *Youth Violence: Program and Prospects*. New York: Pergamon.

Gordon, D.A. and J. Arbuthnot. 1982. "Individual Group and Family Interventions." In H.C. Quay (ed.), *Handbook of Juvenile Delinquency*. New York: Wiley and Sons.

_____, and G.J. Jurkovic. 1987. "Personality." In H.C. Quay (ed.), *Handbook of Juvenile Delinquency*. New York: Wiley and Sons.

Gordon, T.J., R. Grallo, M. Deutch, and C.P. Deutch. 1985. "Long Term Effects of Early Enrichment: A Twenty Year Perspective on Persistence and Change." *American Journal of Community Psychology* 13:393-415.

Gottfredson, D.C. 1985. "Youth Employment, Crime Schooling: A Longitudinal Study on a National Sample." *Developmental Psychology* 21:419-432.

Gottfredson, M.R., S.D. Mitchell-Herzfeld, and T.J. Flanagan. 1952. "Another Look at the Effectiveness of Parole Supervision." *Journal of Research in Crime and Delinquency* 19:277-298.

Gottschalk, R., W.S. Davidson. L.K. Gensheimer, and J.P. Mayer. 1984. "Community-Based Interventions." In H.C. Quay (ed.), *Handbook of Juvenile Delinquency*. New York: Wiley and Sons.

Graves, K., and J. Arbuthnot. 1987. "Prevention of Adult Criminal Behavior Using Family Therapy for Disadvantaged Juvenile Delinquents" Manuscript submitted for publication.

Greenwood, P.W. and F.E. Zimring. 1985. *One More Chance The Pursuit of Promising Intervention Strategies for Chronic Juvenile Offenders*. Santa Monica Rand.

Gresham, F.K. 1985. "Utility of Cognitive-Behavioral Procedures for Social Skills Training with Children: A Critical Review." *Journal of Abnormal Child Psychology* 13:411-423.

Griest, D.L. and K.C. Wells. 1983. "Behavioral Family Therapy with Conduct Disorders in Children." *Behavior Therapy* 14:37-53.

Groth, A.N., R.E. Longo, and J.B. McFadin. 1982. "Undetected Recidivism Among Rapists and Child Molesters." *Crime and Delinquency* 28:450-458.

Gunn, J. and G. Robertson. 1982. "An Evaluation of Grendon Prison." In J. Gunn and D.P. Farrington (eds.), *Abnormal Offenders, Delinquency and the Criminal Justice System*. London: Wiley and Sons.

Haber, G.M. 1983. "The Realization of Potential by Lorton, D.C. Inmates with UDC College Education Compared to Those Without UDC Education." *Journal of Offender Counselling Services and Rehabilitation* 6:37-55.

Harris, P. 1983. "The Interpersonal Maturity of Delinquents and Non-Delinquents." In W.S. Lanfer and J.M. Day (eds.) *Personality Theory, Moral Development and Criminal Behavior.* Lexington: Lexington.

Harvey, O.J., D.E. Hunt, and H.M. Schroder. 1961. *Conceptual Systems and Personality Organization.* New York: Wiley and Sons.

Hebison, F.E. 1986. "Differential Treatment: A Follow-Up Study of Treatment Success." *The Differential View 14.* Montreal: International Differential Treatment Association.

Henderson, M. and C. Hollin. 1983. "A Critical Review of Social Skills Training with Young Offenders." *Criminal Justice and Behavior* 10:316-341.

Hirsch, B.J. 1985. "Adolescent Coping and Support Across Multiple Social Environments." *American Journal of Community Psychology* 13:381-392.

Hirschi, T. 1969. *Courses of Delinquency.* Berkeley: University of California Press.

Hippchen, L.J. 1976. "Bio-Medical Approaches to Offender Rehabilitation." *Offender Rehabilitation* 1: 115-123.

Hoffmann, P.B. and B. Stone-Meierhoefer. 1979. "Applications of Guidelines to Sentencing." In L.E. Abt and I.R. Stuart (eds.), *Social Psychology and Discretionary Law.* New York: Van Nostrand Reinhold.

Hoge, R.D. M. Baitz, D. Robinson, J. Hollett, and R. Stewart (in press) "Case Classification and the Risk Principle." *Canada's Mental Health.*

_____, and J.J. Kiessling. 1980. "Program Structure and Effective Correctional Practices: A Summary of the CAVIC Research." In R.R. Ross and P. Gendreau (eds.), Effective *Correctional Treatment.* Toronto: Butterworths.

Homant, R.J. 1984. "Employment of Ex-Offenders: The Role, Prisonization and Self-Esteem." *Journal of Offender Counselling Services and Rehabilitation* 8:5-23.

Huizinga, D., and S. Ageton. 1985. *Explaining Delinquency and Drug Use.* Beverly Hills: Sage.

Huizinga, D., and B. Morse. 1986. "Self-Reported Violent Offending: A Descriptive Analysis of Juvenile Violent Offenders and Their Offending Careers." *Journal of Interpersonal Violence* 4:472-514.

Hunter, J.E., F.L Schmidt, and G.B. Jackson. 1982. *Meta-Analysis: Cumulating Research Findings Across Studies.* Beverly Hills: Sage.

Hurley, D. 1985. "Arresting Delinquency: Early Intervention Can Reduce the Chance That Certain High-Risk Children Will Become Criminals." *Psychology Today* 18:63-68.

Jackson, P.C. 1983. "Some Effects of Parole Supervision on Recidivism." *British Journal of Criminology* 23:17-34.

Jeffrey, R. and S. Woolpert. 1974. "Work Furlough as an Alternative to Incarceration: An Assessment of its Effects on Recidivism and Social Cost." *Journal of Criminal Law and Criminology 65:404-415.*

Johnson, D.L. and J.N. Breckenridge. 1982. 'The Houston Parent-Child Development Center and the Primary Prevention of Behavior Problems in Young Children." *American Journal of Community Psychology* 10:305-315.

Johnson, B.D. and R.T. Goldberg. 1983. "Vocational and Social Rehabilitation or Delinquents: A Study of Experimentals and Controls." *Journal of Offender Counselling Senteces and Rehabilitation* 65:43-60.

Jones, M.B. and D.R. Offord. 1987. "Reduction of Antisocial Behavior in Poor Children by Nonschool Skill Development." Manuscript submitted for publication.

Jurik, N.C. 1983. "The Economics of Female Recidivism." *Criminology* 21:603-622.

Jurkovic, G.J. 1980. "The Juvenile Delinquent as a Moral Philosopher A Structural-Developmental Perspective." *Psychological Bulletin* 88:709-727.

Kamin, L.J. 1986. "Is Crime in the Genes? The Answer May Depend on Who Chooses What Evidence." *Scientific American* 254:22-25.

Kassebaum, G., D. Ward, and D. Wilner. 1971. *Prison Treatment and Parole Survival: An Empirical Assessment.* New York: Wiley and Sons.

Katz, J.F. and S.H. Decker. 1982. "An Analysis of Work Release: The Institutionalization of Unsubstantiated Reforms." *Criminal Justice and Behavior* 9:229250.

Kazdin, A.E. 1985. *Treatment of Anti-Social Behavior in Children and Adolescents.* Homewood: The Dorsey Press.

Kelly, R.J. 1982. "Behavioral Reorientation of Pedopheliacs: Can it be Done?" *Clinical Psychology Review.* 2:387-408.

Kendall, P.C. and L. Braswell. 1982. "Cognitive-Behavioral Self-Control Therapy for Children: A Components Analysis." *Journal of Consulting and Clinical Psychology* 50:672-689.

Kiessling, J.J., S. Mickus, and D. Robinson. 1986. "The Construct Validity of Interview-Based Risk Assessment in Corrections." *Canadian Journal of Behavioral Science* 18:460-471.

Kiessling, J.J., D. Robinson, and S. Mickus. 1986. "The Risk Principle of Case Classification: An Outcome Evaluation with Young Adult Probationers." *Canadian Journal of Criminology* 28:377-384.

Kirigin, K.A., C.J. Braukmann, J.D. Atwater, and M.M. Wolf. 1982. "An Evaluation of Teaching-Family (Achievement Place) Group Homes for Juvenile Offenders." *Journal of Applied Behavior Analysis* 15:1-16.

Klein, N.C., J.F. Alexander, and B.V. Parsons. 1977. "Impact of Family Systems Intervention on Recidivism and Sibling Delinquency A Model of Primary Prevention and Program Evaluation." *Journal of Consulting and Clinical Psychology* 45:469474.

Kobrin, S. and M.W. Klein. 1983. *Community Treatment of Juvenile Offenders The D.S.D. Experiment.* Beverly Hills: Sage.

Kohlberg, L. 1969. "Stage and Sequency: The Cognitive Developmental Approach to Socialization." In D.A. Goslin (ed.), *Handbook of Socialization* Chicago: Rand McNally.

Lanyon, R.I. 1986. "Therapy and Treatment in Child Molestation." *Journal of Consulting and Clinical Psychology* 54:176-182.

Lee, R. and N. Haynes. 1980. "Project Crest and the Dual-Treatment Approach to Delinquency: Methods and Research Summarized." In R.R. Ross and P. Gendreau (eds.), *Effective Correctional Treatment.* Toronto: Butterworths.

_____, and S. Olejnik. 1981. "Professional Outreach Counselling Can Help the Juvenile Probationer A Two Year Follow-Up-Study." *The Personnel and Guidance Journal* 60:445-449.

Lerner, K., G. Arling, and S.C. Baird. 1986. "Client Management Classification Strategies for Case Supervision." *Crime and Delinquency* 32:254-271.

Leschied, A.W., P.G. Jaffe, and G.L. Stone. 1985. "Differential Response of Juvenile Offenders to Two Detention Environments as a Function of Conceptual Level." *Canadian Journal of Criminology* 27:467-476.

_____, and K.E. Thomas. 1985. "Effective Residential Programming for "Hard to Serve" Delinquent Youth: A Description of the Craigwood Program." *Canadian Journal of Criminology* 27:161-177.

Lewandowski, L.J. and B. Forsstram-Cohen. 1986. "Neurological Bases of Youth Violence." In S. Apter and A. Goldstein (eds.), *Youth Violence: Program and Prospects.* New York: Pergamon.

Lewis, R. V. 1983. "Scared Straight—California Style: Evaluation of the San Quentin Squire Program." *Criminal Justice and Behavior* 10:209-226.

Lichtman, C.M. and S.M. Smock. 1981. "The Effects of Social Services on Probationer Recidivism: A Field Experiment." *Journal of Research in Crime and Delinquency* 18:81-99.

Lightman, E.S. 1982. "The Private Employer and the Prison Industry." *British Journal of Criminology* 22:36-48.

Linden, R. and L. Perry. 1982. "The Effectiveness of Prison Education Programs." *Journal of Offender Counselling Services and Rehabilitation* 6:43-57.

———, and L. Perry. 1984. "An Evaluation of a Prison Education Program." *Canadian Journal of Criminology* 26:65-73.

Lipsey, M.W. 1985. "The Paradox of Effect Size: Too Small to Detect, Too Big to Neglect." Paper presented at the Canadian Evaluation Society, Evaluation Network and the Evaluation Research Society, Toronto.

———, 1986. "Research Plan: Meta-Analysis of Juvenile Delinquency Treatment Research." Unpublished manuscript. Claremont Graduate School.

———, G.S. Cordray, and D.E. Berger. 1981. "Evaluation of a Juvenile Diversion Program: Using Multiple Lines of Evidence." *Evaluation* Review 5:283-306.

Loeber, R. and M. Stouthamer-Loeber. 1986. "Family Factors as Correlates and Predictors of Juvenile Conduct Problems and Delinquency." In M. Tonry and N. Morris (eds.), *Crime and Justice* 7 Chicago: University of Chicago *Press.*

———, and M. Stouthamer-Loeber. 1987. "Prediction." In H.C. Quay (ed.), *Handbook of Juvenile of Juvenile Delinquency.* New York: Wiley and Sons.

Lochman, J.E., J.F. Curry, P.R. Burch, and L.B. Lampron. 1984. "Treatment and Generalization Effects of Cognitive, Behavioral and Goal Setting Interventions with Aggressive Boys." *Journal of Consulting and Clinical Psychology* 52:915916.

———, J.B. Lampron, P.R. Burch, and J.F. Curry. 1985. "Client Characteristics Associated with Behavior Change for Treated and Untreated Aggressive Boys." *Journal of Abnormanl Child Psychology* 13:527-538.

Lorion, R.P., P.H. Tolan, and R.G. Wahler. 1987. "Prevention." In H.C. Quay (ed.), *Handoook of Juvenile Delinquency*. New York: Wiley and Sons.

Lukin, P.R. 1981. "Recidivism and Changes Made by Delinquents During Residential Treatment." *Journal of Research in Crime and Delinquency* 10:101-111.

Lundman, R.J. 1986. Beyond Probation: Assessing the Generalizability of the Delinquency Suppression Effect Measures Reported by Murray and Cox." *Crime and Delinquency* 32:134-147.

Maletsky, B.M. 1980. "Assisted Court Sensitization." In D.J. Cox and R.J. Daitzman (eds.), *Exhibition: Description, Assessment and Treatment*. New York: Garland.

Marlowe, H., J.B. Reid, G.R. Patterson, and M. Weinrott. 1986. "Treating Adolescent Multiple Offenders: A Comparison and Folow-up of Parent Training for Families of Chronic Delinquents." Unpublished manuscript.

Martinson, R. 1979. "New Findings, New Views: A Note of Caution Regarding Sentencing Reform." *Hofstra Law Review* 7:242-258.

_____, and J. Wilks. 1977. "Save Parole Supervision." *Federal Probation* 41:23-27.

Mayer, G.R., T. Butterworth, M. Nafpaktits, and B. Sulzer-Azanoff. 1983. "Preventing School Vandalism and Improving Discipline: A 3-Year Study." *Journal of Applied Behavior* 16:355-369.

Mayer, J.P., L.K. Gensheimer, W.S. Davidson, and R. Gottschalk. 1986. "Social Learning Treatment Within Juvenile Justice: A Meta-Analysis of Impact in the Natural Environment." In S. Apter and A. Goldstein (eds.), *Youth Violence: Program ard Prospects*. New York: Pergamon.

McGlothlin, W., M.D. Anglin, and B.D. Wilson. 1977. "An Evaluation of the California Civil Addict Program." *NIDA Sciences Research Monograph Series*. Washington: U.S. Government Printing Office.

McPherson, S.J., L.E. McDonald, and C.W. Ryer. 1983. "Intensive Counselling with Families of Juvenile Offenders." *Juvenile and Family Court Journal* 34:27-33.

Megargee, E.I. and M.J. Bohn. 1979. *Classifying Criminal Offenders*. Beverly Hills: Sage.

Meichenbaum, D. and D. Turk. 1976. "The Cognitive-Behavioral Management of Anxiety, Anger and Pain." In P. Davidson (ed.), The *Behaviorial Management of Anxiety Depression and Pain*. New York: Brunner/Mazel.

Menzies, K. 1986. "The Rapid Spread of Community Service Orders in Ontario." *Canadian Journal of Criminology* 28:157-169.

Miller, W.B. 1973. "Ideology and Criminal Justice Policy: Some Current Issues." *Journal of Criminal Law and Criminology* 64:141-161.

Miller, W.R. and R.K. Hester. 1986. "The Effectiveness of Alcoholism Treatment: What Research Reveals." In W.R. Miller and N. Heather (eds.), *Treating Addictive Behaviors: Processes of Change.* New York: Plenum.

Motiuk, L.L. 1984. "Offender Classification Systems: Psychometric Properties." Unpublished manuscript. Carleton University, Ottawa.

_____, J. Bonta, and D.A. Andrews. 1986. "Classification in Correctional Halfway Houses: The Relative and Incremental Predictive Criterion Validities of the Megargee-MMPI and LSI Systems." *Criminal Justice and Behavior* 13:33-46.

Murray, C.A. and L.A. Cox Jr. 1979. *Beyond Probation: Juvenile Corrections and the Chronic Delinquent.* Beverly Hills: Sage.

Nathan, P.E. and A. Skinstad. 1987. "Outcomes of Treatment for Alcohol Problems: Current Methods, Problems and Results." *Journal of Consulting and Clinical Psychology* 55:332-340.

Newman G. 1983. *Just and Painful: A Case for the Corporal Punishment of Criminals.* London: Collier Macmillan.

Novaco, R.N. 1975. *Anger Control The Development and Evaluation of an Experimental Treatment.* Lexington: Lexington Books.

O'Donnell, C.R., T. Lydgate, and W.S.O. Fo. 1971. "The Buddy System: Review and Follow-up." *Child Behavior Therapy* 1:161-169.

Offord, D.R. and M.B. Jones. 1983. "Skill Development: A Community Intervention Program for the Prevention of Anti-Social Behavior." In S.B. Guze, F.J. Earle and J.E. Barrett (eds.), *Childhood Psychopathology and Development.* New York: Raven Press.

Orsagh, T. and M.G. Marsden. 1985. "What Works When: Rational Choice Theory and Offender Rehabilitation." *Journal of Criminal* Justice 13:269-277.

_____, and A.D. Witte. 1981. "Economic Status and Crime: Implications for Offender Rehabilitation" *Journal of Criminal Law and Criminology* 72:1055-1971.

Palmer, T. 1968. "Recent Research Funding and Long Range Developments at the Community Treatment Project." Community Treatment Project Research Report, No. 9, Part 2. Sacramento.

_____, 1975. "Martinson Revisited" *Journal of Research in Crime and Delinquency* 12:133-152.

_____, 1983. "The Effectiveness Issue Today An Overview." *Federal Probation* 47:3-10.

_____, 1984. "Treatment and the Role of Classification: A Review of Basics." *Crime and Delinquency* 30:245-267.

_____, and R.V. Lewis. 1980. *"A Differentiated Approach to Juvenile Diversion."* Journal of Research in Crime and Delinquency 17:209-229.

Patterson, G.R. 1982. *A Social Learning Approach Coercive Family Process.* Eugene: Castalia.

_____, 1986. "Performance Models for Antisocial Boys." *American Psychologist* 41:432-444.

_____, P. Chamberlain, and J. Reid. 1982. "A Comparative Evaluation of a Parent Training Program." *Behavior Therapy* 13:638-650.

Pearson, F.S. 1985. "New Jersey's Intensive Supervision Program: A Progress Report." *Crime and Delinquency* 31:393-410.

Petersilia. J., S. Turner, J. Kahan, and J. Peterson. 1985. "Executive Summary of Rand's Study,. Granting Felons Probation: Public Risks and Alternatives." *Crime and Delinquency* 31:379-397.

Piaget, J. 1965. *The Moral Judgement of the Child.* New York: Free Press.

Pithers, W.D., J.K. Marquis, C.C. Gibet, and G.A. Marlett. 1983. "Relapse Prevention in the Sexual Aggressions: A Self-Control Model of Treatment and Maintenance of Change." In J.G. Green and I.R. Stuart (eds.), *The Sexual Aggressor: Current Perspectives on Treatment.* New York Van Nostrand Reinhold.

Platt, J.J., G.M. *Perry* and D.S. Metzger. 1980. "The Evaluation of a Heroin Addiction Treatment Program Within a Correctional Environment." In R.R Ross and P. Gendreau (eds.), *Effective Correctional Treatment.* Toronto, Butterworths.

Quay, H.C. 1977. "The Three Faces of Evaluation: What Can Be Expected to Work?" *Criminal Justice and Behavior* 4:341-351.

_____, 1979. "Classification." In H.C. Quay and J.S. Wcerry (eds.), *Psychopathological Disorders of Childhood.* New York: Wiley and Sons.

Quinsey, L. 1984. "Sexual Aggression: Studies of Offenders Against Women." In D. Weisstub (ed.), *Law and Mental Health International Perseptives.* New York: Pergammon.

_____, 1986. "Men Who Have Sex with Children." In D. Weisstub (ed.), *Law and Mental Health. International Perspectives.* New York: Pergammon.

_____, T.C, Chaplin, and W.F. Carrigan. 1979. "Sexual Preferences Among Incestuous and Non-Incestuous Child Molesters." *Behavior Therapy* 10:562-565.

Rawls, J. 1971. *A Theory of Justice.* Cambridge: Belknap.

Reamer, F.G., and J.P. Lynch. 1981. "Deinstitutionalization of Status Offenders: Individual Outcome and System Effects." *Journal of Research in Crime and Delinquency* 15: 4-29.

Reitsma-Street, M. 1984. "Differential Treatment of Young Offenders: A Review of the Conceptual Level Matching Model." *Canadian Journal of Criminology* 26:467-476.

_____, and A.W. Leschied (in press) "The Conceptual Level Matching Model in Corrections." *Criminal Justice and Behavior.*

_____, and L. Zager. 1986. *Information on Several Classification and Treatment Systems.* Philadelphia: International Differential Treatment Association (C/O Dr. P. Harris, Department of Criminal Justice, Temple University).

Rickel, A. 1986. "Prescriptions for a New Generation: Early Life Interventions." *American Journal of Community Psychology* 14:1-15.

_____, A.K. Eshelman, and G.A. Loigman. 1983. "Social Problem Solving Training A Follow-Up Study of Cognitive and Behavioral Effects." *Journal of Abnormal Child Psychology* 11:15-28.

Robinson, D., and M. Balla. 1986. "Risk Principle of Case Classification and the Prevention of Residential Placements: An Outcome Evaluation of the Share the Parenting Program" *Journal of Consulting and Clinical Psychology* 54:203-207.

Rojek, D.G. and M.L. Erikson. 1982. "Reforming the Juvenile Justice System: The Diversion of Status Offenders." *Law and Social Review* 16:241-264.

Rolf, J.E. 1985. "Evolving Adaptative Theories and Methods for Prevention Research with Children." *Journal of Consulting and Clinical Psychology* 53:631-646.

Romero, J.J. and L.M. Williams. 1985. "Recidivism Among Convicted Sex Offenders: A 10-Year Follow-up Study." *Federal Probation* 49:58-64.

Rosecrance, J. 1986. "Probation Supervision: Mission Impossible." *Federal Probation* 50:25-31.

Ross, R.R. and E.A. Fabiano. 1985. Time to Think: A Cognitive Model of Delinquency Prevention and Offender Rehabilitation. Johnson City, Tenn.: Institute of Social Sciences and Arts, Inc.

————, and P. Gendreau. 1980. *Effective Correctional Treatment.* Toronto: Butterworths.

————, and L V. Lightfoot. 1985. Treatment of the Alcohol-Abusing Offender. Springfield: C.C. Thomas.

————, and H.B. McKay. 1978. "Treatment in Corrections: Requiem for a Pancacea." *Canadian Journal of Criminology* 20:279-295.

Rossi, P.H., R.A. Berk, and K.J. Lennihan. 1980. *Money Work and Crime. Some Experimental Results.* New York: Academic Press.

Rotman, E. 1986. "Do Criminal Offenders Have a Constitutional Right to Rehabilitation?" *Journal of Criminal Law and Criminology* 77:1023-1068.

Rouleau, J. and J. Cunningham-Rathner. 1984. "Sexually Aggressive Behavior." In W. Curren, A.L. McGarry and S. Shah (eds.), *Modern Legal Psychiatry and Psychology.* Philadelphia: Davis.

Rowe, D.C. and D.W. Osgood. 1984. "Heredity and Sociological Theories of Delinquency: A Reconsideration." *American Sociological Review* 49:526-540.

Rutter, M. and H. Giller. 1983. *Juvenile Delinquency: Trends and Perspectives.* New York: Penguin.

Safer, D.J., R.C. Heaton, and F.C. Parker. 1981. "A Behavioral Program for Disruptive Junior High School Students: Results and Follow up." *Journal of Abnormal Child Psychology* 9:483-494

Samenow, S.E. 1984. *Inside the Criminal Mind.* New York: Times Book.

Sanchez-Craig, M., H.M. Annis, A.R. Bornet, and K.R MacDonald. 1984. "Random Assignment of Abstinence and Controlled Drinking. Evaluation of a Cognitive-Behavioral Program for Problem Drinkers." *Journal of Consulting and Clinical Psychology* 52:390-403.

Sarbin, T.R. 1952. "A Preface to a Psychological Analysis of Self." *Psychological Review* 59:11-22.

Sarason, I.C. 1978. "A Cognitive Social Learning Approach to Juvenile Delinquency." In R.D. Hare and D. Schalling (eds.), *Psychopathic Behavior: Approaches to Research.* New York Wiley and Sons.

Schaus, A.G. 1980. *Diet Crime and Delinquency*. Berkeley: Parker House.

Schneider, A.L. and P.R. Schneider. 1985. "The Impact of Restitution of Recidivism of Juvenile Offenders: An Experiment in Clayton County, Georgia." *Criminal Justice Review* 10:1-10.

Schoenthaler, S.J. 1983. "Diet and Delinquency: A Multi-State Replication." *International Journal of Biosocial Research* 5:70-78.

Schumacher, M., G. Kurz, and L. Moulson. 1985. "A Diversionary Approach for the 1980's." *Federal Probation* 49:4-12.

Seashore, M., S. Haberfield, J. Irwin, and K. Baker. 1976. *Prisoner Education: Project Newgate and Other College Programs*. New York: Praeger.

Sechrest. L., S.O. White and E.D. Brown. 1979. *The Rehabilitation of Criminal Offenders: Problems and Prospects*. Washington: National Academy of Sciences.

Selke, W.L. 1982. "Diversion and Crime Prevention: A Time Series Analysis." *Criminology* 20:395-406.

Serna, L.A., J.B. Schumaker, J.S. Hazel, and J.B. Sheldon. 1986. "Teaching Reciprocal Social Skills to Parents and Their Delinquent Adolescents." *Journal of Clinical and Child Psychology*. 15:64-77.

Severy, L.J. and M.J. Whitaker. 1982. "Juvenile Diversion: An Experimental Analysis of Effectiveness." *Evaluation* Review 6:753-774.

Shadish Jr., W.R. 1984. "Policy Research: Lessons From the Implementation of Deinstitutionalization." *American Psychologist* 39:725-738.

Shawver, L., T.L. Clanon, D. Kurdys, and H. Friedman. 1985. "Predicting and Improving Parole Success with PAS." *Federal Probation* 49:34-37.

Shichor, D. and H. Binder. 1982. "Community Restitution for Juveniles: An Approach and Preliminary Evaluation." *Criminal Justice Review* 7:46-50.

Shorts, I.D. 1986. "Delinquency by Association? Outcome of Joint Participation by At-Risk and Convicted Youths in a Community-Based Programme." *British Journal of Criminology* 26:156-163.

Simpson, D.D., G.W. Joe, W.E.K. Lehman, and S.B. Sells. 1986. "Addiction Careers: Etiology, Treatment and 12-Year Follow-Up Outcomes." *Journal of Drug Issues* 16:107-121.

Skovron, S.G., J.E. Scott, and V.S. Burton, Jr. (in press) "Public Support for Correctional Treatment: The Tenacity of Rehabilitative Ideology." *Criminal Justice and Behavior*.

_____, and L.F. Travis. 1984. "Work as an Avenue of Prison Reform." *New England Journal on Criminal and Civil Confinement* 10:45-64.

Smith, R.R. 1980. "Longitudinal Behavioral Assessment of Work Release." *Journal of Offender Counselling Services and Rehabilitation* 5:31-39.

Snyder, J. and G. Patterson. 1984. "Family Interaction and Delinquent Behavior." In H.C. Quay (ed.), *Handbook of Juvenile Delinquency.* New York: Wiley and Sons.

Solnick, J.V., C.J. Braukmann, M.M. Bedlington, K.A. Kirigin, and M.M. Wolf. 1981. "The Relationship Between Parent Youth Interaction and Delinquency in Group Homes." *Journal of Abnormal Child-Psychology* 9:107-119.

Spergel, I.A. 1984. "Treatment of Antisocial Youths: Review of a Conundrum." *Social Work Research and Abstracts* 20:3-7.

Spivack. G., J.J. Platt and M.B. Shure. 1976. *The Problem Solving Approach to Adjustment: A Guide to Researcy and Intervention.* San Francisco: Jossey-Bass.

Staff. 1984. "Sexual Crimes and Treatment of Sexual Offenders" *Liaison* 11:15-20.

_____, 1985. "Victim-Offender Reconciliation Programs may be an Effective Alternative to Incarceration." *Criminal Justice Digest* 5:1-6.

_____, 1986. June 16. "Advances Found in Specialized Treatment of Sex Offenders." *Criminal Justice Newsletter* 17:5-6.

_____, 1986. July 1. "New Interest in Rehabilitation Predicted by Reform Group." *Criminal Justice Newsletter* 17:6-7.

_____, 1986. August 11. *Time* p. 15.

Stanton, M.D. and T.C. Todd. 1982. *The Family Therapy of Drug Addiction.* New York: Guilford.

Strain, P., P. Steele. T. Ellis, and M. Timm. 1982. "Long Term Effects of Oppositional Child Treatment with Mothers as Therapists and Therapist Trainers." *Journal of Applied Behavior Analysis.* 15:163-169.

Sykes, G.M. and P. Matza. 1957. "Techniques of Neutralization: A Theory of Delinquency." *American Sociological Review* 22:664-670.

Tavris, C. 1975. "The Experimenting Society: To Find Programs That Work, Government Must Measure Its Failures." *Psychology Today* 9:47-56.

Thornton, D., L. Curran, D. Grayson, and V. Holloway. 1984. "Tougher Regimes in Detention Centres: Report of an Evaluation by the Young Offenders Psychology Unit." London: Home Office.

Truax, C.B. and R. Carkhuff. 1967. *Toward Effective Counselling and Psychotherapy*. Chicago: Aldine.

Turner, S., and J. Peterson. 1986. *Prison Versus Probation in California Implications for Crime and Offender Recidivism*. Santa Monica: Rand.

Tweedale, M., and S. Kennedy. 1987. "The Realities Involved in the Punishment of Offenders." Manuscript submitted for publication.

U.S. Department of Justice. 1981. *Programs for the Serious and Violent Juvenile Offender*. Office of Juvenile Justice and Delinquency Prevention.

Van Den Hagg. E. 1982. "Could Successful Rehabilitation Reduce the Crime Rate." *Journal of Criminal Law and Criminology* 73:1022-1035.

Van Voorhis, P. 1985. "Restitution Outcome and Probationers' Assessments of Restitution: The Effects of Moral Development." *Criminal Justice and Behavior* 12:259-287.

_____, 1987. "Correctional Effectiveness: The High Cost of Ignoring Success." *Federal Probation* 51, March:56-62.

Vito, G.F. 1954. "Developments in Shock Probation: A Review of Research Findings and Policy Implications." *Federal Probation* 48:22-27.

_____, 1985. "Putting Prisoners to Work: Policies and Problems." *Journal of Offender Counselling Services and Rehabilitation* 9:21-34.

_____, and H.E. Allen. 1981. "Shock Probation in Ohio: A Comparison of Outcomes." *International Journal of Offender Therapy and Comparative Criminology* 25:70-76.

Wahler, R.G. and J.E. Dumas (in press) "Family Factors in Childhood Psychopathology: A Coercion-Neglect Model." In T. Jacob (ed.), *Family Interaction and Psychopathology*. New York: Plenum.

Walsh, A. 1985. "An Evaluation of the Effects of Adult Basic Education on Rearrest Rates Among Probationers." *Journal of Offender Counselling Services and Rehabilitation* 9:69-76.

Walter, T.L. and C.M. Mills. 1980. "A Behavioral-Employment Intervention Program for Reducing Juvenile Delinquency." In R.R. Ross and P. Gendrewau (eds.), *Effective Correctional Treatment*. Toronto: Butterworths.

Warren, M.Q. 1969. "The Case for Differential Treatment of Delinquents." *The Annals of the American Academy of Political and Social Science* 62:239-258.

Webb, L. and J.R. Scanlon. 1981. "The Effectiveness of Institutional and Community Based Programs for Juvenile Offenders." *Juvenile and Family Court Journal* 32:11-16.

Webster-Stratton, C. 1984. "Randomized Trial of Two Parent-Training Programs for Families with Conduct-Disordered Children." *Journal of Consulting and Clinical Psychology* 52:666-678.

_____, 1985. "The Effects of Father Involvement in Parent Training for Conduct Problem Children." *Journal of Child Psychology and Psychiatry and Allied Disciplines* 26:801-810.

Wexler, H.K., D.S. Lipton and K. Foster. 1987. "Outcome Evaluation of a Prison Therapeutic Community for Substance Abuse Treatment: Preliminary Results." Manuscript submitted for publication.

_____, and R. Williams (in press) "The "Stay 'N Out" Therapeutic Community: Prison Treatment for Substance Abusers." *Journal of Psychoactive Drugs.*

Wilks, J. and R. Martinson. 1976. "Is the Treatment of Criminal Offenders Really Necessary?" *Federal Probation* 40:3-8.

Wilson, C.T. and S.J. Rachman. 1983. "Meta-Analysis and the Evaluation of Psychotherapy Outcome: Limitations and Liabilities." *Journal of Consulting and Clinical Psychology* 31:54-64.

Wilson, H. 1980. "Parents Can Cut the Crime Rate." *New Society* 4:456-458.

Wilson, J.Q. and R.J. Hernnstein. 1985. *Crime and Human Nature.* New York: Simon and Schuster.

Winterdyk, J. and R. Roesch. 1981. "A Wilderness Experimental Program as an Alternative for Probationers: An Evaluation." *Canadian Journal of Criminology* 23:39-49.

Wormith, J.S. 1984. "Attitude and Behavior Change of Correctional Clientele: A 3 Year Follow-Up." *Criminology* 22:595-618.

Yochelson, S. and S.E. Samenow. 1976. *The Criminal Personality: A Profile for Change.* New York: Jason Aronson.

Yu, P., G.E. Harris, B.L. Solovitz, and J.C. Franklin. 1986. "A Social Problem-Solving Intervention for Children at High Risk for Later Psychopathology." *Journal of Clinical Child Psychology* 15:30-40.

Zeisel, H. 1982. "Disagreement over the Evaluation of a Controlled Experiment." *American Journal of Sociology* 88:378-389.

CHAPTER 20
Getting Connected:
Becoming a Street Hustler

L.A. VISANO

INTRODUCTION

Prostitution consists of a wide spectrum of differentially constituted activities. The activities of getting connected, staying connected and disconnecting represent empirically related but analytically distinct levels of accomplishments. Thus, this career taxonomy provides a framework within which an organized account of careers can proceed. Each career stage of this social enterprise represents an interplay of identity formations, interactions, and social contexts.

Specifically, a number of contingencies shape movement through career stages. As a sensitizing concept (Becker, 1963; Prus, 1984), a career contingency involves the integration of objective and subjective elements (Shover, 1983). The former factors include aspects of social structure, affiliations, resources, and skills. The latter contingencies reflect ideology, general orientations or perspectives, motivations and rationales, and self-concept. Consequently, our interest is to examine structural and experiential factors which contribute to relatively patterned occupational activities.

The primary purpose of this chapter is to clarify the process by which individuals enter an occupation. By exploring the unfolding drama of how boys get connected to prostitution, we unravel the circumstances under which these boys set themselves apart from conventional society and perceive themselves as part of the street culture. We follow an approach to becoming a hustler that focuses on two general contexts: pre-occupational experiences of dislocation and exposure, and the development of street relations. Getting connected to hustling requires a collective effort wherein the interests and involvements of "significant others" are central.

"Becoming A Street Hustler" was reproduced by permission of the author.

SETTING THE STAGE: PRE-ENTRY EXPERIENCES
THE STREET AS A SOLUTION:
ACCOUNTING FOR IDLENESS

A starting point of inquiry focuses on early street experiences and contingencies influencing choice of roles. Before one can take up street hustling: a number of contingencies need to exist which enable actors to assess their immediate situations.

Boys arrive on the street from a variety of social backgrounds. Boys depict the street as their most common setting. As street transients, newcomers enter the street hierarchy in positions of least prestige. In order to provide a clearer insight into pre-occupational experiences, we need to analyze how "hitting the street" is considered a solution to school and family problems. Historical reconstructions, therefore, become basic tasks in any study of careers (Leyton, 1979). These boys choose to approach their pre-occupational experiences from two different, though obviously related points of view. Accounts are framed within dual forces of dislocation and exposure. In reconstructing and coordinating their biographical maps, they rely exclusively on factors that "push" them out of respectable society and factors that "pull" them towards the seemingly more attractive alternatives of the street. The logic of their accounts hangs together and is contingent upon the available stock of information and the relevant socialization immediately preceding their early street involvements.

Admittedly, background factors, as Heyl (1979) explains, are static in the sense that they alone do not deal with ongoing adjustments, turning points, or entry processes. Nonetheless, antecedent conditions are instructive precisely because they serve to legitimize early street involvements. To ignore what these boys consider as crucial factors invites facile interpretations that often border on crude reductionism. It is argued that these accounts, however distorted, are assigned an actuality (Holzner, 1968) or "objective facticity" within the boys' interpretive framework. What they say, imagine, or believe is very much an integral part of their real life as newcomers.

Linguistic devices that boys employ to evaluate their early street life take the form of excuses. Excuses, as Lyman and Scott (1970: 112-14) note, are accounts expressed in socially approved vocabularies in which one admits the act in question is bad, wrong or inappropriate but denies full responsibility. Newcomers, for example, attribute the problem of being on the street to deterministic causal factors with specific reference to faulty personal relationships that allegedly propel them to move "outside" their familiar environments. It is on the basis of such articulation about difficult experiences with parents, teachers or lovers that they begin to relate to the street as an immediate solution. Such a biography becomes incorporated into a perspective that can be manipulated (Willis, 1980). Family violence, school failures and delinquency often become badges a boy flashes in an effort to demonstrate his membership on the street. Due to these experiences, a boy feels that he has paid his dues and rightfully belongs on the street. Favourable impressions of the present are acquired by advancing unfavourable accounts of the past.

Background factors alone contribute little to learning how boys come to perceive themselves specifically as hustlers. Their preoccupation with these factors as causes of their dislocation is, however, relevant to any understanding of their general orientation. Family and school involvements are presented as contextual experiences from which an initial assessment of career options, and shaping of self occurs. In this section, therefore. we consider how the "street" is interpreted as a meaningful social response to perceived situational difficulties. Both the immediate experiences of recently arrived newcomers to Main Street and the reflections of more seasoned prostitutes are described.

From the outset, in both informal conversations and focused interviews, these boys immediately set themselves apart from families, school and/or lovers. Throughout our exchanges boys tend to detail unsolicited indictments against the family. Family difficulties seem to accelerate their interests in leaving home. According to the case histories that they were asked to construct, there are only a few references to positive family experiences.

Interestingly, these subjects project themselves as victims of misunderstanding, neglect, or violence. They consistently provide evidence to suggest that prior to their actual departure from their families they engaged in active ongoing appraisals of their difficult circumstances. Consider the following account given by fifteen-year old Alfred (No. 4) who, at the time of our exchange, had been on the street for only two days:

> Like man, it's no fucking picnic. When I was, like at home it's a
> fucking circus. I used to shit my pants worrying about splitting. You
> know, I really thought about it. No shit! It's still worser there!
> (private interview, September 15, 1982)

In fact, twenty-two boys indicate that they selected the street option only after their parents rejected their conciliatory gestures. For ten gay or openly homosexual boys, the heterosexuality of their families sanctioned against disclosures. Despite threats of punishment, these boys tried to share their inti-

mate feelings of guilt and confusion with their parents. The following comments, by Rudy (No. 24), Graham (No. 28), and Rocky (No. 21) respectively,
indicate how boys resolved their familial difficulties by assuming an accommodating and compliant demeanor:

> I put up with all the horse shit. I listened to them, I read Ann
> Landers. I even went to a counselor. Can you believe it? If they
> wanted me to feel ashamed, well then I did. I kept giving in, always. I
> split when I couldn't take in. That's it,
>
> (private interview, October 17, 1982)

> I promised to change my so-called funny habits. They said it was a
> passing phase. I went along. Like, they told me to start acting like
> other boys. You know, I even got laid by some bitches too, you
> know, see if they were right. You name it. I was doing it just for
> them.
>
> (private interview, September 16, 1982)

> I used to do all the rapping 'cause they blamed themselves. They
> were head-cases when I talked about how I was feeling. The old lady
> would always lay this trip—check it out. "It's pretty awful what
> you're doing to your father". What about me? Did anybody care?
> What a fucking family. It pisses the shit out of me.
>
> (private interview, December 12, 1982)

While living at his parental home, Glen (No. 27) felt an increasing unwill-
ingness to compromise on "something as basic as who I am." Negotiations in
identity are extremely problematic when parents refuse to be flexible or, as
Greg (No. 29) succinctly describes, "when they just don't come across themselves." Consequently, a greater attenuation of family bonds occurs. As this
estrangement persisted, ten subjects passively rejected the socializing influences of their families. Abandoning a conflict-ridden family situation is
extremely difficult, especially during a process of more active self-discovery.
George (No. 26), a nineteen-year-old seasoned prostitute, explains:

> Coming to terms is scary in the best of times. Imagine it. Slowly
> accept who you are when you're just a kid at home, and the only
> people around treat you like a freak. You don't know where to go.
> You turn to your parents and they just drain you. But you still care
> for them. I had a man-to-man talk with my dad—he told me I was no

man. That flipped me out.

(personal interview, December 16, 1982)

A frequently cited method of avoiding potentially hostile family interactions involves the concealment of one's interests in homosexual identity and activities. General anxieties concerning disclosure to parents generate an even greater isolation for these boys. Open admission of homosexuality was often met with emotional abuse, such as ridicule, guilt and confusion. The consequences of "being found out" by parents, however, claimed an even greater degree of hostility. The following excerpts from interviews with four boys reveal the more violent features of familial relations which ensue when parents discover on their own their son's homosexuality:

> I covered my tracks good. I thought I did. They found out from another kid. Before they disowned me I got a bad beating. They kept saying I was out of control. It's not that I was gay, you know, it's that I wasn't something they wanted. I'm glad I got beaten up. I knew what I had to do.
>
> (Gus, No. 30, private interview, September 30, 1982)

> I was told the truth hurts but lies kill. That's a crock of shit. They wanted me to be a hypocrite. When I put my ass in high gear and they found out, they sent me to a shrink and when that didn't work out, the bastard knocked my lights out. I kicked him in the balls. Now I'm glad—just another good looking stud.
>
> (Robin, No. 20, private interview, December 2, 1982)

> "Do this you queer! Do that!" Fucking right I am. I got caught at school. I paid this little prince a couple of bucks. He told his parents—they called the pigs. I got thrown down the stairs and out the door.
>
> (Gary, No. 25 informal conversation in Ken's presence in restaurant A, December 18, 1982).

> It was a drag. Back-handers. I told the jerk to screw off. That was a world war. He threw a screw-driver at me. It missed. So he slapped me around. I said I'll call the cops. He threw the phone at me. I didn't even know what I did. He probably found out like when my buddy phoned me and he was tuning in on the extension.
>
> (Rodney, No. 22, private interview: December 8, 1982).

In general, the boys hold their parents responsible for these unsatisfactory family relations. The most prevalent explanation for being on the street concerns these competing claims over appropriate identity and behaviour. According to this logic, conflict results from parental rejections of their son's sense of growing independence and maturing identity.

In sum, gay prostitutes emphasize more complex identity issues as contributing to their sustained physical and emotional abuse. By contrast, both newcomers and seasoned hustlers who deny defiantly their homosexuality simply advance more deterministic accounts. they consistently single out the generally violent personality attributes of their parents as the cause of family difficulties. Running away from home is viewed as a reasonable response to a situation in which violent parents permit little or no autonomy. Excerpts from the field notes (Rooming house B, November 21, 1982) show Sandy (No. 8) and Sam (No. 7) proudly comparing their family difficulties:

> Sandy opens the discussion enthusiastically by saying that it was his mother's fault: "She's an uptight bitch, always spying. A real basket case".
>
> Sam's opening move was even stronger: "That's peanuts. The shit kicked my ass in. The old man too, when the slut starts hollering".
>
> The exchange continues: Sandy: Me too, I got my ass kicked in. The slut had rules—no dope, no tail. Sam to L.V.: Check this out will ya. Write it down if you want.
>
> L.V.:   As long as you don't mind and as long as you're not saying it for my benefit.
>
> Sam: Fuck off. I got nothin' to hide. Like I told ya before. As long as you don't shit me, it's cool. No hassles.
>
> L.V.:   It's a deal.
>
> Sam: Write what the fuck you want. Like maybe you let me see everything. O.K. 'Cause somebody should write about all the crap with our families. Like I say, I pissed them off and I got the belt.
>
> Sandy: I got my ass kicked 'cause I was in (interrupting) space city. The mother fucker put me away. I did time, you know.
>
> L. V.:   For what?
>
> Sandy: No reason.
>
> Sam: Yeah no reason just 'cause they know nothin', sweet dick all. They didn't like you doing you're thing.

On another convivial occasion (Park 1, October 15, 1982), Stan (No. 12) joined Simon (No. 10) in a discussion of family violence. The following excerpt from the field notes describes the presentation and negotiation of indictments against the family. This exchange is typical in the sense that it expresses the tendency of these boys to shape difficulties according to common background features:

Simon: I got caught boosting. The parents pigged out on me. The cops were nicer to me than my old man. When the pigs left, the old man hammered my head.

L.V.:   Why?

Simon: I guess I went to far. I broke a couple of his rules. No big deal, like smoking dope and swearing all the time.

Stan: (Stan did not mince words nor was he willing to be upstaged) So What! Don't make me puke with that shit. I caught my old man throwing the blocks to our cleaning lady.

Simon: Big shit!

Stan: Let me finish ass-hole. So I caught them, right? My old man's a lawyer—a real religious nut. Get this—I told my old lady. The douche bag called me a liar. I called them a bunch of phonies. Then they both went to town on me:

Simon: They're all bastards! You said you gotta kid?

L.V.:   That's right.

Simon: Remember this—he could be like us if you don't get too uptight. Be loose. If he starts fucking around, don't throw him out like some garbage. 'Cause he'll split like us.

Stan: Parents are too fucking crazy. They blow hot and cold. They get hot if you're pulling your wire. It's O.K. for them to do it—you know, get laid but no good for you to do it.

Simon: (directed to Stan) You're not as stupid as you look. I know where you're at with your parents. We're right you know, parents don't want to let go. If you try, you get smacked and really hard. I got no teeth, see that's where I got punched out.

The importance of this background information is captured tersely by Sylvester (No. 15) who describes his early violent experiences as "battle wounds". Images of violence predominate in these recollections. Moreover, these details function to provide evidence of their strength and perseverance. When queried about the tendency of boys to talk at great lengths about their abusive families, Scott (No. 9) elaborates:

> What else have they got. They were hurt bad. Now they're smart. What it says is, "Listen Jack, I didn't take this from my old lady, so I ain't going to take it from anybody else". It makes them feel tougher. That's why. It gets them ready for anything. They'll dish it out to their tricks, even to other kids. Don't think they just talk about it to you, no way. They rap about it to their buddies, all the time
>
> (private interview, November 27, 1982).

This background information helps to justify their immediate responses, allowing them to use violence on the street generally or in their work setting. This sentiment is expressed by Rodney (No. 22) who suggests that violence becomes part of a street kid's general orientation. He also provides unsolicited remarks about the consequences of failed romantic relationships:

> Even in a sour love affair, these boys aren't going to take much crap. It's important because they know they're not going to take any shit from a john. You don't forget how you were treated, it helps the business to know you can be pretty rough. You've been through it. Not going to take any more shit.
>
> (private interview, December 2, 1982)

According to more seasoned street prostitutes, these early experiences as victims enable boys to acquire a general conflict perspective, which they can readily invoke in legitimating violence against threatening colleagues and non-compliant clients.

In the above section, we have examined various reasons actors offer for being on the street especially in reference to family problems. Table 1 summarizes information obtained from interview questions which ask for a comparison of types of abuse boys claim to have suffered while at home. From column comparisons, it is evident that gay prostitutes offer emotional abuse as a dominant explanation. In contrast, boys who deny homosexuality select physical violence as a foremost feature of their family relationships.

Table 1
Nature of Family Abuse and Types of Hustlers

Nature of Abuse	Gay Prostitute	Street Hustler (defiantly straight)	Total
Physical	4	12	16
Emotional/Mental	11	1	12
Both	3	2	5
Total	1%	15	33*

*Includes three informants

In addition to the family, school experiences are frequently singled out as a "pushing" influence. Although the school offers a measure of escape from abusive families, it too exacts a price. The most explicitly stated resentment of school concerns boredom. Whatever their motivations for being in school, twenty subjects argue that school occupies an irrelevant place between the constraints of family life and the freedoms of the street. According to all boys, complete withdrawal from school is difficult unless they are prepared to leave home.

All boys employed a number of coping strategies that minimized the meaningless of school. These responses, which range from acquiescence to direct confrontation are described as "jacking off", "scoring" or "shoving it". "Jacking off" expresses a minimal level of participation in the classroom. Boys attend classes only to "pass the time". They engage in considerable daydreaming, come to school "wasted" on drugs, or just use school to plan evening activities. "Scoring" denotes a more direct form of subversion whereby boys attend classes in order to "score points" with their buddies by disrupting lessons, distracting other students by "clowning" around, and ridiculing others. Seven boys talked about using their school to "score" dates and drug deals. Lastly, five subjects report that they rejected school altogether by withdrawing episodically, by going to "parties", and committing truancy. Consider the following remarks by Albert (No. 2), and Alfred (No. 4) respectively:

> Man I just pissed my time away. I'd goof off. Too much bullshit.
> Who cares about history. This is more important [pointing to his
> crotch]. I wanted more. I started to screw around and deal.
>
> (informal conversation, November 13, 1982)
>
> It was torture. The same shit and same shit-heads.
> Was I bored! Nagging about this and that. What about teaching us
> how to get laid. It's all useless; getting your rocks off—that's all. So
> me and my pals kissed it good-bye. We got expelled for just farting
> around—skipping you know.
>
> (informal conversation, September 15, 1982)

Only eight boys favourably assess the value of formal education. Their schooling, however, was quickly disavowed of any serious relevance when they discovered that their teachers were becoming more directly implicated in their
family lives. These boys malign the rapport teachers developed with parents
and castigate them for informing parents of their poor progress at school.
Teachers, therefore, are perceived as potentially troublesome as they align
themselves with the boys' parents. In essence, they are regarded with great
disdain primarily because their negative evaluations of the boys' school performance are part of the arsenal of reasons parents invoke in inflicting punishment against them. The socialization process, which tends to discourage subjects from challenging parental power (Lee, 1982: 603), spills over to the
school and is shared by teachers. To the chagrin of these boys, teachers who
were once quite encouraging soon demonstrate a growing disinterest in their
well-being. Accordingly, boys cite two common situations which exacerbate
their relations with teachers. Firstly, teachers are too reticent about reprimand-
ing pernicious taunts of other students regarding a boy's homosexuality. And,
secondly, boys consider teachers too anxious in referring homosexual boys to
special counselors, under the dubious pretext of "help".

For all subjects, the exigencies of family problems, namely, physical and
emotional abuse, interfered with their school performance. Their preoccupation with the realities of conflict-ridden family relationships often resulted in a
decreasing interest in school work and a greater recognition of the insignifi-
cance of education. Boys define their involvements at school as even less
meaningful once they realize that these experiences fail to provide them with
an immediate escape from family problems.

These accounts certainly do not suggest that school failures are necessarily
pivotal to the process of becoming a prostitute. Rather, withdrawal from
school is an event seen as a significant condition of their pre-entry process.

That is, family and school experiences bring into focus a variety of legitimations designed to make good their claims that the street represents freedom. These reflective shreds and patches provide a common vision of what they understand as factors "pushing" them out of conventional normative bonds. The street, therefore, is conceptualized as an option which is immediately available and easily appreciated in light of the limited future their familiar world holds for them.

Freedom from boredom figures prominently in these claims. Notions of freedom are constructed out of a constellation of meanings that they divine within the twin contexts of past estranged experiences and current predicaments.

Table 2
Variations in Perceptions Regarding Boredom

Locus of Boredom	Gay Prostitute*	Street Hustler*	Total
Family	11	8	19
Lovers	2	—	2
Peers	2	—	2
School	1	7	8
Boredom not an issue	2	—	2
Total	18	15	33*

*Informants included

Table 2 presents the context of boredom. Although boys overwhelmingly identify family life as the locus of boredom, there are apparent differences regarding school. Only one gay prostitute considered school as boring whereas seven defiantly straight street hustlers repeatedly describe it as dreary. Yet our focus is not based on the veracity of these assertions. Rather, it is directed towards the degree to which this quest for freedom and independence is incorporated into their central meaning patterns. Consider, for example, Greg's (No. 29) brief comparison of a constraining home life and the promise of freedom he discovered on the street.

> Supper at seven, homework at eight. Bed at ten. Every single day. I
> wanted more. There was nothing but hassles at home. So I went
> looking for freedom and I found it in my lover. I figure he can give
> me more than my parents—more love and freedom. He made my
> life easy. What's the point staying home dying—that's how I figure
> it.
>
> (private interview, December 11, 1982)

In addition to the "pushing" influences of family and school "hassles", boys refer to the "pulling" forces of the street, notably its variety and excitement. The psychic lure of the downtown glitter, of "fast lanes", appears strong, especially for boys who have learned to resent their many daily mundane rounds. Twenty-five boys characterize their first few hours on the street in terms of a spirit of adventure. They are intrigued to explore this new world and use a variety of images to portray themselves as special "survivors", "hunters" and "trappers" out in the "jungles" and "trenches" searching for "the action". Both this search for prohibited pleasure-seeking activities and the existential state of uncertainty about what direction their lives are going to take, contribute to this stimulation. A blatant example of this justification comes from Sam (No. 7), who, in a surge of enthusiasm, indicates:

> At fifteen I hiked all over the country. I tried a lot of ass, did all the
> dope around. I saw a hell of a lot more than anybody my age. You
> name it, I did it. Out in the big city. No more hick towns.
> [When asked about what Main Street represents, he added:]
> Freedom [shouting], that's it! No more curfews, no more head
> games, no more goofs around. If I want to sniff gas or even glue and
> some powder or do acid, I can do it.
>
> (private interview, November 23, 1982)

Likewise, Scott (No. 9) focuses on sexual freedoms: "I'm pretty good now. I'll get into heads, switches, splashes, jobs. My joint has never been busier". Andy (No. 6), a fifteen-year old who has been on the street for only a week at the time of our exchange, describes:

> It was just being here. Even when I froze my ass it was fun. It's a
> high out here. I guess, I'm like a fucking rebel. Christ, the more I last
> out here, the tougher I feel. That's pretty neat. All the action.
>
> (informal conversation, December 4, 1982)

Expressions of freedom and adventure serve to further extricate boys from their unpleasant and boring family and school experiences. Interestingly, these boys project what Matza and Sykes (1970) refer to as a billiard ball concept of self. Accounts tend to remain clearly within a normative framework that is particularly sensitive to the immediate context of their trouble. In addition, they offer melioristic impressions of the street which legitimate their decisions to leave home. These boys seldom arrive on the street scene unfamiliar with what awaits them. On the basis of their own limited week-end excursions and information shared with friends at school, they acquire favourable impressions of the excitement of Main Street. As the downtown becomes projected as an attractive alternative, the temptation to be on the street and to abandon family, school and/or lovers increases. Seventeen boys enjoyed well over a dozen all-night week-end excursions on Main Street before actually deciding to move out permanently. Four subjects indicate that during their stay at a group home they were exposed to various contacts who detailed the nature of sexual marketplaces, profitability of street activities, and locations of hostels and missions.

These sketches, however, provide a misleadingly positive appraisal of street life. The language in which these accounts are cast, risks eliding expressions of hardships boys encounter during these early days on the street. The street as a problem is often glossed over and blithely ignored. The nature of sociology, however, requires a more rigorous interpretation of these legitimations in light of other evidence collected. Data collected from conversational interviews on the street and from observations of newcomers suggest widespread difficulties.

THE STREET AS A PROBLEM: PARADOXES OF MARGINALITY

Aside from exaggerated notions of excitement that awaits them, these boys generally do not have comprehensive role maps, information and knowledge about how to manage problems concomitant with "survival" on the street. Initially, newcomers experience considerable hardships in trying to fit into the street environment. For the solo or solitary adventurers, this early period is marked by trial and error. Irrespective of their previous entanglements at home or at school, newcomers are not integrated into a meaningful web of friendship patterns on the street. They exist on the border of conventional and "deviant" worlds. They are "on" the street, but not "of" the street.

Upon arrival, boys do not participate in the conventional society, gay community or in street subcultures. Their attitudes and behavioural patterns remain on the fringe. On the one hand, newcomers partially relinquish former cultural traditions. And, on the other hand, they have not won acceptance in the culture toward which they are beginning to drift. Although they have forsaken familiar associations, they have not carved out a place in their newly found and seemingly attractive street lifestyle.

During this initial phase on the street, newcomers become impoverished street transients. Their experiences begin to assume a solitary quality. Despite the advantages of being free, as newcomers, they soon realize that they are all alone "trying" to make it. In discussing their first few days on the street, subjects repeatedly single out difficulties in securing fundamental amenities of food and shelter. Alfred (No. 4) and Allen (No. 5), two recent arrivals on the street, describe their initial problems as follows

> I was no better than a fucking bum—checking out garbage, sleeping anywhere. I made my Big Mac stretch. I was starving. I remember I didn't eat for two days straight.
> (Alfred, conversational interview,
> September 15, 1982)

> Man, we're only talking about a week ago. I was in the fucking gutter. Just like a rat or something. But don't get me wrong, I was my own rat.
> (Allen, conversational interview, October 9, 1982)

All newcomers expect to overcome these obstacles by simply seeking aid from social service agencies. Observations of boys at welfare agencies, however, illustrate that the delivery of welfare provisions is not automatically forthcoming, as noted in the following excerpt from field observations at agency A (November 12, 1982):

> Although bereft of any financial resources, Albert (N. 2) refuses to appreciate the agency's administrative follow-up in dispensing cash. The following exchange is overheard while Albert is at the counter and I am sitting in the waiting room writing up the conversation:
>
> Albert: I got no place. I need some fast money.
> Social Worker   O.K. Give me some particulars. I'll need your

	name and address.
Albert:	I told ya, I got no place.
Social Worker:	O.K. Your previous address.
Albert:	What for?
Social Worker:	We just can't give you money like that. We'll send out a worker to your home—you know a community assessment.
Albert:	[raising his voice] I told ya I got no place.
Social Worker:	All we need is an address of a place you'll be staying at and we'll give you an emergency advance.
Albert:	I need the money now!
Social Worker:	I understand [becoming irritated], we'll have emergency assistance when you return tomorrow and in the meantime you can stay at the shelter. They'll put you up. I'll give you a letter to take with you. Let's fill out this form first. How old are you?
Albert:	Sixteen. Sixteen and a half.
Social Worker:	Is that all. This presents a problem. I'll have to talk it over with my supervisor. I don't think you're eligible.
Albert:	Forget it. I need the money. Don't jerk me around—talking to this guy, tomorrow. Screw it!
Social Worker:	Well, I'm sorry but you just can't come in and demand money.
Albert:	[extremely indignant.] Shove it! Who needs this shit?
Social Worker:	Grow up will you. You keep this up, we'll have to bar you.
Albert:	I'm shaking. (He turns to me and we both leave.)

In a follow-up discussion outside this agency, Albert explains that he does not want "any hassles with the cops". Nine other boys also mention that in addition to food and shelter, survival depends on the boy's ability to avoid detection, especially from the police and youth workers. They fear the consequences of discovery, which usually include returning the boy to his family home, to a group home, or training school. Thus, a reliance on welfare workers jeopardizes the likelihood of succeeding on the street, especially since agencies seek to reconcile a boy with his family. These boys quickly learn that agencies are also compelled to notify the police if youths are under sixteen. What emerges is a fear of exposure that presumably follows from divulging information to case workers. According to Alex (No. 3), a clever fifteen-year old from another part of the country:

> Like, they watch me, you know. Like, I fake it. You know, these social workers, yeah that's what they call them. Like, they're pretty tight with the fuzz. I showed up, like at this hostel, right. They called the cops on me 'cause I was pretty stupid for telling them I was fifteen.
>
> (private interview, November 30, 1982)

Initially, newcomers to the street try to avail themselves of any employment prospects. Eighteen boys admit that most jobs searches are extremely frustrating because of continual rejections from potential employers. They discover in a matter of days that there are very few legitimate opportunities. Because of these early negative employment contacts, they quickly become discouraged, and abandon further job applications. In discussing their inability to secure employment, however, they seldom focus attention on their limited skills. Instead, they articulate lengthy rationalizations in terms of their negative evaluations of work in general.

Work is translated as a restriction on their mobility and, subsequently, on their "fun" activities. Newcomers feel that they did not leave their homes in order to embark on yet another constraining commitment. Securing a full-time legitimate job occupies little significance and is also cast as an irrelevant concern. Although in need of money, they refuse to be "stuck" in what they perceive as meaningless or boring activities such as working in loading areas of warehouses, or washing dishes and sweeping floors in restaurants. These jobs are described as time-consuming, poorly rewarding and, more importantly, in conflict with their sense of adventure. Moreover, neither their family nor school experiences prepare these poorly educated and unskilled boys to function in the legitimate workplace. A typical explanation boys give for refusing the more painstaking task of finding legitimate work is provided by Kevin and Ken, respectively:

> All I want is instant cash. I'm not going to stand in line for any goof who's going to tell me to get lost anyway. And if he hires me, I'm not going to take any shit. Working for a couple of pennies like a slave. All I want is no rules, man; and some fast bread.
>
> (joint interview with Clarke, September 11, 1982)

I checked into this place at six in the morning. Casual work. They
wanted some scabs. The boss gave me shit because I had no socks. I
was cold and really famished. He goes, "looks like you never worked
before. We need somebody who can work hard loading trucks." And
then he goes like "I don't know if we could trust you" and told me to
screw off.

(private interview, January 12,1983)

Initially, the experiential reality that these solitary newcomers construct for
themselves is nothing short of a meager subsistence. They learn to rely on
their wits to structure and seize upon any opportunity to fend for themselves
as best they can. According to recent newcomers, survival requires them to be
constantly "on the prowl" and ready to "score" by "rolling" a drunk, "boosting", "smashing and grabbing" anything of value, or simply panhandling.

The term marginality, therefore, accurately reflects the general conviction
that they are somehow set apart from society and yet not fully part of street
groupings. Marginality, however, is a structural concept that does not simply
refer to surface characteristics of a population. Marginality is related to deeper
processes that underlie a newcomer's limited dislocation and exposure.
Essentially, the determination of marginality is related to the street context in
which they are implicated and the degree to which this setting is socially and
economically peripheral to the larger urban setting (Kapferer, 1978: 288).
Marginality refers to the fact that a social group has little influence in the
mainstream of social and economic life. (Clairmont and Magill, 1971: 480).

For newcomers, the general structures of age, class and sexual orientation
characterize their marginality. According to Hollingshead (1975: 5), adolescents occupy a temporal period in life when the society in which they function
refuses to regard them as children, and yet denies them full adult status. Since
many newcomers are under sixteen years of age, accommodation and welfare
services are not available to them. In terms of class affiliations, these adolescent wanderers have no place in the class structure. Although they are unem-
ployed, newcomers are-outside of social labour and share no loyalties to the
working class or the class hierarchy of their parents. That is, they have no
consciousness of their existence as a class. As "lumpenproletariat" (Fanon,
1968: 130; Matza 1975; Brake, 1980: 87, 98), they prey on all classes.
Lastly, as adolescent homosexuals, they continue to remain marginal and
shunned by their familiar heterosexual world. Furthermore, community agencies are reluctant to offer formal supportive services to under-age homosexual

street transients.

In brief, the above sections identify the general context within which boys get connected. An analysis of the process of exposure, to which we now turn, remains inadequate without describing this background of dislocation. The purpose of this discussion is not to discount the affinity of family and school experiences but to illustrate how these accounts mesh with the actors' decisions to become involved on the street. These early experiences indicate how boys orient themselves generally, and become involved in prostitution specifically. The status of marginality is central to seeking supportive relations on the street. The paradox of being "on" the street and not "of" the street does not solely determine directions to pursue. But, it is against these background accounts that newcomers justify the development of street relations. Early difficulties on the street, especially in reference to securing food and shelter, contribute to a lowering of defenses and a greater susceptibility to involvements with more seasoned boys, who are willing to offer even a modicum of support. Just as the street was perceived as a solution to prior family and school difficulties, street relations are also held to be a solution to immediate problems of survival for the solitary newcomer. While the previous sections examine initial dislocations, the following discussion deals with the newcomer's exposure to the socializing influences of street relations. By focusing on these interactions, we explore the process of admission into the world of prostitution. Becoming a hustler requires a collective accomplishment. Hustling emerges out of the various social relations that newcomers develop on the street. As a form of secondary socialization, becoming a hustler consists of both self-induction or enlistment and recruitment by others. The street, therefore, is an unique social setting facilitating "seekership" (Prus, 1984) and encouragement.

The circumstances of being "on the street" is a starting point for our analysis primarily because it is a consistently invoked feature identified by all boys. Boys are able to distinguish these early days when they "just hit the streets" from those days when they sought street contacts. This is not to suggest that early solitary street experiences causes prostitution. Rather, this early exposure to the street is a significant prerequisite for initiating street connections, which eventually introduce newcomers to prostitution as an attractive alternative.

ESTABLISHING STREET RELATIONS:
THE SOCIAL ORGANIZATION OF ENTRY

Street life is a complex amalgam of interactions which are influenced by a wide variety of social, environmental and interpersonal factors. A kaleidoscope of street activities provides many significant contacts for newcomers. Specifically, the social organization of Main Street includes a variety of overlapping activities, fluid and fleeting relations, and numerous roles and rules. The structure of street relations is a contingency that shapes the newcomer's self-image and his understanding of prostitution as an appropriate response to situational difficulties. Therefore, the street offers both limitations to, and possibilities for, survival.

In general, newcomers arrive at the edge of spatially located street relations. Relations are sought which help solve some of the problems associated with being a solitary street transient. Newcomers discover a number of street alignments by gravitating towards different "hang-outs". During their frequent visits to arcades, parks, coffee-shops, hostels and street-corners, newcomers make contacts and come to the attention of more seasoned "street kids". Newcomers gradually become enmeshed in pre-existing social relations. Newcomers learn to sort out more comfortable associations of unacquainted peer groups. Five boys, however, indicate that they preferred to interact with many different street contacts rather than simply drift towards a more specific congenial grouping.

While "hanging out", "goofing off" and "making rounds" with a group of three or four boys, newcomers gain an increasing familiarity with different activities such as selling drugs, stolen merchandise, and sex. During these episodes of exposure, identities are disclosed and receptivities of others tested. This early stage involves the learning of a newcomer's role, especially with its emphasis on naiveté and subservience. Recent arrivals organize their responses around the preliminary reactions of strangers with whom they form loose, fleeting and casual streetcorner groupings or "clusters" (West, 1978). An important contingency involves the experience of being publicly accepted. In the course of their interactions, newcomers pick up the requisite jargon and listen attentively to the legends, successes and conflicts that seasoned boys communicate to them. As a result of their common situation, previously unacquainted street boys develop bonds with each other. These relationships function to provide general assistance and provisions of support for newcomers. The latter become informed about shelter, food and detection of police. Considering their prior experiences and difficulties as solitary street transients, it is not surprising that the simple pleasures of a generalized street fellowship are enough to bind them. Consider, for example, Ray's (No. 16) comments regarding the benefits of forging an alliance with loose groupings:

> I used to spend hours hanging around with these kids, listening to what they said and watching them. I think I had to do that, you know. It's like paying your dues. I knew I couldn't shoot my mouth off. I couldn't be pushy. But look at how they helped me. These strangers put me up, gave me smokes and were really nice.
>
> (informal conversation, September 5, 1982)

The process of introducing themselves to an existing reference group is not without difficulties. Not only are newcomers expected to defer to more seasoned "street smart" kids, but also their acceptance is based on the performance of certain tasks. In many of these streetcorner groupings, newcomers are regarded with caution and suspicion. They are subjected to considerable manipulation by older boys attempting to "test" their loyalties. Both Robert (No. 19) and Reid (No. 17) elaborate:

> When you're checking it out, you don't know what shit is going down. You don't know who you're fucking with—could be pimps, maybe pushers. When they say fuck off, you split 'cause you don't know them and maybe don't want to know them.
>
> (private interview, September 2, 1982)

> I got beat up when they found out I was gay. They grabbed me and took my five bucks. They punched me out in the alley. So I got lost fast and found some other kids goofing around. You see, you gotta be careful when you're still fresh meat. It's scary if they don't like you.
>
> (private interview, September 23, 1982)

More significantly, it is in the context of loose and fleeting peer acquaintances that newcomers begin to discover inviting street associations. "Hanging out" contributes to the expansion of opportunities and contacts. Street-corner groupings constitute the most important means for enlistment or recruitment. According to sixteen boys, hanging out at arcades enables them to initiate contacts actively, to make direct inquiries, and make themselves available for street activities. By contrast, seventeen other boys indicate that as aspirants they were invited to tag along and participate in unskilled tasks, the completion of which led to an apprenticeship.

According to our data, two fundamental issues concerning seekership emerge. First, boys are not simply propelled in a "pre-ordained" (Matza 1969: 101) manner. They are involved in meaningful interactions with their street worlds. The process of affiliation is purposive and rational. A second, related issue concerns the social construction of choice. Choices are made according to the evidence available and the attractiveness of various options. Newcomers drift into a reference group for whom their limited street experience makes them eligible candidates. Fortuitous encounters are undoubtedly responsible for many initial introductions. Nevertheless, the process of enlistment, or what Matza (ibid) refers to as the "ordaining of self" is an active human accomplishment. Despite the unanimous view held by all six senior case workers interviewed that newcomers are "forced" or compelled into prostitution, all thirty-three boys maintain that it was upon their own initiatives in seeking out supportive relationships that they chose to associate with more seasoned hustlers.

Older seasoned hustlers typically go out of their way to help newcomers. In addition to sharing food and shelter, newcomers are invited to participate in various play or leisure pursuits. Admittedly these relations are no different from general adolescent associations wherein boys retrospectively discuss parties, alcohol, drugs and sex. During initial streetcorner encounters, seasoned boys usually discuss hustling only after newcomers express an interest in "hanging around" and remaining on the street. Four seasoned prostitutes, however, established links with unacquainted newcomers only after collectively sharing their experiences. After they were all-chased out of a shopping plaza for loitering, refused accommodation at a hostel or arrested, older boys initiated encounters with their new "street buddies". The following comments by Rick (No. 18) and Roger (No. 23) describe their introduction to other street boys:

> I tried looking for some buddies first. So I just travelled you know, like by myself. I go to this pin-ball place and I look at this guy running some good points, free games. So he goes like, "Where you from", pretty friendly. Like, he could go like "screw off"; but he didn't. He splits and goes, "Let's get out of here". So we moved around like together. We did some stuff and crashed at the fleabag hostel. He's my buddy.
>
> (informal conversation, September 26, 1982)

I met David when I was just bumming around. I was washing my hair
in this washroom. He started to talk—he's a neat guy. I told him I
was strapped. He said he could use a partner. He bought me a milk-
shake and put me in touch with other guys. I stayed at his place.

(private interview, November 16, 1982)

There are several important features of this socialization process that are quite
instructive in understanding apprenticeship. By spending an inordinate number of hours "checking out his chick" or "fresh fish" in order to secure a
degree of loyalty, the seasoned street hustler begins to act like a sponsor.
Once the newcomer is accepted, the seasoned boy recommends him
favourably to his friends and informs him about general situational uncertainties inherent in hustling. Although a general mood of excitement characterizes
these encounters wherein interests and experiences are compared, a dependency relationship emerges. In the company of these seasoned hustlers, newcomers generally submit to this imbalance in exchange for scarce resources
such as food, shelter, and hustling skills. The following excerpt of an observation further demonstrates the development of an asymmetrical relationship.

While leaning against a telephone pole talking to Sonny (No. 11),
Alex (No. 3), a recent arrival approaches us slowly. Sonny notices a
young boy carrying a shopping bag.

Sonny:	What the fuck do you want?
Alex:	Nothing, why?
Sonny:	Because I'm asking fuck face. Got any bread?
Alex:	Five bills, why?
Sonny:	Don't get smart. Fork it over. I'll pay you back.
Alex:	Shit, that's all I got.
Sonny:	You don't need it. Listen, I'm not asking.
Alex:	O.K. What about—what am I going to do for food?
Sonny:	We'll square it later. Just hang loose.
L.V.:	What's he going to do?
Sonny:	It depends. If he's smart, he'll hang around with us—he'll be O.K. If he's not. I'll come back and score again.
Sonny to Alex:	C'mon chicken. I'll fix you up.

(October 28, 1982)

Interestingly, Alex "hung out" with Sonny for five days. Relationships characterized by positive emotional bonds and extensive interactions inevitably lead
to a more serious commitment to apprenticeship. Apprenticeship entails a
social obligation that goes beyond hanging around and listening to general
"hustles". As a result of an escalating trust, a repertoire of specific "trade
secrets" and legitimating devices are communicated to the role incumbent.
Alfred (No. 4) elaborates on this process of getting connected:

> You just don't go and say, "Listen Mac, teach me how to survive".
> The older kid knows where you're at. He'll make the move.
>   (informal conversation, September 15, 1982)

Typically, the method used for "breaking in" or integrating a newcomer into
hustling is through "on-the-job" observation and participation. That is, the
requirements of hustling are learned by direct assistance, imitation, and repeti-
tion. Subsequently, progress is effected by approval, encouragement and monetary rewards. The following excerpt from field notes demonstrates this socialization:

> In coffee-shop B with Robin (No. 20), a seasoned hustler, on
> December 3, 1982. At approximately 1:30 AM, we were joined by
> Andy (No. 6). During the course of our conversation, Robin inter-
> rupts and directs his attention to Andy.

Robin:	How many times I got to tell you, be smart? I saw you flashing some bread after you left the trick. What kind of a fucking idiot are you?
Andy:	No big deal. Nobody saw me.
Robin:	Don't you know what you're doing? Man, you're hustling your ass and telling the world. You really piss me off. Sometimes I can't figure why I waste time telling you things.
Andy:	All right. I read your lips. Check this out. The jerk gave me his watch.
Robin:	Let me see. What did you do for it? It's a cheap Timex—a couple of bucks. It's shit. What about bread? We need bread for the rent tomorrow.
Andy:	I'll pick some up tomorrow. Don't worry.

> Robin then introduces me to Andy.

Robin:	You see I showed him the ropes. He's good but pretty dumb.
Andy:	Fuck off.
Robin:	What you do for the watch?
Andy:	Not in front of him.
Robin:	He's all right. Don't worry. Anyway I told him he could hang around with you.
Andy:	Just down on him.
Robin:	Good, that's all this shit is worth.
L.V. to Andy:	Where did you learn how to get into this?
Andy:	From him. He's O.K., but gets pissed off too much.
Robin:	Next time, I'll set you up. That way I know you'll get cash.

For twenty-one boys, the process of acquiring technical skills is relatively easy and usually occurs within the first three weeks on the street. Apprenticeship, as a form of positive support, depends on the nature and frequency of these contacts. Virtually all "on-the-job" instructions are anchored in friendship associations of two to three boys. As attachments grow, seasoned hustlers become role models within a framework of sociability. Role incumbents begin to identify with their instructors. They gain a vague feeling that they are maturing as street hustlers. This sense of self as a hustler is reinforced repeatedly during this training period. Ray (No. 16) comments on his training:

> My friend Bobby taught me a couple of things. I guess I was like a kitten. So I watched him hustle his buns. We used to do it together and them try a menage with a trick. It's like a business—renting your dick. It's not just screwing. You gotta learn how to tease it. Practice makes perfect. Bobby showed me how to fake it, how to handle poppers when I do it. It takes time and practice.
>
> (private interview, September 5, 1982)

Newcomers become caught up in reciprocal expectations that facilitate apprenticeship. Norms of reciprocity (Gouldner, 1960) require these role incumbents to assist those boys who have guided them. Specific expectations are defined in terms of actual and perceived benefits to be gained. Although nineteen boys agree that there are numerous benefits to be derived from an apprenticeship, they hasten to add that an appreciation of specific guidelines soon wanes. After several weeks of apprenticeship they refuse to act like newcomers and begin to seriously question their tutors' assumptions. They seek to dismantle their circumscribed newcomer identity and reject the expected subservience. Despite the immediate benefits of initial street companionship, twelve gay prostitutes are circumspect about the nature of this training by instructors who are strident about their heterosexuality. According to these gay boys, their training period faltered miserably in preparing them for actual participation in prostitution. Instructions about specific client relations were replete with contradictions. Romanticized notions of fun conflict with the practice of "bashing queers". Moreover, these boys report that the rhetoric of a general street brotherhood sharpy contrasts with the violence that they witness against other street kids. They are especially dismayed with the flagrant disdain their tutors demonstrate towards gays in general. As these boys become less impervious to outside street contacts, notably with members of the gay community, they are more inclined to abandon apprenticeship altogether. They strive to move beyond hustling as a collective peer activity and towards a more solitary entrepreneurship. Stu's (No. 14) remarks introduce a number of issues, to be explored in subsequent chapters, which attest to the dilemmas faced by gay newcomers interacting with homophobic street hustlers:

> My buddy was good to me at first. Then it started to get bad. But, you don't split 'cause he'll call you a goof. Anyway I had nowhere to go. So I put up with all the shit about gays. I was mad. I needed him. So I faked it. Like he talked about poking faggots. I go along smiling. If I said something then he knows I'm gay.

In conjunction with determining how boys develop street relations during this initial stage, we also investigated the motives of newcomers and seasoned street hustlers for supporting each other. The most common motives evinced in the data are: promise of money, companionship, and fun. Initially, interest ties bind actors in an apprenticeship relationship. For seasoned boys who act as instructors, personal gain is operationalized according to the following benefits they receive. Firstly, during early instructions newcomers are expected to perform many undesirable jobs including: luring tricks into backalleys or parks where seasoned boys would be waiting and ready to rob or "score" these potential clients; acting as messenger boys, running errands; serving as "front men" by obstructing shoppers and store clerks, or causing a distracting flurry of activities while older boys would shoplift; and carrying drugs or weapons for older boys since their age and inexperience would result in a more lenient treatment if apprehended by the police. Secondly, newcomers act as "lookouts" and help reduce the probability of getting caught. They would "watch the backs" of older boys during sexual transactions by observing from a distance or even recording licence plate numbers and addresses of clients. In the event that their tutors do not return on schedule at a pre-arranged location, newcomers would notify the police. Most importantly, newcomers are regarded as probable sources of income for seasoned hustlers. These protégés may be stronger in one area or demonstrate more marketable assets, namely youthfulness, attractiveness and naiveté, where seasoned regulars may be weak. The revenue newcomers make would be shared with their "street buddies", often to defray the costs of rent, groceries, drugs, or bail. And lastly, seasoned hustlers nurture these relations in order to ensure a smooth circulation of goods and services. Apprenticeship enables them to protect their established business interests against the potential competition of unbridled newcomers frequenting common job sites.

Newcomers are also motivated by self-interests. They arrive on the street in a state of confusion. On the one hand, they are impressed with the novelty of independence and a general wanderlust of the "street scene". And yet, they suffer from a poor self-image and lack the confidence necessary for street survival. Getting into street relations is perceived as a means of reconciling this dilemma. Boys are anxious about learning methods of survival, while sustaining a sense of excitement. Consider the following interpretations of Adam (No. 1) and Allen (No. 5) which highlight the difficulties confronted by newcomers:

> Man I was beat. I saw kids hanging around. I said to myself, maybe they got a handle. Anyway, I was really scared and lonely. I wanted to trip around with somebody.
>
> (conversational interview, October 7, 1982)

> I wanted action. I wanted some guy to show me around. Like I was hungry. I told this kid that I was desperate. He helped me out. I swapped my old man's address and we B and E'd it. Now we're like brothers.
>
> (private interview, October 9, 1982)

The relevance of these associations is not simply limited to making money or securing a street education. In addition to interest-based motives, there are also friendship-oriented sentimental ties. Once immediate situational difficulties are overcome, boys concentrate on the more emotionally rewarding aspects of being on the street—companionship, sociability and recreation. For eighteen boys these initial street companions were their closest and only friends. Furthermore, seven boys were sexually intimate with their "street buddies". During these introductory weeks on the street, this companionship provides them with a considerable degree of support, strength and protection. A sense of altruism or benign fraternalism leading seasoned hustlers to adopt newcomers, by sheltering and feeding them is illustrated in the following comments by Steve (No. 13) and Simon (No. 10), respectively:

> I saw this skinny kid. Paper-thin jeans hassled by the cops. Shivering. So I said to myself, if I didn't help him, nobody is going to. No strings attached.
> (conversational interview, October 26, 1982)

> We is all in the same shit. You see yourself in these fish. They're scared. Pretend to be tough but still scared. I'm not blind. I'm human too. I'm tough too, but a pussy cat when I see a really young boy looking around. No place to go. They's just cruisin' for a bruisin'
> (conversational interview, October 3, 1982)

All subjects were asked to evaluate the involvements of significant others who encouraged them to become hustlers. During interviews all subjects were provided with a lengthy list of possible significant sponsors or tutors. They were asked to rate perceptions and involvements in terms of simple percentages. For example, all were asked the following: "What percentage of boys become prostitutes because of their involvements with older heterosexual adults?" Individual responses for each question were averaged out and compared with all other boys. In addition to simple percentages, Table 3 includes actual involvements as reported by all thirty-three boys. The perceptions of representatives of agencies, who interact routinely with street hustlers, are inconsistent with those general projections and actual reported involvements of boys. What appears noteworthy is the degree to which social workers and police officers implicate others in this process of becoming a hustler, notably adults, pimps or homosexuals. For instance, police officers indicate that newcomers become involved in prostitution primarily because of their contacts with adult homosexuals who exploit them. Boys, on the other hand, are quick to attribute their involvements in prostitution to friendship ties with other boys. As will be elaborated in chapter six, the interpretations held by police officers have serious implications for social control.

In brief, we have explored the social organization of street relations as a context in which learning to become a prostitute occurs. In the following section we analyze the substance of what is transmitted in these encounters.

Table 3
Variations in Perceptions Among Agency Representatives and Boys Regarding the Involvement of Significant Others
(and Actual Involvement as Reported by Boys)

Significant Others as Tutors/Instructors	Boys (%)	Social Workers (%)	Police Officers (%)	Actual Involvements Reported by Boys
Street Hustler: friend	80	20	10	23
Street Hustler: acquaintance	15	10	5	7
Other Newcomers	—	20	—	2
Pimps	—	20	25	
Adults: homosexual	5	20	50	
Adults: heterosexual	—	10	10	
Total	100	100	100	33

HUSTLING AS A PERSPECTIVE:
EMERGING CULTURAL ORIENTATIONS

Hustling, as a generalized frame of reference, emerges as a result of effective and continued interactions newcomers experience with more seasoned colleagues. Newcomers learn a pragmatic orientation to survival. A hustling framework becomes a method of making sense of, and coping with realities of the immediate environment. Hustling structures, and is structured by, the nature of experiences and relationships. General propositions related to street activities, rules, and roles serve to classify information. Hustling, as a form of symbolism denoting words and objects that have particular references to survival, allows boys to locate themselves in reference to available options. Hustling refers to more than a means of making "quick cash"; it symbolically incorporates a common way of life (Prus and Irini, 1980: 207) or world vision.

As a perspective, hustling is a set of concepts which can be easily manipulated in order to control definitions of the situation. Seasoned boys attempt to project authority over newcomers and clients alike by ceremoniously parading a number of hustling attributes. This enables them to transcend situational features by relating them to a broader context. A particular picture of reality is advanced for buttressing their *status quo*. As a motivation, hustling is bifurcated to include immediate and ultimate means and ends, which can be used to legitimate activities and identities. By retracing their street experiences, boys justify hustling according to the following reasons: satisfying relationships, sense of belonging, elements of danger, demands for services, and the economic rewards. But most importantly, boys single out the valued role of a hustler as a powerful influence which gives their street status a sense of integrity. The nascent formation of a hustling identity marks a decisive phase in street socialization. Although this justification is admittedly tautological, it is not without meaning for these boys. That is, the assertion, "I hustle because I'm a hustler", is significant because this justification acts as a mechanism which signals to others and to themselves a commitment to a constellation of street values.

Hustling values are consequences of past accomplishments. Newcomers incorporate these values as rules.

What then are these rules that extol the values of hustling? Within the normative framework of hustling, there are two kinds of rules: generally accepted guidelines that are applicable to all contexts of the street, and more specific situationally-defined norms of conduct. Boys distinguish rules according to the generalized notions of "street justice". For example, informing the police of the identities and activities of other hustlers calls for extreme violence. But, the client is often disciplined by disparaging comments and mild censure.

Specifically, a hustling orientation consists of the following three specific values and their attendant rules of behaviour: the ethos of individualism, themes of survival, and a "game" perspective. An omnipresent ideology of individualism pervades street hustling relations. According to this individualistic and self-oriented perspective, a newcomer learns that, as a hustler, he is his "main man" and is forever "looking out for number one". He is expected to take pride in his own independence. Hustlers engage in cooperative ventures only if they are satisfied that two conditions are minimally met: that loyalty is secured, and that the probability of immediate and personal advantage exists. Even in these collective practices, cynicism prevails as they learn to expect very little from others. The following are statements boys offer in explaining this individualism:

> You always need buddies. But you know, they'll sell you out. What I learned is that everybody's out to shaft you. You get ready to stick it to them. You gotta stay alive.
>
> (Sandy, No. 8; informal conversation, Nov. 21, 1982)

> You're always looking out for number one. That's the most important rule. After you do that, you can party with other guys.
>
> (Sylvester, No. 15, private interview, December 23, 1982)

> My friend taught me how to swim. When you make it on your own, then you're a real hustler. Don't get me wrong, you still like your friends. But they're swimming too.
>
> (Ken, private interview, January 12, 1983)

The above comments on individualism are related to notions of survival. The theme of survival is consistently repeated in interactions on the street. Within this discourse of survival, boys continually talk about money and street wisdom. Money is viewed as a powerful and positive reinforcement as well as an ongoing rationalization. "Fast money" assumes an exaggerated significance. Aside from the immediate benefits they associate with money, such as partying, drugs, alcohol, and a lavish consumerism, money also serves to determine friendship patterns, status and respect. Sandy (No. 8) elaborates:

> Money talks loud. You do it for the money. If you got no bread, nobody wants to hang around with you. But you blow it fast. I take cabs everywhere, splash it on records, maybe restaurants, you know, booze, you name it, for my buddies you know.
>
> (conversational interview, November 21, 1982)

Newcomers learn that to be a hustler, they must be "street smart", that is, alert and resourceful. They must be prepared to take advantage of or seize upon any opportunity that offers a "fast buck". By being constantly "on the prowl", there is little separation between work and leisure. Newcomers are taught to acquire a constant interest in street opportunities and a curiosity about street knowledge. Carmichael (1975) describes this street knowledge as information on criminal behaviour, street expectations, and clients. Stan (No.

12) expands on this issue:

> A hustler's gotta be smart. Phoney names. If you're not smart,
> you're stupid. You move around. See what's doing. Check it out.
>   (private interview, October 15, 1982)

A "smart hustler" presents himself to newcomers as a tough-minded oppor-
tunist who lives on his wits and avoids the humiliation of a regular job. One
possible reason for the pre-eminence of this trait is its scope for opportunities,
as indicated by Karl's explanation:

> You see, a smart hustler checks out his trick. His eyes are always
> moving around. He's ready to score something. So when the sucker,
> a dummy, leaves the hustler maybe for a second alone in his pad,
> the kid's going to swipe, maybe a wallet or maybe a watch. That's
> why he's there in the first place.
>   (private interview, April 21, 1983)

According to these boys, learning to be smart requires coolness and tough-
ness. Lyman and Scott, (1970: 145) defines coolness as:

> the capacity to execute physical acts, including conversation, in a
> concerted smooth, self-controlled fashion in risky situations, or to
> maintain affective detachment during the course of encounters
> involving considerable emotion.

Coolness on the street refers to the boy's ability to maximize gain and minimize effort while structuring relations in a way that impresses favourably. With
this "cool" orientation, newcomers are encouraged to adopt a presentist attitude. Presentism is the lack of perseverance in the pursuit of long term projects (Cusson, 1983: 126, 164). Newcomers learn to orient their lives to the
immediate pleasures of the present. This existential approach may, however,
be a realistic appraisal of their predicament given the uncertainties about the
future directions of their lives.

Violence is also part of a newcomer's growing repertoire of "cool" techniques. Hustlers consider fighting as a legitimate technique for resolving disputes on the street. A more extreme example of the use of violence is
explained by one inveterate street hustler:

Like, you're not at church now. Everybody squares off. This ass hole
was, you know, flexing his muscle. I didn't know him. So like, he's
flexing. He's calling. So I thumped him. When he was down, I hit
him harder. It's part of life here. That's all. Don't get mad, just get
even. Even the score.
> (Sonny, No. 11, conversational interview, October 28, 1982)

Lastly, a game-oriented perspective is another salient feature of the socialization of newcomers. Essentially, games make apprenticeship more exciting and pleasurable. Games are useful in sustaining the involvements of newcomers with more seasoned hustlers. In addition to acquiring money, hustling offers a degree of entertainment. A newcomer learns that survival is entrenched in this orientation. It is, therefore, fair game to "take the edge" by altering the rules. That is, as long as other players are considered "marks" or "tricks", hustlers can be innovative in this game of adventure. Images of play predominate, especially when older hustlers celebrate their success or "scores" with their newcomers. In the course of these interactions, the latter appear all too willing to learn how to play the game of survival.

Aside from reinforcing consensus, the view of hustling as a game serves to protect the identity of hustlers against possible spoilage. Lofland (1969: 13) suggests that games are used by actors to defend themselves against mistrusted and suspicious others. Hustling provides newcomers with a number of masks designed to secure favourable encounters.

MASKS AND MARGINALITY

In many street corner groupings, there are constant displays of heterosexual masculinity (Whyte, 1955: Liebow, 1967; Harris 1973). Youthful associations are obsessed with a heterosexual orientation (Brake, 1980: 132) and portray gays virulently, in jokes and profanities. What is of interest is the penetration of the dominant heterosexual culture on groups which claim to sever ties from conventional society. As Willis (1980: 148) cogently observes: "The dominant ideology does enforce aspects of itself on subordinate behaviour". In their discussion of drift, Matza and Sykes (1961) note that juvenile delinquents do not repudiate the imperatives of the dominant normative system, despite their failure to follow them. Street transients are more integrated into conventional order in regard to homosexuality than is often presumed.

Gay disclosures are not encouraged by seasoned street kids. Newcomers learn that only a small fraction of street kids are involved in selling sex. Of those who are involved in gay sex, the majority deny that they are gay. Moreover, newcomers continually hear boys bragging about luring a homosexual in some alley and turning on him with a couple of friends. Although their buddies provide considerable information about how to manage their discredited identity as prostitutes by alluding to the general framework of a game, they are not taught how to cope with their own homosexual identity.

Newcomers are usually drawn into homophobic associations. Consequently, they learn to deny their gayness and to "pass as straight". The heterosexual mask is assumed by the newcomer not necessarily because he is insecure about his homosexuality but because failure to embrace masks leads to violent encounters with more seasoned straight hustlers. The following excerpts illustrates a gay newcomer's denials of his homosexuality in potentially dangerous situations:

> In this encounter, Roger (No. 23), in front of Bar 2, November 15, 1982 openly admitted he was gay. As we strolled down Main Street we were approached by two boys whom he had recognized. He directed his attention to the older boy who asked him what he was up to. The following brief conversation took place:

Older boy:	So what's doing? Picking up queers?
Roger:	Get lost. That's not my fucking bag.
Older boy:	These fucking queers are all over the place.
Roger:	Yeah.
Older boy:	It pisses me off. I'd like to get a broom and slam it up their asses.
Roger:	That's cool.
Older boy:	Who's the shit with you, a queer or something?
Roger:	Just a friend. You don't have to be a queer to hang around here.
Older boy:	Sure. Catch you later, girls! [left laughing]

The above illustrates an extremely problematic situation: gay newcomers may not fully subscribe to hustling and yet be required to pass as straight. They find it painfully difficult to adjust to the expectations of straight street hustlers. The suggestion that these boys have no conception of themselves as homosexual (Reiss, 1961: 63) is not supported by our data. In private discussions, boys openly admit their homosexuality but realize that denials are necessary at this stage of their street involvements. During this initial stage, gay newcomers are confronted with a limited reference group of straight hustlers. Once gay youths move beyond these associations and "turfs", into a more congenial environment, disclosures are less threatening. Even in gay neighbourhoods, the street is not the most appropriate forum for disclosures, especially with the decline of gay cruising on the street and the growing fears about acquired immune deficiency syndrome (A.I.D.S.). The anonymity of street contacts remains a potential liability for disclosures. Heterosexuality is staged by boys who become increasingly proficient in manipulating appearances. By disguising their homosexuality they minimize the social risks concomitant with disclosures. The game perspective provides a framework for disavowing any negative labels.

Gay youngsters, who follow the routings of gay tutors, pay less attention to the interpretations of straight hustlers. In general, the admission of homosexuality is usually delayed until newcomers discover supportive relationships. Disavowals are more strident by boys who consider themselves straight and by boys who belong to a tighter street reference group. The importance of these denials is succinctly stated by Sam, (No. 7):

> Listen man, I'm just trying to make it here. Me and my buddies aren't queers. No way. Anybody says so, including you gets his eyes poked out. I don't do any of their shit. Let's get that straight—I'm good only for a blow—they go down on me. I screw more broads than Jack the Ripper. Do it for the money, that's it. I'll bash his fucking head in if the goof thinks I'm queer. Just a fucking game.
> (private interview, November 23, 1982)

Additionally, newcomers learn to project hard luck stories to social workers. They misrepresent themselves to the police as victims exploited by adult homosexuals. They also lie about their age and experience to clients in the hope of increasing their fees for service.

This game is ordered by-means of a vocabulary that newcomers acquire, which is grounded in a general street argot. Language, as Berger and Luckmann (1967) describe, is any sign that typifies experience. Street vocabularies become expressions of their knowledge base. A street argot signals to other hustlers the level of street affiliation. An argot reaffirms to newcomers themselves their growing commitment to hustling. Their language disguises the game to be played from outsiders. But, similar means of expression do not necessarily imply a tightly cohesive social organization or rigid collectivity of a gang structure. Nevertheless, the data indicate considerable support for the assertion that newcomers interpret relationships according to a common hustling perspective. Consider, for example, the following comments by both a defiantly straight and a gay prostitute, respectively, which reflect a typical interpretation of this game orientation:

> The game is to fake it. You're told how to con your mark—any mark. All of life is a game. It's no different. For me, everything is a hustle.
>
> (Stan, No. 12; conversational interview October 14, 1982)

> What I teach my chicks is that everything's a circus —a big game. In a circus you got clowns and tricks too. It's the same shit here. Like, kids got to pick the game up fast, 'cause it' s no matter where you go.
>
> (Rocky, No. 21; conversational interview December 11, 1982)

HUSTLING AS ACTIVITY

Becoming a hustler refers to socially constructed responses to problems street youths confront in their immediate environments. These responses consist of both perspectival and applied approaches. The former is concretized in the latter. As Holzner (1968) notes, orientation precedes experience. Initially, newcomers are exposed to a few general guidelines regarding hustling. With increased hustler-client contacts, however, general street values are subject to negotiation, and are transformed into many situationally-qualified and more clearly enunciated rules.

In general, hustling is a comprehensive term for various street activities. As Carmichael (1975: 140) explains, hustlers are persons who scheme to make money by manipulating impressions of reality, by skillfully appraising and adjusting odds on events of chance, and by providing scarce or illicit services and goods. Essentially, a hustler is a person who endeavours to obtain money outside the conventional world of legitimate work (Horton, 1975: 30; Harris, 1973: 37-38; Allen, 1980). Moreover, Smith and Stephens (1976: 156) argue that hustling, as income-generating behaviour, includes a plethora of "con" games such as panhandling, welfare frauds, shoplifting, stealing, dealing in drugs and stolen goods, and prostitution. During the boy's introduction to the street there does not appear to be strong evidence of task specialization. Twenty-seven boys note that they experimented in other "hustles" while dealing in sex.

On-the-street socialization exposes newcomers to a variety of enterprises. In general, prostitution exists within a dominant hustling perspective. That is, hustling sex is socially learned and subjectively interpreted in a manner that blends consistently well with the fabric of general street hustling. Newcomers strive to define prostitution as an expression of this more favourable larger orientation. Newcomers derive an initial understanding of prostitution from their larger street reference groups to which they relate practically and symbolically. In both private interviews and group discussions boys admit that they are becoming hustlers and not prostitutes. Newcomers view hustling sex not only as a barter of sexual resources, but also as a "scam", "ripoff" or an extortionate transaction. Without these legitimating qualifications, newcomers perceive prostitution as physically and morally disgusting.

During this getting connected stage, there are only a few subjects who restrict their learning to specialized sex hustles alone. In reference to the diversity of hustles, Gary (No. 25) and Steve (No. 13) explain:

> I didn't start shanking. Like, I was a hustler first. I was no whore. I do boosting, copping and stashing hot stuff, too. Like, I hustled any shit. Play the field. Sure I used to spread. Like, on some days I deal dope, I pulled other scores as well.
>
> (private interview, December 18, 1982)

> Giving tail is just another scam you pick up. I followed my pal and ripped off here and there. I went with a rich bitch, not just for the loot but to do a rip-off.
>
> (private interview, October 26, 1982)

Seasoned prostitutes were asked to clarify these hustler-prostitute distinctions. According to gay prostitutes, newcomers assign a distorted sense of importance to hustling primarily because of the close attachments newcomers establish with straight boys. As Graham (No. 28) notes:

> It's not hard to figure these punks out. They say they're hustlers and not prostitutes because they want to be trade. They figure that a prostitute does his thing and lives pretty happy with the money. But, when they say they're hustlers, what they're saying to you is they want to get more than what the sex act is worth. It's like they don't

want the bread, they want the whole fucking bakery.

(private interview, September 17, 1982)

The reasons for selecting prostitution are varied. An analysis of the entry process defies simplistic explanations. According to Akers' (1977) psychological approach, prostitution is better explained by the relative rewards if offers. Most newcomers select prostitution as a result of their immediate needs which include income, adventure, and affection.

The decision to hustle sex is contingent upon options available and the advice proffered by contacts whom they have learned to trust. What emerges out of these relationships is the realization that sex, like many other hustles, can be manipulated to obtain financial rewards. The relationships newcomers develop offer considerable social reinforcement about the use of sex as a marketable commodity. Undoubtedly, this instrumental gain is a major inducement for boys protect boys from negative imputations of homosexuality. Newcomers are also reminded to distance themselves from clients by treating them derisively. Considerable time is spent detailing the physical violence inflicted on recalcitrant clients. As one seasoned hustler describes tersely, "If you can't trick your mark, then you mark your trick". In other words, it is a commonly accepted practice to treat the client as a "sucker" or "target" who, even in the best of times, deserves to be treated with disdain. Violent retaliations against non compliant clients is not only expected but perceived as a collective response, which other hustlers feel compelled to enact. According to seasoned gay prostitutes, clients are disliked by newcomers because they remind boys of their own repressed homosexuality. This conclusion is shared by three clients interviewed who point out that intimacy is too threatening to the fragile identities of these boys. As one married, fifty-nine-year-old client describes:

> They have a fierce and demented contempt for us. I've been going out with them for about ten years and I always hear these denials. They murder you, if you act in a stupid way. You can't disagree. You have to let them come out by themselves.
>
> (Charles, private interview, December 15, 1982)

There is another noteworthy group—boys who develop bonds with older gay prostitutes. Unlike newcomers who are instructed by older homophobic hustlers, these boys are exposed to a more elaborate training. They acquire a more specific set of instructions regarding client-management, diversity of sex-

ual services, fees, hygiene, grooming, and locations. The following segments
of interviews with Robert (No. 19) and George (No. 26) illustrate this:

> You hear from other kids, the punks, stupid things like to get ahead
> you gotta give head; it's not what you know, but who you blow.
> That's stupid. They're just clowns. For me, its learning a trade. I
> don't like that word but your hammer is your tool. You learn how to
> use it.
>
> (private interview, September 2, 1982)

> You learn how to spot your trick, how to stand, make the eyes
> work, and strut your stuff. My lover was my teacher. No monkey
> business. How to handle your basket. We practised.
>
> (private interview, December 17, 1982)

Regardless of these gay or "straight" distinctions, all newcomers learn a number of fundamental techniques. All newcomers are encouraged to adopt an
emotionally detached demeanour with clients. By objectifying sexual acts they
convey a style that is consistent with street hustling. Boys distance themselves
form clients by withholding information about their identities.

The above sections do not suggest that a cultural framework of prostitution does not exist. Rather, prostitution is overshadowed by a hustling perspective. Prostitution, for these newcomers, is not a serious business around
which they organize their lives. In general, the learning of hustling values hin-
ders, as much as it assists the development of a career in prostitution.

REVIEWING THE FIRST ACT

The actual performance of sexual services constitutes a basic experiential
stage in becoming a prostitute. It is in their personal encounters with clients
that newcomers are able to assess the adequacy of acquired perspectival and
technical approaches to hustling.

According to all boys, all other events in this process of becoming a prostitute pale in significance to the first act of prostitution. There are two reasons
boys cite in explaining their abilities to recall vividly their first paid sexual
exchanges. Firstly, they allude to the intense anxieties, replete with insecurity
and fear, they experienced during this act. And secondly, boys spend considerable time celebrating this accomplishment with their friends. Insecurity and

fear are prominent features of these recollections. Unlike other hustles, prostitution generally requires newcomers to be alone with strangers whom they have learned to treat derisively. Newcomers remain confused primarily because their rudimentary knowledge overlooks many significant details about the sex act and client management. Although they have been taught by older hustlers to shield information about themselves from clients, newcomers find it extremely difficult to act with a degree of confidence. Commenting on the inadequate instructions he received, Stu (No. 14) describes:

> What the older kids tell me was crap. These assholes don't got all the answers. Like, they think they're smart. Like, they go, like go "sell you meat". Nobody says nothin' about like, how you get your head together. You know, in gear. I was really out of it in my first go at it. A bit of a basket case.
>
> (private interview, September 19, 1982)

In general, anxieties about self-image are not readily overcome in instances where clients respond favourably and sensitively. Reid (No. 17) explains:

> We checked in at a hotel. I got peanuts—no guff, thirty smackers only. It was a bad trip 'cause the crazy guy was really decent, like pretty neat. This shook the shit out of me. He wasn't supposed to be that nice. That's hard to handle.
>
> (private interview, September 24, 1982)

Boys who are adamant about their heterosexuality express disorientation especially when they discover homosexual activity to be less displeasing than originally anticipated. Consider Steve's (No. 13) reactions:

> The bozo went down on me. I don't know if it's because of the dope we did or what. But you know, it was O.K. I was ready to kick his balls in, you know. Instead, I was fooling around too. I don't know if I should bash his head in if I see him or what? I'm no fag—I just don't know why I got into it like that.
>
> (private interview, October 26,1982)

Newcomers who venture out with expectations of restricting their services to passive fellatio alone soon find themselves deriving some pleasure from receiving and giving stimulation. As one regular prostitute recalls:

> It was different. I got fifty bucks. The goof took pictures. You know,
> he cleaned my clock a couple of times. Shit! I cleaned his too. Can
> you believe it. That's odd!
>
> (Private interview, October 17, 1982)

This evidence is further corroborated by accounts offered by clients who detail reciprocal satisfaction in sexual involvements.

In addition, clients and regular prostitutes cite the offensive demeanour towards clients and the ardent declarations of heterosexuality as reflective of the fears and uncertainties newcomers experience during the first act. In private interviews, newcomers frequently express the following fears: excessive generosity to their clients, apprehension by police, and violence by clients. Evidently, only two subjects mention that as newcomers they threatened to use physical force on their clients. In both of these cases clients refused to accept the boys heterosexual claims.

Aside from the emotional impact of the first act, details are also easily remembered because newcomers frequently reconstruct this event for their older friends. Details are ceremoniously paraded and earnings from these acts are flashed as evidence of having proved their mettle. Newcomers who have successfully passed this trial are accorded with a different role. By moving from observers to participants, newcomers don the mantle of a hustler. The following sanguine remarks are made by recent arrivals to the street after their first paid sexual encounter:

> Man, I made it. I'm in the big leagues.
>
> (Adam, No. 1, October 7, 1982)

> I felt good. No more a fish. Now I'm a shark.
>
> (Albert, No. 2; November 13, 1982)

> It was better than passing at school.
>
> (Alex, No. 3; November 30, 1982)

> After that, I walked around like a big stiff. Who says
> I'm not tough.
>
> (Andy, No. 6; December 4, 1982)

Nonetheless, the impact of the first act of street prostitution is contingent upon the newcomer's subjective identification with his emerging role. What is important is the conception newcomers create for themselves as a result of this act and its attendant consequences. The development of a hustler's identity is related to the meanings newcomers assign to such concepts as prostitution and homosexuality. These meanings are directly influenced by the stock of meanings generally available to them in their immediate environment. Consequently, the term hustler is not intended to be an ontological expression of their essential condition. Rather, it refers to a limited aspect of the newcomer's self-image. We, therefore, cannot affirm that this first act alone or, for that matter, subsequent acts of prostitution create an all-encompassing identity. Likewise, the acquisition of a certain identity is not always consistent with images appropriated for newcomers by their peers. This is clearly demonstrated in cases where newcomers pass as "tough straights", but privately project their first act of prostitution in a manner that is incompatible with their friends' expectations. In all situations observed and reported, newcomers publicly adopt a view of this act completely within a "hustling" perspective. Prostitution signifies weakness whereas hustling denotes cleverness, assertiveness and manipulation. This identity-assuming process emerges from an interplay of the individual and his immediate audiences. Identity consists of multiple roles that change according to an actor's social location. Identities are largely shaped by attending the responses of influential others.

A striking difference exists between the identities developed by boys who have strong emotional bonds to a few close friends and that of boys who enjoy a wide array of weak relations. With the former category, newcomers carefully retrace details of the first act by locating this sexual behaviour in a more acceptable street framework. Denials of homosexual and prostitute identities are based on a desire to impress close friends of the immutability of their hustling orientation. These newcomers hurry back to boys with whom they share living arrangements and leisure pursuits in order to collaborate stories of their hustling successes. Their reconstruction of the first act is replete with accounts of excessive violence, denials of intercourse, and denigration of clients; "closure" plays a significant role for straight boys. Consider, for example, the following comments by Sonny (No. 11) at his flat in the company of his two room-mates:

> It made me puke. I didn't like it. Who does? You see, I'm straight. I told the jerk I was straight—no monkey business or I'll shove your head through the windshield. No way he's gonna think I'm queer. The goof deserves to have his hose cut off.
>
> (October 27, 1982)

Later, while alone out on a streetcorner, Sonny offered the following interpretation:

The money wasn't bad—twenty bucks for the throw. The guy was all right. He told me a lot of good things. I learned a lot from him. He was cool. I didn't know what to do and he helped me out. I was a bit scared. He helped me out anyway. A nice guy. I don't mind getting it on with him again.

(October 27, 1982)

When queried about these inconsistencies he was embarrassed and simply retorted, "It's a big game, that's all." He was not willing to pursue it further and felt increasingly uncomfortable that he already provided too much information which he feared could easily be misinterpreted as a violation of a loyalty to his friends. The general threat inherent in perceived discordance is given pointed expression by still another comment he expressed the next day.

You know, I gotta live with these jerks. They talk garbage. You know, I'm more scared of them than the tricks. I just give them what they wanna hear. They'll never know how I really think anyhow.

(private interview, October 28, 1982)

This juxtaposition of competing value systems is articulated by newcomers who concur with homophobic evaluations of older boys from whom they routinely receive generous assistance. Scott (No. 9) indicates that heterosexuality dominates the street relations and any emphasis on positive aspects of prostitution is subject to ridicule:

Your buddies get pissed off if you say your trick was O.K. They laugh and say you're a fag. You bullshit them. You tell 'em you went for ten minutes only. My first go, I was gone for two hours. I didn't tell 'em that. They'll punch my lights out 'cause if you're, you know, gay or something, they'll get pissed off.

(private interview, November 27, 1982)

Insecurity is further exacerbated by the problematic reactions of clients. It would be more preferable for these newcomers to have clients behave less compliantly and more abusively towards them. According to newcomers, negative responses from clients guarantee further disaffection of homosexual clients. In subsequent exchanges with fellow hustlers, newcomers feel compelled to distort the nature of actual interactions with clients. In private interviews, however, newcomers indicate little or no displeasure with cooperative clients. They conceal favourable assessments from their street associates who typically impute debased identities to newcomers who fail to discredit clients.

In contrast, there is another category of newcomers differentiated by all street hustlers, clearly on the basis of negatively evaluated attributes. This group consists of gay newcomers who resist the ascribed identity of a "straight hustler" in favour of their achieved identity as a male prostitute. Their differential commitment to general hustling activities represent an important factor in setting themselves apart from street hustlers. These gay newcomers have the following characteristics: pejorative treatment by "straight" hustlers, an emerging sensitivity to gay issues, and a growing attenuation of relationships with street hustlers. Gary (No. 25) who presents himself as a sage critic of peer pressures on the street, describes the confusion newcomers experience:

> The thing you gotta remember in your study is that these kids like to talk about their first time. But they can't discuss it with their street pals. So what can they do? It's awkward. They're nervous. Then they find out it's a big game they have to play, not with the trick but with their friends. A big scam. All these fresh faces play it. It's typical until they move on, on their own.
>
> (private interview, December 19, 1982)

Many gay newcomers disagree with their street colleagues about the following issues: homosexual identity, client management, and prostitution as a viable hustle. According to older gay prostitutes, street comer associations do not help newcomers define themselves as gay. Within a matter of several weeks, gay newcomers perceive Main Street as an ill-defined "no man's land". This hiding place offers little escape from recriminations. By remaining more isolated from street reference groups, they become less vulnerable to negative evaluations. During their first acts of prostitution, they engage in more blatant violations of hustling norms. In these encounters not only do they seek assistance from clients, but they set themselves apart from street kids by projecting themselves as gay prostitutes, a generally discredited identity on Main Street. Unlike "straight" newcomers who allude to an inventory of street hustles, gay newcomers primarily focus on the sex hustle. This clash of values further weakens their attachments to other street hustlers. Consequently, they avoid conflict by finding streetcorners or "sites" that are less threatening. These movements enhance their freedom to choose social relations. For gays, relations grounded in the streetcorners of Main Street are less emotionally supportive than those available in spaces adjacent to gay facilities.

Despite the above distinctions, there is an overwhelming degree of consensus regarding the first act. All boys perceive the first paid encounter as rewarding financially and emotionally. For example, all boys indicate that their clients paid considerable attention to them. Clients took the initiative in carefully instructing newcomers about price, locations, and specific techniques. In addition, the data suggest a theme that has been overlooked in studies of prostitution—the impact of clients as agents of socialization. Additionally, very little effort has been made to examine the role of clients in generating the newcomer's sense of identity. In private interviews, clients suggest that many newcomers are limited by their ignorance. Clients discourage furtive encounters in alleys and encourage boys to meet them at their residence, advise them to concentrate on task requirements, and reinforce a more positive orientation to prostitution.

The following excerpt from field notes outlines Allen's (No. 5) first act of prostitution:

> At approximately 10:30 p.m., I was sitting with Allen on the steps outside an office building across the street from Bar B. Throughout the afternoon Allen (No. 5) talked about wanting to "score" his first trick. Apparently his friends were becoming annoyed with his freeloading. He was given an ultimatum by his best friend either to share in rent and groceries or move out of the apartment.

> For approximately fifteen minutes Allen was eagerly peering into a couple of slowly moving automobiles. Finally, a driver of a late-model sports car smiled and motioned to him. He sauntered towards the car, now parked on curb lane, motioned to the driver to wait and quickly returned to me. I was approximately ten feet away from the vehicle. I noticed a well-dressed, slightly built man in his early thirties.

> Allen to L.V.:   Here goes nothing. I really don't know what the shit I'm supposed to do. I guess I'll roll with the punches. Wish me luck.

> Before leaving with his prospective client, Allen arranged to meet me at restaurant C, which was located a block away. I observed Allen and the driver engage in an extended conversation. As the vehicle sped away, both were smiling.

At approximately midnight Allen entered the restaurant grinning.

Allen: Well I did it. I made it.

Initially Allen was reluctant to discuss the event. He ordered a couple of hamburgers for us.

Allen: Aren't you going to ask how it went?

L.V.:   Sure. Only if you want to talk about it.

Allen: Yeah. No sweat. It's really nuts. When I got into his car he said I was pretty cute. He said he liked my tight jeans.

L.V.:   Do you mind if I write some of this down? You see this is one of the few times that I was around when somebody has gone for the first time.

Allen: No sweat. No names, eh?

L.V.:   Of course. Look at my notes if you want.

Allen: I was pretty stupid 'cause I told him it was my first go. I didn't know how much. So he goes, "what d'ya wanna do." Before we took off he said, "Who's that guy." I told him you're my buddy and I promised you I gotta be back in an hour. He said it was cool, so we drive to a playground.

L.V.:   What about the money?

Allen: You know I almost forgot about it. We rapped about it. He gave me a twenty when it was done. That's not bad for a half hour. He would have given me fifty for all-night. For a twenty, he went down. That's it! A bit of jerking too [hesitated]. Don't tell the other guys I went down too. He was a really together guy. He was probably clean. Listen, don't tell my buddies or they'll probably kick me out.

L.V.:   For what?

Allen: They'll think I'm, you know.

L.V.:   Gay?

Allen: Yeah.

Allen: I really dunno if I am. Maybe, maybe not.

L.V.:   What are going to tell your friends?

Allen: What they dunno won't kill them. No sweat. I won't tell them that I did some poppers with the guy. I'll maybe just say I pulled a blade on a jerk. They like that. That's all. I'll give 'em ten bucks for beer. Keep 'em quiet. No sweat.

(observation notes, October 9, 1982)

This finding is further evidence of a positive attitude towards the initial act which later becomes denigrated for the benefit of street colleagues. Allen felt that he had to impress his close associates by re-casting the above event within a heterosexual framework. Identities became ambiguous or ambivalent as a result of these competing evaluations.

Just as "coming out" does not require homosexual relations, homosexual acts do not necessarily require a homosexual self-identity. For fourteen boys, the first paid sex act occurs at a point in time when there is a growing self-affirmation of a homosexual identity. An equal number of boys, however, do not view themselves as homosexuals. Instead, they invoke a general hustling perspective that safeguards against a devalued homosexual identity.

It is argued that newcomers who interact intimately with other street hustlers are more likely to be preoccupied with staging a heterosexual orientation. They routinely embark on relationships which reinforce positive labelling of "straight" stereotypes. These public expressions of heterosexuality are, however, marred by a steadfast homophobia. According to all seasoned gay prostitutes interviewed, homophobia explains many difficulties newcomers face in coming to terms with prostitution. Their general fear of homosexuality is exaggerated and translated into a fear of being identified as prostitutes. Prostitution, as a specialized hustle emphasizing male sex, leaves open to suspicion claims of heterosexuality. Denials of homosexuality, therefore, require further denials of prostitution. Gay newcomers, on the other hand, do not signify homosexuality as central to the way they organize their prostitution. They have acquired information from their many contacts both on and outside of Main Street, which helps to dispel negative feelings about their identities and activities. Their growing acceptance of their identities as homosexuals contributes to a recognition of prostitution as a viable opportunity for securing an income.

Interpretations of the first act are framed within the context of affiliations. The role of "others" is significant in defining the actor and his activity. The process of interpreting the first act is fundamentally related to the wider social context of colleagues, clients and communities in which newcomers are embedded. The process of assuming a street hustler or prostitute identity is an extension of these social orientations. Newcomers who project a heterosexual orientation are more closely involved in homogeneous street groupings. They know each others' contacts intimately. Gay newcomers, however, associate more loosely with street corner groupings and enjoy a wider variety of relations that are not as spatially located.

Since survival is a central concern for newcomers, these early relationships on the street are fundamentally instrumental. During the initial days on the street all newcomers invest considerable effort in trying to secure resources that range from tangible benefits like food, shelter information, and money to more intangible elements such as companionship and emotional support. Gay newcomers define these street associations as increasingly debilitating. They are deprived of supportive relations to which straight newcomers are usually exposed. Since these relations are not positive sources of companionship, gay newcomers become less dependent upon street hustlers. Gay newcomers strive to develop relationships outside Main Street. Unlike street hustlers who tend to establish relations that are spatially and socially concentrated, gay newcomers seek a greater diversity of acquaintances which provide a far reaching range of information, opportunities and experiences.

More important still, the structure of street relations affects the nature of social control. Newcomers, who are more isolated from informal street associations, are less susceptible to the norms of hustling. In loose peer group associations, social control is fragmented, less consistent and less effective. The imposition of social control is better facilitated in dependency relations.

The nature of associations, combinations of colleagues and friends, and intensity of interpersonal relationships shape the information boys use in interpreting the first act. All newcomers objectify the first act and allude to monetary rewards. Boys who define themselves as "straight" experience more difficulties in sustaining the impersonality of this act. They are quick to express emotions of anger and guilt despite their rhetoric of detachment. On the other hand, gay newcomers develop a "market mentality" towards sex wherein the fear of emotional attachment is less problematic, as long as the sex act remains commercialized.

The relationship between homosexuality and prostitution, therefore, continues to be a focus of sociological investigation. Many studies indicate the significance of homosexuality as basic to an understanding of male prostitution (Reiss, 1961; Harris, 1973; Lloyd 1977; Hoffman, 1979). In these studies however, these links remain conceptually threadbare and are reduced to assumptions derived from prevailing cultural values about homosexuality. Homosexuality is often decontextualized and too readily extricated from male prostitution. In contrast, studies on female prostitution ignore heterosexuality and proceed to examine prostitution in isolation (Gray, 1973; Adler, 1975; Heyl, 1979; Bracey, 1979). With a few notable exceptions (Prus and Irini, 1980), studies of becoming a prostitute often understate complex interactions of a variety of relationships. These limitations result from a failure to direct inquiry into multiple heterosexual and homosexual involvements. As has been demonstrated, these associations facilitate and inhibit decisions regarding homosexual identity alone, shape patterns of opportunities and involvements in getting connected to prostitution.

SUMMARY

In this chapter we have identified a number of "near necessary" (West, 1974) factors that are associated with the process of becoming a hustler. Factors which facilitate the likelihood of becoming a prostitute include both subjective and situational contingencies: identity, relationships, perspectives and activities. An emphasis on the interpretations of these contingencies links our diverse findings. Subjective evaluations vary according to interactions that serve to define and organize the appropriateness of action. Interactions with significant others provide a framework for interpreting the substance and structure of this learning process. Interpretations are influenced by the social organization of information, street relations and emerging cultural values of hustling.

Newcomers avail themselves of opportunities for attaching themselves to the street. From the outset, the newcomer typically makes interpersonal contacts with others in the same situation who help the transition from home life to the street. Friendship and acquaintance-based associations provide many benefits to these urban transients. Information is shared concerning the accessibility of assistance regarding shelter, food, protection from official agencies, and companionship. Less experienced newcomers, therefore, seek the attention of many inviting street groupings. This recruitment enhances an "embeddedness" (Prus and Irini, 1980) on the street. Experienced hustlers orient neophytes to various techniques of survival. Street ties are essential for "learning the ropes" and for developing a repertoire of manipulative skills. The accessibility to various street contacts carries serious implications for the social organization of getting connected. Thus, the nature of relations influences plans of action. Having access to a number of street associations increases the newcomer's exposure to street knowledge relationships generally vary in kind and intensity. There are a number of different and continually intersecting associations. At one extreme, there are interpersonal relations based on friendship. At the other extreme, there are relations based on the acquisition of resources. Although more prevalent than the former, the latter associations tend to be short-lived and loosely bound. Once these immediate instrumental ends are attained, there is no longer the necessity to prolong the relation on a continued basis. Bonds appear and disappear quickly. The content of these interactions are shaped by the immediate issues at hand. Gay newcomers, for example, move beyond these limited street groupings when support is not forthcoming. Gay newcomers become impugned with low moral character in these familiar informal street associations. Thus, they seek more meaningful interactions outside of streetcorner groupings that are dominated by street hustlers.

Conceptually what has been detailed in this chapter is a perspective on social order which depicts newcomers as attending to certain features of their respective affiliations. Upon closer scrutiny, it is evident that participation in different street associations influences this process of getting connected. It is argued that the broader the base from which newcomers operate, the greater the likelihood that prostitution will be pursued as a livelihood. As prostitution becomes less controlled by the assessments of "loose peer clusterings" (West, 1978), newcomers are more able to secure continuity in, and commitment to prostitution.

This chapter highlights the acquisition of a general framework of hustling. This perspective cements disparate accommodations to the street by legitimating the acquisition of income from illicit services. Pragmatism unfolds as a "generic feature" of interactions (Prus, 1984). Newcomers develop attitudes towards immediate issues of survival by alluding to this all encompassing framework of hustling. Table 4 summarizes situational and subjective contingencies which influence movements from conventional lives at home and in school to illegitimate street activities.

Table 4
Becoming a Hustler

Situational Contexts	Subjective Features
A. (i) Circumstances of Dislocation (push/pull pressures)	Street as a Solution
(ii) Paradoxes of Marginality (survival)	Street as a Problem
B. Street Relations	
(i) Exposure and Affiliation (recruitment and training)	Relations as a Solution and the Development of a Hustling Perspective (rules, skills)
C. Activities	
(i) Client/colleagues (outside street involvements)	Relations as a Problem
(ii) Involvement (on/outside the street)	Ongoing assessment of associations; (identity paradoxes; prostitution and homosexuality; and prostitution and other hustles)

The general sociological paradigm of this chapter stresses the interactionist aspects of human behaviour. Newcomers shape their responses by taking into consideration differential expectations of those with whom they interact. By tracing various social environments, we seek to determine how the acquisition of thought is interpreted as meaningful. This processual model of becoming a prostitute highlights those interactions in which identities are built, sustained and translated into action. An analysis of significant interactions and their reactions provides insights into socialization. The newcomer's response to social, economic and cultural influences shape subsequent involvements on the street.

This emphasis on subjective interpretations does not underscore the importance of structural perspectives. Interactional contexts of affiliative relationships negotiate larger environmental influences. Such informative structuralist notions of marginality regarding disadvantaged youths, as well as the ideological underpinnings of heterosexuality, permeate situational exchanges, vocabularies, and activities of newcomers. Prostitution and homosexuality are not alien to larger structural concerns. But, the developmental process of moving from conventional norms to illegitimate occupations is not fully captured by structuralist perspectives (Heyl, 1979: 25).

As an initial stage, getting connected influences subsequent processes. As a general contingency, this stage informs newcomers of what is available and prepares them either to continue or to drop out. In this stage, actors routinely ground themselves in general street values. They develop techniques for projecting themselves as street hustlers. Although hustlers are the subject of this chapter, they are examples of a much larger group of actors—marginal people in marginal work. A theme which not only recurs in this chapter but is also corroborated in subsequent chapters, concerns the limited and conflictive nature of relations in marginal involvements such as work.

REFERENCES

Adler, F., 1975. *Sisters In Crime*, New York: McGraw Hill.

Allen, D., 1980. "Young Male Prostitutes: A Psychosocial Study" *Archives of Sexual Behaviour* 9 (5), (Oct.): 339-426.

Akers, R., 1977. *Deviant Behaviour: A Social Learning Approach*, Belmont: Wadsworth.

Becker, H., 1963. *Outsiders*, New York: Free Press.

Bracey, D., 1979. *Baby-Pros: Preliminary Profiles of Juvenile Prostitutes*, New York: John Jay Press.

Brake, M., 1980. *The Sociology of Youth Culture and Youth Subculture*, London: Routledge and Kegan Paul.

Carmichael, B., 1975. "Youth Crime in Urban Communities—A Description Analysis of Street Hustlers and Their Crimes", *Crime and Delinquency*, 21 (2): 139-148.

Clairmont, D. and Magill, D., 1971. "Nova Scotia Black: Marginal People in a Depressed Region", in Gallagher, J. and Lambert, R. (eds.), *Social Process and Institution: The Canadian Case,* Toronto: Holt, Rinehart and Winston.

Cusson, M., 1983. *Why Delinquency?*, Toronto: University of Toronto Press.

Fanon, F., 1968. *The Wretched of the Earth*, New York: Grove Press.

Gouldner, A., 1960. "The Norm of Reciprocity", *American Sociological Review*, 25 (April): 161-178.

Gray, D., 1973. "Turning Out: A Study of Teenage Prostitution", *Urban Life and Culture*, 1 (4) (Jan.): 401-426.

Harris, M., 1973. *The Dilly Boys*, London: Groom Helm.

Heyl, B., 1979. *The Madam As Entrepreneur*, New Brunswick: Transaction.

Hoffman, M., 1979. "The Male Prostitute", in Levine, M. (ed.), *Gay Men: The Sociology of Male Homosexuality*, New York: Harper and Row.

Hollingshead, A.B., 1975. *Elmtown's Youth and Elmtown Revisited*, New York: John Wiley.

Holzner, B., 1968. *Reality Construction in Society*, Cambridge: Schenkman.

Horton, J., 1975. "Time and Cool People" in Hernslin, J. (ed.), *Introducing Sociology*, New York: Free Press.

Leyton, E., 1979. *The Myth of Delinquency*, Toronto: McClelland and Stewart.

Lee, J.A., 1982. "Three Paradigms of Childhood", *Canadian Review of Sociology and Anthropology* 19 (4): 591-608.

Liebow, E., 1967. *Tally's Corner*, Boston: Little, Brown.

Lloyd, R., 1977. *Playland*, London: Blond and Briggs.

Lofland, J., 1969. *Deviance and identity*, Englewood Cliffs: Prentice-Hall.

Lyman, S. and Scott, M., 1970. *A Sociology of the Absurd*, New York: Appleton-Century-Crofts.

Matza, 1970. "Techniques of Delinquency" in Wolfgang, M., Savitz, L. and Johnston, N. (eds.), *Sociology of Crime and Delinquency*, New York: Wiley.

Matza, D. and Sykes, G., 1961. "Juvenile Delinquency and Subterranean Values", *American Sociological Review* 26.

Prus, R., 1984. "Anthropological and Sociological Approaches to Deviance: An Ethnographic Prospect", Paper presented at Deviance in a Cross-Cultural Conference, Waterloo: June.

Prus, R. and Irini, S., 1980. *Hookers, Rounders and Desk Clerks: The Social Organization of the Hotel Community*, Toronto: Gage.

Reiss, A., 1961. "The Social Organization of Queers and Peers", *Social Problems* 9 (Fall): 102-120.

Smith, R.B. and Stephens, R.C., 1976. "Drug Use and Hustling: A Study of Their Relationships", *Criminology* 4 (2).

West, W.G., 1974. "Serious Thieves: Lower Class Adolescent Males in a Short-Term Deviant Occupation" unpublished doctoral dissertation, Northwestern University.

West, W.G., 1978. "The Short-Term Careers of Serious Thieves", *Canadian Journal of Criminology* 20 (2): 169-190.

Whyte, W.F., 1955. *Street Corner Society*, Chicago: University of Chicago Press.

Willis, P., 1980. *Learning to Labour*, Westmead, Farnborough: Gower.

CHAPTER 21
Youth Gangs: Criminals, Thrillseekers or the New Voice of Anarchy?

KEVIN FOWLER

Canadians have the dubious pleasure of watching criminal trends in the United States escalate into major law enforcement problems. In Los Angeles, California, despite an ever-increasing anti-gang patrol, crime associated with youth gangs comes in like the flooding tide of the Pacific, Black, Hispanic, White, Asian—gangs fester in an endless cycles of violence and crime.

While receiving a great deal of media attention, Los Angeles is not alone when considering the youth gang phenomenon. New York City, Toronto, Chicago, plus many other major urban centres, experience gang problems to varying degrees. Small towns and suburbs are, by the same token, susceptible to gang activity. No geographic location is immune and no socio-economic class is precluded from being the source of gang deviance. Unpredictable random violence, vandalism and crime among youth gangs is no longer limited to the occasional isolated incident, but has become an alarmingly regular statistic. As a consequence of a typically 1980s fascination with convenience and speed, the gangs have even popularized a term: the drive-by shooting.

While experiencing unprecedented growth in the last two decades, youth gangs are not new. As far back as 1827, New York City Police had been experiencing problems with organized youth gangs in the area now known as lower Manhattan Island. In the 1950s, typified by a "West Side Story" mentality, fighting gangs massed for large scale rumbles. Around the same time, England's "Teddy Boys", smartly-dressed thugs, roved in packs and harassed unwitting citizens. Later in England, Mods and Rockers formed rival, distinct groups and battled each other for territory and kicks. Pill-popping Mods, clad

"Youth Gangs: Criminals, Thrillseekers or the New Voice of Anarchy?" was reproduced by permission of Kevin Fowler and the RCMP Gazette, Vol. 51 (7 and 8). Copyright © 1989 by the RCMP Gazette.

in army fatigue jackets and riding scooters, fought leather-clad, motorcycle-riding Rockers.

In the 1960s, gang behaviour appeared to experience a sharp decline. Theorists have attributed this to the maelstrom of political, cultural and social upheaval of the time. The peace crusade, the civil rights movement, Viet Nam, the hippie counterculture and the growth of politically militant organizations were believed to have provided youth with sufficient distractions to account for the curtailed gang activity in that decade. Others have argued that this decrease in activity was simply the result of a preoccupied media, and that the problem still persisted.

The 1970s saw the resumption of intensified gang activity, and not exclusively within large urban centres; the suburbs were also alive with the symptoms of disaffected youth.

In a book detailing gang activity in a suburban area. The Losers[1] presents a case study in social deviance. The book recounts the growing tension between the community, police and a youth gang, tagged "The Losers". In a predominantly affluent area, a group of misfits meld together in response to what they feel is an oppressive ruling class. Despite community outcry and an intensified enforcement campaign by local police, the gang grows and becomes more active and violent. The civic pressure only "contributed to a feeling of group identity...an esprit de corps developed that made the group even more attractive to participants and potential participants"[2]

"The Losers" situation arose from factors that still exist in many communities. Kids from lower income families, living in areas of a community that are easily identified as being less prosperous, experience prejudice as early as elementary school. This may not occur all the time, but the cruelty of the playground is legendary. When the youths become older, these feelings of inadequacy and isolation grow into acts of vandalism, harassment of citizens, and eventually bombing vehicles belonging to the chief of police and the high school vice-principal. Shorewood Heights (a fictitious name) is a quiet, clean, prosperous place, but every community has its troublemakers. Because of poor foresight and analysis, the situation is allowed to escalate, and the gang's rebellion is fuelled by the very measures undertaken to control the problem.

Inner-city gangs are formed out of the same dissatisfaction with what is perceived as the existing power structure. Prospective gang members are usually disenchanted with the educational system, have been given little guidance or encouragement, or can see no future for themselves as academics. Youths may join gangs for identity or recognition; an opportunity to attain status and respect impossible outside the gang. Some perceive themselves as warriors or soldiers defending their neighbourhood or turf. Others may join for protection from rival gangs, a guarantee of support in case of attack, and retaliation against any transgressors. Lacking perhaps a stable home environment, other youths may seek the sense of family and cohesiveness that a gang provides. Youths may also be intimidated into joining, particularly if a gang is at war and recruiting is fierce.

Gang organization, depending on the level of sophistication, is much the same as a corporation or an outlaw motorcycle gang, with a hierarchy of hard-core members (senior partners), underlings (associates) and aspiring candidates (trainees). Initiation will usually involve some sort of action by the prospective member to prove his/her mettle to the rest of the gang. "Jumping in" involves several gang members physically beating the hopeful, testing the individual's courage and fighting prowess. The prospect may also have to commit a criminal act as a way of gaining acceptance of other members.

A disturbing trend among more advantaged youth is also emerging. No longer the sole property of the poor (if such a distinction ever existed), youth gangs of relatively affluent kids are becoming more active. Rather than a means of physical survival, some gangs are being formed along ideological lines. In Californian stoner gangs, members are linked by common bonds; abuse of drugs; alcohol and an anti-establishment stand reminiscent of the 1960s hippie counter-culture, but less inclined towards peaceful ideals.

Some stoner gangs have been known to practice bizarre, masochistic initiations or satanic rituals. Other reports have linked them as allies with more traditional street gangs. Neo-fascist skinhead gangs, advocating white supremacy or other racist nonsense, are roving packs of junior anarchists that prey on unsuspecting citizens. With total disregard for society and authority, the skinheads preach hate and disguise it as a cause. Abuse of illegal drugs and inhalants have been reported with skinhead and stoner groups, and funds for drug habits can account for some of their criminal activities.

Female participation in youth gangs has long been analysed using a stereotypical mindset. The "girls in the gang" are viewed as sex objects, fuel for inter-gang rivalries, or as promiscuous luggage in a male dominated structure. In some cases, this theory may be credible, but in the majority of youth gangs, female roles will form a sub-chapter within the larger gang. They will protect their own interests against any rivals and engage in traditional gang activities. There are also situations where an all-female gang will form and operate independently. Before the advent of women as police officers, females were often used as couriers for a gang's weapons or drugs because of search restrictions imposed on male officers.

Females within male dominated youth gangs are often prisoners of the same values they have rebelled against. A gang, as mentioned previously, will frequently adopt a conservative organizational structure while group ideology runs toward the reactionary. The females in such a situation become victims of traditional chauvinistic attitudes. If they conform to a support role, they can become little more than property. If they attempt to assert themselves like their male counterparts, they are often labelled as trouble. Within many traditional youth gangs, male sexual conquest or physical aggression is equated with the expected macho posturing; females wishing to act the same way may be considered tramps, tomboys or questioned about their sexual preference. Seeking to escape from the repressive "straight" world, females involved with youth gangs often experience this intensified double standard. Female skinheads, or Chelseas, dress like their male counterparts, and often leave a tuft of hair in the front of their shaved heads.

Skinhead gangs, or skins, have their roots in Britain, France, and other countries in Europe. Skinheads are notorious for their violent behaviour and are quite proud of this reputation. Skinheads, as the moniker implies, can be identified by their closely cropped hairstyles, suspenders, white supremacist or nazi accoutrements (swastikas, nazi cagle, iron cross) and "Doc Marten" boots—viewed as status symbols among skinheads. Doc Marten boots, designed by a German podiatrist forty years ago, look like a heavy-soled army boot. The black, red, or blue boots, with anywhere from eight to twenty-four eyelets, can have white (signifying white supremacy) or red (nazi) laces. Skins will challenge "posers" or pretenders to "up the docs", or give up their boots. Hardcore skins will fight for another's boots (which can cost up to $120) because the "docs", like the reputation, must be earned. Skins will prey on citizens or other street kids for money, and, usually working in groups, inflict severe beatings, using their "docs" to hammer home their violent message. Skins usually aim their "docs" at a victim's head.

Montreal Urban Community Police Department Situation

There are currently about 250 "Skinheads" in the Montreal Urban Community Police area of jurisdiction. They are always visible, especially in the centre region, and particularly in district 33. Since early 1987, this group has been involved in about a hundred crimes, varying from armed robbery and assault to sexual assault. Followed by the arrest of several members, an investigation of this group led to a decrease in crime. We are, however, witnessing another surge of violence concentrated in district 33.

MUCPD investigators believe that there are currently three categories of "Skinheads" in their territory: recruits, hardcore members and the "OI", who are reportedly pro-Nazi; by far the most violent, and apparently use "OI" as their rally cry. They are easily identifiable by their shaved heads and "Doc Marten" boots. Their ages range from 15 to 25. They wear suspenders, etc., and often carry knives. Some members of this group, especially the "OI", have no fixed address, sleep in factories or abandoned houses and live off the proceeds of crime.

At present, this group is without a hierarchy or leader. It does not have an defined goals and some members do not understand the meaning of the movement.

This group does not, therefore, fit into the organized crime category as defined by the Organized Crime Section. Their type of crime should be classified as nothing more than crime committed by adolescents or young adults, the duration of which shall be determined by such certain factors as the appearance of a leader who could organize them.

Patrol officers should be thoroughly informed about this type of person and asked to report the presence of "Skinheads" to the appropriate personnel, who can then monitor the evolution and movements of the group within the Montreal Urban Community territory.

Submitted by MUCPD

The most disturbing and dangerous manifestation of skinhead aggression is a tendency towards racially-motivated violence. Homosexuals, Blacks, Hispanics, East Indians, Jews, Asians, even TV talk show hosts—anything other than the Aryan ideal—are all potential victims of skinhead attacks.[3] The fanatic fascism of the skinheads can be regrettably equated with the policies of Nazi Germany and skins have been linked with neo-Nazi fringe groups as well as the Ku Klux Klan. Some skinheads wear patches with "88" on them, signifying the eighth letter in the alphabet or "HH" (Heil Hitler), in tribute to Adolph. One skinhead described his haircut as a statement. "My shaved head is like a balled fist."

The skinheads, driven by their right-wing tenets and preferred music (an equally inane brand of frenzied rock laced with white supremacist lyrics), abhor anything non-skinhead. Other street gangs, punkers, stoners or preppies are all labelled the enemy of the skinhead. There has been noise from some skinheads of the need to organise themselves, to band together. The very nature of these gangs and their transient membership would seem to discourage organization, but determined, hard-core members are preaching this ideal. Estimates on skinhead population vary; individuals may appear authentic but can be merely adopting the "look" as a fashion statement. Suffice it to say that hard-core skinheads are a noticeable police problem in some major Canadian cities, and are involved in actively recruiting younger individuals to join their gangs.

Along with this grassroots desire of skinhead groups to become better organized, traditional street gangs have been reported to be attaining this goal. In an effort to expand their drug empires, California gangs, like the Bloods and Crips, are branching out to Portland, Seattle, Omaha, Oklahoma City, the Eastern U.S., even Anchorage, Alaska.

Police in the Toronto area have been alerted to a loosely organized group calling themselves the Untouchables. Reports tag them as "young, preppie and mostly middle-class but also vicious, arrogant and aimless." Mostly high-school aged and of both sexes, gang members indulge in robbery, theft, vandalism and extortion. Often using a technique called swarming, the Untouchables will surround a victim (sometimes outnumbering the victim twenty to one) and provoke a fight, or threaten violence if they want a victim's belongings. What the Untouchables lack in courage they make up for in strategy.

Accounts of the Untouchable's formation differ according to what faction you listen to, but again the driving force stems from a desire to belong to a group and the security that numbers will provide.

Reports out of Vancouver have linked rival youth gangs, namely the Red Eagles (also known as Alley Boys or Gumwah) and Los Diablos with violent crime. One incident had two carloads of opposing gang members engaged in gunplay, while another involved a drive-by shooting at a gang member's home. No one was injured in either instance. An earlier battle, believed to have provoked the later violence, saw three gang members taken to hospital with gunshot wounds.

Breaking the cycle of gang involvement is a difficult task. A gang member will be reluctant to trust any authority figure outside the gang; gaining an individual's confidence is difficult but vital. The longer an individual is associated with a gang, the more difficult it will be to dissuade him/her that the gang is a dead-end. The emphasis should therefore be placed on alternatives to the gang's criminal activities. A review of various programs suggests these initiatives to guiding youth away from gang involvement:

- athletic programs, starting at age 10-12;

- employment or meaningful, applicable educational prospects;

- assistance with job applications;

- counselling on developing good work habits, with periodic follow-up; and

- drug and alcohol counselling, helping ex-offenders resocialize and find employment.

From an enforcement standpoint, helping the L.A.P.D. (Los Angeles Police Department) provides this breakdown on the objectives of the CRASH (Community Resources Against South Bureau Hoodlums) program.

1.   Eliminate gang-related violence.

2.   Identify and apprehend violent gang members.

3.   Work with victims, witnesses, parents and neighbours to eliminate gang problems.
     The methods used by Crash team members also deserve discussion. Officers handle to completion all gang incidents that occur on their beat and also gather and co-ordinate intelligence on all gang activities. The focus of the CRASH program is on breaking the organizational network of violent gangs.

The problem of violent gangs is one that, if unchecked, quickly escalates into very serious trouble. Once a gang develops a reputation among its potential recruits as being powerful, "cool" or prosperous, those recruits will see the gang as a viable alternative; an opportunity for respect and acceptance that they think they can never get from outside.
     The reasons that youths become involved with violent gangs are innumer-

able, but all stem from some sort of personal dissatisfaction with, or alienation from, an established social order. The preventive key is in early intervention—before that individual becomes totally indoctrinated into violent gang group psychosis, including distrust of anything non-gang. Gang members, of course, must have personal convictions to want to help themselves, to seek a way out of the cycle of crime and violence. Police officers are faced with a very complicated problem, one that surfaces on the street but has its roots in schools, families and peer groups. The best course of action, though often time-consuming and frustrating, lies in personal, one-on-one communication with youth gang members in an attempt to help them—before they become a statistic for court and correctional systems.